T0073653

THE MODEM WORLD

KEVIN DRISCOLL

The Modem World

A PREHISTORY OF SOCIAL MEDIA

Yale UNIVERSITY PRESS   NEW HAVEN AND LONDON

Published with assistance from the Louis Stern Memorial Fund.

Yale University Press books may be purchased in quantity for educational, business, or promotional use. For information, please e-mail sales.press@yale.edu (U.S. office) or sales@yaleup.co.uk (U.K. office).

Set in Scala & Scala Sans type by Newgen North America, Austin, Texas.
Printed in the United States of America.

Library of Congress Control Number: 2021943963
ISBN 978-0-300-24814-2 (hardcover : alk. paper)

A catalogue record for this book is available from the British Library.

This paper meets the requirements of ANSI/NISO Z39.48-1992 (Permanence of Paper).

10 9 8 7 6 5 4 3 2 1

For Eva Marigold

CONTENTS

THE MODEM WORLD

Recalling the Modem World

THE INTERNET BECAME AVAILABLE TO Richard Scott Mark in 1994. After hours spent installing new communications software, configuring his modem, and connecting to his new internet service provider, he double-clicked on Mosaic and ventured out onto the World Wide Web. As he wandered from page to page, an odd sense of loneliness and isolation overtook him. The much-hyped information superhighway was full of images but empty of people. Digital billboards flew by, but there was nowhere to pull over: no exits, no rest stops, no roadside attractions. "I was there," he remembered thinking, "but where was everyone else?"[1]

In 1994, the web was still brand new.[2] But Richard Mark was no newbie. He had spent the previous decade building personal computers and exploring communication networks from his home in Gainesville, Florida. Since 1987, he and two friends—Paul Martin and Dave Tieman—had run Dragon Keep International, a dial-up online service known as a "bulletin board system," or BBS.[3] They originally launched Dragon Keep with a secondhand computer, $25 worth of software, and a commitment to creating a fun, respectful environment for their users.[4] By 1994, their BBS had grown into a lively community serving more than four thousand members from around the city.[5] Every night, dozens of people dialed in from their home PCs to chat, trade files, play games, read the forums, and post messages of their own. In 1996, Mark described it as a thriving "cyber-city."[6]

The experience of running Dragon Keep shaped Mark's early encounters with the internet and his expectations for the World Wide Web. Logging into a popular BBS could feel like stepping into an electronic nightclub. You were visiting a real place with real people, personality, and vibe. The web of 1994, by contrast, felt less like a place than a thing. Mark compared surfing the web to flipping the pages of an "endless magazine."[7] The technology was impressive, the aesthetics were cool, and the information was engaging, but the overall experience felt static and lifeless.[8] After months of hype, Mark was underwhelmed. "In its present form," he concluded, "[the web] is simply noninteractive."[9]

Mark was not alone in his disappointment. From the late 1970s until the dot-com boom of the 1990s, dial-up BBSs were the prevailing form of social computing for PC owners. Built by amateurs using off-the-shelf parts and regular telephone lines, this "modem world" offered an open, grassroots alternative to the closed, institutional networks sponsored by state agencies, research universities, and multinational corporations. In North America alone, more than a hundred thousand BBSs served millions of people on systems ranging from fewer than ten to more than ten thousand active members.[10] In the early 1990s, when privatization opened the internet to everyone with money to spare, these BBS enthusiasts were among the first to open their checkbooks. Big BBSs like Dragon Keep International, ECHO, Exec-PC, and The WELL hitched themselves and their dial-up communities to the global information infrastructure. Former BBS users ran popular mailing lists, moderated newsgroups, and commercialized the web. From private BitTorrent trackers to Facebook groups, the fundamental social structures of the modern internet were forged on a dial-up BBS.

HOW DID THE INTERNET BECOME SOCIAL?

Today, the internet mediates all aspects of social life, from the most intimate to the most mundane. Digital communication networks are the infrastructures through which we keep in touch with family, argue about politics, find romantic connection, look up health information, and seek emotional support. Social media services provide online counterparts to the café, shopping mall, library, cinema, confessional booth, barbershop, and nail salon. Blending commerce and community, they are the gathering places of the online world, spaces of social encounter where we observe other people, express ourselves, and collectively make sense of the world. From school to work, the bedroom to the public square, the rhythms of everyday life resonate through networks of copper cabling, optical fiber, and electromagnetic waves that seem to charge the very air around us with the spark of communication.

And yet the social internet, in spite of its ubiquity, is short on social history. The best-known histories of the internet focus on either the engineers who developed the core technologies or the businesspeople who profited from them. Neither offers a satisfying explanation for the rise of computer networks as platforms for popular culture and public life. The prehistory of social media unfolded not in the office parks of Silicon Valley or the meeting rooms of military contractors or the labs of university researchers. Instead, we must peer into the improvised workshops of millions of hobbyists, volunteers, activists, and entrepreneurs who—for fifteen years prior to the opening up of the internet—hosted small-scale online systems in cities and towns throughout North America.

The modem world began in the late 1970s. Amateur technologists appropriated the residential telephone network as an infrastructure for data communications, trading electronic files and messages through circuits originally designed to carry the human voice. Within a few years, dial-up BBSs had become the dominant form of networking among personal computer owners, especially those who were excluded from other media systems. It was on these grassroots networks that computer enthusiasts started to use their machines for popular communication and community building. Their experiences and experiments with anonymity, identity, privacy, sexuality, and trust generated many of the technologies and practices that Silicon Valley later reproduced and sold as commercial social media.

Lost in the transition from hobbyist telecommunication to commercial social media was the intimacy of the modem world. Whereas today's social media systems are characterized by ambiguous terms of service agreements, uncertain privacy guarantees, mass surveillance, and widespread abuse and harassment, bulletin board systems operated under very different technical, cultural, and political-economic regimes. BBSs were local affairs, serving small numbers of people living in relative proximity. The administrators, known as "system operators" or "sysops," were responsible for maintaining the tech, paying the bills, setting the rules, and resolving disputes. Regular users and sysops came to know each other personally, often meeting up to tinker with computers, trade software, party, or just hang out. Ownership accrued to the edges of BBS networks, making sysops accountable to their users as members of a shared community rather than representatives of a corporation or self-interested investors.

This is a book about how the internet became social. The people who built and maintained dial-up BBSs in the 1980s laid the groundwork for millions of others who would bring their lives online in the 1990s and beyond. Along with writing code and running up their phone bills, these modem enthusiasts developed novel forms of community moderation, governance, and commercialization. As some of the only people to enter the dot-com boom with practical experience running online communities, many BBS sysops found employment in the internet economy of the 1990s. Some transformed their BBSs into internet service providers (ISPs). Others applied their expertise to the World Wide Web. Over time, countless social media platforms have reproduced the social and technical innovations of the BBS community.

Recovering the history of dial-up BBSs also helps us to imagine a world after social media. Endlessly modifiable, BBS technology afforded sysops a remarkable degree of expressive flexibility. From the visual design of BBSs to their organizational structure, each BBS represented an idiosyncratic dream of what cyberspace could be, a glimpse of the future written in code and accessible from your local telephone jack. When commercial internet access finally came to the public, tens of thousands of BBS networks were already in operation, providing computer enthusiasts across the continent with networks of their own. This is not to romanticize the past—many users happily abandoned BBSs for the web—but to recover a sense of wonder about the internet of today. Immersing ourselves in a period of experimentation and play makes the internet seem strange again. By changing how we remember the internet's past, we can change our expectations for its future.

WHAT IS THE INTERNET?

The purpose of this book is to change how we talk about the history of the internet. But what is "the internet"? If you ask a network administrator, they will tell you something about protocols, standards, gateways, or peering agreements. In a technical sense, this is correct. Nearly every mobile phone, laptop, tablet, and "smart" thing in the world runs a standard set of software programs known as the internet protocol suite, or TCP/IP, and every ISP exchanges packets with peer networks through IP gateways.[11] But a typical user doesn't think about the internet in terms of datagrams shuttling between switches and routers. A strictly technical definition doesn't capture what we mean when we talk about "the internet."[12] Learning about the architecture of TCP/IP won't help us to understand the diversity of user practices that have emerged since the 1970s.[13] Like the notion of "the movies," the internet is an invention of our social imagination, as much an idea or a feeling as a technology. The internet means something different depending on who, when, and where you are.

Today's vernacular use of "internet" reflects a transformation in meaning from the technical to the social, from programs and protocols to people and practices. For much of the 1970s and 1980s, "internet" was just a shortened form of "internetwork," an adjective used by network engineers to classify technologies that spanned multiple communication systems, for example, "an internetwork gateway."[14] As internetwork gateways became more common in the late 1970s, researchers needed a word to describe the resulting networks-of-networks. Louis Pouzin, director of the experimental CYCLADES network in France, proposed "catenet," the concatenation of dissimilar networks. Others used organizational adjectives to distinguish particular internetworks such as "the Xerox internet" or "the ARPA internet."[15] The capitalized, singular "Internet" remained relatively rare, even in technical literature, until late in the 1980s, when a flood of new data networks—national videotex systems like Minitel and Telidon, international commercial services like CompuServe and Tymnet, and worldwide cooperative networks like BITNET and USENET— created a need for better documentation and a more precise definition.[16] In 1990, John S. Quarterman, a former ARPANET engineer, published *The Matrix*, a 750-page atlas of data networks.[17] According to *The Matrix*,

The worldwide "metanetwork" of communication and information services, according to data published by John S. Quarterman in 1990. This diagram depicts more than 227 systems operating in forty-one countries, from international commercial services and cooperative email systems to national research networks and secure military infrastructures. The edges between nodes indicate a gateway. The size of each node corresponds to its number of connections. Redundancies and gaps reflect the practical difficulties of documenting this dynamic period. Around the world, new networks were coming online, existing networks were merging, and old networks were being phased out.

"the Internet" referred to a particular family of experimental networks used by state agencies, universities, and corporations with roots in the United States.[18] Like Pouzin, Quarterman focused on the concatenation of heterogeneous networks. Accordingly, "the Internet" of 1990 was just one component of a rapidly growing "metanetwork" of remote computing and conferencing systems.[19]

By 1994, the term "internet" had escaped from the specialized vocabulary of computer experts, and a more expansive, metaphorical meaning had taken hold in the language of politicians, advertisers, and the popular press. At the start of the year, there were fewer than one thousand sites on the public web, but cyberspace was already becoming a topic of popular curiosity. America Online (AOL) had mailed out a quarter million starter diskettes by the time President Bill Clinton namechecked the "information superhighway" in his second State of the Union Address.[20]

Self-Reported Populations of Commercial
Online Services, 1995

America Online	3,800,000
CompuServe	3,540,000
Prodigy	1,720,000
Microsoft Network	200,000
Delphi	125,000
eWorld	115,000
GEnie	75,000
Mnematics Videotex	65,000
ImagiNation Network	62,000
Reuters Money Net	33,000
AT&T Interchange	25,000
Interactive Visual	25,000
Digital Nation	15,000
The WELL	12,000
Computer Sports World	10,200
Multiplayer Games Network	10,000

Source: Adapted from Jack Rickard, "Editor's Notes," *Boardwatch*, December 1995, 65.

In July, the cover of *Time* magazine—stocked in grocery-store checkout lanes across the country—promised readers an introduction to "the strange new world of the internet."[21] The "metanetwork" described by Quarterman was expanding rapidly to include bulletin boards, commercial online services, and public data networks.[22] In this period of convergence, the TCP/IP internet served as a convenient go-between, conveying packets across otherwise-rigid political and organizational boundaries. *The Economist* dubbed it "that Grand Central of cyberspace," a transit station for the online world.[23]

With the World Wide Web as the primary interface, the internet of 1994 lost its sense of being a metanetwork or network-of-networks. Mouse in hand, the web made the internet feel like one massive system. Every digital thing was a click away from every other thing. By obscuring the complex routing of packets behind a simple point-and-click interface, the web dissolved the boundaries between networks on the internet. In early 1995, just weeks before the NSFNET backbone was retired, the ARPANET veteran David Crocker attempted to resolve the conflict between the two meanings of the "internet."[24] According to Crocker, a person sending internet mail from behind a corporate firewall or posting on USENET from an AOL account should be considered "on" the internet, even if their machine was not. The internet wasn't just a network; it was *the* network.

Today, the internet is no longer the object of fascination that it was in 1995. There is no sense of there being a world of networks outside the internet. All networks are assumed to be internet networks. For the majority of Americans living with ubiquitous broadband, the internet is not a particular network or networking technique but a context for social activity.[25] Every bit of communication, from mundane telephone calls and credit card payments to television series and breaking news, flows through an internet connection. Furthermore, Americans believe that the internet has had a positive effect on their lives and say that it would be difficult to give up.[26] The internet is how they keep in touch with family, read the news, seek health information, look for jobs, listen to music, play games, flirt, pray, celebrate birthdays, and mourn the dead.

WHERE DID THE INTERNET COME FROM?

Since 2016, I've asked dozens of students to write down, in a sentence or two, where the internet came from. Year after year, they recount the same stories about the US government, Silicon Valley, the military, and the threat of nuclear war. They remember learning about the early internet in another course or hearing about the "dot-com boom" in a documentary film. A few mention the ARPANET by name. Several get the chronology wrong, placing the World Wide Web before the internet or expressing confusion about the invention of email. Others mention "tech wizards" or "geniuses" from Silicon Valley firms and university labs. No fewer than four students have simply written, "Bill Gates."

Despite the internet's staggering scale and global reach, its folk histories are surprisingly narrow. This mismatch is the result of the unstable meaning of "the internet." The fragments of internet history that filter into popular television and film, political discourse, and tech PR tell the story of an internet that hasn't existed since 1994. When nonexperts look for internet origin stories, they want to know how the internet as they know it came to be. But the internet of today was created through the convergence of hundreds of networks during the mid-1990s, only one of which was previously referred to as "the internet."

The internet swept into US popular culture as a technology out of time, simultaneously new and old.[27] The same magazine articles and TV news reports that described the internet as the revolutionary, generation-defining medium of the 1990s made sure to remark on its origins in the Cold War research labs of the 1960s. This tension between novelty and history prompted a burst of historiography during the 1990s.[28] As Americans took their first steps into cyberspace, bookstores were overrun with how-to guides and reference materials. Scholars, journalists, and longtime users undertook tremendous historiographic labor to meet the demand for information about the origins of the internet. By convention, nearly all mass-market how-to books included brief histories in their introductory chapters.[29] Longtime internet advocates such as Ed Krol, author of *The Whole Internet: User's Guide & Catalog*, framed their microhistories as a bulwark against the ahistorical rush of the dot-com boom: "To most people, the Internet seems to have sprung fully formed on the world some time after 1990. That is not the case."[30]

The historiographic frenzy of the 1990s centered on the family of packet-switching networks descended from the ARPANET project. Early narratives were collected and shared on USENET newsgroups like alt.folklore.computers and alt.culture.internet. A 1993 essay by the science fiction author Bruce Sterling offers a characteristic example. Transcribed from *The Magazine of Fantasy & Science Fiction*, the piece opened with a dramatization of the internet's military origins: "Some thirty years ago, the RAND Corporation, America's foremost Cold War think-tank, faced a strange strategic problem. How could the U.S. authorities successfully communicate after a nuclear war?"[31] For more than a decade, the essay circulated across various BBS networks, USENET newsgroups, FTP sites, and the web under the title "A Short History of the Internet."[32]

The Cold War "survivability" narrative has been the best-known story in internet history since the 1990s. Yet the focus on military strategy rankled some of those who were involved in the early internet. In 1996, *Where Wizards Stay Up Late*, by the journalists Katie Hafner and Matthew Lyon, gave voice to former ARPANET engineers who felt misunderstood.[33] Drawing on extensive interviews, *Wizards* directly challenged the Cold War mythology.[34] In its place, *Wizards* offered a cast of brilliant oddballs far removed from the deadly considerations of their funders.[35] From this perspective, any regard for the potential military use of the network was a bureaucratic formality, required for the continuation of ARPA funding but not a meaningful influence on the research.[36] Despite these disagreements, the best-selling *Wizards*—subtitled *The Origins of the Internet*—did little to dislodge ARPANET as the narrative core of internet history.[37]

In 1999, the historian Janet Abbate published *Inventing the Internet*, tracing the continuous reinvention of packet-switching networks from the experimental ARPANET to the internetworks of the 1980s and consumer services of the 1990s.[38] In an overt response to the historiographic explosion of the previous decade, *Inventing the Internet* focused on the organizational cultures and political-economic forces that shaped networking projects like ARPANET.[39] This approach revealed a complex period characterized by competing visions of the future, international competition over standards, and the simultaneous invention of fundamental techniques. While ARPANET flourished, contemporary networks in France and the United Kingdom floundered due to a lack of institutional support.[40] And, whereas earlier histories tended to dismiss the formal processes of standardization as dull and bureaucratic, *Inventing the Internet* suggested that useful research may have been swept aside in the rush to establish TCP/IP as a de facto standard. Whether the computer science researchers working on ARPANET day to day could see it or not, their internet was produced by and for a diverse range of stakeholders, many of whom stood to benefit strategically and financially if the network developed along certain paths.

From informal essays to mass-market paperbacks to scholarly monographs, the writers and historians of the 1990s produced a common set of stories about the origins of the internet. After decades of repetition, the sociologist Tom Streeter dubbed these narratives the "standard folklore" of the internet.[41] When I ask my students where the internet came from, many of them know the standard folklore. And yet these histories were written at a moment when the internet itself was undergoing a transformation, swallowing up commercial online services and university networks, mutating into something bigger, more commercial, and more accessible to the nonexpert. The internet of 1999 was a different system—in culture, technology, economics, and policy—from the internet of 1992. Why hasn't the standard folklore kept up?

It is worth noting that referring to the historiography of the 1990s as "folklore" or "mythology" is not meant to discredit the people, institutions, or technologies involved. The veracity of these histories is not in question. Rather, mythologies provide us with an explanation of how the online world came to be the way it is. The trouble is that histories of ARPANET or Silicon Valley on their own cannot account for the mass adoption of internet access, the commercialization of the web, or the emergence of social media. The standard folklore can tell us why our smartphones run TCP/IP, but it can't tell us why we carry them. The histories we know aren't wrong. They are incomplete.

WHAT WAS THE "MODEM WORLD"?

Personal computers, or PCs, are virtually absent from the standard folklore of the internet. ARPANET predated consumer PCs by nearly a decade. The internet protocols were not designed for single-user PCs. Microsoft did not release an official version of TCP/IP until 1994.[42] Yet most people have experienced the internet through a personal computing device such as a laptop or smartphone. To understand how the internet became a medium for everyday life, we need a history that accounts for the creation of personal computer networks and their convergence with the internet.

At the core of such a history will be a rather strange peripheral: the dial-up modem. In the 1980s, "modem" referred to a device for converting a stream of digital pulses from a computer into an audible signal for transmission over a standard telephone line.[43] Personal computers did not include a modem by default until the mid-1990s. As a result, the modem became a technology of distinction among computer enthusiasts of the 1980s. Modem owners knew themselves as a separate class of computer users, capable of traversing the emerging byways of cyberspace. The networks that they frequented came to be known, collectively, as the "modem world."[44]

The modem world relied on the diffusion of the personal computer as a cultural form and economic category. For most of the twentieth century, computers were not seen as personal devices for individual people to use. In popular culture, computers were depicted as massive "electronic brains" responsible for the automation of society.[45] In films ranging from *Desk Set* in 1957 to *2001: A Space Odyssey* in 1968, computers represented the domination and de-skilling of human beings. These representations reflected the prevalence of "mainframe" computers sold by firms like IBM to large corporations and state agencies. Although mainframes were hidden in the basements of large buildings and accessible only to specialized staff, everyone felt their presence in the rising quantification of daily life. Interest rates, income taxes, credit ratings, and draft cards were all linked to the "computerization" of society.[46] Yet, in the 1980s, small-scale PCs offered a new model of computing. Instead of an electronic brain to power a whole organization, firms like Apple and Microsoft marketed the PC as a single-user device. No longer displacing human beings, the personal computer was sold as a tool to empower individuals, foster creativity, and increase productivity.

Historians of technology trace the transition from mainframes to personal computers through two overlapping technical cultures of the 1960s and 1970s, time-sharing and hobby computing. Time-sharing began in the early 1960s as a modification of the mainframe paradigm by university researchers.[47] The name referred to a clever programming technique that distributed a single computer's processing power among a network of attached terminals, giving multiple users the illusion of exclusive access to the computer's resources.[48] Early advocates of time-sharing promoted a vision of computing as a public utility comparable to residential electricity.[49] In the future, they reasoned, a single computer might offer enough computing "power" for a whole community.

Time-sharing proved especially successful in educational settings. In hundreds of university computer labs and K–12 classrooms, time-sharing enabled the flourishing of creative, cooperative cultures of computing. At Dartmouth University, the BASIC programming language offered an accessible point of entry for beginners, and at the University of Illinois, the PLATO system provided interactive games, educational software, forums, and chat rooms.[50] The experience of time-sharing combined an invigorating feeling of individual control with a sense of collective obligation to one's fellow users. The historian Joy Lisi Rankin describes the participants in these time-sharing communities as "computing citizens."[51] By the start of the 1980s, hundreds of thousands of students had become citizens of a time-sharing community.

As time-sharing systems flourished in the 1970s, electronics hobbyists began to experiment with building computers of their own. Steeped in the technical culture of amateur radio, hobbyists valued hands-on learning, practical expertise, and fellowship among amateurs.[52] Mail-order "microcomputer" kits like the MITS Altair 8800 in 1975 presented hobbyists with a new challenge to their do-it-yourself (DIY) skills.[53] Soon groups of microcomputer enthusiasts formed clubs, published newsletters, shared programs by mail, and added computers to their ham radio stations.[54] Equipped with a BASIC interpreter, microcomputer owners benefited from the deep catalog of fun, accessible software created for time-sharing systems.

By the end of the 1980s, hobby computing no longer required proficiency with a soldering iron. Kit computers like the Altair gave way to prebuilt "home computer" products like the Radio Shack TRS-80 and Commodore PET. The burgeoning personal computer industry drew on its hobbyist roots for talent and countercultural bona fides. Yet, despite brisk sales, "micros" were not seen as competitors to mainframes or minicomputers until spreadsheet programs like VisiCalc began to drive interest among business users. In 1981, IBM introduced its own PC, lending further credibility among corporate decision-makers. Within a few years, "IBM-compatible" had become a de facto industry standard, drawing many hobbyists away from earlier platforms.[55] By the end of the decade, the popular image of the computer was no longer an imposing mainframe but an approachable desktop PC.

The modem world developed at the crossroads of these two cultures. Hosted on home-built micros and off-the-shelf PCs, the first bulletin board systems combined the cooperative sensibility of time-sharing with the accessible infrastructure of microcomputing. Whereas time-sharing computers were typically owned by an institution, most BBSs were run out of the homes of amateurs who maintained their systems through tinkering and experimentation. Crucially, bulletin boards served a different population from contemporary time-sharing systems. The earliest BBSs were populated by microcomputer enthusiasts, trading technical information and chatting about their hobby. Later, however, BBSs linked a more diverse group of PC owners, covering a wider range of interests and identities beyond the tech hobbyist. Time-sharing demonstrated the potential for community to form around a computer network. Dial-up BBSs made it accessible to the peripheries of computer culture.

BBSs emerged during the famously snowy winter of 1978, when Ward Christensen and Randy Suess created the Computerized Bulletin Board System, or CBBS, using a home-built S-100 microcomputer and a brand-new Hayes modem. Christensen and Suess were members of a local microcomputer club, known as the Chicago Area Computer Hobbyist's Exchange, or CACHE. The club's newsletter was a vital source of information; but club members had to be cajoled to submit new articles, and there was no easy way to provide access to earlier issues. Inspired by a cork bulletin board used for public notices at CACHE meetings, Christensen and Suess set about building an online database of newsletter articles.[56] They installed the system at Suess's place and had it running by early February. Almost immediately, hobbyists from outside Chicago began to call in to check out the system and swap messages with one another, transforming the "computerized" bulletin board into a public forum. Within a few months, CBBS was fielding dozens of calls from around the country, and new bulletin boards had sprouted up in Atlanta and San Francisco.[57]

CBBS was the archetypal dial-up BBS. It was a clever technical system with an accessible interface and friendly personality. The CBBS "host" computer was hooked up to a single telephone line and could handle just one user at a time. To get online, potential users needed a telephone modem and some kind of data terminal. Early on, most people called in from paper-based teleprinters, but these were soon replaced by video displays and "terminal emulation" software. Upon successfully connecting to CBBS, one's terminal would spring to life, hammering out, "WELCOME TO CBBS/CHICAGO . . . WARD AND RANDY'S COMPUTERIZED BULLETIN BOARD SYSTEM."[58] The welcome message also included instructions on navigating the system and encouraged new users to call Christensen or Suess at home to report any problems with the hardware or software. They were told to jump right in: "Feel free to leave a message on any hobbyist computer related subject."[59]

The functional simplicity of CBBS belied its power as an organizing tool for the hobbyist community. In November 1978, *Byte* magazine ran a special issue on communications featuring an article by Christensen and Suess that explained the technical architecture of CBBS and invited readers to take the system for a spin.[60] Thousands of readers took up their invitation, and soon new bulletin boards were being announced around North America and Europe. Each new BBS tweaked the core concept of the computerized bulletin board, adding features for trading files or playing games, implementing rules regarding user behavior, and expressing the local culture and personality of its owners. Most were free to use, save for the cost of placing a long-distance call. BBS enthusiasts ran their phone bills into the hundreds of dollars just to experience these novel outposts on the electronic frontier.

Hobbyists weren't the only ones building online systems. In 1979, two new commercial online services launched with the hope of attracting PC owners.[61] By the end of the year, The Source, based in Northern Virginia, boasted three thousand customers dialing from 260 US cities. Subscribers paid an hourly rate of $15 during the day and $2.75 at night for access to international news, stock market data, real estate listings, and restaurant reviews. Meanwhile, the time-sharing firm CompuServe Inc. created MicroNET, an online service aimed at personal computer enthusiasts. Whereas The Source emphasized access to information, MicroNET promised access to computing power. From 6 p.m. to 5 a.m., MicroNET subscribers paid $5 per hour to write and run programs on mainframe computers attached to the CompuServe network.[62] Yet it was neither information nor access to computers that kept subscribers paying the hourly fees. CompuServe and The Source became important community spaces for early modem owners. The discussion forums, software archives, and "CB simulator" chat channels on these systems served as a kind of informal backbone to the emerging network of local BBSs.

The summer of 1983 brought about the rise of a new stereotype: the tech-savvy teen. In movie theaters, the Cold War thriller *WarGames* showed its two young protagonists using a modem and microcomputer to change their grades, download games, and (almost) start World War III. It was the first time that Hollywood had depicted computers and computer networks as tools of exploration, play, personal identity, and teen mischief.[63] Over the next year, BBSs and commercial services alike saw a surge in new users as teens attached modems to their home computers. But what did the middle-aged hobbyists and teen newcomers have to say to each other? And what teenager could afford to pay for the commercial services? Soon, modem-equipped teens were hosting bulletin boards of their own, adapting the technology to meet their interests and needs.

Unlike the nationwide commercial services, bulletin board systems tended to serve a local population of users since few hobbyists could afford to routinely call long-distance.[64] System operators were keenly aware of the local nature of BBS culture. In a sense, sysops were inviting strangers into their homes. With the host computer sitting on a nearby desk or in a closet, they could hear the whirr of the hard drive and see the flickering lights of the modem as callers dipped in and out. Most boards encouraged the use of pseudonyms or "handles," but relationships between users and sysops frequently crossed the boundary between on- and offline. Many sysops hosted parties at their homes or a favorite watering hole where users of their BBS could hang out. These opportunities for face-to-face interaction shaped the social norms of the BBS. Trolling and flame wars took on a different character when the person on the other side could be your neighbor, classmate, coworker, or friend.

Through the 1980s, the distribution of BBSs roughly followed the distribution of people. Modem owners living in densely settled cities had a broader choice of local BBSs to call than people living in smaller towns did. In metropolitan areas, the concentration of boards encouraged sysops to specialize, resulting in BBSs that served particular groups of

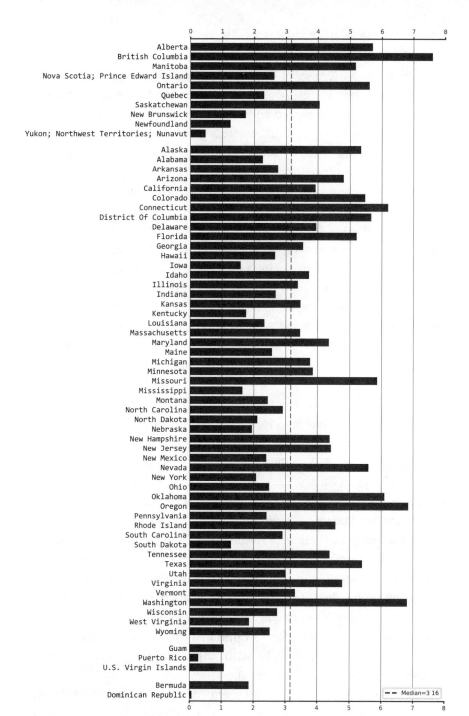

Approximate number of BBSs per ten thousand people in regions served by the North American Numbering Plan (median = 3.16). Estimates based on 106,288 telephone numbers associated with a BBS between 1978 and 2010, including at least one BBS in each of the 158 area codes in service prior to 1996.

people and communities of interest within the city. People who wanted to talk about amateur astronomy found their way to one board; people who wanted to trade pirated software found another. Those who were interested in both topics could create separate profiles on each board, thereby selecting, revealing, and disclosing different aspects of their online identities. No such luck for rural users: if you were the only amateur astronomer in your area, there might not be anyone on the local boards for you to chat with.

To bring users from different regions together, bulletin board system operators needed a way for users of one board to communicate with users of another without placing a long-distance call. In the early twentieth century, amateur radio operators solved this problem by organizing a network of cooperating stations to voluntarily "relay" messages around the country.[65] The ARPANET email system relied on a similar "store-and-forward" technique to transmit data between machines in the network, albeit without the need for human operators in the middle.[66] Other institutional networks used the Unix-to-Unix Copy (UUCP) protocol to transmit messages between time-sharing systems.[67] But as with CBBS, it was a fellow amateur who finally started writing code and organizing intercity links to transmit messages and files between BBSs.[68]

The first inter-BBS connections radiated out of the Bay Area home of Tom Jennings in early 1984. Previously, Jennings, a microcomputer expert, dog lover, and self-described "weirdo fag punk," had released a BBS host program known as "Fido" for the IBM PC platform.[69] By the summer, a dozen or so BBSs were running Fido, and Jennings kept in touch with their sysops via telephone. With the help of John Madill, a sysop in Baltimore, Jennings added an experimental feature that allowed two BBSs running Fido software to call each other and trade data automatically. After a year in operation, more than a hundred BBSs were active on the network, and "FidoNet" became an open standard for exchanging files and messages between BBSs. By the end of 1985, "netmail" messages were bouncing from Maryland to St. Louis, Texas to Hawaii, England to Indonesia. With its open standards and clever design, FidoNet became a platform for experimentation. A group of sysops in St. Louis created a hierarchy to more efficiently route messages across long distances, and internetwork gateways ferried mail between BBSs and the burgeoning internet. By the start of the 1990s, the international FidoNet was unmatched among computer networks for its low barriers to entry and global reach.

The social and technical environment of the dial-up BBS gave rise to new forms of computational art and literature. The primacy of text rewarded users who took pleasure in written communication. Many sysops provided space for collections of plain-text documents, or "textfiles." While some were simply transcriptions of hard-to-find print material, the textfiles phenomenon developed into a distinct genre of electronic publishing akin to DIY fanzines and underground comics. As early as 1983, groups of textfile authors banded together into writing collectives, producing hundreds of collaborative files and "e-zines."[70]

Digital text also shaped the visual culture of BBSing.[71] To ensure compatibility with teleprinter terminals, early BBS interfaces were constructed from the limited set of symbols available on the typical typewriter. By the mid-1980s, however, the widespread adoption of IBM-compatible "clone" PCs provided a common medium for "textmode" artists—80 columns, 16 colors, and 256 characters. Soon, BBS interfaces and textfiles were adorned with wildly colorful "ANSI art" graphics. ANSI art collectives such as ACiD and iCE began to circulate "artpacks" alongside existing textfile groups.[72] These high-resolution text-mode graphics also enabled the production of BBS "door" games. Installed as extensions by the BBS sysop, door games ranged from simple casino simulators to complex strategy games and multiplayer virtual worlds.[73]

As the 1980s wore on, personal computers became more accessible, modem prices fell, and BBSs spread beyond techies to groups of people with a practical need for alternative communication media. Bulletin boards for queer communities, fan cultures, and political activism were especially vibrant spaces for socializing, organizing, and sharing resources. In 1984, Arthur Kohn opened the Backroom, which led to the formation of GayCom, a network of BBSs for gay and lesbian people.[74] Political organizers in the United States and United Kingdom formed EcoNet, GreenNet, and PeaceNet for the peace and environmentalist movements.[75] And in 1985, The WELL—perhaps the best-known BBS—provided virtual space for members of the Bay Area counterculture, including hundreds of Grateful Dead fanatics.[76] Of course, the political potential of BBS technology was not lost on white power groups, militias, anti-Semitic conspiracy theorists, and other far-right

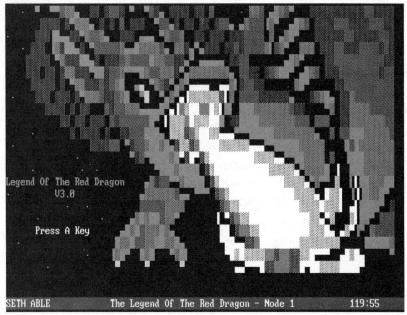

Legend of the Red Dragon, or *LoRD*, was a multiplayer fantasy role-playing game written in Turbo Pascal by Seth Able Robinson in 1989. Robinson hoped that *LoRD* would
attract more callers to his BBS, and the mechanics of the game rewarded players who
frequently dialed in. Each day, players were allowed a limited number of actions—
exploring, trading, dueling, hunting, and hanging out in the tavern—and each night,
this allotment was reset. As *LoRD* grew in popularity, Robinson encouraged enthusiasts
to enhance and modify the game, enabling sysops to adapt *LoRD's* mechanics and
aesthetics to the local culture of their boards.

extremists.[77] Some of the earliest coverage of BBSs on US TV news focused on the adoption of BBSs by neo-Nazi groups in the United States
and Canada.

We will never know exactly how many BBSs there were or precisely
how many people used them. The data that exist are messy and hard
to interpret. But even a rough estimate reveals that the scale of these
amateur networks outstripped many better-known commercial services.
In cities and towns across North America, more than one hundred thousand bulletin boards served at least two and a half million callers.[78] And
the geography of BBSing extended far beyond tech hubs like Silicon Valley or Northern Virginia. From Alaska to Bermuda, Puerto Rico to Saskatchewan, every telephone area code in the North American Numbering Plan played host to at least one dial-up BBS.[79] The roots of today's

social media are in in the interconnection of these local communities and small-scale networks.

The demographics of BBS users appears to have tracked with the broader adoption of personal computers in the United States, skewing in favor of white men. Between 1989 and 1993, the US Census Bureau asked American computer owners about their use of bulletin boards and electronic mail. Although the survey did not distinguish commercial services from BBSs or university networks, it remains one of the few comprehensive accounts of the early online population. In 1989, the bureau reported that approximately 5–7 percent of all computer owners used bulletin boards and electronic mail. While there was little variation by age and income, single, white men were nearly twice as likely as other groups to report using bulletin boards. In the early 1990s, a jump in computer ownership brought more Americans into the modem world. In 1993, the bureau found that Black and white computer owners used bulletin boards in roughly equal measure, nearly 9 percent, and that email usage had jumped to approximately 32 percent. Black users were somewhat more likely to use email than other groups were. Yet women were still underrepresented online. Nearly twice as many men reported using bulletin boards as women, a disparity reflected in women's firsthand experiences of the period.[80]

In 1991, when future vice president Al Gore described the "information superhighway," many longtime computer users imagined a

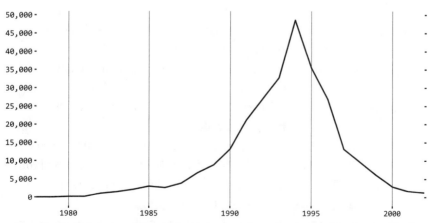

Trend in North American BBS activity, 1978–2002. Annual estimates based on archived BBS lists and retrospective self-reporting.

souped-up network of BBSs. At the time, only about a fifth of Americans had access to a computer at home, and even fewer knew how to get online.[81] As people struggled to make sense of cyberspace, many BBS enthusiasts saw an opportunity to convert their technical hobby into a source of income. How-to books and trade shows promised to teach sysops how to turn their BBSs into businesses. In the summer of 1994, a BBS convention in Atlanta, Georgia, drew four thousand attendees—double the previous year—prompting the *InfoWorld* columnist Bob Metcalfe to declare an imminent "explosion" of BBSs on the internet.[82] Around the country, BBSs promoted themselves as a local, friendly alternative to nationwide systems like CompuServe, Prodigy, or AOL. They would be the on-ramps, rest stops, and service stations on the information superhighway.

But the process of privatization was messy. Lacking any central authority or advocacy organization, the BBS community had no voice in the roiling debates about the future of the internet.[83] As commercial service providers tussled with the administrators of university networks, the interests of BBS users and sysops were hardly considered at all. Compounding the lack of representation, longtime internet advocates were generally unfamiliar with the technology and culture of dial-up networks. Packet-switching systems like NSFNET ran on a fundamentally different infrastructure from consumer-oriented BBS networks, and relatively few people were expert users of both.[84] By and large, BBSs were not ignored by institutions of power so much as they were overlooked. Finally, when a moral panic over "cyberporn" threatened to burst the dot-com bubble in 1995, BBSs provided a convenient scapegoat.[85] BBSs were old and dirty; the internet and the web were new, clean, and safe for commerce. Facing this stigma, many enterprising BBS operators quietly rebranded. Seemingly overnight, thousands of dial-up BBSs vanished, replaced by brand-new "internet service providers." In the United States, the term "BBS" fell out of use. In 1997, the Bureau of the Census dropped the term "bulletin board" from its questionnaire, replacing it with "internet."

The BBS movement was short-lived, but its influence persisted. From running local ISPs to establishing new communities on the web, former BBS users and sysops played key roles in shaping the public internet. So who were they? On average, the demographics of the modem world fit the stereotype of the 1980s computer geek: young, white, middle-class

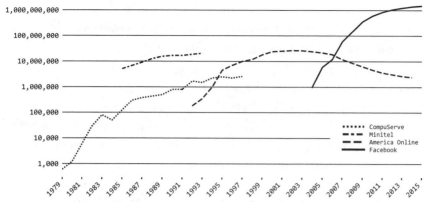

Comparative growth of selected online services, 1979 to 2015. Estimates based on
self-reported data published by the trade press or disclosed in annual reports submitted to the US Securities and Exchange Commission. All estimates are assumed to
be international in scope except for Minitel, which was exclusive to residents of France.
Minitel remained in service until 2012, but usage statistics were only published through
1993. America Online acquired CompuServe in 1998. Facebook population estimates
are inferred from the "monthly active users" metric.

men and boys. At the peak of the BBS era, many BBSs were used exclusively by men. Even overtly queer BBSs tended to serve primarily gay
men.[86] Yet the decentralized structure of the modem world facilitated
considerable variation from system to system. The organizers of individual BBSs and BBS networks freely adapted BBS technology to serve
different communities of computer owners. In New York City, ECHO
sysop Stacy Horn cultivated a community with a majority of women;
other BBSs such as The Oak Tree in Colorado and 10% Connection in
Chicago sought to create women-only spaces; and the member boards of
TGnet were dedicated to transgender identity, health, and culture.[87] Likewise, AfroNet connected more than two dozen BBSs for wide-ranging
discussions of Black interest.[88] On balance, Black American households
were less likely than whites to own a computer in the early 1990s, but
Black computer owners reported similar rates of BBS use.

　　Making sense of this prehistory requires us to confront contradic-
tions in scale, moving between individual users' firsthand experiences
and the aggregate characteristics of a widespread grassroots movement.
Dial-up BBSs both were overwhelmingly populated by middle-class white
boys and, at the same time, provided vital counterpublic spaces for computer owners excluded from other media systems. Reckoning with the

conflict between these two aspects of the modem world is fundamental to understanding the failures of social media in the platform era and essential to imagining the worlds that will come after.

HOW DO WE KNOW WHAT WE KNOW?

The stereotype of digital media is that they are sterile and precise. It costs nothing to make a copy of this book and email it to a friend. This faith in the immateriality of digital media is evident in the metaphor of "the cloud."[89] Each time we store a vital bit of personal data in the cloud, we indulge in the fantasy that there is no cost—human or environmental— to building and maintaining a global network of data centers. In the 1980s and 1990s, however, computer networks were tangible things, made of copper wires and whirring disk drives. Their materiality was impossible to ignore.

At the outset of the modem world, computer-mediated communication functioned more like broadcast media than software.[90] Ephemerality was embedded in its architecture. Just as many TV studios routinely erased their old tapes to make space for new recordings, many BBS programs erased old posts to make space for new messages. BBS users understood that there was no guaranteed future for their online activities. Bulletin board systems were never crawled by Google or captured by the Internet Archive's Wayback Machine. There were no search engines, portals, or digital directories to consult. When a BBS went offline, it vanished from cyberspace, taking all of the files and messages created by users along with it. Data storage was expensive. Most sysops either could not afford or did not think it was necessary to create backup copies of their systems. Often, the best way to record the visual culture of a BBS involved pointing a camera at the computer and making a literal "screen shot." Home videos occasionally turn up on YouTube.

Further complicating the material history of the modem world is that it was decentralized in its administration as well as its technical design. Each BBS functioned independently, and individual user accounts were not linked from one BBS to the next. Even relatively large BBS associations such as FidoNet, which kept records out of technical necessity, represented a small subset of the overall BBS world. Enthusiasts published hundreds of reference guides and BBS lists, organized by region and theme, but there was no single, central authority keeping track of the overall network.[91] While state-sponsored contemporaries like Mini-tel and NSFNET kept central records for the purposes of accounting, BBS operators were not bound by any record-keeping mandate: there were no annual reports to be filed, no grants to be renewed, no stock-holder notices or conference proceedings. Privately held commercial services like CompuServe and The Source surely kept records of their subscribers, but these data are not available to the general public. With the exception of the US Census, a handful of academic papers, and a few market-research reports, there were no representative surveys of the on-line population published during the 1980s and 1990s.[92] In the place of formal documentation, there are notes meant for contemporary readers, such as FAQs and README files. The stories of people and their com-munities lie in the margins of these gray literatures.

Today, the material record of the modem world remains scattered and messy, but it is stubbornly growing. Traces persist in shoeboxes of floppy disks, stacks of waterlogged magazines, deaccessioned library books, unmarked VHS tapes, and pirated software. Although they have not been systematically collected by libraries, museums, or other archi-val institutions, they survive at ham radio swap meets, in eBay auctions, and in the closets of former users. Over the past twenty years, a loose network of self-archiving "retrocomputing" hobbyists have made their personal collections accessible on the public web. Any effort to write histories of the BBS era depends on the expertise, labor, and material resources of this enthusiast community.[93] In the absence of institutional support, hobbyists pay hosting fees out of pocket, scan and upload im-ages from magazines and catalogs, and learn specialized forensic tech-niques to recover data from aging floppy disks.

The single most important resource for modem world research is textfiles.com, a digital archive that has been maintained by the self-described "rogue archivist" Jason Scott since 1998.[94] Textfiles.com began with Scott's personal collection and grew to include a range of newslet-ters, technical documents, computer programs, and other ephemera of 1980s BBS culture.[95] Today, the site hosts over fifty thousand files, in-cluding more than eleven thousand homespun periodicals or e-zines.[96] In addition to textfiles.com, Scott also directed *BBS: The Documentary*, an eight-episode documentary series about BBS technology and culture. From 2001 to 2005, Scott documented the production process on a blog and in periodic posts on forums like *Slashdot*. This unusually transparent approach served as an explicit invitation for former BBS enthusiasts to reach out and share their memories. Rather than present a personal memoir, Scott aimed to represent the plurality of the BBSing movement, from for-profit commercial platforms to small-scale hobby BBSs.[97] Consistent with the spirit of the original project, Scott has since posted over two hundred hours of unedited interview footage to the Internet Archive.[98] These interviews are the principal source of oral histories related to the modem world.

Beyond "born digital" sources such as the textfiles.com collection, print media have also been crucial vessels for the preservation of BBS history. Between 1983 and 1998, the tech press produced a handful of how-to books and technical manuals about BBSs and PC communications. Although these books tended to focus on technical implementation, the authors often included firsthand observations about the experience of using a BBS. From the late 1970s, computer hobbyist magazines such as *Byte*, trade periodicals like *InfoWorld*, and special-interest TV programs like *Computer Chronicles* regularly covered PC networks. The late 1980s saw the emergence of several magazines specifically for BBS users, including *Boardwatch*, *BBS Callers Digest*, and *Sysop News . . . and CyberWorld Report*. For readers without access to a local user group, computer magazines served as vital gateways into the growing community of computer enthusiasts. Through reader letters and classified ads, these magazines featured the voices of newbies and nonexperts alongside industry professionals and longtime hackers.[99]

In addition to these archival and methodological challenges, anyone handling the material history of BBS culture will eventually confront difficult ethical questions.[100] BBS communities thrived in relative obscurity. With good reason, users behaved as though they were hanging out in a private club. The feelings of security and anonymity offered by BBS networks facilitated their adoption by marginalized groups of people. As the inheritors of this culture, we have a moral obligation to understand and preserve these historical circumstances whenever possible. Throughout this book, I have sought to balance a desire to identify and celebrate the contributions of individual BBS participants with a respect for the original contexts in which they lived.

The informal archives of BBS history combine memoir and materiality in equal measure. The scanned pages of a magazine contain handwritten notes and a shipping address. A BBS advertisement is stowed away in a ripped CD-ROM of 1990s shareware. Telephone numbers appear on the title screen of a pirated PC game. These bits of digital marginalia remind us that these are histories of technology-in-use. These surviving data were not made to last. They were smuggled into the future.

WHY NOT ANOTHER INTERNET?

Before social media, the dot-com boom, and "10 free hours" on America Online, dial-up bulletin board systems provided an accessible platform for computer owners to meet one another, share resources, and make community. The history of this modem world offers a new explanation for how the internet became social, a complement to histories focused on the US military, academic research, or Silicon Valley. Building on a long tradition of amateur media, the hobbyist groups that built dial-up BBSs in the 1970s transformed the idea of the computer network from a tool of work into a space for communication, culture, and play. Through the creative appropriation of the North American telephone network, BBSs of the 1980s provided a low-cost alternative to commercial packet-switching systems and closed research networks. Rather than reliability or profit, the design of BBS networks reflected the social needs of human communities. By the end of the decade, thousands of people and organizations that had been excluded from other media systems were running BBSs in cities and towns throughout North America. From music fandom and fantasy gaming to queer activism and political advocacy, these communities developed norms and practices that continue to shape the social media systems we rely on today.

Bulletin board systems were cheap, interoperable, and explicitly social—everything that their institutional contemporaries were not. They proliferated in cities and towns far from conventional centers of tech power, such as Silicon Valley or the Route 128 corridor. They were hosted on PCs that sat on kitchen tables, on workbenches, and in the spare closets of homes and offices of dedicated volunteers. And BBSs were accessed by a more diverse population of people living under a wider variety of socioeconomic conditions than the comparatively homogeneous research networks were. As the characteristic problems of online community—sustainability, privacy, governance, and free speech—inevitably arose, the plurality of the BBS ecology afforded more opportunities for experimentation and democratic participation than would have been possible in a less diverse environment.

For early modem users, cyberspace was first and foremost a local BBS. Embracing this grassroots origin story should change how we engage with social media systems today. The concentration of power in a handful of platforms and providers is a departure from the longer tradition of decentralized networking, local ownership, translocal cooperation, and mutual accountability. To imagine a better future for the internet, a future that comes after social media, we need a more robust account of internet history, one that includes the abandoned prototypes and paths not taken of a more experimental era. What cultural, technical, and regulatory conditions enabled the flourishing of BBSs? How did potential users learn about the modem world? Who was welcomed to participate and who was excluded? How did longtime BBS users respond to the dot-com boom of the 1990s? What social practices and technical innovations carried over to the participatory web? Why do so many histories overlook the BBS phenomenon? How might the memory of yesterday's BBS embolden us to demand justice for tomorrow's internet?

CHAPTER TWO

Computerizing Hobby Radio

ON JANUARY 12, 1978, snow began to fall across the midwestern United States, and within a few days, more than a foot blanketed the region. Power lines were downed, freight trains derailed, and hundreds of cars stranded alongside treacherous roadways.[1] The brutal storm clobbered cities and towns from Michigan to Massachusetts for more than five days, leaving thousands of people stuck inside with unplowed streets and unreliable power.[2] On the morning of Monday, January 16, Ward Christensen and Randy Suess were among those Chicagoans facing another day out of work. Feeling restless, Christensen phoned his friend and suggested that the two begin building a "computerized bulletin board system" for their computer club, the Chicago Area Computer Hobbyist's Exchange (CACHE). Christensen had been toying with the idea for a while, and now, with little but shoveling to distract them, the two men set to work.[3] By the end of the day, they had settled on a rough design, and after a few weeks of assembling, soldering, programming, and testing the system in their spare time, the two were ready to present "CBBS" to the rest of the club's members. By February 16, 1978, the first homegrown dial-up bulletin board system was up and running in Suess's basement, waiting to accept a call from anyone with a computer terminal and a modem.

True to its name, the Computerized Bulletin Board System worked like a cross between a telephone answering machine and cork-and-pins community bulletin board. Accessing the system required a terminal, modem, and phone line—a tall order for all but the hardcore hobbyist in 1978. Lacking computers of their own, the earliest users relied on teleprinters such as the Teletype Model ASR-33.[4] To establish a connection using such a terminal, a user held the telephone handset to their ear, manually dialed 312-528-7141, and waited for the machine in Randy Suess's basement to answer. Upon hearing CBBS respond with a tone, the user placed the handset on a special cradle and pressed the terminal's "carriage return" key a few times. If this arcane rite was performed successfully, it brought their printer to life, and the clacking machine would begin to bang out a message:

*** WELCOME TO CBBS/CHICAGO ***
*** WARD AND RANDY'S COMPUTERIZED BULLETIN BOARD SYSTEM ***

As you might imagine, this system was hardly foolproof. A noisy line, quirky modem, or bug in the software could break the connection. Christensen and Suess routinely updated the system on the basis of feedback from their users, but the nascent modem world was as unpredictable as it was exciting.[5] With a virtual shrug, Christensen and Suess made no guarantees, advising would-be users, "Feel free to hang up and try several times if you have problems."[6]

The design of CBBS reflected the state of the art for DIY microcomputer technology.[7] Christensen mocked up the system software in BASIC and rewrote it in 8080 assembler language, and Suess custom-built the hardware using an S-100 motherboard that he bought at "some flea market."[8] The machine connected to the phone line using a brand-new modem from D. C. Hayes Associates, the first computer modem built by and for hobbyists.[9] Unlike most modems available at the time, the Hayes modem was programmable. Taking advantage of these hackable features, Christensen and Suess rigged up a clever mechanism to detect incoming calls and "cold boot" the system directly into the CBBS software, which would wake up the modem and answer the call. When the caller disconnected, the system shut itself down completely—a crude but effective way to recover if a user dropped the line without logging off.

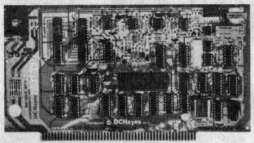
Ad for the 80-103A modem, the first product from D. C. Hayes Associates, Inc. Aimed at the burgeoning hobbyist market, the Hayes modem enabled microcomputers to exchange data over the telephone network using the Bell 103 protocol from AT&T. In addition to the modem's ability to access time-sharing systems, its manual suggested a range of applications including telecommuting, multiplayer gaming, electronic mail, home and office automation, and running an online database. The circuit board was designed to fit into the S-100 expansion bus used by popular microcomputers such as the Altair 8800 and IMSAI 8080. (*Byte*, November 1978)

In addition to Christensen and Suess sharing news of their creation with the members of CACHE and the makers of the Hayes modem, Christensen mailed announcements to *Dr. Dobb's Journal of Computer Calisthenics & Orthodontia* and *Byte*, magazines reaching over one hundred thousand hobbyists throughout North America and Europe.[10] The editors of *Dr. Dobb's* simply printed the original text of Christensen's letter, complete with a note that anyone having trouble with the system should give him a call at home.[11] The editors of *Byte*, meanwhile, published a short commentary about CBBS under the title "What Might Be Called CACHE's On Line Graffitti [*sic*]." In addition to a brief description of the system's architecture, they provided step-by-step instructions for dialing in and joked that readers should be prepared for a busy signal because of "all the other people reading this notice" who would be trying to log in at the same time. At the end of the piece, they included a partial log of their session on CBBS dated March 19, 1978. The editors encouraged readers to try out the system for themselves, promising "a long and fascinating interactive communications session."[12]

The response to CBBS was immediate and overwhelming. While the system had already been receiving calls from outside Chicago through word of mouth, the announcements in *Byte* and *Dr. Dobb's* brought immediate attention to the computerized bulletin board, and Suess's phone line started to register calls from all over the United States and beyond.[13] The founding editor of *Byte*, Carl Helmers, was so inspired by CBBS that he published an eight-page editorial speculating about the future impact of the modem on hobby computing.[14] "Computer-to-computer communications via the dialup phone network are a very real possibility for the personal user," he enthused. Helmers urged readers to think beyond the typical time-sharing paradigm and toward smaller-scale group communication. To the hobbyist, computer-mediated communication offered a new space for collaboration. Helmers imagined that systems like CBBS would flourish whenever "a few people share a common goal and live far enough away from one another."[15] Instead of long drives and occasional meetings, he suggested, a bulletin board offered a means for regular communication among communities of interest.

After several months of testing, modification, and repair, Christensen and Suess submitted an article to *Byte* magazine detailing the architecture of the new system.[16] Published in November 1978 under the

```
TERMINAL NEED NULLS?  TYPE CTL-N WHILE THIS TYPES:

          ***   WELCOME TO CBBS/CHICAGO   ***
     ***  WARD AND RANDY'S COMPUTERIZED BULLETIN BOARD SYSTEM  ***


-----> CONTROL CHARACTERS ACCEPTED BY THIS SYSTEM:

     DEL/RUBOUT  ERASES LAST CHAR. TYPED (AND ECHOS IT)
     CTL-C       CANCEL CURRENT PRINTING
     CTL-K       'KILLS' CURRENT FUNCTION, RETURNS TO MENU
     CTL-N       SEND 5 NULLS AFTER CR/LF
     CTL-R       RETYPES CURRENT INPUT LINE (AFTER DEL)
     CTL-S       STOP/START OUTPUT (FOR VIDEO TERMINAL)
     CTL-U       ERASE CURRENT INPUT LINE

-------------------- BULLETIN  --------------------
       PROBLEMS WITH THE SYSTEM??
HARDWARE: RANDY (SUESS), (312) 935-3356
SOFTWARE: WARD (CHRISTENSEN), (312) 849-6279
-------------------- BULLETIN  --------------------
)
-------------------- BULLETIN  -  --------------------
---> ALL USERS:  BE FAMILIAR WITH MESSAGES 3, 6, AND 60

               N O T E
-----> AS OF 4/8/78, MESSAGES PACKED AND RENUMBERED <-----
-------------------- BULLETIN  --------------------
```

Log of a typical session on CBBS during its first year in operation. Many early users accessed the system from a teleprinter terminal, so these interface elements would have been hammered out onto a reel of paper rather than scrolling up the glass of a video screen. (*Byte*, November 1978)

title "Computerized Bulletin Board System," the article explained how to assemble the hardware and code the software required for running an autonomous bulletin board system of one's own. Beyond the technical instructions, their article also tacitly established several norms—social as well as financial—for the protean BBS culture. Playing around with CBBS was fun and interesting, but it wasn't free. Hardware cost money to buy and software took time to write, so they had to consider the financial as well as technical challenges of running an online community out of your home.

From the outset, CBBS provided an open gathering place for hobbyists curious about computers and communication. A file called "WELCOME" contained text to be sent out each time a new caller connected to the system. The CBBS WELCOME file conveyed a sense of friendly informality. Beneath a short set of instructions for operating the system, a bulletin—"PROBLEMS WITH THE SYSTEM??"—invited users to call Christensen and Suess at home to discuss hardware and software issues.

The convivial tone of the WELCOME message made CBBS feel less like a high-tech experiment and more like an easygoing computer-club meeting.

Christensen and Suess also hoped that CBBS would provide a model for other computer clubs to build virtual meeting places. The *Byte* article equipped readers with all of the information they would need to assemble a computerized bulletin board system of their own. In a letter to *Dr. Dobb's*, Christensen noted that he had already shared the CBBS software with Dennis Hayes, maker of the Hayes modem, and Dave Caulkins, head of the People's Computer Company networking committee (PCNET).[17] Documentation for the software emphasized the fun of "getting on the air" with CBBS and joked that while users were "on their own," they were welcome to call up the authors for the "occasional chat."[18]

On top of all this free sharing, Christensen and Suess were also concerned with the legal complications and commercial potential of CBBS. Christensen noted that the software was protected by copyright to limit commercial uses, but "something should be able to be worked out" in the case of noncommercial use.[19] Shortly after, they began to sell copies of CBBS.[20] Christensen joked that selling the software should prevent people from "bugging him" for a free copy. On Caulkins's recommendation, Christensen set the price at $50 and gave all of the proceeds to Suess.[21] "After all," reasoned Christensen, "[Randy] put up all the money—all I'd put up was time."[22] Buyers received two eight-inch floppy disks containing the 8080 assembly code and related documentation formatted for the CP/M operating system.[23] According to memory, they sold approximately two hundred copies of the software.[24] By the end of 1981, three years after the publication of the *Byte* article, more than two dozen other systems were running CBBS in cities and towns from Vancouver, British Columbia, to Tallahassee, Florida. Countless others were using software inspired by CBBS, such as ABBS for the Apple II and FORUM-80 for the Radio Shack TRS-80.[25]

So what drove Christensen and Suess to build CBBS? Could they imagine inspiring thousands of others? Did they dream of changing the world or maybe getting rich? Or was it all just a goof? When asked directly about their motivations, Christensen and Suess demurred. In

Christensen's initial announcement to *Byte*, he reported that he kept the system up twenty-four hours a day "just to see what happens."[26] Later, he joked that CBBS was just something fun to do during a snowstorm: "all the pieces are there, it is snowing like @#$%, let's hack."[27] While these statements reflect Christensen's self-deprecating sense of humor, they are also consistent with an ethic common among postwar technical culture: innovation for its own sake.[28]

Of course, there was also a practical dimension to the computerized bulletin board. As the system itself informed callers, it was designed for "message communication between computer hobbyists."[29] By 1978, the club to which Christensen and Suess belonged, CACHE, had already begun to appropriate media technologies for sharing information about the club's hobby. It published a monthly newsletter, titled *The CACHE Register*,[30] and maintained an information "hotline" using an answering machine stored in Christensen's basement.[31] Rather than replace these systems, CBBS offered a new opportunity to extend the lively dialogue that was already taking place in meetings, newsletters, and phone calls.[32] And, unlike more ephemeral interactions, the questions, answers, announcements, and articles posted to CBBS remained available for future retrieval.

The founding of CBBS marked the beginning of the "modem world," a period of time from roughly 1978 to 1998, during which the use of computers for communication remained a niche, peripheral activity in the broader culture of personal computing. Although this period overlaps chronologically with the interconnection of many computer science research facilities in the United States, notably those with financial support from the Department of Defense's Advanced Research Projects Agency (ARPA) or the National Science Foundation (NSF), such institutional computer networks remained almost wholly inaccessible to the typical personal computer owner. Indeed, from the perspective of a microcomputer enthusiast in 1978, the ARPA- and NSF-funded networks simply did not exist.

But CBBS did not fall from the heavens with the Chicagoland snow, fully formed and without precedent. Instead, it was created amid a generative historical conjuncture in which policy, infrastructure, and popular culture converged to reimagine the PC as a medium for communication

NOVEMBER 1978   VOLUME 3, Number 11

$2.00 in USA
$2.40 in CANADA

BYTE

the small systems journal

Cover of a special issue of *Byte* magazine dedicated to data communication. A painting by the artist and software engineer Ken Lodding depicts a satellite and two microcomputer terminals orbiting a bright blue-green Earth. Red lines connect the terminals and satellite to the planet's surface. Keen readers may have recognized the satellite's three-point star shape as a prototype spacecraft under development by the Radio Amateur Satellite Corporation (AMSAT). Feature articles detailed the opportunities for combining amateur radio, microcomputing, and satellite communications. Tucked in the middle, a piece by Ward Christensen and Randy Suess described a "computerized bulletin board" built atop the existing telephone network. (*Byte*, November 1978) rather than a tool for computation. Further, a long tradition of amateur telecommunications created a context for grassroots innovation and a community eager to experiment with novel forms of data networking. Technical hobbyists were already in the habit of exchanging information by radio, by mail, at swap meets, and in club meetings. Indeed, the very same issue of *Byte* that carried the CBBS article featured a cover story about adapting amateur radio repeaters to build a global system for "intercomputer communication."[33] With photos of shiny satellites and diagrams of ionospheric propagation, this article presented a breathtaking vision of computer hobbyists around the world exchanging messages with one another through the ether. In contrast, the system outlined by Christensen and Suess must have seemed downright simple. Yet CBBS struck the right balance of accessibility and difficulty to inspire readers to break out their soldering irons. Creating a bulletin board was not easy, but it was possible; and unlike more outlandish proposals, a BBS offered immediately practical benefits—especially for members of hobbyist clubs and organizations.

The CBBS origin story is a treasured bit of BBS lore.[34] Christensen and Suess are humble, relatable heroes, and the blizzards of 1978 provide a perfect backdrop for the start of their adventures. At first blush, this tale of two friends sparking an accidental revolution seems to follow a familiar Silicon Valley innovation narrative—but CBBS was not a business enterprise like Apple or Microsoft.[35] Rather, Christensen and Suess aimed to provide a platform for communication and collective intelligence among their fellow computer enthusiasts. As Christensen later recalled, the inspiration for CBBS came from his club's newsletter and a cork bulletin board posted up during club meetings.[36] Further development of the system was driven by the pleasure of technical mastery and pride of craftsmanship common to so many men's hobbies of the US postwar period. In this sense, the CBBS story provides a convenient point of origin for an alternative mythology of the internet. The social, technical, financial, and legal constraints that shaped the early years of CBBS foreshadowed areas of conflict and creativity that would animate the next two decades of personal computer networking. Likewise, CBBS drew on nearly a century of amateur tinkering with radio technology and the telephone network. CBBS may have been a literal computerization of the community bulletin board, but it marked an even more significant transformation: the computerization of telecommunications by the grassroots.

At the end of the 1970s, a confluence of social, technical, and regulatory activity in the United States created a favorable environment for grassroots networks like CBBS. First, the nationwide telephone network known as the "Bell System" provided a reliable, accessible, and relatively open infrastructure for hobbyists to experiment with data communications.[37] For nearly half a century, AT&T had enjoyed a de facto monopoly over telecommunications in the United States, but in the 1960s and 1970s, this arrangement was under increasing scrutiny.[38] By the end of the latter decade, regulators were moving to break up "Ma Bell" and open telephony to private competition. In this period of transition, the gradual opening of the Bell monopoly enabled the formation of independent dial-up networks. Without the ten-digit telephone number and standardized RJ-11 wall socket, there could be no BBS networks or PC modems.

To imagine the Bell System as an infrastructure ready for appropriation depended on a broader cultural context. The technical culture of dial-up BBSs drew directly from a tradition of amateur experimentation that had been developing for decades around radio communications. During the 1970s, hobby radio was experiencing a revival in the United States thanks to newly affordable two-way FM equipment and a bloom of interest in Citizens Band (CB) radio. Previously, amateur (or "ham") radio activities were limited by the complexity, cost, and availability of equipment using vacuum tubes. But in the 1960s, advances in microelectronics resulted in simpler radios and radio kits based on integrated circuits and other solid-state components. These same innovations drove the production of new portable and handheld VHF radios in the 1970s, reducing the technical and financial barriers to participation in both ham and CB radio.[39] Ham radio clubs around the United States built "repeaters" that served as virtual gathering places for casual communication.[40] By the end of the decade, the practice of chatting over the air with nearby strangers had become familiar. Numerous Hollywood films and television shows depicted characters operating radio equipment, and CB slang leaked into casual talk.

Meanwhile, the popularization of two-way radio communication in the mid-1970s coincided with the emergence of a new arena of amateur experimentation: microcomputing. Although small groups of enthusiasts had been experimenting with amateur computing since the mid-1960s, the introduction of do-it-yourself kits in the mid-1970s opened microcomputing up to a broader population of technology enthusiasts.[41] Kit computers such as the Altair 8800 were featured in magazines of general technical interest, such as *Popular Electronics*, as well as publications aimed at amateur radio operators, such as *QST* and *73*. Kit computers were notoriously difficult to build and operate, but computer hobbyists frequently carried over expertise from their prior experiences with amateur radio, model rocketry, and hi-fi stereo equipment. With the availability of prebuilt microcomputers after 1977, a secondary market emerged around hardware peripherals, including devices for telecommunications. As a result, the basic technical requirements for building a BBS—a phone line, modem, and PC—were available to most Americans by the start of the 1980s and no longer required a soldering iron or background in electrical engineering.

The modem world appeared at a moment of social, political, and technological change. Christensen and Suess brought CBBS online amid the conjuncture of several systems in flux: a telephone network preparing for liberalization, a recent fad for CB, a revolution in amateur radio practices, and an emerging marketplace for microcomputer products. Briefly, these changing systems provided a context in which amateurs could begin to build a new data infrastructure from the bottom up. On the afternoon that Christensen and Suess decided that a computerized bulletin board would be a fun project for a day off work, elsewhere in the United States, songs about CB radio were climbing the pop charts, economists were arguing for the end of the AT&T monopoly, ham radio operators were erecting antenna towers, and computer enthusiasts were turning their hobby into an industry. To understand this unusually generative moment, we should step back to a moment before electrified communications had become commonplace.

MAKING CONTACT WITH RADIO HOBBYISTS
For someone in 1975 to imagine that the Bell System could serve a function other than voice telephone calls required a playful relationship with

the media environment. But to actually build an alternative communication system on top of Ma Bell also required a certain hubris about your right to modify the architectures of everyday life. In 1978, Randy Suess and Ward Christensen exhibited both of these qualities in their work on CBBS. By remaking the telephone network as a medium for grassroots data communications, they were acting in a tradition of amateur telecommunications stretching back more than a century. From adolescent amateur press associations and "wildcat" rural telephone operators to community television systems and radical "videophile" networks, enthusiasts have consistently pushed telecommunications in new directions by finding unexpected uses for existing media technologies.[42]

Beginning with the earliest experiments in wireless communication at the end of the nineteenth century, amateurs have adopted, modified, and repurposed industrial information and communication technologies for the purposes of community building, resource sharing, collective intelligence, and public safety. Alongside the forces of regulation, commercialization, and militarization, these amateur activities played a critical role in shaping social computing practices and platforms of the 1980s and 1990s. Unlike their peers in academia, industry, or the military, the typical middle-class American amateurs worked out of their homes using the "free" time and money left over from their commitments to work and family. While the work of professional researchers was rationalized, bureaucratized, and archived by virtue of their institutional affiliation, the work of amateurs was either self-archived or, more often, lost to time. As a result, the contributions of amateurs have been obscured, overlooked, and ignored by popular histories of media and communication. Yet, to make sense of the creation of CBBS in the late 1970s and the subsequent rise of the modem world, it is necessary to understand the norms, values, and visions motivating technical hobbyists across North America.

The microcomputer hobbyists building and exploring networks like CBBS were closely tied to the technical cultures of amateur (ham) and Citizens Band radio.[43] Ham and CB are legally and culturally distinct forms of radio communication, but they each experienced a boom in participation during the 1970s. By the end of the decade, participants in both types were in the habit of appropriating new media technologies to extend their hobbies. Military surplus and cast-off consumer products provided a steady stream of raw materials for hands-on learning and experimentation. In addition to on-air interactions, CB and ham radio enthusiasts throughout North America belonged to local and regional clubs that met regularly in person, published newsletters, and managed shared technical infrastructures. By the late 1970s, the technical repertoire of radio amateurs provided a ready-to-hand set of metaphors and communication frameworks for computer hobbyists building online communications. Indeed, many of the practices that we now associate with computer-mediated communication have a prehistory in the annals of hobby radio.

Unlike AM/FM broadcasting, CB and ham radio are peer-to-peer, noncommercial forms of wireless communication. There is no audience, no news or entertainment programming, no advertising. Rather, hobbyist radio practices like these consist of home-built or store-bought stations transmitting on particular frequency "bands" of the electromagnetic spectrum. For example, since the late 1920s, amateurs have used the ten-meter "high frequency" band to send and receive Morse code messages around the world. During the 1970s, ham radio and CB radio were two of the most common technical hobbies in the United States.

Historically, ham radio and CB radio have been quite distinct technical cultures. They operate on different frequencies, using different equipment, according to different regulations. However, participants in the two forms of radio share in a larger sociotechnical imaginary that values hands-on knowledge and democratic access to communication technology. Ham and CB operators each take pleasure in the rather unusual practice of reaching out across the airwaves to communicate with unseen strangers. One joy of hobby radio is to make contact for its own sake, to establish a communication bond without any expectation of transmitting useful information.[44] Despite the meaningful differences between amateur radio and CB radio, both played a key part in shaping the emerging technical culture of the modem world.

VIRTUAL COMMUNITY ON THE LOCAL REPEATER

In the United States, "amateur" denotes a special class of radio operators licensed by the Federal Communications Commission (FCC) to operate certain types of equipment on a set of clearly defined frequencies.[45] Federal legislation guarantees amateur access to valuable regions of the electromagnetic spectrum to encourage bottom-up experimentation and innovation. For more than a hundred years, amateur radio operators have built and maintained countless networks ranging from public-service systems to experimental satellite communications. Their trials and achievements provided the cultural context for the appropriation of other communication and information technologies during the 1970s. In a very material sense, dial-up BBSs grew out of preexisting amateur radio networks.

The ham radio origin story is about the stubborn creativity of amateur technologists. In the (metaphorical) wake of the sinking *Titanic*, Congress passed the Radio Act of 1912. The act both introduced an official "amateur" radio license and also severely restricted the activities of amateur operators.[46] Newly licensed amateur stations were restricted to transmitting on wavelengths of two hundred meters or less, a region of the electromagnetic spectrum considered useless at the time. The days of unrestricted experimentation were over. Yet hobbyists embraced the term "amateur" as a collective identity and sought out new opportunities to communicate with each other, on and off the air. Among the newly classified amateurs was a forty-three-year-old automobile engineer and radio hobbyist named Hiram Percy Maxim.[47] In 1914, believing that a lack of political representation was to blame for the severe restrictions of the Radio Act, Maxim proposed the creation of a "league" of local clubs to represent the amateur radio hobby community. In addition to its political purpose, the Amateur Radio Relay League (ARRL) aimed to create a nationwide communication network of cooperating wireless stations. Using a store-and-forward networking technique, participating amateurs could exchange messages over far-greater distances than would have been possible under the technical restrictions of the Radio Act. By 1917, the ARRL had grown to more than three thousand members across the United States and Canada. On March 8, a message made the round trip from Los Angeles to New York and back in less than two hours, a technical and organizational feat unmatched by either commercial or military wireless systems of the period.[48]

Over the next half century, as radio and television technology diffused into homes and automobiles throughout the United States, hams continued to push the boundaries of wireless telecommunications. In the 1960s, ham radio clubs around the United States began to build a new type of cooperative network known as a "repeater." Repeaters are autonomous stations installed at high elevation that automatically retransmit the signals of nearby hams in order to extend their geographic range. Unlike the relay networks, which required substantial human organization and sought to cover large territories, repeaters are local resources. In the 1970s, ham radio clubs built and maintained repeaters in cities and towns throughout the United States. Today the ARRL produces repeater databases listing locations, frequencies, ownership, and other details to help visitors "key up" the repeater. The repeater provides an informal gathering place on the air for hams living nearby or passing through the area.

The explosion of repeater activity was stimulated by changes in the technology and regulation of amateur radio. In the late 1960s, the consumer electronics industry went micro, using small self-contained components known as integrated circuits or "chips" to replace full-sized transistors, resistors, and capacitors.[49] Integrated circuits enabled the production of smaller, simpler equipment that could be assembled and sold at a dramatic discount. Meanwhile, the FCC changed the allocation of wireless spectrum above 30 MHz, known as the "very high frequencies" (VHF), rendering a significant amount of commercial FM radio equipment (of the sort found in police cruisers and taxicabs) obsolete.[50] Hams eagerly bought up this discarded gear and modified it for use on the new amateur radio frequencies. By the early 1970s, amateur activity on VHF had become so popular that electronics manufacturers such as Motorola began to produce new VHF transceiver equipment specifically aimed at the amateur market.[51] With short VHF antennas and tiny integrated circuits, many of these new radios were small enough to be handheld, enabling a new mobility for ham radio operators.[52]

While VHF radios offered greater mobility and improved audio quality, their range was considerably shorter than other operating modes— approximately five to fifteen miles.[53] Building repeaters allowed ham radio enthusiasts to overcome this limitation. Approximately the size of an office filing cabinet when fully assembled, a repeater is composed of an antenna, a transceiver, a microcomputer for operating the radio autonomously, and a "duplexer" that allows the system to simultaneously transmit and receive information on a single antenna. Antennas placed at higher altitudes reach a much larger area, so hams sought out hilltops, ridges, and space on existing radio towers for their repeater installations.

In practice, operating a repeater feels like joining a chat room or a party line. Only one participant can speak at a time, and the repeater typically enforces a short pause between each transmission. With the advent of repeater culture in the 1970s, ham radio operators began to keep a radio tuned to the local repeater all day, waiting for friends to show up for a short chat. Numerous clubs used (and still use) repeaters to hold weekly on-air discussions, or "nets," as a way to keep in touch during the gaps between their in-person meetings. An active repeater provides a gathering point in the ether, a rest stop on the electromagnetic spectrum.

A repeater is a collective good of significant value to its users. In Elkhart, Indiana, for instance, the Elkhart County Radio Association (ECRA) has continuously operated a VHF/FM repeater for nearly fifty years. In the early 1970s, Elkhart was home to Crown International, an electronics firm owned by a Christian minister and radio amateur named Clarence Moore (W9LZX). Moore provided his employees with an amateur radio station to support their interest in radio communications and experimentation. However, members of the local club remember that the company's low-band station was little used until Moore's fellow amateurs "kindled a burning desire" in him to add a VHF repeater.[54]

Initially, the ECRA repeater's antenna was installed on a "modest" eighty-foot tower outside Moore's home. From this location, the repeater became an important infrastructure in the ongoing social life of the Elkhart club and came to symbolize the members' technological ambition and collective commitment to experimentation. Following Moore's death in 1978, the repeater's antenna was moved to a new five-hundred-foot antenna erected in his memory and ceremonially activated on January 1, 1980. The new antenna was said to fulfill the late founder's dream of reaching "50 miles in all directions" and led to considerable growth of the club, as the repeater invited participation from an even greater geographic range.[55]

Amateur radio repeaters of the 1970s such as the Elkhart system represented a different type of telecommunications network from the ARRL's store-and-forward messaging system from half a century earlier. Whereas the decentralized ARRL network moved messages efficiently across the continent, the centralized repeaters represented hubs of local communication.[56] The work of building and maintaining a local repeater strengthened the relationships between hams in the local community. Furthermore, by publicizing the repeater's location and frequency, local clubs made themselves audible to traveling hams, extending a kind of fraternal hospitality into the ether.

Structurally, ham radio repeaters provided a ready-to-hand conceptual model for the architects of grassroots computer networks such as CBBS. Both systems acted as hubs for local networks of hobbyists. The autonomy of repeaters and BBSs depended on the availability of programmable microprocessors to control communication interfaces and convey messages between users of the system. Functionally, repeaters and BBSs provided virtual gathering spaces for users of a larger telecommunications infrastructure. Repeaters were located at particular frequencies on the VHF band; BBSs, at particular numbers on the telephone system. Potential users learned about these spaces through word-of-mouth recommendations or publications aimed at communities of shared interest. Once up and running, however, the themes and interests discussed on BBSs ranged much more broadly than the technically minded chat on ham radio repeaters. Indeed, the open-ended discussions on dial-up BBSs more closely matched the playful, provocative discourse of CB channels.

GETTING WILD ON THE CITIZENS BAND

Whereas ham radio was steeped in history and tradition, CB radio flashed into US popular culture of the 1970s as a fun, accessible form of grassroots communication. The radio historian Kristen Haring characterizes the difference in terms of social norms and barriers to participation: "the culture of CB radio was as free as amateur radio's was restrictive."[57] Although the spectrum was allocated in 1948, the Citizens Band, as we know it, came into being with the creation of twenty-three distinct "channels" in 1958. During the 1960s, the falling price of two-way radio gear spurred adoption among enthusiasts and commercial users alike. The cover of the 1965 *Radio Shack Catalog* depicted two men at the beach chatting over handheld radios: "No license. No kit building! Ready to talk."[58] Officially, CB radio required a license, but CB regulations were scarcely enforced. Hardly any CB owners bothered to register with the FCC.[59] In the mid-1970s, a prebuilt CB radio from a nearby Radio Shack—or garage sale—was the only requirement for getting on the air. At the height of the craze, CB radio participation outstripped ham radio by an order of magnitude. More than four million CB radios were sold in 1975 alone.[60]

Due to the low barriers to entry, the discourse on CB was more free-wheeling than on the ham radio bands. Whereas hams tended to follow orderly on-air procedures, CB radio could be rollicking and chaotic with frequent interruptions, trash talking, and endlessly mutating slang. If amateur radio could feel like a friendly classroom or workshop, tuning into CB radio could be like wandering into a late-night saloon. As a result, the popular image of CB radio took a dramatically different shape from earlier forms of amateur telecommunications. Ham radio operators were civic-minded nerds. CBers, in contrast, were telecom outlaws in muscle cars and tractor-trailers. On film and TV, CB operators flagrantly violated FCC regulations, broke the new interstate speed limits, and revved their engines at the global shortage of crude oil. According to the FCC, CB operators were supposed to identify themselves on the air by their call signs and avoid transmitting foul language, music, advertising, or malicious interference—but, like the licensing requirement, these regulations were difficult to enforce and largely went ignored by the everyday CB operator.

During the mid-1970s craze, country and western recording artists brought the sounds and slang of the Citizens Band over to the AM/FM airwaves. A slew of "trucker" songs included the crackling sound of CB to convey the sonic experience of the open highway. In 1972, Dolly Parton and Porter Wagoner recorded an early CB-themed song, titled "10-4 Over and Out." In "10-4," Parton and Wagoner play out a series of escalating arguments between a wife and her chronically late husband as though they were sung over the air. In the second verse, Parton demands to know why her husband isn't home, and Wagoner warbles his reply, claiming that he can't hear her due to interference. The song's romantic twist is that the couple only fights on the air. When they're home, they shut off the radio and love each other, telling the rest of the world "over and out." As the population of CBers grew, so did this frisson between voyeurism and performance.

Although the duet between Parton and Wagoner suggested equal participation in CB among men and women, other popular media portrayed CB communication as a predominantly male practice. In blockbuster films such as *Smokey and the Bandit* (1977) and *Convoy* (1978), long-haul truckers adopt the CB as part of a rugged, macho counterculture. *Convoy* was adapted from an earlier country-western song, the 1975 hit "Convoy" by C. W. McCall. The film and the song describe a fictional on-the-road protest in which long-haul truck drivers evade highway patrol officers and the National Guard through their tactical use of CB. McCall's story was enhanced by snippets of CB chatter, peppered with nearly impenetrable lingo. As the record crossed over from country-western radio to mainstream pop, it boosted the hype for CB across the country. Whereas Parton and Wagoner's bickering portrayed CB as a space of daily chatter, "Convoy" portrayed it as a form of mass resistance. Microphone in hand, these truckers "just ain't a-gonna pay no toll." In a departure from the geeky masculinity of ham radio, "Convoy" positioned the CB radio alongside the eighteen-wheeler, the .38 Special revolver, and the American muscle car as icons of roadhouse masculinity.

The popular perception of CB radio as an ungovernable space was also reflected in the use of CB for gender play and sexual exploration. Beyond the cute drama of "10-4" and outlaw masculinity of "Convoy," the Citizens Band offered an opportunity for anonymous flirtation among nearby strangers. As Ernest Dickinson reported in the *New York Times* in 1976, some CB communities informally set aside one channel for this type of communication, in his words, "a singles bar of the airwaves."[61] The uncertain audience for radio transmissions offered an additional exhibitionist thrill for those who were engaging in the sexier side of the Citizens Band, and popular coverage of the CB craze frequently remarked on the use of CB radios among sex workers.

Occasionally, representations of sexuality on the Citizens Band took on a distinctly queer character, as in Rod Hart's novelty song "CB Savage," a minor hit in 1975. The vocal performances on "CB Savage" sit in polysemy between the homophobic and homoerotic. In spoken narration, Hart recounts the story of a pair of bored truckers interrupted by flirty come-ons from a lisping male voice over their CB radio. The mysterious stranger flips the typical radio slang, exploiting the double entendre in common CB terms like "hammer" and "handle." The two truckers are flustered by the suggestive transmissions, and their reactions invite a queer misreading. The narrator describes his copilot blushing and smiling like "a big old bird-fed cat." Liner notes on the record sleeve took pains to describe Hart as a "good ole, straight ole country boy," but Plantation Records seemed to acknowledge more ambiguous reading of "CB Savage," issuing the seven-inch single with a pink label in place of its conventional green.[62]

While the popular representation of CB tended toward the sensational, quotidian CB use was surely tamer. In 1975, at the apogee of the CB radio "boom," Harvey A. Daniels from the Education Department at Rosary College in River Forest, Illinois, encouraged K–12 English teachers to bring CB radios into their classrooms. The unusual vocabulary and dynamic lexical choices of CB slang, Daniels argued, offered a unique opportunity for students to think critically about the relationships among language, culture, and communication. In suburban Chicago, Daniels noted, "the most common phonological judgment made by first-time CB listeners is that 'they all sound like southerners.'"[63] Although the predominance of southernness "defied demographic reality," Daniels observed a surprising harmony among speakers exhibiting different phonological characteristics: "There does not seem to be any conflict or discrimination between speakers whose phonological patterns do reveal different social or regional backgrounds. Blacks and whites, northerners and southerners, and all other possible combinations of speakers, converse more peacefully and more often on the radio than they ever would in person. I have never heard any linguistic discrimination or put-downs of anyone's language as long as both sides were employing the basic CB dialect—and this is a medium where wisecracks are more the rule than the exception."[64] Daniels was careful to note, however, that this tolerance had its limits and that languages other than English were often poorly received. In one interaction, an operator transmitting briefly in Spanish was criticized harshly by another, who stated, "Somebody forgot they're in America." Clearly, the egalitarian possibilities of the Citizens Band were not equally accessible to all users.

In addition to the "southern" characteristics of the CB dialect, Daniels also observed linguistic habits that suggested comparisons with "Black English." Not coincidentally, CB radio was already widely adopted among middle-class Black Americans by the time that the 1976 "boom" brought CB radio into the homes and cars of millions of white Americans. Whereas hams were often drawn to radio out of technical curiosity, Black American CBers were additionally compelled by the sonic qualities of radio communication. In a landmark 2011 article on the origin and growth of Black CB radio culture for *American Quarterly*, Art M. Blake describes Black CB culture emerging out of a preexisting Black "aural-oral sphere" at the conjuncture of Black-interest radio, jive talk, and jazz and blues lyricism.[65] Even as the mobility of Black bodies remained socially and politically constrained, the active, omnidirectional antennae of the Black CBers emanated Black voices and Black cultural concerns without restraint.

The motivations for Black CB radio adoption were explicitly connected to the civil rights struggles of the 1960s, and the future political implications of CB radio use were no less explicit.[66] In 1976, *Ebony* published a statement from Berkeley G. Burrell, the president of the National Negro Business League and adviser to President Nixon, celebrating the potential applications of Black CB radio for political organizing and economic development. "With the strength of thousands of Black CBers," enthused Burrell, "they could be organized to do almost anything."[67] Two years later, Burrell repeated this appeal to an audience of over ten thousand Black CB radio enthusiasts at the fifth annual convention of the African American radio club the Rooster Channel Jumpers.[68] Within a few months, this political potential was demonstrated in the city of Boston as the public crisis over desegregation and busing erupted into street violence. Residents, white and Black, in the neighborhoods of Roxbury and South Boston employed CB radios to coordinate political and public-safety activities with their neighbors.[69]

In spite of CB's rapid adoption and pop visibility, the CB craze did not last long. Kristen Haring speculates that a combination of uncertain technical standards and unfavorable atmospheric conditions may have contributed to a decline in the reliability of CB communication.[70] What fun is CB if you can't hear anyone? Furthermore, the FCC specifically prohibited the operation of repeaters on the Citizens Band, so even tight-knit CB communities were unable to (legally) engineer solutions to the rising interference and limited range.[71] Without the freedom to experiment guaranteed to licensed amateurs, CBers were at the mercy of forces out of their control. And with declining functionality, many CB radio owners may have simply abandoned the habit.

Ham and CB radio complemented each other during the 1970s, resulting in a bloom of hobby radio activity across the United States. Each offered multiple forms of legitimate participation, from demonstrating expert on-air operating to repairing secondhand equipment. This variety reflected a broader rise in participatory cultures concerned with technology and innovation, such as amateur film and photography, hot rod and lowrider car clubs, and science fiction and fantasy fandoms.[72] CB also attracted different groups of people to the airwaves. Amateur radio had traditionally been a homosocial activity promoting intergenerational mentorship among middle-class white men.[73] Organized club activities such as erecting new antennas or running "field day" events provided opportunities for hams to form intimate fraternal bonds without breaking the restrictive norms of postwar masculinity.[74] The Citizens Band, meanwhile, welcomed a population of hobbyists who were more diverse in race, ethnicity, and socioeconomic class than their ham radio contemporaries.

After more than half a century of ham radio activity, the accessibility and popular pleasures of the Citizens Band finally opened amateur telecommunications to participation on a mass scale. Furthermore, the lower barriers to entry made CB a more appropriate tool for political organizing among communities of people with variable technical expertise. As a result of these features, CB radio culture included participants from a greater range of racial groups and socioeconomic classes than were welcomed into the rather homogeneous society of amateur radio. This diversity was audible in the unrestrained slang, regional colloquialisms, and racially specific discourses that listeners encountered across the Citizens Band. CB radio facilitated a much more playful, spontaneous, and, at times, subversive, on-air culture than its older cousin did. A visit to a crowded CB channel offered humorous commentary and entertaining personalities. These performative aspects of the hobby were valued just as highly as the engineering of a crisp signal was.

Finally, the CB craze overlapped chronologically with the emergence of affordable, accessible computing. How many microcomputer enthusiasts heard the galloping rhythm of McCall's "Convoy" on their drive down Interstate 40 to Albuquerque, New Mexico, for the first World Altair Computer Convention in March 1976?

THE COMPUTERIZATION OF HOBBY RADIO

While the 1970s airwaves buzzed with two-way radio activity, a new technical culture was forming around a different microelectronic medium: the computer. Although data processing was already part of corporate America's information infrastructure and the time-sharing industry was beginning to boom, hands-on access to computers remained rare, especially outside of university research labs.[75] Participatory time-sharing systems such as the Minnesota Educational Computing Consortium demonstrated the potential of amateurs and nonexperts to shape the future of computing, but these remained shining exceptions during the 1970s.[76] Rather, scarcity stimulated the curiosity of tech enthusiasts, giving rise to a popular computing culture that revered computers as mysterious and exciting. For teen ham radio operators such as the future microcomputer designer Steve "Woz" Wozniak, computers became objects of unmet boyhood desire—Woz hung computer posters on his bedroom walls and "dreamed" of owning his own minicomputer.[77] Such fan practices were encouraged by hobbyist magazines and science fiction stories that offered speculative glimpses of a more participatory future for computing. As a result, unrestricted access to computer technology became a driving concern and fundamental value of the new technical culture.[78] Radio was accessible. Computing was aspirational.

Amateur access to computers happened in fits and starts. As early as the mid-1960s, some amateurs enjoyed informal access to a computer thanks to the beneficence of a local institution. But widespread access was hard to imagine before the introduction of affordable "microprocessor" chips in 1971.[79] A microprocessor is an integrated circuit designed to perform a set of basic arithmetical operations. Its utility depends on the architecture into which it is deployed. In the 1960s, Intel imagined that its microprocessors would be built into household appliances like coffee-makers and washing machines to automate simple, predetermined tasks. But as had been done many times before, experimenters and entrepreneurs found an unexpected application for these new materials: to build cheap computers. By 1975, microprocessors formed the basis of several do-it-yourself "microcomputer" kits available from mail-order catalogs and enthusiast magazines.

Ham radio operators and CB enthusiasts were among the earliest adopters of microcomputers. Kit computers, occasionally referred to as "hobby computers," were sold through the same mail-order catalogs and retail stores as amateur and CB radio equipment. Magazines of interest to amateur radio operators—for example, *Popular Electronics*, *Radio-Electronics*, *QST*, and *73*—featured articles on computing and advertisements from microcomputer makers. Promotional photos of microcomputers frequently depicted them among the larger technical apparatus of a ham radio "shack." For many hobbyists, amateur radio and microcomputing required similar skills and offered similar technical pleasures. These were hands-on hobbies for people who enjoyed the smell of burning solder.

Microcomputing was especially attractive to radio hobbyists frustrated by the limited tinkering potential of radios built around integrated circuits rather than discrete electronic components.[80] Ham radio magazines promoted computer kits as an extension of amateurs' existing technical practice, while also presenting digital logic and software development as wholly new challenges. Between 1974 and 1976, *73* magazine ran a series of articles on the fundamentals of computer science: number systems, binary arithmetic, discrete logic, serial communications, and memory addressing.[81] Behind the scenes, Wayne Green, editor of *73*, was hard at work on a new magazine dedicated to the computer hobby: *Byte*.

Beyond the inherent pleasures of learning a new technical field, hobby computing promised to expand the scope of hams' existing radio practices. In an article titled "Computers Are Here—Are You Ready?," Green positioned microcomputing as a complement to the latest amateur radio techniques: "More and more amateurs are tackling the new inexpensive computer kits and coming up with very usable results. Some are using the units to aim their antennas for moonbounce, some to predict or even aim antennas at Oscar, some to operate a virtually automatic RTTY station, some to run a repeater or even a system of repeaters."[82] If microelectronics threatened ham radio's tradition of hands-on technical expertise, hobby computing promised a renewal.

By 1976, thousands of amateurs were working on building a computer of their own. That year, Green published an anthology of microcomputing articles aimed at amateur radio operators. At first glance, the book's cover looked like a typical ham radio operator's workbench. Instead of transceivers or amplifiers, however, the photograph depicted a typical hobby computing setup: a home-built keyboard, cassette tape recorder, small television and video interface, and MITS Altair 8800 computer. Based on the Intel 8080 microprocessor, the Altair was not the only or the latest kit computer on the market in 1976, but its bright-blue case and blinking red LEDs had come to symbolize the technical culture of microcomputing. Indeed, MITS, the firm responsible for the Altair, had previously sold model rocketry components and electronic calculators.[83] Truly, the Altair was a computer by and for the technical enthusiast.

Designed to resemble more expensive minicomputers like the DEC PDP-11, the Altair 8800 promised both practical business and scientific applications and fun challenges for the technical hobbyist.[84] A cover story in the January 1975 issue of *Popular Electronics* declared the Altair a "minicomputer kit to rival commercial models."[85] This claim was accurate insofar as a fully functional Altair could replace a minicomputer in many industrial and commercial settings, but it did not at all reflect the usability of the kit alone. While time-sharing systems offered real-time interaction and terminals with QWERTY keyboards, the Altair user interface was limited to one row of red LED lights and a bank of on/off switches. Without the additional purchase of a teletype terminal and tape reader, programming the machine was a slow, difficult task. And without a floppy-disk or cassette-tape interface, the machine's memory would be lost each time it was shut down.

As painstaking as building and programming an Altair may have been, the experience brought computer hobbyists into close contact with the digital logic of the microprocessor. Whereas microelectronics had introduced a layer of opacity between radio operators and their equipment, kit computers brought the hobbyist back down "close to the metal." Early microcomputer programmers needed to express their ideas using the limited set of instructions etched into the Intel 8080.[86] Eight of the switches on the face of the Altair corresponded to the eight digits that could be read at a time by the eight-bit microprocessor. The "on" position indicated a "1" and the "off" position a "0." Though considerably less efficient than the programming and debugging tools available on more sophisticated systems, this interface forced the hobbyists to "speak" the same language as the microprocessor.

The enthusiastic adoption of the Altair by hobbyists in 1975 and 1976 presaged a boom in the microcomputer market stretching into the 1980s.[87] Just as the CB craze expanded access to two-way radio communication beyond the limited domain of the technical hobbyist, prebuilt "home" and "personal" computers brought microcomputing to a broader population. Between 1977 and 1983, multiple manufacturers brought computers to market for a wide range of prices, users, and applications.[88] Radio Shack featured the low-cost TRS-80 Color Computer in its annual catalog, while Apple Computer maintained a premium rate for the Apple II. Atari and Commodore sold computers with rich graphics and sound as entertainment machines, while IBM packaged its PC in silver and beige for the serious business user. Meanwhile, the BASIC programming language became the lingua franca of personal computing, and a torrent of BASIC workbooks and programming magazines encouraged users to write their own software.[89] By the end of the 1980s, microcomputing no longer required facility with a soldering iron, but the values and interests of radio amateurs continued to shape the growing technical culture.

Radio hobbyists saw the microcomputer as a device for communication, rather than information processing or automation. By incorporating microcomputer technology into their hobby, radio amateurs anticipated the diffusion of computers across the field of telecommunications. In the hands of ham radio operators, microcomputers came to serve three key functions. First, microcomputers extended the technical affordances of amateur radio stations by, for example, automating the control of a directional antenna or interpreting incoming Morse code messages. Second, hams used office applications such as database management systems and word processing software to organize hobby activities outside of radio communication, for example, printing a club newsletter or organizing one's contact history. And, third, microcomputers offered wholly new telecommunication modalities that were not previously possible.

Amateur radio enthusiasts were uniquely suited to the technical challenges of computer-mediated communication. Although they would not have described their activities as "digital," hams of the 1970s regularly communicated in code. Until 2003, all licensed amateurs were

required to demonstrate minimal proficiency with copying and transmitting messages in Morse code. Furthermore, a popular activity within
amateur radio since the 1940s included adapting cast-off teletype equipment for "radio teletype," or RTTY, operations.[90] Radio teletype stations
could even be configured to receive messages semiautonomously, providing RTTY operators with a kind of proto–bulletin board function. It
was easy to imagine adding a microcomputer to such a system. Indeed,
one popular application of microcomputers to amateur radio was to
translate messages from the Morse code sent by human operators to the
ASCII and Baudot codes used by RTTY stations.[91]

Local and regional amateur radio club meetings were also important
venues for microcomputing enthusiasts to meet one another. By the late
1970s, many amateur radio clubs were also actively engaged in hobby
computer activities. In 1983, the "Club Corner" section of *QST* magazine
specifically addressed this area of contact between the two hobbies in a
column by Sally O'Dell (KB1O) titled "Clubs and Computers: A Simple
Interface." O'Dell compared the early days of ham radio with the nascent personal computing movement and encouraged club members to
make computing a more central feature of their activities. As a place to
start, she suggested finding access to desktop publishing tools, noting
that at least 25 percent of ARRL-affiliated clubs were already producing
a computer-generated newsletter. O'Dell further portrayed hobby clubs
as crucial spaces for learning and sharing technical information about
new technologies such as home computing. O'Dell also urged club organizers to reach out to local computer users' groups: "it may well be that
computer enthusiasts are as interested in Amateur Radio as you are in
computers."[92] Finally, O'Dell announced that two microcomputer videos
were added to the ARRL film library and were available for rent by any
affiliated ham radio club.

Along with magazines and club meetings, amateur radio also provided a few additional venues for the nascent microcomputing community: on-air "nets" and regional swap meets. Amateur radio "nets"
are on-air meetings in which hams gather on a prearranged frequency
or repeater to share information and socialize. In 1980, *QST* magazine
published a short note from David P. Allen (W1UKZ) of Scituate, Massachusetts, inviting readers to join several computer hobbyist nets.[93] A
Boston-area net met on Wednesday nights, an East Coast net for Apple

owners met on Saturday nights, and an international Atari net was held on Tuesday evenings. In Southern California, the W6TRW Amateur Radio Club began hosting a monthly swap meet in the parking lot of an aerospace company where many club members were employed.[94] Although a valid amateur radio license was required to rent a table, the swap meet's organizers specifically allowed participants to sell computer parts along with amateur radio gear. Amateur radio nets and swap meets provided valuable spaces for informal socializing among hams interested in learning about hobby computing.

During the 1970s, the established technical culture of amateur radio provided a nurturing context for the formation of hobby computing. Not all of amateur computing originated in ham radio, of course, but the two hobbies served as valuable complements to each other. In particular, the existing values, practices, and structures of amateur radio provided useful models for the organization of amateur computing's technical culture. For those computer enthusiasts who were hams, however, amateur radio also significantly shaped their expectations of the microcomputer. Beyond the advertised uses of microcomputers as tools for business and entertainment, the amateur radio operator encountered the home computer first and foremost as a technology for communication and community organization.

FROM THE AIRWAVES TO THE TELEPHONE LINE

The creation of CBBS in 1978 marked the beginning of the modem world. By publishing the details of the system in *Byte*, Christensen and Suess laid the groundwork for thousands of similar "computerized bulletin boards" to pop up across North America.[95] By 1983, more than 275 boards were up and running across forty-three states.[96] *Byte* continued to play a central role in the emerging modem world, routinely covering new developments in BBS technology and publishing dozens of reader letters about modems and telecommunications.[97]

Despite CBBS's origins in the eerie quiet of a snowy city shutdown, it was not formed in a vacuum. Rather, Christensen and Suess worked at a particularly generative conjuncture of technological, cultural, and regulatory change in telecommunications. The Bell System infrastructure had recently been opened to experimentation, microcomputer kits based on the Altair architecture were becoming increasingly reliable, and the technical culture of hobby radio encouraged a playful, participatory engagement with telecommunications. CBBS represented a convergence of these three parallel phenomena, a culmination of more than fifty years of amateur and professional telecommunications in the United States.

The technical culture of the modem world exhibited many of the norms and values of earlier forms of amateur telecommunications, not all of which were positive. While early bulletin boards exuded the same spirit of technical exploration and collaboration that had motivated radio amateurs before them, the social and material barriers to entry were high. Unlike the open and accessible culture of CB radio, the early modem world more closely resembled postwar amateur radio. For more than a decade, participation was largely limited to white middle-class men, many of whom seemed happy to escape from the complex social reality of the 1970s into an alternative world of protocols, software, and transistor-transistor logic. Eventually, the political, economic, and cultural circumstances of the 1980s opened the modem world to more diverse publics. But in the very early days, the population of most bulletin boards was relatively homogeneous—especially in contrast to CB radio and other racially diverse technical hobbies.

Amateur and CB radio nevertheless provided the firmament for grassroots computer networks like CBBS to grow and flourish. Their appropriation of the Bell System for data communications was consistent with the creative pragmatism of radio hobbyists who built their stations out of secondhand military equipment and discarded commercial hardware. Likewise, early online systems reproduced many networking concepts and cultural norms from hobby radio. Dial-up BBSs came to serve a similar function for local computer hobbyists as the amateur radio repeater did for local hams. Even the slang overlapped. Terms like "channel" and "handle" were borrowed directly from CB radio. In 1980, the nationwide online service CompuServe made the connection explicit by naming its chat system the "CB Simulator." In a very direct sense, the computerization of hobby radio in the 1970s produced the modem world of the 1980s and 1990s.

CHAPTER THREE

Building an Internet for Everyone

IN 1983, JOHN MADILL WORKED at the Pikesville ComputerLand store in Baltimore, Maryland.[1] At the time, ComputerLand was promoting the DEC Rainbow, a competitor of the IBM PC, and Madill bought one for himself. As he learned to use the new computer, he started looking around for communications software with the goal of running his own BBS. Although DEC designed the Rainbow for compatibility with MS-DOS, it didn't provide the same "interrupts" that most DOS software used to interface with the modem, so many widely available BBS programs wouldn't run. A friend recommended that he reach out to Tom Jennings, the sysop of "Fido's BBS" in San Francisco. Jennings specialized in writing low-level code to make DOS run on non-IBM hardware. While working for Phoenix Technologies in Boston, he had written the compatibility layer for numerous PC "clones" including the Rainbow. His own machine—nicknamed "Fido"—was "a real mongrel," running MS-DOS on a Motorola 68000 microprocessor.[2]

One night, Madill gave Fido's BBS a call—long-distance from Baltimore to San Francisco. He left a message for Jennings, and the two began chatting about computers and communications. Jennings provided Madill with Rainbow-compatible versions of two utilities he had written for terminal emulation and file transfer.[3] Over the next few weeks, they spent a lot of time chatting about how to port Fido's underlying BBS software to the Rainbow. Out in San Francisco, Jennings had no access to the Rainbow, so they often wound up on the phone, late at night, with Jennings dictating code for Madill to key into the machine. Jennings later described it as "the most painful code I have ever written."[4] After several "gigantic telephone bills," Madill had a working copy of Fido's BBS running on his DEC Rainbow.[5]

Despite Jennings and Madill's success, the collaboration had not been easy. Living in different time zones and area codes, they were keenly aware of the costs involved. As they continued to tinker with Fido and call each other's boards, they began to discuss a new feature that would allow one Fido to automatically place a call to another Fido, quickly exchange new messages or files, and hang up. This would minimize the duration of each long-distance call and enable them to schedule the calls for late at night, "off peak" hours when the long-distance rates were cheapest. At the time, there were only two Fidos, so they designed a simple "point to point" networking scheme in which each system was assigned a number—Jennings was #1, Madill was #2, and so on—and each system kept a file listing the telephone numbers associated with each node number. If you wanted to send a message to the sysop of another Fido, you needed only to know their node number. Your Fido would wake up in the middle of the night and deliver the message while you slept. With off-peak calls running about $13 per hour, they estimated that a "coast to coast" transfer would cost about $0.01324 per message.[6] Early in the summer of 1984, Jennings sent a software update to Madill's Fido. Soon after, the first "FidoNet" connection was made between San Francisco, California, and Baltimore, Maryland.[7] "[It was] a big giant hack," recalled Jennings; "the hack value was very high."[8]

The big giant hack was about to get much bigger. Jennings had also been communicating with Ben Baker, a computer hobbyist based in St. Louis.[9] Baker was planning to start a BBS for the employee computer club at the aerospace firm McDonnell Douglas. The club had a Rainbow 100 on loan from DEC to host the system, which led Baker to discover the port of Fido BBS being written by Madill and Jennings. In March, Baker set up a new Fido BBS on the Rainbow, and in April, the new system became Fido #10.[10] Over the next few weeks, Fido BBSs continued to pop up around the country. By June, there were five in St. Louis's 314 area code alone—including four running on DEC Rainbows.[11] As Jennings continued to work on the Fido software, he kept in touch with all of the sysops running a Fido BBS, regularly leaving messages on their boards, uploading files, and chatting with them on the phone. In June, Jennings passed around an updated version of Fido along with two new components: "FIDONET" and "NODELIST.BBS." Overnight, every board running Fido had been transformed into an addressable node in an autonomous, grassroots messaging network.

THE PROBLEM OF LONG-DISTANCE DIALING

To understand the financial and technical constraints that inspired Jennings and Madill's collaboration, it is helpful to explore several key aspects of the nationwide telephone network on which dial-up BBSs depended.

The modem world is a telephonic history of the internet.[12] Without the availability of reliable telephone service throughout the United States, neither the institutional nor the hobbyist computer networks of the 1970s and 1980s would have been possible. State-supported networks like ARPANET ran over special long-distance "leased lines" that created a dedicated connection between points in the network, freeing ARPANET engineers to focus on higher-level concerns.[13] Hobbyists enjoyed no such luxury. Modem users remained keenly aware of the conditions and constraints of their residential telephone service. Line noise, busy signals, and the competing interests of other members of the household were common sources of frustration for BBS users and sysops.

The computerized bulletin board emerged at a particularly opportune conjuncture in the history of the telephone. For nearly half a decade, AT&T had enjoyed a de facto monopoly over telecommunications in the United States, but by the early 1980s, regulators had broken up "Ma Bell" and opened telephony to private competition. While the gradual opening of the Bell monopoly enabled the formation of independent dial-up networks, the system that AT&T had created was a technological and organizational marvel. In 1978, nearly every home in the United States was accessible from every other home through a convenient, easy-to-use telephone terminal.

However, some telephone calls were far pricier than others. During the twentieth century, US telephone services depended on a division of space into "local" and "long-distance" regions, with long-distance "trunk" lines connecting local network exchanges. Since the 1920s, long-distance calling rates have been set relatively higher than local rates in the United States. The rationale for this arrangement is that local network infrastructure is required for callers to access long-distance services—a long-distance call literally depends on a larger component of the network.

So by 1978, nearly everyone could *receive* a telephone call, confident in the knowledge that it cost nothing to answer. Dialing out, however, required a mental calculation of distance, time, and cost. The telephonic spatial imaginary sorted the geography of one's social life according to rates set by telecom regulators. It might be free to call your son's school downtown but cost five cents a minute to call your friend across the state and twenty cents a minute to call Uncle Larry in Walla Walla. Accidentally ringing up a massive bill was, unfortunately, a common experience for many new modem owners. The combination of long-distance dialing, hourly fees, and premium services could be confusing, and users might not realize their mistake until the end of the month, when the telephone and credit card bills arrived by mail. While professional adults could afford to joke about the cost of getting online, similar usage by a teenager could result in significant intrafamily conflict.

The ten-digit telephone number was the result of a thirty-year effort on the part of AT&T to create a fully automatic network spanning the continent of North America. Central to this project was the organization of the network into the North American Numbering Plan, or NANP, in 1945.[14] By enforcing a universal numbering scheme across the network, telephone users from around the country could imagine themselves as members of a single integrated system. The first three digits of any North American telephone number contain the "area code." Since the introduction of area codes in the 1960s, they have been markers of collective identity, recognizable around the country and brandished with pride by longtime residents of cities like Los Angeles, Manhattan, and Miami. Although area codes do not always align neatly with the system of local and long-distance calling rates, lists of BBSs were nevertheless typically sorted by area code, reflecting users' desire to avoid long-distance charges.

Whether or not BBS users were willing and able to pay, long-distance calling fees substantially structured the network imaginary of the modem world. The prevalence of regional BBS lists reflected the extent to which BBSing remained an exclusively local activity. Callers seeking special-interest boards may have been more inclined to pay a long-distance fee than were those looking for general-interest chat, but toll calls could easily overwhelm the careless modemer. BBSs with adult content, particularly original images and video clips, typically charged a monthly access fee, but the authors of *Erotic Connections*, a how-to book aimed at readers curious about "love and lust" on BBSs, cautioned their readers to be mindful of their telephone bills: "Even a free board . . . can get expensive to use if it's an out-of-state call."[15]

The steep cost of long-distance dialing meant that the aggregate growth of BBSs did not necessarily translate into equal access for all computer owners. Faced with the ten opaque digits of a telephone number, there was no way—short of dialing—to know what was waiting at the other end.[16] For some people, this ambiguity lent BBSing an attractive air of mystery, a sense of participating in an underground society. For others, it was costly and frustrating, enough of a barrier to keep them out altogether.

BECOMING FIDONET

Early on, FidoNet employed a simple point-to-point networking scheme and a fixed schedule for transmitting messages between nodes. The NODELIST.BBS file was a human-editable list of BBSs in the Fido network. Each night, at 4 a.m. Eastern Time, the FIDONET program took over the host PC. If there were outgoing messages to be sent, it looked up the destination BBS in the NODELIST and placed a call. If it got a busy signal, it moved on to the next message in the queue. Meanwhile, it paused between calls in case a remote board was trying to call in. The telephone company billed long-distance in one-minute increments, and a typical message was just a few hundred bytes in length. Even at 300 bits per second, most Fido-to-Fido connections were over in less than one minute. Yet, as more Fidos came online and more sysops began to experiment with the inter-BBS messaging feature, the network started to fall out of sync. Busy signals were coming up more often, and messages weren't getting through. The net needed a more sophisticated system for routing and scheduling mail.

In addition to network traffic jams, the management of the nodelist itself was becoming a problem. At first, everyone in FidoNet knew each other, and the entire nodelist fit on a single piece of notebook paper. Node numbers were assigned on an ad hoc basis. Anyone who registered their copy of Fido BBS received a printed manual with a unique node number handwritten on the cover.[17] But as the network grew beyond thirty nodes, there were strangers involved, and the node-list required daily care and attention. By July 1984, recalled Jennings, the nodelist was falling apart, and the network was "starting to deterio-rate."[18] Each week, the list grew longer, creating more opportunities for error. In the absence of any formal process for joining the network, new sysops simply reached out to Jennings and asked to be included. Bogged down developing the software itself, Jennings couldn't keep up with the interest. Errors weren't just frustrating to the hobbyists involved with the network. A wrong number in the nodelist meant that dozens of BBSs would be dialing out to that number every night. In one case, a typo resulted in a "poor old lady" being woken up every night at 4 a.m. to her telephone ringing off the hook for an hour. Realizing the error, Jennings called up to apologize, only to find himself in the unpleasant situation of trying to explain FidoNet to "an extremely tired, extremely annoyed person."[19]

With six active nodes in the local calling area, St. Louis became the unofficial testing ground for the future of FidoNet. In August, St. Louis sysops Ken Kaplan, Mike Mellinger, and Jon Wichman took over main-tenance of the nodelist. By that point, the list was "in shambles."[20] After several weeks of verifying the accuracy of each record, they released a thoroughly revised nodelist on September 21, 1984. They also declared that all future requests must be submitted through FidoNet itself, a mechanism that ensured that all new nodes had correctly installed and configured their BBS software.[21] Simultaneously, several other sysops including Madill, Tony Clark, Danny Feinsmith, Jim Ryan, Ben Baker, and Vern Crawford continued to work with Jennings to develop and test the design and implementation of FidoNet. They added binary file trans-fers, cost accounting, and system security features. They also began to work out a scheme for routing mail among local nodes in the network.[22] Instead of point-to-point networking, a single board would act as a gate-way into the area code and redistribute mail locally. In this "store-and-forward" arrangement, a message would take multiple short "hops" to reach its destination, cutting down on the number of long-distance calls

```
                                                  6/84  15   7/84
  * 2. CLP-BBS  Pikesville, MD John Madill        (301)-484-2831           32
  * 3. MICRONET Atlanta, GA Lane Fowler           (404)-979-5105
  * 4. Chance Load Mgt St. Louis, MO Tony Clark   (314)-895-6471
    5. Batie's Backyard Corvallis OR Alan Batie   -DOWN-
    6. CastleNet Corvallis OR Lee Damon           -DOWN-
  * 7. Strictly Software Waimea, HI Bob Overlock  (808)-338-1277
  * 8. Demon  New York, NY Danny Feinsmith        (212)-591-4487 10p - 3p
  * 9. Silver Screen  Danbury, CT Jim Ryan        (203)-748-5146 8p - 8a
  *10. MDC/RCC St. Louis MO Ben Baker             (314)-234-1462 5p - 8a
  *11. PRO-TECH Sanford Zelkovitz                 (714)-898-8634
  *13. Vern's Fido San Jose, CA Vern Crawford     ( 408)-923-5565 when not in use
      *14. WayStar Marlboro, MA Kevin Porter      (617)-481-7147
      *16. Mikes Board Mike Mellinger  St. Louis, MO (314)-726-3448
      *17. DCA_BBS Jon Wichman St. Louis, MO      (314)-962-0395
      *18. Steve Hedlund  Van Nuys, CA            (415)-989-2415
      *22. PCLUG St. Louis, MO Ken Kaplan         (314)-576-2743
       23. ComWorx  Encino, CA Paul Levy          (818)-986-1673 930a-11p +wkends
      *25. Take-A-Byte Anaheim, CA Robert Collins (714)-995-2428
      *26. MicroFonePC Fresno, CA Bob Robesky     (209)-227-2083 5p-9a +wkends
      *27. ??? Gardner, MA David Rene             (617)-632-1861
      *28. World Control Baltimore MD Rob White   (301)-653-2074
      *31. ??? John Warren Riverside, CA          (soon)
      *32. George Gilbert Artesia, CA             (213)-402-6217
       33. Rod Smallwood  England                 44-635-4680
      *34. CrossFire Todd Savar Philadelphia, PA  (215)-576-5009
      *35. ConsultNet Jim Turley Saratoga, CA     (408)-867-5078 11p - 3a
      *36. Rainbow Data  Los Angeles, CA          (Aug 15)
      *38. Bill Thousand Jr Madison WI            (608)-274-6377 330p - 830a
      *39. Karl Regier Reedley CA                 (209)-591-7464 630p - 100a
      *40. Ron Crain Birmingham MI                (313)-646-5159 11p - 6a
      *41. reserved
      *42. reserved
      *43. Seequa Computer Odenton MD             (301)-672-3627
      *44. NECS Arlington, MA Dave Mitton         (617)-646-3610
```

The FidoNet nodelist from June to July 1984, including handwritten updates by Tom Jennings. (Original materials courtesy of Tom Jennings)

throughout the system.[23] Jennings and others dreamed of one day routing messages coast to coast using only flat-rate local calls.[24]

Under the new system, the network continued to grow. In the final four weeks of 1984, the nodelist climbed from 108 to 134 nodes. Less than a year after the release of version 1, Fido BBSs were operating in forty-one area codes of the NANP. St. Louis was no longer the only area code with a network of local boards. New clusters were forming in wealthy suburbs like Route 128 in Massachusetts, Orange County in California, Northern Virginia, and the Houston Beltway in Texas. Beyond these high-tech hubs, the network was taking hold in regions that were especially disadvantaged by long-distance dialing. Four nodes were trading mail from the islands of Hawaii, three served BBSs in Ontario, and one BBS in the small town of Petersborough, New Hampshire, brought FidoNet into the offices of *Byte* magazine.[25] Outside of Canada and the United States, international links were established with BBSs in England, Indonesia, and Sweden. Calls from North America to Europe cost approximately one to three dollars per minute, so exchanging messages computer to computer was cheaper than talking by telephone and faster than mailing a conventional letter.[26]

With increasing reliability and geographic reach, FidoNet was becoming as much a social organization as a technological project. On December 1, 1984, Jennings launched *FidoNews*, a weekly electronic newsletter distributed to every node in the network.[27] In a short introduction, Jennings laid out a vision for the newsletter. Each issue would include "human-readable" copies of the nodelist and routing map along with classified ads and articles written by other Fido sysops. "ANYTHING is fit for the newsletter," he assured readers, "a description of your board, problems found, questions, jokes, fixes, horror stories about wrong FidoNet numbers, things for sale, etc etc etc."[28] Over the next year, the newsletter served as a forum for the Fido community, on topics ranging from highly technical discussions of network protocols to an alarming piece about the emergence of neo-Nazi BBSs.[29] As the only authoritative source of technical information about the rapidly changing network, *FidoNews* was essential reading for all Fido sysops.[30] "*FidoNews* is the only thing that unites all FidoNet sysops consistently," wrote Jennings. "Please keep up to date on it, and stock it for your users if you have the disk space."[31]

FidoNet is closely associated with Tom Jennings. As the sysop of Fido #1 and author of Fido BBS, he was accepted as the creator of FidoNet, and many other sysops deferred to his judgment about its future. Online and off, Jennings was gregarious, opinionated, charismatic, and outspoken. He could easily have positioned himself as the final authority

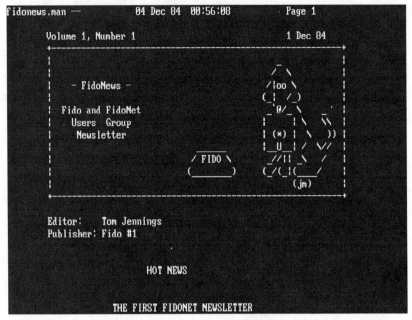

Masthead from the first issue of *FidoNews* featuring the ASCII art dog logo created by John Madill. (Original materials courtesy of Tom Jennings)

on FidoNet. But time and again, he disclaimed any control over the network. Instead, he invited others to collaborate, focused attention on their contributions, and gave up positions of power. In the electronic pages of *FidoNews* and in later interviews, he characterized his refusal to exercise central control as an expression of his politics—radical, anarchist, queer, punk. Jennings regarded the decentralization of the preexisting modem world as a virtue: "Every bulletin board was completely different, run by some cantankerous person . . . the way that they saw fit, period."[32] The original design of FidoNet sought to maintain the autonomy of individual boards. A sysop could cut themselves off from others by editing their copy of the nodelist, but they couldn't force anyone else to accept their changes. Conversely, the Fido software did not require the use of the St. Louis nodelist. With a copy of Fido, any two sysops could start a new network in parallel to, in competition with, or in defiance of the original. Early documentation for the system made this point clear: "You get to control absolutely everything that FidoNet does."[33]

In the spring of 1985, after a year in operation, FidoNet was becoming many things: a set of protocols, a collection of programs implementing

FidoNet bumper sticker with a gap for Fido sysops to write in their node numbers. Sold at cost through *FidoNews* at the start of 1985. (Original materials courtesy of Tom Jennings)

those protocols for different platforms, a network of interconnected BBSs, and a community of sysops and users. This multiplicity of meanings foreshadowed the transformation of the internet a decade later. Sure, anyone could use the Fido software to create a new network, but there was only one "FidoNet."[34] Overwhelmed by hundreds of requests for help, Jennings handed off editorial control of the weekly newsletter to Thom Henderson, an early Fido sysop.[35] In his first editorial, Henderson encouraged readers to take ownership of *FidoNews*. "Don't think of this as 'my' paper, or even as Fido's," he wrote. "Think of it as YOUR paper."[36] FidoNet was a collective, participatory project, and Fido sysops were already beginning to identify with the network. Jennings printed up five hundred bumper stickers featuring a dog and a blank space for sysops to write in their node numbers.[37]

REORGANIZING FIDONET

As the growth of the nodelist continued to accelerate, FidoNet was again racing toward disaster. Despite the success of the new routing system, the latest version of Fido could only index 250 nodes, and the nodelist was projected to hit the limit sometime in mid-April 1985.[38] The nodelist was also becoming an unreasonable burden on its volunteer administrator, Ken Kaplan. Ben Baker argued that an amateur network should be driven by pleasure: "[For Kaplan,] FidoNet is rapidly becoming work, not fun."[39] Ultimately, Kaplan represented a single point of failure in a system with dozens of participants. "FidoNet is too large to be managed from a central point," wrote Jennings in an article for *FidoNews*.[40]

A fundamental revision of the FidoNet addressing scheme was urgently needed. In 1985, there were no models for organizing a cost-conscious computer network at an international scale. FidoNet was an anomaly. "Fido wasn't designed," Jennings had remarked to *Byte* the previous October. "It was just built."[41] But the stakes seemed higher than they had even a few months before. Every night, hundreds of people sent mail through the network, and each week, a dozen boards joined the system. Could they rebuild the network while it was running? Or would it all fall apart?

The opportunity to redesign FidoNet came in April 1985. The McDonnell Douglas computer club invited Jennings, Henderson, and *Byte* magazine's West Coast editor, Ezra Shapiro, out to St. Louis for a special joint meeting with the local chapter of the Digital Equipment Computer Users' Society.[42] Henderson wasn't available, but Jennings and Shapiro took the five-hour flight from San Francisco to the nerve center of FidoNet in the US Midwest. The club meeting was held on Thursday night, but Shapiro and Jennings stuck around. That weekend, they convened with several St. Louis sysops at the home of Ken and Sally Kaplan to discuss the future of FidoNet.[43] Jennings turned up with a skateboard and knapsack full of maps of North America. They spread the maps out on the floor, passed around a felt-tip pen, and carved the continent into ten "regions."[44] For eleven hours, no one left the Kaplans' living room. They talked about software problems and administrative difficulties, drew potential maps and routing diagrams, and discussed how the network should function differently. Jennings later called it "the most productive meeting" he'd ever attended.[45] Late that night, they said good-bye and headed out with a plan.

On April 22, Thom Henderson sent out a special issue of *FidoNews* dedicated to the outcome of the meeting in the Kaplans' living room. Anticipating the pushback from sysops happy with the status quo, Henderson opened the newsletter with an excited editorial. "FidoNet has just grown too big too fast," he wrote. "Something that started out as a way for a small circle of friends to swap files back and forth has grown into a nationwide (even worldwide) electronic mail network, with hundreds of subscribers."[46] In a pair of articles, Jennings and Baker laid out their vision for the remaking of FidoNet. "Don't panic yet," assured Jennings; "it will be easier and better for everyone."[47]

The principal outcome of the St. Louis meeting was a reorganization of the network from an "amorphous" topology to a two-tiered "multinet." In the multinet, each individual BBS was still a node, but now every node also belonged to a region or a net.[48] Regions were defined strictly by geography, while nets also included an agreement to route mail locally. Ideally, all nodes would eventually belong to a net, but nodes in remote areas often started out as a member of a region. For example, while Region 17 covered a geographic area bounded by Alaska, Saskatchewan, Oregon, and Wyoming, most nodes in Region 17 belonged to one of seven nets organized around the cities of Portland, Vancouver, Alberta, Seattle, Regina, Saskatoon, and Eugene. For continuity, existing nodes kept their numbers, which left traces of the earlier topology in the new nodelist. Tom Jennings's original Fido BBS, located in the Bay Area's Net 125, became 125/1. John Madill's board, Fido #2, joined Metro DC's Net 109 and became 109/2. Under the net/node system, fewer messages would be sent directly over long-distance calls. Instead, Node 0 would act as a gateway. Any messages sent to Node 0 would be routed to the appropriate local node.

The regional schema represented a novel reconfiguration of space. For FidoNet purposes, the net/node number actually superseded the telephone number as a BBS's primary address. To convey the purpose of net numbers to the community, Baker and Jennings compared them to telephone area codes. In fact, an early prototype of the Fido map adopted area codes directly from the NANP.[49] At first blush, it might have looked to some sysops like they were reinventing the telephone numbering plan. But unlinking the network's addressing schema from the NANP allowed FidoNet to grow independently of the underlying telephone infrastructure. Just as the cluster in St. Louis had formed organically around the McDonnell Douglas computer club, future nets would be created according to the social and economic needs of a local community.

Breaking FidoNet into regions did more than fix a technical problem. The two-tiered system effectively decentralized administrative control of the network. Jennings characterized the new architecture as "anarchy through computers," a noncoercive approach to internetwork communication.[50] Instead of relying on a single person to manage the nodelist, each net and region nominated a voluntary "coordinator," known as the "NC" and "RC."[51] The coordinators were responsible for assigning new node numbers, distributing issues of *FidoNews*, resolving technical problems, and maintaining a regional nodelist. Each week, if there were any changes within the region or net, the coordinator would send an updated list to the sysop at Node 1/0. This position, initially held by Ken Kaplan, involved simply compiling the regional lists into a global nodelist and sending it back to the NCs. Jennings characterized the new top-level position as "grunt-work . . . no creativity involved."[52] Crucially, the net coordinator positions were designed with hobbyists in mind. Each NC was responsible for just a handful of nodes.[53] The network no longer depended on the beneficence of a single coordinator. Errors and failures would be contained within nets and regions.

Splitting up the nodelist enforced an interdependence among sysops in each calling area. The architects of the net/node plan did not prescribe how the net coordinators were to be chosen. This hands-off approach gave political control to the regional nets, enabling a flourishing of regional cultures. The practical need to find a volunteer NC implicitly encouraged local sysops to identify with their regional nets as much (or more) than with FidoNet as a whole. In July 1985, Henderson invited everyone in Net 107 (NYC_Metro) to spend a day on his boat for "sun, suds, surf and sysoping."[54] The next issue of *FidoNews* featured a humorous account of the party: "Picture a bus load of Fido Sysops with a printed text file as a guide scooting north on the Garden State Parkway."[55] Joining a net meant joining a community of peers.

The transition to "multinet" Fido was not immediate, and its creators anticipated that it might be rocky. Soon after the meeting in April, Kaplan announced that the nodelist was frozen.[56] New applicants would have to wait for the transition and apply to their new net coordinators. In late May, after more than a month of testing, Jennings released the first version of Fido with support for regional nets.[57] Now, when a user entered the FidoNet messaging area to create a new message, they were prompted to first select a net and then a node within that net.[58] Sysops were instructed to get the new version of Fido installed before June 12, 1985.[59] On that date, a new nodelist would go into effect. To make the transition, each sysop needed to download the new nodelist and set their system's net and node numbers. "I was expecting total chaos," recalled

Geographic structure of FidoNet after the "multinet" transition in June 1985. These original ten regions were "dreamed up" by several key FidoNet sysops during a marathon meeting in St. Louis and included every active area code in the North American Numbering Plan. Using felt-tip markers on large paper maps, the sysops constructed each region intuitively, aiming for segments of approximately equal population. The results provide a sense of the prevailing spatial imaginary among BBS sysops of the period, as well as a snapshot of the geographic reach of the telephone network. Not pictured: Region 18 also included area code 809, which was used by Puerto Rico, the US Virgin Islands, Bermuda, the Dominican Republic, and the fifteen island nations of the Commonwealth Caribbean.

Baker. "I was not at all prepared for just how smooth the transition happened!"[60] After weeks of anticipation, FidoNet carried on with barely a blip. Bemused, Baker later joked, "The mail kept flowing as if nothing had happened!"[61]

The successful upgrade marked an evolution in the collective identity of FidoNet's sysops. In the same sense that amateur radio operators discussed the coast-to-coast relay project of the 1910s, the transition to multinet Fido became a source of pride for the FidoNet community. "We've done an incredible thing here," remarked Thom Henderson in *FidoNews* a few months after the transition.[62] In comparison to other major networks requiring reorganization around the same time, the remaking of FidoNet was remarkably uneventful. When ARPANET transitioned to TCP/IP, it had taken six months for all of the nodes to adopt the new protocols. USENET's "Great Renaming" involved months of acrimonious debate. For Fido sysops, the experience of working together on a big technological problem seemed to deepen their commitment to FidoNet. "[The transition] took a good deal of coordinated effort by a great many people," recalled Baker in 1987. "It proved we COULD function as a body!"[63]

Over the next year, the net/node architecture remained stable, and FidoNet grew to nearly one thousand nodes—including more than one hundred outside of North America.[64] In November 1985, the Hobbycomputerclub (HCC) of Holland flew Jennings to Utrecht for a large computer show and a meeting of European Fido sysops.[65] According to a report Jennings published in *FidoNews*, the HCC included approximately twenty-five thousand members, and the room was packed for his presentation on FidoNet.[66] Despite the enthusiasm for microcomputers and BBSs, however, Europe presented unique challenges to FidoNet's growth. Whereas Americans paid a flat rate for local calls, Europeans paid per minute, regardless of distance. Additionally, variations in line quality and the availability of consumer modems complicated the construction of international connections. In the short term, countries outside North America were represented by national regions and nets, and local coordinators determined the best way to route mail within each country. By October 1986, there were nineteen regional networks operating outside North America, including nodes in Indonesia, Australia, Singapore, and Hong Kong.

REENGINEERING FIDONET

Although the transition of June 1985 distributed administrative control of FidoNet to the regional subnets, one critical aspect remained highly centralized: the Fido software itself. Tom Jennings originally created Fido BBS as a lark—it was 1983, he'd just moved across the country, and he had the time to write code for a few weeks. That owners of the DEC Rainbow flocked to the system was unexpected. That it would become an international messaging network was ridiculous. After two years and dozens of updates, Jennings was burning out. "It's crazy!" he told a DEC computer magazine. "There are 250 or 300 nodes, and I'm the only person maintaining them."[67] The pressure to release updates increased with the size of the network. In October 1985, just a few weeks after the release of version 11, a well-intentioned Fido sysop circulated a "wish list" of features he'd like to see in version 12. "Tom Jennings has MUCH to be proud of," he wrote. "Maybe he'll be able to teach Fido some of [these] 'tricks.'"[68] Tom didn't finish version 12 until August 1987.

Fortunately, the structure of Fido BBS invited tinkering. Fido had always been a software system rather than a single monolithic program. Future innovations to FidoNet came from outside Fido itself. A typical Fido was composed of a copy of the FIDO executable program, a set of directories on disk, and a collection of custom scripts. The initial configuration was difficult, but a functional Fido BBS was relatively easy to understand. Fido used the standard MS-DOS file system to define its message and files areas, providing sysops an unusual degree of control over its internal operations. Sysops frequently authored and swapped small utilities to automate the maintenance of their BBSs and add features to the system. Participants in FidoNet began experimenting around the edges of the network, building new components to replace parts of the default Fido system. In April 1986, the Houston-area sysop Richard Polunsky tracked down 133 Fido utilities, many of which automated maintenance tasks such as managing the nodelist and culling old email.[69] By 1987, it was possible to run a fully functional FidoNet node without running any of the original Fido software at all.

Tom Jennings, meanwhile, was living in a San Francisco warehouse with a crew of queer punks, artists, activists, and skateboarders.[70] In just under a year, the warehouse had become a hotbed for political organizing, underground publishing, and countercultural events. Jennings directed any revenue generated by Fido shareware fees toward rent and groceries for the collective, but his companions were only peripherally aware of what he was doing with his computer. One former housemate described him, lovingly, as a "mad scientist."[71] Jennings continued to support the Fido community from a workbench in the warehouse, but his attention was increasingly occupied by the queer punk culture blossoming around him. Soon, he stopped running his own bulletin board. As other sysops took on more responsibility, Jennings reduced his role, allowing FidoNet to take on a life of its own.

Compiled versions of Fido BBS were freely available for a range of platforms—FIDO_IBM.EXE, FIDO_DEC.EXE, and so on—but the source code was not. Fido's code included proprietary routines that Jennings was not at liberty to distribute.[72] In March 1985, Jennings had begun raising the alarm: "This is a grassroots, low cost, hobbyist network, the first and only one of its kind. It is truly the forefront of technology; you can ride along for free and see it collapse by Fall, or you can start things going, even better than it is."[73] A new Fido-compatible BBS program was needed to keep the network going in the event that he "dropped dead."[74] Plus, Fido was hardly perfect: "It is huge, cumbersome, and consumes disk space like a congressional subcommittee consumes money."[75] In response, FidoNet began to move further away from Fido as the default.[76] By the end of 1985, several dozen nodes were running bits and pieces of Bob Hartman's Fido-compatible ROVER project.[77] But cloning Fido was not the only way to remove Jennings as the single point of failure for FidoNet. If other BBS software could generate the same message "packets" as Fido, the network would continue to grow on its own.[78] At least two programs—SEAdog and Colossus (aka "Collie")—were already offering limited support for FidoNet mail thanks to their authors' painstaking efforts to reverse-engineer the Fido data format. Forget the Fido code: the future of FidoNet depended on its protocol.

Ideally, publishing a standard FidoNet protocol independent of the Fido software would open the network to thousands of new participants. In 1985, countless developers—from hobbyists to professionals—were writing BBS programs that could potentially join FidoNet, if only they had access to accurate information about the protocol.[79] The challenge, of course, is that any technical standard is more than a mere document. Standards are complex social objects, laden with cultural values and political commitments.[80] In the case of telecommunications, the values embedded in a networking protocol shape the relationships between people, places, and things.[81] In the mid-1980s, such "protocological" forms of social control were top of mind for networking researchers in Europe and the United States. A protracted battle over internetworking standards had split the community between advocates of TCP/IP and the Open Systems Interconnection (OSI) model.[82] But whereas TCP/IP and OSI both represented the interests of universities, corporations, governments, and other large institutions, the FidoNet protocol would serve an open-ended, loosely affiliated network of amateurs. The financial stakes may have been lower, but the debates were just as fierce. Notoriously independent, BBS sysops were not used to being told what to do.

Despite Fido BBS's cutting-edge networking features, by the end of 1985, its user interface was starting to look positively ancient. Messages and menus rendered in monochromatic text rolled up the screen like the output of a teleprinter, just like the bulletin boards of the late 1970s. Jennings defended the spartan interface on the grounds that it was economical, interoperable, and easy to learn. "It was done ugly on purpose," he told *InfoWorld* magazine.[83] Indeed, Fido worked with virtually any available computer platform—including screen readers for the visually impaired—but the rest of the modem world was moving to colorful, animated interfaces similar to videotex systems like Minitel. The diverging aesthetics presented a quandary for Fido sysops. Couldn't they have the network without the ugly?

Elsewhere in the modem world, a more beautiful Fido was already under way. At the urging of friends, the Dallas-based programmer Wynn Wagner III started working on a FidoNet-compatible BBS called Opus.[84] Rather than replace the previous system, Wagner conceived of Opus as "an evolutionary step" forward.[85] Opus used the same support files, message areas, and networking tools as Fido, making it easy for sysops to switch. But whereas Jennings had resolutely stuck to the minimal interfaces of an earlier era, Wagner encouraged sysops to adopt "blazing color" and "lavish widgets."[86] To create its animated graphics, Opus relied on the sixteen-color "ANSI art" technique characteristic of MS-DOS and the IBM PC platform.[87] For callers with compatible hardware, Opus could display dynamic, moving visual images. For everyone else, the system fell back on plain ASCII text.

Opus sent a shock through FidoNet's increasingly bureaucratic culture. Irreverent quotations and references to cyberpunk science fiction appeared throughout the user manual. FidoNet was "the matrix," programmers wore "mirror shades," and the whole project was "militantly" anticommercial.[88] Wagner, a gay man, insisted that anyone running Opus in a for-profit context send $50 to support AIDS-related research and care services.[89] In January 1987, after a year of testing, Opus version 0.1 was released, sparking a frenzy of calls into North Texas. "So many people were using modems to get to the Opus sites in Dallas," recalled Wagner, "that the telephone network couldn't handle the load."[90] Within

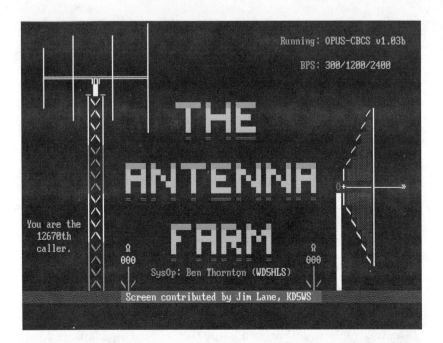

Welcome screens for BBSs running Opus software. These colorful images were made for the text mode of an IBM-compatible PC by arranging the built-in semigraphical characters and ANSI escape codes. "The Antenna Farm" was created by Jim Lane (KD5WS) (silent key) for the ham radio BBS run by the sysop Ben Thornton (NI5B; formerly WD5WLS). "The Private Oak Lawn Exchange" was bundled with Opus to demonstrate its graphical capabilities. The name of the BBS refers to the Oak Lawn neighborhood of Dallas, Texas, a hub for the city's gay community. (The Antenna Farm courtesy of Bennett Thornton)

months, a large majority of FidoNet nodes had switched over from Fido to Opus. The Fido network was becoming a mongrel.

With the emergence of Fido alternatives like Opus, the need for a common definition of FidoNet was becoming urgent. The first coordinated effort at standardizing FidoNet began in the summer of 1986.[91] Randy Bush, a Fido sysop and the author of several BBS utilities, announced the formation of the FidoNet Standards Committee.[92] The initial purpose of the committee was to document the existing protocol and create a standard for future "FidoClones." The announcement listed several familiar names—Ben Baker, Ken Kaplan, Tom Jennings, and Thom Henderson were all involved, as well as programmers Gee Wong and Bob Pritchett. The committee planned to share a first draft of the standard at an upcoming FidoNet convention planned for August in Colorado Springs, Colorado. Henderson assured readers of *FidoNews* that the committee was concerned only with the technical definition of FidoNet, not its administration or organization: "just the stuff that goes over the phone line."[93] At the convention, Bush presented the committee's draft standard to a rapturous reception. The longtime Fido sysop Allen Miller described the standardization project as "the most meaningful contribution to the world of telecommunications that I could have imagined."[94] A few weeks later, Hartman invited the committee to visit him in southern New Hampshire, where they outlined an "extended addressing" scheme to better handle the growth of international traffic and internetwork gateways connecting FidoNet to USENET and ARPANET.[95] Existing net/node addresses would be expanded to include optional zone and point numbers. Zones represented large, continental-scale constructs, and points referred to nodes with just one user. For example, Henderson's 107/6 address would be extended to 1:107/6.1. Days after the meeting, Henderson offered cautious optimism in his report to *FidoNews*: "Kludge it may be, but it's simple and straightforward."[96]

The FidoNet Standards Committee, later known as the FidoNet Technical Standards Committee, or FTSC, adopted similar decision-making practices as the emerging internet community. FidoNet standards were published in plain ASCII text, circulated on the network for discussion, and frequently updated by the committee.[97] Like the internet's "Request for Comments" documents, FidoNet standards blended policy considerations with technical specifications, an unavoidable characteristic of

Evolution of the FidoNet Zone System, 1987–1995

ZONE	YEAR	NAME
1	1987	N._America_Coord
	1988	Intl_FidoNet_Co
	1989	North_America
2	1987	Europe
	1991	Europe/Soviet_Union
	1992	Europe_etc
	1995	Europe_&_more
3	1987	Oceania
	1993	Australia_NZ_PNG
4	1989	America_Latina
5	1990	Africa
6	1991	Asia

Note: Zone names extracted from archived FidoNet nodelists through 1998.

any telecommunications protocol.[98] As Randy Bush explained in an early draft of the standard, compliance with the standard protocol was a "social obligation" between cooperating participants in the network.[99] The stakes reflected the amateur community's reliance on the spatial and economic structure of the telephone network. Failing to receive an incoming packet represented not only a breakdown in communication but an unfair financial burden on the sysop placing the call. The FidoNet standards were written by people who paid their own telephone bills.

In 1987, shortly after the meetings in Colorado and New Hampshire, the FidoNet Standards Committee produced its first standard, "A Basic FidoNet(tm) Technical Standard." Labeled FSCoo1 and credited to Randy Bush, the standard established the bare minimum requirements for a node to fully participate in the network.[100] In plain language, the purpose of FSCoo1 was to ensure a "reasonable chance" that any two nodes could successfully exchange mail.[101] Ideally, every node on the nodelist would meet the criteria laid out in the standard. Bush based his definition of FidoNet on the messages and packets produced by Fido version 11w and SEAdog version 3. To make the standard legible across the amateur and institutional boundary, he adopted the same "layered" protocol model as the OSI.[102] Among other technical details, FSC001 outlined the byte-for-byte structure of a message "packet" and modeled the exchange of packets between nodes as a finite state machine.[103] Crucial components of the network, such as the format of the nodelist, were set aside to be defined in a future standard. The goal of FSC001 was to provide all of the details necessary to replicate the networking features of Fido BBS.

This standardization effort occurred in parallel with the creation of "continuous mail" and "Echomail," two extensions of FidoNet built by members of the community. Continuous mail, also known as "crash" mail, enabled boards to exchange messages at times other than the late-night FidoNet Mail Hour. Nodes supporting continuous mail could send and receive FidoNet packets throughout the day, dramatically speeding up the spread of messages through the network and providing sysops with more fine-grained control over their expenses. Continuous mail first appeared early in 1984, when Thom Henderson introduced SEAdog, an email program that implemented Fido's network protocol but none of the BBS features. SEAdog could either run alongside a standard Fido installation or act as a stand-alone node for a single user.[104] In the complementary configuration, SEAdog answered the phone instead of Fido. If the incoming call was from another SEAdog node, then the two programs would rapidly exchange packets and hang up. If not, SEAdog would hand over the call to Fido.

"Front-end mailers" like SEAdog transformed the temporality of FidoNet. The late-night Mail Hour remained sacrosanct, a technocultural ritual holding the network together, but a growing number of nodes traded mail throughout the day. From 1987 to 1992, the number of nodes accepting continuous mail rose from approximately 54 percent to 85 percent.[105] During this period, new mailer software such as Binkley-Term, Dutchie, and FrontDoor altered the structure of BBS communications by enabling individual PC owners to read and write mail in "offline mode."[106] Sysops of popular BBSs encouraged frequent callers to adopt mailer programs to reduce the amount of time that each person spent on the board, thereby freeing up the line for other callers.[107] Mailers also provided sysops with tools to determine when and how to send data around the network. For example, a sysop might set a high priority on a few long-distance boards and send mail to them immediately, despite the cost, while leaving the rest of the mail for late at night.

Echomail, the second major extension of FidoNet, used the underlying networking facility to create a public conferencing system similar in purpose and structure to USENET newsgroups or CompuServe forums.[108] The standard Fido BBS featured several separate "areas" organized around different topics. The manual suggested technical themes such as "IBMPC," but sysops were free to create their own ontologies—Jennings's board featured areas dedicated to graffiti and music.[109] Yet the standard Fido software allowed only one of the message areas to carry FidoNet mail. As a result, FidoNet mail was used primarily for person-to-person messaging between sysops, rather than open-ended discussions between the users of different BBSs.

Echomail emerged out of the same lively BBS community in Texas as Opus. Sysops around Dallas and Ft. Worth were tight-knit and chummy, meeting regularly for pizza parties and picnics. At one such gathering in late 1985, several sysops had been talking shop, complaining about long-distance bills and irksome users causing trouble on their boards.[110] They began to wonder aloud about an online space for local sysops to compare notes. Why not use FidoNet? Jeff Rush, one of the sysops, took a few ideas from their bull session and came up with the basic structure of Echomail. Instead of depositing all incoming FidoNet messages into the same message area, Rush introduced two additional programs—a "scanner" and a "tosser"—to manage the distribution of messages among multiple networked areas. The Dallas-area sysops Chuck Lawson, Jon Sabol, and Wynn Wagner agreed to test out the new system. Within a week, they added a link to Harv Neghila's BBS in San Francisco.[111]

The defining feature of Echomail is the topical conference, or "echo." Each echo was identified by a unique nickname that appeared in the list of message areas on participating BBSs. The Dallas group started with SYSOP and TECH. After a week, they added CHATTER and POLITICS, foreshadowing a proliferation of topics far afield of tech and telecom. Like FidoNet itself, Echomail was a decentralized communication system, managed from the edges of the network. There was no official list of echoes or approval process to create a new conference. Rather, the growth of Echomail was informal and ad hoc. To create a new conference, two sysops would agree to "carry" the topic on their boards, voluntarily swapping messages back and forth. If another sysop wished to join in, they would request a "feed" of new messages from one of the established participants.[112] To generate interest in a new echo, participants circulated electronic memos to other sysops inviting them to carry the feed. By August 1986, new echoes were popping up every week on topics including genealogy, ham radio, record collecting, science fiction and fantasy fandom, witchcraft and neopaganism, polyamory and other "alternate lifestyles," support for Vietnam veterans, disability, and countless computer platforms, software systems, and programming languages.[113]

Compared with conventional FidoNet mail, Echomail was very easy to use. Indeed, the interface was so transparent that a new user could jump into a discussion without initially realizing that they were trading messages with people on other BBSs.[114] Upon close inspection, however, telling details were appended to every remote message. Like a postmark on a traditional letter, the body of an Echomail message included two or more lines of "control information" used to route the message through the network. The "origin line" spanned a single line with a maximum of seventy-nine characters—excessive control information was considered wasteful—and indicated the name and address of the BBS from which the message originated.[115] Creative sysops seized on this technical requirement as an opportunity for promotion and self-expression, packing the origin line with ASCII art, jokes, puns, and other silly messages. Soon, individual users joined in, extending the automatically generated text to include their own signature "taglines." In practice, taglines and control lines were easy to ignore, but they provided a regular reminder that Echomail conferences did not exist in some abstract cyberspace— FidoNet was a network of real computers, each one plugged into a wall somewhere on Earth.

Echomail spread so quickly and so thoroughly throughout the network that FidoNet almost collapsed under the sudden increase in activity.[116] Within weeks of Echomail's release, Thom Henderson joked, "[It] will greatly expand the whole meaning of FidoNet, if it doesn't break it first."[117] By summertime, the Dallas clique had released a new version of Opus with built-in support for Echomail, lowering the bar for participation even further.[118] In August 1986, Jeff Rush showed up at the annual FidoNet convention wearing a shirt emblazoned with a bull's-eye and the words "ECHOMAIL CREATOR." During the opening session, he stood up from the audience for a round of applause as Ben Baker and Thom Henderson pretended to shoot him with imaginary arrows from

```
--- ReadMail
 * Origin: tomj@fidosw.fidonet.org / World Power Systems  (1:125/111)

--- msged 2.07
 * Origin: STARCOM - Milwaukee, WI - Your Midwest Echo Hub (1:154/69)

--- Maximus 2.01wb
 * Origin: On a Clear Disk You Can Seek Forever (1:225/1)

--- QuickBBS 2.80 Ovr (Gamma-5)
 * Origin: Music Lovers' Board (885-9531) (6:700/7)

... TELEGARD Conference Moderator and Author of Telegard (Retired)
--- Blue Wave/TGq v2.02/C+ Beta
 * Origin: The I/O Bus - TG_BETA Conference Moderator (1:120/187.0)

... OFFLINE 1.35 * Recycle! For us... and them...
--- Maximus 2.01wb
 * Origin: Permaculture 1 BBS * Northcote_Aust * +61-3-482-2942 (3:632/376)


---
 * Origin: Rights On! - Privacy #1 Right! - Titusville_FL_USA (1:374/14)

--- Where Friends Meet!!
 * Origin: RecoverNet * The Recovery Corner * TX * (817) 447-1619 (1:130/911)

---
 * Origin: GAIA/GALAXIA BBS Aylmer QC Canada 1-819-684-6187 V.FC (1:163/262)

--- Nothing special
 * Origin: Edifying Cat Point Station (2:5020/140.1)

... "Man has the one true religion.  Several of them!" -- Twain
___ Blue Wave/QWK v2.12
--- TriToss (tm) 1.01 - #22
 * Origin: End of the Line, Austin,TX, (512-459-4693) (1:382/208)

--- Heaven [2 Node/ANSi]
 * Origin: h e a v e n - better than bad, it's good! - 613.732.1616

--- GoldED+/LNX 1.1.5
 * Origin: Rusty's BBS - Bloemfontein, Free State, South Africa (5:7105/1)
```

Taglines, tear lines, and control lines appearing in Echomail conferences between 1987 and 2002. The "tear line," beginning with three leading dashes, marked the division between a user's message and the required Echomail control information. The tear line often included the name and version number of the "mailer" program used to send the message. The "origin line" indicated the BBS from which the message was sent, typically with the FidoNet address listed in parentheses. This list includes messages sent from Australia, Canada, Hong Kong, South Africa, and the United States. Many Echomail programs also allowed users to add an additional "tagline" just before the tear. Taglines included shout-outs, quotes, social commentary, and single-line ASCII art illustrations.

the stage.[119] An overwhelming majority of the sysops in attendance had adopted Echomail, mere months after its release. To handle the new traffic, participants informally agreed to shrink the size of their transfers using compression software, to limit redundant Echomail packets, and to prioritize person-to-person mail over conference messages.[120] FidoNet survived; Echomail thrived.

Due to the decentralized structure of the network, there are no authoritative lists of Echomail conferences or comprehensive archives of Echomail messages. However, as with the broader BBS movement, several Echomail users stepped up to create their own information resources regarding the new network. In May 1986, the Fido sysop Thomas Kenny announced his plan to create a public database of Echomail conferences, available from his BBS in Tom's River, New Jersey.[121] At the start of 1987, Kenny published a first draft of the list, including contact information for 133 active echoes and twenty-three proposed topics.[122]

In January 1987, Echomail was just one year old. Yet Kenny's list reveals an emerging awareness of FidoNet as a medium for cross-regional communication. A few echoes focused on particular geographic regions—an unmoderated conference for gossiping about Florida's Suncoast BBS scene, a "cosmopolitan" conference for talking books with Metro Boston modemers, a proto-foodie conference for DC-area restaurant reviews.[123] But many more aimed to overcome the constraints of long-distance dialing. Two of the earliest echoes, GAYNET and BIBLE, specifically sought users from different parts of the modem world to create translocal communities of interest.[124] Wynn Wagner created GAYNET with his boyfriend, Rick, from their home in Oak Lawn, a historically gay neighborhood of Dallas.[125] Just as the gay residents of Oak Lawn might visit friends in Boystown, Chicago, or vacation in Provincetown, Massachusetts, Echomail enabled an alternative mapping of the modem world, organized by shared interest and identity rather than area code or computer platform. Whether connecting the residents of gay enclaves or the adherents of a particular religion, Echomail provided a common meeting place for geographically distributed communities of interest.

For longtime FidoNet sysops, Echomail was a revolution they had been working toward for nearly two years. Ben Baker, after "banging his head against the wall" and "pleading" with users to try FidoNet, was thrilled by the sudden enthusiasm for Echomail.[126] Tom Jennings believed

Selected Echomail Conferences, 1987–1991

CONFERENCE	DESCRIPTION
ABLED	disABLED users information exchange
ASIAN-AMERICAN	Asian-American Community happenings
BIBLE	Christian conference
C_ECHO	C language programmers
DOGGIES	Fido clones & compatibles
FEMINISM	A discussion conference on feminism and gender issues
FIRENET	Fire/Rescue/EMS news and information exchange
FOR-SALE	A nationwide flea market
GAYNEWS	Gay/Lesbian news echo
GENEALOGY	Family ties
HAM_TECH	Amateur (ham) radio technology conference
HEALTH	Health related issues (MDs participating)
IFNA	International FidoNet Association members
IPR	InterPersonal Relationships plus moral, ethical, social issues
JOBSHOP	Nationwide help wanted
JUDAICA	General Jewish discussions
LIFESTYLE	Aging hippies, probably
MEADOW	Opus sysops
PARK	US National Park Service only
RECORDS	Record collecting and music in general
RECOVERY	Members of Alcoholics Anonymous
RELIGIOUS DEBATE	Born again vs secular humanists
S&M	Consensual power exchange
SF	Science fiction and fantasy literature
SYSOP	THE National Sysop conference. Sysops ONLY!
TECH	General computer talk
VIETNAM VETS	Vietnam veterans' conference
WILDLIFE	Discussion of nature, outdoors, hunting, fishing, conservation

Sources: Michael G. Fuchs, "Echomail Conference List Report," FidoNet on the Internet, July 1, 1991, http://www.textfiles.com/fidonet-on-the-internet/e1991/elist107.txt; Thomas Kenny, "The First Echomail Conference List," FidoNet on the Internet, January 13, 1987, http://www.textfiles.com/fidonet-on-the-internet/e1987/elist701.txt; Kenny, "The First Echomail Conference List," *FidoNews*, March 9, 1987, http://www.textfiles.com/bbs/FIDONET/FIDONEWS/fido0410.nws; Wynn Wagner, "OPUS Computer-Based Conversation System Version 1.0," ed. John Miller, June 14, 1987, archived at http://cd.textfiles.com/masterdisc/SS/CMM/0004/OPUSDOC.TXT.

that Echomail alone drove the adoption of FidoNet during the late 1980s. "It spread like wildfire," he recalled. "The traffic was just enormous."[127] New sysops were joining FidoNet specifically to access Echomail.[128] Several sysops volunteered to form a high-volume Echomail "backbone" network to ensure the availability of the most popular echoes.[129] Between 1986 and 1989, the nodelist more than quadrupled, and by one estimate, the network carried nearly five hundred public Echomail conferences.[130] To manage the rising cost of running a node, sysops experimented with novel long-distance products from Sprint and MCI and tunneling over commercial packet-switching networks like Telenet's PC Pursuit. They worked directly with modem makers including US Robotics, Telebit, and Microcom on the design of faster, more flexible PC modems.[131] And in 1992, they moved a large proportion of FidoNet traffic off the telephone network altogether and onto the Planet Connect satellite network.[132] Yet the growth of FidoNet and Echomail continued to outpace these innovations. In 1993, the sysop Roy Timberman reported paying $2,500 per month to move data through his Kansas City gateway.[133] That was a big number for an individual hobby, but it was a steal when it came to running a global data network.

THE INTERNATIONAL FIDONET LIVES UP TO ITS NAME

By 1988, the FidoNet community had stubbornly built its own online world, independent of the corporate or academic networks springing up around North America. The grassroots BBS network provided a set of services comparable to the nascent internet—email, file transfers, and discussion forums—without any of the institutional support. The clever hack that enabled Tom Jennings and John Madill to trade bits of code in 1984 had become a worldwide network of cooperating bulletin board systems, carrying everything from geeky jokes to vital medical information. Gateways eroded the boundaries between FidoNet and the institutional networks connecting large corporations and universities.[134] As people outside the modem world learned about FidoNet, many came to see it as a "training ground" rather than a legitimate information system of its own.[135] This dismissive view of FidoNet reflected a common prejudice against microcomputers and a failure to appreciate the unique social, technical, and economic challenges that the international amateur network had already overcome. Echomail wasn't a substitute for USENET any more than FM was a substitute for AM radio. As Zone 1 coordinator George Peace reminded an internet-hungry audience at a BBS convention in 1993, FidoNet was a different technology meeting different needs for different people.[136]

Above all, FidoNet remained an independent, cooperative computer network. Unlike commercial platforms or institutional networks, there was no central authority governing the technological or social behavior of FidoNet users and sysops. A resistance to hierarchy was baked into the very core of the network's original design, an explicit expression of Tom Jennings's anarchist values. Yet the lack of authority posed new difficulties. As FidoNet attracted tens of thousands of new users, its key challenges were administrative, rather than technological. In late 1986, several well-known early sysops—including the original St. Louis crew— had attempted to form a nonprofit membership organization to oversee the nodelist and represent the network. The organization, known as the International FidoNet Association, or IFNA, faced an immediate backlash from dozens of self-described "grunt sysops" who objected to the legalistic incorporation process and a perceived loss of individual autonomy.[137] On January 1, 1988, a splinter group—including *FidoNews* editor Thom Henderson—announced the creation of Alternet, a parallel BBS network using the same technology as FidoNet but governed by a different set of policies and principles. Over the next year, Alternet provided empirical proof of the durability of Fido's decentralized architecture.[138] Sysops were free to participate in FidoNet, Alternet, or both. By 1989, several other groups of sysops had followed the Alternet example, creating additional "othernets" to run alongside the original FidoNet.[139] This process of replication revealed FidoNet to be a functional network-of-networks, adaptable to dynamic political and infrastructural conditions.

Despite the political turmoil in North America's Zone 1, the geographic expansion of FidoNet continued. From 1988 to 1993, the network nearly doubled each year, with substantial growth coming from beyond the affluent, English-speaking hobbyist communities of North America.[140] In eastern Europe and South America, the creation of newly democratic governments enabled some citizens to participate more freely in international telecommunications. For sysops in these environments, building a networked BBS was more than an enjoyable technical challenge. The net/node system offered an alternative arrangement

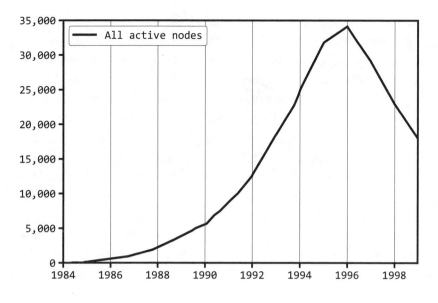

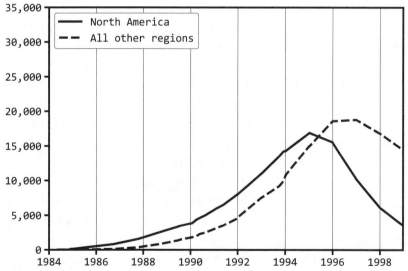

Growth of FidoNet as measured in active nodes, from May 1984 to December 1998.
The international FidoNet peaked around thirty-four thousand nodes in 1996. However,
the rate of growth differed by region. The number of nodes in North America declined
faster and earlier than the rest of the network, falling from nearly seventeen thousand
in January 1995 to approximately ten thousand in January 1997. Over that same period,
the rest of FidoNet continued to grow, expanding from about fifteen thousand nodes in
January 1995 to almost nineteen thousand in January 1997 before beginning to decline.
This lag reflects differences in the culture, technology, regulation, and political economy
of communication networks across the globe.

of communication power. Each FidoNet node number represented an addressable location in a global network of computer enthusiasts. For computing fans cut off from Western infrastructures and institutions, FidoNet offered a place in cyberspace.

In 1987, Poland became the first communist country with a FidoNet region number. With the help of the Dutch Hobbycomputerclub and the support of FidoNet sysops in the United States, Poland joined Europe's Zone 2.[141] Whereas most FidoNet nodes were located in the homes of individual hobbyists, the Polish BBSs on FidoNet were run out of private computer firms and the offices of *Komputer* magazine.[142] In 1989, the Polish sysop Jacek Szelozynski arranged for an Echomail feed from a BBS in the Netherlands run by Arjen Lentz, providing access to a growing community of Polish PC "fanatics" in Gdansk, Krakow, and Warsaw.[143] According to Szelozynski, the appearance of messages from beyond the Iron Curtain caused "quite a sensation" in techie conferences like C_ECHO and ZMODEM.[144] And as revolution spread across the Eastern Bloc, computer enthusiasts in other cities followed the Polish model, adopting FidoNet technology to build translocal communication networks in the absence of institutional infrastructure.[145]

Meanwhile, in 1987, a BBS in Johannesburg became the first FidoNet node on the continent of Africa, exchanging mail through a gateway in Europe. The decision to grant the node number was the subject of debate among sysops in Europe and North America who objected to the racial terror of the apartheid regime.[146] Anticipating the cyberutopian rhetoric of the 1990s, the debate seems to have turned on a belief that the possibility of communication itself might contribute to the cause of liberation. Don Daniels, president of IFNA, expressed a commitment to "the free and open exchange of information" and a hope that participation in FidoNet would "in some small way" benefit the antiapartheid movement.[147] In retrospect, their optimism seems naïve, but by 1992, FidoNet had already become a critical communication infrastructure for NGOs and universities in South Africa.[148] Gateways created by Randy Bush and others enabled activists and academics in Africa to exchange email and files with colleagues in the United States and Europe even if their home institutions were not connected to the packet-switched internet.[149]

At the same time that FidoNet was extended into Johannesburg, the Argentina-based sysop Pablo Kleinman was creating TangoNET around the city of Buenos Aires.[150] TangoNET exchanged mail with the rest of FidoNet through a BBS in Southern California run by the sysop Travis Good and became a gateway for other regions of Latin America. Juan Davila, a sysop in San Juan, broke off from a regional network in the southeastern United States to form an independent net in Puerto Rico. Together, Davila, Good, and Kleinman began promoting a Spanish-language conference on Echomail called LATINO, translating FidoNet documentation, and publishing the first non-English articles in *FidoNews*.[151] Eventually, the sysops in Latin America and South Africa broke away from Europe and North America altogether and formed Zone 4 and Zone 5, respectively. By 1991, Zone 6 reached into areas of Southeast Asia and China.[152]

After 1995, the increasing availability of commercial internet access eroded some of the appeal of FidoNet in North America. FidoNet did not stop running—indeed, thousands of nodes continue to exchange mail and files today—but the costs and constraints of a telephone-based network eventually pushed a majority of the users and communities off BBSs and onto internet mailing lists and web forums. Of course, there was a social cost to this change in infrastructure, too. While the internet discouraged people from thinking too much about geography, FidoNet constantly reminded users that they were people living in place. The unique net/node numbering schema engendered a translocal imaginary of cyberspace as a network of local communities rather than a global village or virtual reality. Internet advocates envisioned cyberspace as an escape from the physical world. FidoNet provided a means to tunnel through it.

CHAPTER FOUR

Sharing Files with Strangers

IN THE SUMMER OF 1982, Rich Schinnell's phone rang and rang and never stopped ringing. Day and night, calls came from PC owners around the country trying to get through to Schinnell's new bulletin board. By November, he estimated that he'd received more than six thousand calls at his home in Rockville, Maryland.[1] At the time, Schinnell's BBS, known variously as the Software Exchange or Software Library, was a novelty in the modem world.[2] Rather than sharing messages or technical tips, callers to the Software Exchange were on the hunt for real, working programs to download. Using host software written by fellow members of the Capital PC User's Group, Schinnell's BBS acted like a robot storekeeper, automatically accepting uploads and queuing downloads for the system's callers.[3] Four floppy disk drives whirred and clicked endlessly, serving up games, utilities, and other applications for the new IBM PC platform. At 300 baud, downloads were slow and unreliable—Schinnell joked that early data-transfer routines merely "threw the bits out the communications port"—but the files were rare and the users were stubborn.[4] A profile in *InfoWorld* magazine described Schinnell's board as "a simple revolution."[5]

The allure of free files was irresistible to many early PC owners. A year after Schinnell put up the Software Exchange, *InfoWorld* ran a cover story on the online file-trading phenomenon. A long-exposure photo of California's Interstate 280 depicted a new off-ramp between San Francisco and San Jose. Hanging over the freeway, a green sign read "FREE SOFTWARE" in bright white letters.[6] "It's no scam," exclaimed a blurb inside; "you can get software for free (or almost free) from user's groups and bulletin board systems all over the country." Describing BBSs like the Software Exchange as a "junkyard of software spare parts," the feature story lauded the "creative," "experimental," and "rare" programs available online.[7] Byron McKay, the sysop of PicoNet BBS in Silicon Valley, reported receiving eight megabytes of new software each month: "60% crap, 10% so-so, 10% you'd use once in a blue moon and 10% absolute gems."[8] Like hot-rodders prowling the junkyard for auto parts, hunting for software gems offered its own intrinsic pleasures. "One of my favorite sports has become bagging some of the megabytes of free software that can be had for the price of a (sometimes extended) phone call," joked *InfoWorld* staffer John Markoff.[9] (Of course, he confessed, all this modeming was easier when your employer picked up the bill at the end of the month.)

Moving data from one machine to another was one of the fundamental challenges of early personal computing. Prior to the popularization of modems and BBSs, microcomputer owners were stuck with just two methods of exchanging files. First, they could transfer their data to a cassette tape or floppy disk and physically carry it over to another machine—the proverbial "sneakernet." Or, second, they could write down the source code longhand and manually type it back into the other computer. Neither solution was ideal. Both were prone to error, floppy disks weren't cheap, and manual entry was tedious.

The modem offered a third way to exchange data between microcomputers. By connecting directly over a telephone line, two modem owners could trade files in real time, streaming data over Ma Bell's copper wires. BBS host software removed the need for coordination between users. BBSs became central nodes in an emerging network of file-sharing strangers. More than a convenience, BBSs served as rich data depots, makeshift libraries for the file-hungry culture of 1980s computing.

In the shift from sneakernets to dial-up BBSs, the human beings trading files with one another became increasingly estranged. Files took on lives of their own. Rather than handing a floppy disk to a friend or fellow computer-club member, pseudonymous file traders uploaded and downloaded without any expectation of forming a relationship. File-oriented BBSs became gathering places for data as much as for people. The files sitting in their download directories may have been copied numerous times before, long predating the systems that played host to them. Files jumped from BBS networks to USENET newsgroups, from commercial online services to CD-ROMs. Users dialing long-distance carried files across the invisible borders of telephone area codes, enabling data to spread semiautonomously through the decentralized network of regional BBSs. Popular files traveled farther than their authors, reaching distant BBSs that would have been prohibitively expensive to dial directly. Even today, files originating on a local BBS from the 1980s accumulate in the dusty corners of the web, reappearing in search results after years of neglect.

The enthusiasm with which BBS users set about copying files from place to place raised difficult questions about the legal status of computer software and the moral obligations of computer owners to share (or not to share) the data in their possession. The notion that software represented an immaterial form of "intellectual property" remained in flux throughout the start of the microcomputer industry, and there were few ethical norms governing the small-scale exchange of files. In the 1970s, representatives of the film and music industries could argue that media-sharing practices like "home taping" were hurting the owners of cinemas and record stores, but there was no similar retail infrastructure for consumer software. Indeed, the dominant computer firms of the period, such as IBM, did not consider software a part of their product lines at all. Rather, as the historian Paul Ceruzzi puts it, software was "what the company did to get people to buy hardware."[10] The norms and values of hobby computing culture reflected this perception as well. Many hobbyists—particularly those who belonged to clubs and user groups—were accustomed to trading software freely with friends. In 1975, Bill Gates infamously challenged this social norm in an "open letter to hobbyists" criticizing the unauthorized duplication of Microsoft's first product, Altair BASIC.[11] Gates's letter sparked a nationwide debate about the value of software and the future of the software industry, but it did not fundamentally alter the norm of free exchange.[12]

Debates over "software piracy" have distorted the history of file sharing. The outsized attention paid to piracy has obscured other file-sharing
cultures and practices. While unauthorized copying stimulated internet
adoption and challenged traditional media industries, it was not the
only form of peer-to-peer file sharing on early networks. As file sharing
moved online in the mid-1980s, the practice of trading programs with
other computer owners gave rise to novel aesthetic forms and economic
practices. From the electronic publications known as "textfiles" to free-
to-try "shareware" applications, modem users glimpsed a fundamentally
different future for computer software than the media industries that
came before. Even within the history of software piracy, a competitive
culture of "cracking" gave rise to the worldwide "warez" subculture, with
its own customs, values, arts, language, and lore.[13]

The cultural history of file sharing is imbricated with the technological history of communication by modem. The file-sharing practices and types of files in circulation at particular times and places
reflected the speed and pricing of modems, the sophistication of serial-
communication and error-correction protocols, and the efficiency of
data-compression algorithms. For example, the same piece of software
that would have taken several hours to download with a modem from
1980 took only a few minutes in 1990. Between 1978 and 1998, the data-
transfer rates between consumer modems rose from 300 bits per second
to 56 kilobits per second, the theoretical maximum transfer rate for the
standard twisted pair of copper telephone lines. Each step in the typical
upgrade path for a BBSer in the 1980s—from 300 to 2,400 to 9,600 bits
per second—represented a massive increase in data throughput.

For computer owners of the 1980s and 1990s, buying a new modem
opened up entirely new areas of online activity that were previously inaccessible. Friends who had only communicated by email and chat could
suddenly exchange photos. Gamers satisfied with turn-based games and
text-mode interfaces could participate in real-time graphical worlds such
as *Doom*. Computational art practices such as demoscene programming
and sample-based "tracker" music flourished as fast modems carried
their work to new audiences.[14] For internet users accustomed to broadband, the phenomenological experience of upgrading one's modem during this period of rapid innovation is difficult to comprehend. It would
be like buying a new set of tires that turned your car into an airplane.

Approximate download times for different modem speeds (in hours and minutes). Estimates based on ideal conditions. Real-world download times were longer due to connection problems such as telephone-line noise.

Beyond the efficiency of individual file transfers, faster data rates altered the collective temporality of the modem world. The owners of faster modems downloaded files differently from the owners of slower modems. Someone with a fast modem could sample new programs and download files out of curiosity without worrying about tying up their telephone line for hours on end. In turn, faster connection speeds enabled BBSs to accommodate more callers per telephone line, allowing more users to download more files at lower cost and in less time. By the late 1980s, hundreds of software authors were creating programs to circulate on BBS networks, altogether bypassing the retail and mail-order markets. Together, the producers and consumers of BBS files created a data ecology that functioned on a different temporal scale and commercial logic than its offline counterparts did.

Files and messages are the twin foundations of BBSing. Nearly every bulletin board in history has offered a combination of both. Yet, as Rich Schinnell's Software Exchange BBS illustrates, newcomers were drawn to the online world by the promise of free files. And indeed, they were not disappointed. Files were abundant—from unique applications to pirated games to risqué images. Yet those who came seeking files were also exposed to the communication and community functions of BBS networks. Many file seekers became active participants in the messaging side of their local boards. For some, online forums offered opportunities to discuss their file-collecting hobby and seek technical support. For others, the mystery and joy of virtual community far exceeded the value of free downloads. Files were an engine that drove many thousands of PC owners to venture online for the first time. Meeting strangers and becoming part of a community were the experiences that kept them coming back.

AT 300 BITS PER SECOND

Early on, the heartbeat of the modem world pulsed at a steady 300 bits per second. Streams of binary digits flowed through the telephone network in 7- and 8-bit chunks, or "bytes," and each byte corresponded to a single character of text.[15] The typical home computer, hooked up to a fuzzy CRT monitor, could display only about a thousand characters at once, organized into forty columns and twenty-four rows. At 300 bits per second, or 300 "baud," filling the entire screen took approximately thirty seconds. The text appeared faster than if someone were typing in real time, but it was hardly instantaneous.

In the late 1970s, the speed at which data moved through dial-up networks followed a specification published by Ma Bell nearly two decades before. Created in the early 1960s, the AT&T Data-Phone system introduced a reliable technique for two-way, machine-to-machine communication over consumer-grade telephone lines.[16] Although Data-Phone was initially sold to large firms to facilitate communication between various offices and a single data-processing center, it soon became a de facto standard for commercial time-sharing services, online databases, and amateur telecom projects.[17] In 1976, Lee Felsenstein of the People's Computer Company designed a DIY modem kit offering compatibility with the AT&T system for under $100.[18] And as newer tech firms like Hayes Microcomputer Products in Atlanta and US Robotics in Chicago began to sell modems for the home computer market, they assured consumers of their compatibility with the "Bell 103" standard. Rather than compete on speed, these companies sold hobbyist consumers on "smart" features like auto-answer, auto-dial, and programmable "remote control" modes.[19] A 1980 ad for the US Robotics Phone Link Acoustic Modem emphasized its warranty, diagnostic features, and high-end aesthetics: "Sleek . . . Quiet . . . Reliable."[20]

To survive, early PC modem makers had to sell more than modems. They had to sell the value of getting online at all. Today, networking is central to the experience of personal computing—can you imagine a laptop without Wi-Fi?—but in the late 1970s, computer owners did not yet see their machines as communication devices. Against this conventional view, upstart modem makers pitched their products as gateways to a fundamentally different form of computing. Like the home computer itself, modems were sold as transformative technologies, consumer electronics with the potential to change your life. Novation, the first mover in this rhetorical game, promised that its iconic black modem, the Cat, would "tie you into the world."[21] Hayes soon adopted similar language, describing the Micromodem II as a boundary-breaking technology that would "open your Apple II to the outside world."[22] Never mind that these "worlds" did not yet exist in 1979. Modem marketing conjured a desirable vision of the near future, specially crafted for computer enthusiasts. Instead of driving to an office park or riding the train, modem owners would be the first truly autonomous information workers: telecommuting to meetings, dialing into remote databases, and swapping files with other "computer people" around the globe. According to Novation, the potential uses for a modem like the Cat were "endless."[23]

In practice, 300 bits per second did not seem slow. In fact, the range of online services available to microcomputer owners in 1980 was rather astonishing, given their tiny numbers. A Bell-compatible modem like the Pennywhistle or Novation Cat offered access to searchable databases such as Dialog and Dow Jones, as well as communication services like CompuServe and The Source. Despite the hype, microcomputers alone could sometimes seem underwhelming to a public primed by visions of all-powerful, superhuman "world brains."[24] Yet, as one *Byte* contributor recounted, the experience of using an online "information retrieval" service felt like consulting an electronic oracle. The oracle accepted queries on virtually any topic—"from aardvarks to zymurgy"—and the answers seemed instantaneous.[25] "What's your time worth?" asked another *Byte* writer, comparing the breadth and speed of an online database to a "well-stocked public library."[26] Furthermore, exploring electronic databases was *fun*. A representative for Dialog likened searching its system to going on an "adventure" and joked that it was "much less frustrating" than the computer game of the same name.[27] Indeed, many early modem owners came to believe that online information retrieval would be the killer app propelling computer ownership into the mainstream.[28]

Yet it was not access to other machines but access to other people that ultimately drove the adoption of telephone modems among microcomputer owners. Just as email sustained a feeling of community among ARPANET researchers and time-sharing brought thousands of Minnesota teachers and students into collaboration, dial-up modems helped to catalyze a growing network of microcomputer enthusiasts.[29] Whereas

Cat Calls

How to tie your computer into the world.

All you need is a phone and a Cat™ acoustic modem. A Cat modem takes the data you type into your terminal and sends it out over standard telephone lines to any other compatible computer or terminal within reach of your phone. And it listens too.

So now you can work at home and talk by phone to your office computer. Gain access to data banks. Or swap programs with computer people anywhere. The possibilities are endless—if you have Cat.

It's the fast, accurate, reliable modem that ties you into the world—for less than $199.

Cat by **Novation**

Call for details

(800) 423-5410

In California (213) 996-5060

Available at Hamilton/Avnet, Kierulff Electronics, Byte Shops, Computerland, and your local computer store.
Novation, Inc., 18664 Oxnard Street, Tarzana, California 91356

Advertisement for the Novation CAT modem demonstrating its acoustic coupler interface with the handset of a standard Western Electric Model 500 telephone. ("Cat Calls," *Byte*, December 1979) users of time-sharing networks tended to access a central computer through a "dumb" terminal, users of microcomputer networks were often themselves typing on a microcomputer. In other words, there was a symmetry between the users and hosts of microcomputer networks. The same apparatus—a microcomputer and modem—used to dial into a BBS could be repurposed to host one. Microcomputers were more expensive than simple terminals, but they were much cheaper than the minicomputers deployed in contemporary time-sharing environments.

Like many fans and enthusiasts, computer hobbyists were eager to connect with others who shared their passion for hands-on technology. News and information about telephone networking spread through the preexisting network of regional computer clubs, fairs, newsletters, and magazines. At the outset of 1979, a first wave of modem owners was meeting on bulletin board systems like CBBS in Chicago and ABBS in San Diego to talk about their hobby. In a 1981 article for *InfoWorld*, Craig Vaughan, creator of ABBS, characterized these early years as an awakening: "Suddenly, everyone was talking about modems, what they had read on such and such a bulletin board, or which of the alternatives to Ma Bell . . . was most reliable for long-distance data communication."[30] By 1982, hundreds of BBSs were operating throughout North America, and the topics of discussion were growing beyond the computing hobby itself.[31] Comparing the participatory culture of BBSs to amateur radio, Vaughan argued that modems transformed the computer from a business tool to a medium for personal expression.[32] Sluggish connection speeds did not slow the spread of the modem world.

True to the original metaphor of the "computerized bulletin board," all early BBSs provided two core functions: read old messages or post a new message. At this protean stage, the distinction between "files" and "messages" could be rather fuzzy. In a 1983 how-to book for BBS software developers, Lary Myers described three types of files accessible to users: messages, bulletins, and downloads.[33] While all three were stored and transmitted as sequences of ASCII characters, Myers distinguished "the message file" as the defining feature of the BBS.[34] Available day and night, the message file provided an "electronic corkboard" to the community of callers: a place to post announcements, queries, or comments "for the good of all."[35] Myers's example routine, written in BASIC, identified each message by a unique number and stored all of the messages on the system in a single random-access file.[36] A comment in Myers's code suggested that eighty messages would be a reasonable maximum for systems running on a TRS-80. A caller to such a system requested messages by typing numbers on their keyboard, and the system retrieved the corresponding sequence of characters from the message file. New messages were appended to the end of the message file, and when the maximum number of messages was reached, the system simply wrote over the old ones. Like flyers on a corkboard, messages on a BBS were not expected to stay up forever.

Beyond messages, however, the typical BBS provided access to at least two other types of files, distinguished principally by their contents and use. In Myers's taxonomy, "bulletins" represented a special type of message stored outside the rotating message file but still viewable online. A bulletin might include general information about the BBS, the minutes from a recent club meeting, technical reference material, product recommendations, or advertisements. "Use your imagination," encouraged Myers. "Just remember to keep a close tab on the amount of space you have on your disk."[37]

In contrast to bulletins, "downloads" included software programs and data files that were not meant to be viewed online. The files available from systems like Rich Schinnell's Software Exchange BBS tended to fall into this category. Myers characterized downloads as a type of software circulating outside the commercial sphere: "thousands of programs that have never been seen by the market and probably never will."[38] Typically, homebrew microcomputer software was written in BASIC and stored in the same human-readable ASCII format as messages and bulletins. As a result, Myers recommended using the exact same routine for transferring downloads as for bulletins.[39] It was up to the caller to capture the incoming stream of data and save it to tape or floppy disk.

On early BBSs, the ambiguity between files and messages gave rise to a novel form of electronic literature: the "textfile." Building on the countercultural values and aesthetics of fanzines and underground comics, textfiles were documents that unsettled the boundary between bulletins and downloads. Textfiles were well suited to home computers equipped with 300 baud modems and floppy disks. No special software or technical skills were required to create a textfile, and textfiles could move between otherwise-incompatible platforms. As a distinct form of electronic publishing, textfiles began to take shape in the early 1980s and remained a mainstay of BBS culture throughout the 1990s.

Initially, the term "textfile" was used to distinguish human-readable documents from executable programs. But "textfile" soon came to signify a more specific form of electronic literature. Written for an audience of fellow BBSers, there were few stylistic conventions or constraints on the textfile. Textfiles ranged in tone from the silly to the serious. There were satirical essays, high school rants, political manifestos, conspiracy theories, technical reports, explicit sexual fantasies, and many, many megabytes of teen poetry. Some textfiles were written by a single author, others in collaboration, many using pseudonyms. Some were carefully formatted and illuminated by bits of text-mode art, while others were barely legible. While some textfiles were little more than clippings from a forum or newsgroup, others were organized into "issues" and "volumes" like a print periodical. Textfiles were the broadsides of the modem world, an ephemeral street literature for the information superhighway.

The prevalence and aesthetic form of the textfile are reflected in the default configurations of many BBS host programs.[40] For example, a 1986 version of WWIV automatically created a subdirectory for "general text files."[41] Callers accessed the textfiles area by pressing "G" at the main menu, leading to the use of "g-files" as a synonym for "textfiles."[42] The 1991 version of Oblivion/2 not only created a "TEXTFILES" subdirectory by default but included a set of utilities for authoring textfiles that sysops could invoke from within the BBS.[43] One of the more common BBS modifications during this period was to add an online textfile viewer so that users could preview textfiles on-screen before downloading them. As textfiles grew in visual complexity, so did the special-purpose software for viewing them. DISPLAY, a modification for PCBoard, simply wrote a stream of text to the caller's terminal, while ANSI Gallery, a modification for Oblivion/2, transformed a collection of textfiles into an online "art gallery."[44]

Unlike programming or graphic arts, textfiles provided a low-tech medium for the circulation of new ideas and information on computer networks. No special software was required to view, edit, or create a textfile. As one enthusiast put it, "Everyone can use a textfile on the first try."[45] While some textfiles were transcribed from preexisting print materials—such as a book or magazine—most were original works of creative self-expression.[46] Because textfiles were smaller in size than programs or images, multiple textfiles fit onto a single floppy. A CD-ROM or hard disk drive held thousands. Furthermore, the portability of plain text across heterogeneous computing platforms made textfiles mobile in ways that their readers and authors were not.[47] A textfile originating on one BBS might pass through several others before appearing on a USENET newsgroup, a BITNET discussion list, and a CompuServe forum. Eventually, thousands of textfiles came to rest on the World Wide Web.

Positioned at the intersection of desktop publishing and dial-up networking, textfiles provide a historical bridge between the underground publishers of the 1970s, such as Loompanics Unlimited, and web magazines of the dot-com era, such as *Suck*.[48] Many zine makers of the 1980s were directly involved with BBS culture, and many textfile authors were active in the underground press. Tom Jennings, creator of FidoNet, published seven issues of a radical queer zine titled *HOMOCORE* from 1988 to 1991.[49] Mike Gunderloy, the founding editor of the influential *Factsheet Five*, ran a Factsheet Five BBS out of his home in East Greenbush, New York, from 1988 to 1994.[50] And before *Boing Boing* moved to the web in 1995, its editors—and self-described "happy mutants"—Carla Sinclair and Mark Frauenfelder published fifteen print issues of the cyberculture fanzine.[51] Whether publishing in print or online, this loose network of writers shared a common vision of an alternative media system sustained through the democratization of tools for design, publishing, and distribution.

Textfiles were common, but very few bulletin boards specifically focused on electronic literature. In March 1986, Jason Scott, a teenager in Chappaqua, New York, founded The Works BBS in his childhood bedroom using an IBM PC, a ten-megabyte hard drive, and a Hayes modem.[52] The 914 area code, not incidentally home to IBM corporate headquarters, was already host to a lively modeming scene.[53] Inspired by print zines like *Factsheet Five*, on the one hand, and the early "modem sub-culture," on the other, Scott decided to differentiate his system by designating it "text-files only."[54] Scott's sense of humor and enthusiasm for textfiles pervaded The Works. In a short file pitching the system to new callers, he noted that his pet ferret would serve as "co-sysop" and encouraged his readers to print out the files they found on his system

Advertisement for The Works BBS, included at the end of the second textfile released by the system's homegrown writing group, Octothorpe Productions, in 1986. (Courtesy of Jason Scott)

and to read them "at school or at the job, or even on the beach."[55] After three months in operation, with dozens of callers and over nine hundred textfiles, Scott declared his system "914's Text-file BBS." As one former user recalled, The Works was "a text file HEAVEN."[56]

For BBS callers in North America, the use of the contraction "textfiles," as opposed to, say, "electronic journal," also signaled affinity for a particular subculture. Textfiles flourished among modem users who favored messaging, for whom the wit and wordplay of their fellow callers superseded all other features of the modem world. Unlike activist or evangelical users, these adherents of the textfile, many of whom self-identified as "hackers" or "phreaks," composed their files for an imagined community of like-minded peers. In 1986, several regular callers to The Works formed a "writing group" and began to publish an irregular series of original files under the collective name "Octothorpe."[57] From 1986 to 1988, the group produced fifty-two files, the thematic range of which reflected the interests and sense of humor of the dominant teen hacker demographic. Parody pop lyrics reminiscent of "filk" music and articles copied out of *Playboy* magazine sat alongside inscrutable technical files detailing the inner workings of the local telephone network. Many files satirized the modeming subculture itself with coded in-jokes skewering specific users of The Works. "The Guide to Real Works Users," for example, included a list of one-liners such as, "Real Works Users thrive on

Doritos, Diet Pepsi and dial tones."[58] For the most part, the messages posted to The Works discussion forums have been lost. But the textfiles uploaded to the BBS survive, thanks to Scott's own preservation work, offering a glimpse of the fellowship among users and the day-to-day life of the board.[59]

Beginning around 1990, as the boundaries among various networks began to grow increasingly porous, a new form of textfile took hold. Electronic newsletters, magazines, and "e-zines" mimicked the conventions of a print periodical. They were published on a consistent schedule, and each file was assigned a "volume" and "issue" number. E-zines were a primary channel for communication among participants in the growing hacker subculture. Long-running publications such as *Phrack* and the *Computer Underground Digest* served as online analogues to older print zines like *2600*.[60] Collaborative writing groups like Cult of the Dead Cow published dozens of textfiles, becoming an influential voice for the "computer underground."[61] Starting an electronic periodical was relatively easy; maintaining one was hard. Hundreds of e-zines were assembled and released, but few lasted beyond a handful of issues.[62]

The first textfiles produced by Cult of the Dead Cow, or "cDc," appeared on bulletin boards around Lubbock, Texas, in 1985. Using the pen name "Swamp Rat," the teen computer enthusiast Kevin Wheeler published a satire of the violent recipes found in *The Anarchist Cookbook* titled "Gerbil Feed Bomb," followed by several detailed files about popular games for the Apple II.[63] The combination of ironic humor and technical arcana in Wheeler's first run of files became a trademark of the cDc. Later topics ranged from "Twenty Ways to Disrupt School Assemblies" and "Society Sucks (and what to do about it)" to area-code listings for the North American Numbering Plan and a guide to hacking the Telenet packet-switching network.[64] Sequentially numbered and stamped with an ASCII art rendering of a cow's skull, cDc textfiles became digital collectibles. New readers scoured BBSs for back issues, and fans ranked and debated their favorites. At the outset of the 1990s, bolstered by the visibility of cDc textfiles, the members of cDc became central figures in the booming hacker culture. While others may have written more code, the cDc provided the hacker movement with style and lore—a collective identity and a story to tell about itself.

The hacker panic of the late 1980s also prompted the creation of the *Computer Underground Digest*, or *CuD*. In early 1990, federal grand juries in Chicago and Atlanta indicted four members of the "Legion of Doom" (LoD) hacker group on charges that they planned to disrupt the 911 emergency services of the local telephone system.[65] As discussion of the LoD case threatened to overwhelm the moderators of the otherwise straight-laced TELECOM mailing list, the sociologists Gorden Meyer and Jim Thomas spun off the *CuD* as a new publication dedicated to "the social world of phreaks, hackers, and pirates." Unlike free-wheeling e-zines like *Phrack*, however, Meyer and Thomas characterized *CuD* as an open forum for disagreement and debate. "Although we encourage opinion," they wrote, "we suggest that these be well-reasoned and substantiated with facts, citations, and other 'evidence.'"[66] Despite its mission, *CuD* retained a sense of humor. Thomas and Myer suggested that their editorial ideal was a combination of the "World News" section of *Phrack* and the long-running TV debate program *Crossfire*—as moderated by the stand-up comedian Emo Phillips.

Publishing an e-zine involved an initial upload to one location followed by a decentralized process of diffusion. New issues of *Phrack* appeared first on the Metal Shop BBS, while new issues of *Computer Underground Digest* circulated on a BITNET mailing list. Readers of both publications acted as voluntary relays, manually transferring copies of the newsletters across the gaps between these heterogeneous communities. As a result, e-zines like *Computer Underground Digest* and *Phrack* were accessible to readers throughout the modem world, regardless of their geographic location, computer platform, or access to commercial networks.

The low barriers to entry, tolerance for transgressive content, and predominance of young white men also made BBSs an attractive environment for right-wing extremists. During the 1980s, several producers of racist and anti-Semitic media began to experiment with electronic publishing as a complement to their print and broadcast efforts.[67] George Dietz, publisher of the openly racist *Liberty Bell* magazine and self-described Nazi, was especially active in the adoption of new media technologies. In the 1970s, Dietz claimed to have organized a network of right-wing amateur radio operators, and in the 1980s, he helped to create several American Nazi BBSs.[68] Meanwhile, the neo-Nazi cable TV producer Tom Metzger promoted a California-based BBS to Canadian hate groups as a means to circumvent local hate-speech regulations.[69] In 1985, stories about the neo-Nazi computer networks ran on the ABC and CBS evening news—the first appearance of dial-up BBSs on either program.[70] The rhetoric on these systems was alarming, but the attention they received from journalists far outstripped their reach in the online world. In practice, neo-Nazi BBS networks were small and mostly disconnected from other BBS networks.[71] Textfile enthusiasts appear to have handled the neo-Nazi files of the mid-1980s as offensive oddities—digital contraband comparable to other conspiracy theories. Yet these forays presaged a mass migration of racist publishing from print to digital during the 1990s and a proliferation of white-supremacist material on the World Wide Web.[72]

Not all of the alternative publishing communities of the 1980s were represented in the electronic literature of the modem world. Young women were among the most prolific, dedicated, and innovative creators of print zines during the 1980s and 1990s, but they are scarcely visible in extant textfiles from the period.[73] This absence from the available archives of BBS culture is underscored by an abundance of feminist activity elsewhere online. Feminist forums, chat rooms, mailing lists, and e-zines proliferated on a variety of commercial and noncommercial computer networks including America Online, Prodigy, USENET, and the web.[74] Women-only BBS conferences such as The Women on The WELL (WOW) occasionally produced collective publications, but there were no explicitly feminist textfile writing groups or any analogue to Xeroxed "riot grrl" fanzines on dial-up BBSs such as The Works.

Textfiles emerged out of the earliest microcomputer networks, a vernacular form of electronic publishing shaped by the storage capacity of a floppy disk and throughput of a 300 baud modem. For the computer enthusiasts drawn to this unusual literature, textfiles offered a glimpse into a more participatory future for the media. In the absence of gatekeepers or the material costs associated with print publishing, a cohort of young writers carved out a new space for creative self-expression. Through informal file-sharing networks, their writing reached thousands of readers. Many found kinship with strangers through the exchange of ASCII characters, an electronic epistolary network resulting in lifelong bonds. The shortcomings of the textfile phenomenon—notably, the spread of racist

conspiracy theories and the absence of women's voices—reflect fundamental problems in US cyberculture that would reappear on a much
larger scale in the decades to come. It should be instructive that the only
systems to counter these biases involved active, hands-on moderation.

Textfiles survived the changing infrastructure of the modem world
and adapted to the affordances of new microcomputer technology. Rather
than disappear with the advent of faster modem speeds and cheaper storage, textfiles continued to grow and spread. Some authors adorned their
files with ornate ASCII and ANSI art. Others collaborated with graphic
artists, programmers, and musicians to produce bundles of creative material. Textfiles were the first homegrown files to circulate on the modem
world, but changing technology and an expanding population of participants sparked a second form of electronic publishing: shareware.

Before faster data speeds made their way to the microcomputing
public, however, hobbyists found methods of file sharing that were de-
cidedly low-tech. At 300 baud, the communities built by dial-up BBSs
enabled networks of enthusiasts to trade files that were too large for an
online transfer. As the memoirist Rob O'Hara recalls, the key calculation for file traders was to compare the speed of an online transfer with
the speed of a car traveling down the freeway. In the hours that it would
take to transfer a single floppy disk over a noisy phone line, he could
"drive to the person's house, copy an entire box-load of games, and drive
back home."[75] During his teen years, O'Hara began to routinely visit the
homes of his online acquaintances, and during these unusual meetings, he found himself navigating unfamiliar social terrain. Duplicat-
ing floppy disks was a slow, monotonous activity after all, and the two
strangers were stuck in a room with each other. In O'Hara's recollection,
the first visit to another hobbyist's home usually involved "coming up
with creative ways to fill the awkward silence."[76] Yet, for O'Hara and others, these awkward encounters occasionally resulted in long-term friend-
ships, blurring the boundary between file sharing and social networking.

The prevalence of low-speed and offline file trading also gave rise
to BBS software that dispensed with messaging altogether in favor of a
minimal interface for uploading and downloading. In 1982, Bill Blue and
Mark Robbins wrote ASCII Express II "The Professional."[77] Among its
many features, AE Pro included an "unattended auto-answer" mode that
allowed remote users to browse a local floppy disk, viewing or download-

ing the files stored there.[78] Systems running AE Pro, known colloquially as "AE Lines," were spartan infrastructures that offered few features
for communication between users. Unlike BBSs like CBBS that offered
space for community to grow, AE Lines were little more than anonymous
caches of software hanging out on the public telephone network.

The AE Pro interface was impersonal and efficient: a list of filenames
and a command prompt. In advertisements and BBS lists, AE Lines were
conventionally marked with the initials "AE" next to their phone numbers so that readers would know not to expect thoughtful discussion or
online games. Yet AE Lines offered a convenient file-sharing platform
that appealed to technically sophisticated users. By the mid-1980s, some
Apple BBSs advertised two phone numbers, one for the main system
and one for the AE Line. Others were modified so that callers could jump
into AE Pro for file sharing and then jump back to the main system for
messaging.[79] Despite the limitations of the software, AE users nevertheless found ways to communicate by naming their files with an audience
in mind. Files with names like "README," "HELLO," or "WELCOME"
served as an improvised form of public messaging comparable to the
"bulletins" on Myers's BBS. Even the seemingly businesslike exchange
of files on an AE Line revealed a collective desire to communicate.

2,400 BITS PER SECOND

The standard 300 baud modem was adequate for trading messages and
textfiles and short BASIC programs, but it was clearly too slow for more
substantial files like applications, games, or digital images. When CBBS
came online in 1978, virtually all telephone modems ran at 300 baud.
Within ten years, however, the typical data rate had jumped to 2,400 bits
per second (bps), an eight-fold increase. The expansion in throughput
enabled more real-time communication functions, responsive user interfaces, and, crucially, faster downloads. At 2,400 bits per second, dial-up
BBS networks provided a plausible alternative infrastructure for the distribution of commercial software. As most of the industry struggled with
brick-and-mortar retail sales, the experimental "shareware" movement
took advantage of the growing capacity of the BBS network to convey
files throughout the world.

The shift from 300 bps to 2,400 bps happened gradually. As early as
1981, a minority of BBSs offered 1,200 bps connections, but these faster

speeds always came at a cost. Whereas 300 baud modems universally supported the Bell 103 standard, faster transmission rates lacked a de facto standard protocol. Despite the premium pricing of "high-speed" modems, their performance was inconsistent, and modems from different makers were frequently incompatible with one another. The half-duplex 1,200 bps mode of the Novation Apple-CAT II, introduced in 1981 and favored by computer-game traders, used a relatively uncommon protocol, Bell 202, and required a Novation modem on both ends.[80] Racal-Vadic, meanwhile, supported multiple Bell standards alongside its own proprietary protocols but aimed its devices at corporate customers rather than individuals. Even the cost-conscious Pro-Modem 1200 from Prometheus Products sold for more than twice the average price of a 300 baud model at Radio Shack. For most home computer owners, cost and compatibility kept the modem world running at 300 bits per second through the middle of the decade.

The barriers to faster modem connections were physical as well as political and economic. In 1984, the European standard organization CCITT published the V.22bis standard for 2,400 bps communications over standard telephone lines, resolving some of the fragmentation in the modem market and providing a common protocol for Europe and the United States.[81] At the end of that year, Kim Maxwell, founder of Racal-Vadic, published a feature in *Byte* detailing the technical challenges facing producers of "high-speed" modems for home computer owners.[82] In Maxwell's assessment, the key factor limiting data throughput was the "twisted pair" of copper wires connecting residential telephones to the larger network. The Bell 103 standard achieved simultaneous two-way (or "full-duplex") communication by carving two "channels" out of the audible spectrum, one for each modem. To achieve greater throughput in the same copper medium, "high-speed" modems employed more complex modulation schemes, transmitting multiple bits simultaneously over narrower and narrower channels. Despite theoretical proof of the feasibility of these modulation schemes, the signal processing required to encode and decode the bits often exceeded the computational capability of the attached PCs. Indeed, Maxwell pointed out, the ITU's V.32 standard for 9,600 bps required 2.4 million multiplications per second, an order of magnitude above the processing power of the IBM PC.[83]

Affordable 2,400 bps modems came to market in the latter half of the 1980s. Between 1984 and 1986, semiconductor firms began to manufacture signal-processing hardware specifically for high-speed data communications. By 1986, there were more than a dozen 2,400 bps modems available to consumers, including offerings from market leaders like Hayes and US Robotics.[84] Standardization on the V.22bis protocol led, once again, to competition on special features, design, and price. In the back pages of computer magazines, less well-known brands such as Compu Com Corporation advertised no-frills modems compatible with both the 300 and 2,400 bps standards for as low as $109.[85] Eventually, Radio Shack added a 2,400 bps modem to its annual catalog, a sure sign that the modem world had shifted gears to "high speed."

The material difficulties of moving files from place to place were magnified in the context of commercialization. The developers of PC software were bedeviled by a lack of venues for promoting and selling their products. Computer stores, bookstores, hobby shops, toy stores, and department stores all sold microcomputer software; but shelf space was limited, and logistics were costly. Catalog sales offered greater variety to the customer, but mail order introduced new complexity when it came to handling payments and customer-support requests. Magazine publishers, meanwhile, provided an alternative distribution network. Initially, programs were circulated on the pages of magazines as raw source code for the reader to manually transcribe.[86] Later, "software magazines" such as *Softdisk* published monthly anthologies on floppy disk. In some parts of the world, public radio and television stations broadcast software over the air.[87] With the added burden of unauthorized copying, many software firms preferred to deal exclusively in business-to-business sales, altogether abandoning the consumer market.

Computing folklore pegs the start of the consumer software market to the release of VisiCalc, an attractive spreadsheet program for the Apple II, in 1979.[88] VisiCalc was one of the first applications to attract substantial interest outside hobbyist circles.[89] Not only were existing Apple II owners willing to pay $250 for VisiCalc, but businesspeople with no background in computers were spending thousands on "turnkey" VisiCalc systems that included a brand-new Apple and printer.[90] As the industry analyst Ben Rosen remarked, "[VisiCalc may be] the software tail that wags (and sells) the personal computer dog."[91]

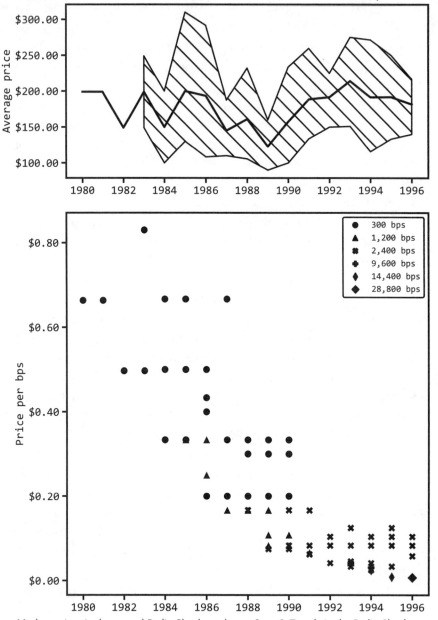

Modem prices in the annual Radio Shack catalog, 1980–96. Trends in the Radio Shack product line provide an approximate index of the technology available to a typical consumer over time. During this period, Radio Shack sold forty-three different modems including acoustic couplers, direct-connect peripherals, internal expansion cards, and travel-sized models. Nearly three-quarters ran at either 300 or 2,400 bits per second (bps). The latter first appeared in 1988 and remained the top speed until the introduction of an "awesome" 9,600 bps modem in 1993. Despite the breadth of Radio Shack's telecommunications line, the average cost of a modem in any given year hung steadily around $150–$200. Yet the bang for your buck rose dramatically as the demand for faster data rates drove down the cost of older (and still quite capable) models.

But most PC software is not like VisiCalc. Whereas a good spread-sheet program is useful to a wide range of computer owners, the major-ity of software products will only be useful to a particular segment of po-tential users. From health to education, hobbies to entertainment, there seemed to be no limit to the applications imagined by microcomputer enthusiasts—but developers had few outlets for promoting, selling, and distributing their software products to these niches.[92] Without access to retail shelf space, smaller-scale developers went DIY—taking out ads in hobbyist magazines, packaging their software in Ziploc baggies with Xeroxed manuals, and fulfilling orders at the post office. With tiny mar-gins and no formal business structure, even successful ventures could be overwhelmed by customer-support requests, returned packages, and bounced checks. The market for microcomputer software had bugs.

Users were even more frustrated than developers by the problems with the early software market. The typical commercial software trans-action required computer owners to take on an unreasonable risk. With little more than magazine reviews, advertisements, or the advice of a store clerk to guide them, consumers paid up front before ever seriously testing out a computer program. Critics called this risk the "shrink wrap problem" and blamed it for sluggish sales across the industry. Mean-while, the pages of popular computer magazines were filled with com-plaints about unfixed bugs and undocumented incompatibilities, evi-dence of users' frustration with the existing software marketplace. It was an unhappy arrangement for everyone.

The uncertainty of the broken software marketplace seemed to bind users together. Word of mouth could make or break a new software product, and BBSs provided a valuable medium for computer owners to meet and discuss their experiences with various games and applica-tions. When computer owners came across a piece of quality software, they were eager to share their discovery with others. Making copies for friends and acquaintances seemed like a natural extension of this peer recommendation system, and the file-sharing function of BBSs pro-vided a mechanism for this exchange. Such unauthorized trades were decried as "piracy" by commercial software developers, who saw each download as a potential loss. Beyond these accusations of theft, how-ever, file-trading activity expressed an important quantum of economic information. The number of unauthorized copies of a given program in circulation positively correlated to the value that it held for users. This principle, which held as true for Microsoft BASIC in 1976 as for Microsoft Multiplan in 1982, provided a compelling puzzle for many small-scale software developers. Could the work of this dynamic network of traders be harnessed for commercial purposes? Might the impulse to share files give rise to an alternative economy of consumer software?

At the intersection of a failing marketplace and a thriving file-trading culture, "shareware" emerged as a novel approach to the business of software. Shareware took advantage of both the infinite reproducibility of digital media and the growing network of file-hungry modem owners. Of all the new types of files cascading through BBS networks in the 1980s, shareware was the most uniquely at home in the modem world. Rather than attempt to restrict access—whether through copy protection or shrink wrap—shareware authors surrendered control to their users, relying on an appeal to morality and a spirit of fraternity to sustain their businesses. Advocates described shareware as a marketing scheme, an ideology, business model, community of practice, genre, and stigma.

The shareware concept was invented by small-scale software developers in response to the ongoing failure of the microcomputer marketplace to provide space for them. Shareware represented an alternative vision for the future of consumer software, built on the technical affordances of the nascent modem world. Instead of fighting with file-swapping enthusiasts, shareware authors encouraged users to make copies and pass their programs along. By allowing users to "try before you buy," they reasoned, a quality shareware program sold itself. Plus, by empowering users to copy programs for friends, they could reach potential customers without spending any money on advertising. In the words of one software publisher, the shareware model offered a new type of marketing: "word of disk."[93]

The typical shareware license granted users a short period during which they were welcome to use the program free of cost. At the end of this evaluation period, the user was obliged to mail a small "registration fee" to the author. Registration fees were conventionally under $25 and often included a printed manual, backup diskette, or promise of future upgrades. Contemporary accounts frequently describe the shareware protocol as a matter of "honor." In the 1995 edition of *The Secret Guide to Computers*, Russ Walter encouraged readers to explore the available shareware but reminded them that they were "honor-bound" to pay the suggested fee for software they found useful.[94] Rey Barry made a similar argument in his *Guide to Free Shareware*, published in the same year. The shareware economy, he argued, is an "Honor System," and as long as users continue to register their software, shareware authors will continue to produce affordable programs of high quality, "as good as any you will find [in a retail shop]."[95]

For approximately fifteen years, shareware was the dominant business model of the modem world, adapted to a range of niche markets, from small business owners to hardcore gamers. Today, the influence of shareware lingers in the form of in-app purchases, premium upgrades, and "Pro" versions of otherwise free utilities. Yet these models lack the moral conviction at the heart of shareware, a belief that some people will voluntarily pay for a product simply because paying another person for their labor is the right thing to do.

Shareware origin stories typically begin in 1982. That year, critics agreed that Andrew Fluegelman's PC-TALK was the best telecommunications program available for IBM PC.[96] Even better, Fluegelman gave away both the program and its source code free of charge. In return, he asked that satisfied users mail a check to his home in Tiburon, California. Meanwhile, Jim Knopf, another hobbyist programmer, out in Bellevue, Washington, had begun to give away a database program called Easy File with a very similar request for support.[97] Within a few months, a user of both programs put the men in touch. Knopf and Fluegelman agreed to embark on a "marketing experiment" together.[98] Easy File was renamed PC-File, the prices of both programs were set at $25, and each programmer added a notice about the other's program to their bundle. Knopf's wife called him "a foolish old man" for thinking that anyone would voluntarily send him money.[99] Soon, however, checks began arriving to the family's mailbox.

As Fluegelman and Knopf's experiment began to take shape, a third programmer independently took up the try-before-you-buy model. In 1983, Bob Wallace of Seattle, Washington, released PC-Write, a word processor for the IBM PC. Wallace believed that users needed to try a program to decide if it was right for them. The shareware model, he believed, "let software explain itself."[100] Not only did Wallace permit users to copy his program, but he offered a financial incentive to file swappers. Wallace paid registered users a $25 commission for converting others into customers.[101] For prominent hobbyists, the arrangement could be quite remunerative. The shareware advocate and frequent file swapper Michael Callahan later recalled converting his $75 registration fee into approximately $500 in commissions.[102]

The unexpected successes of PC-TALK, PC-File, and PC-Write provide the narrative backbone of shareware's origin story.[103] Shareware began as a form of hobby entrepreneurship, but it was never disconnected from the conventional computing industry. In spite of being routinely described as "amateurs," all three of the men at the core of shareware's founding myth were previously employed in computing—Fluegelman was the editor for a major computing magazine (as well as the *Whole Earth Review*),[104] Knopf had worked at IBM since 1967, and Wallace was one of the first employees at Microsoft. But these biographical details should not undermine the authenticity of shareware as a form of user-driven innovation. Rather, the defection of professional programmers from corporate positions to self-employment illustrates how the organization of the software industry was upset by microcomputing. Amateurs and professionals alike saw an opportunity to abandon conventional employment in favor of work that served the computing community.[105] Proponents often described shareware authors "making a living" doing work they love.[106]

By 1984, dozens of programmers were experimenting with free-to-copy online distribution, but there was little standardization from one program to the next. Fluegelman had trademarked the term "freeware"; Knopf preferred "user-supported software"; and Wallace was building a business around the term "shareware."[107] Adding to the confusion, these terms were often used interchangeably with "public domain" (or copyright-free). Tech journalists highlighted the low cost, wide availability, and uneven quality of amateur software. One feature writer wryly acknowledged the rampant disregard for copyright: "Believe it or not, piracy isn't the only way to get free software."[108] Given this tangle of terminology, new computer owners could be forgiven for thinking that any program they downloaded or copied from a user group was free of cost and copyright.

To quell the confusion, Nelson Ford, maintainer of the Public (Software) Library, or PsL, hosted a naming contest through his column in *Softalk for the IBM Personal Computer* magazine. After a few weeks, the results were in: readers preferred "shareware." In 1987, Ford organized a conference in Houston, Texas, for shareware programmers, vendors, and BBS sysops that led to the creation of a trade organization known as the Association of Shareware Professionals (ASP). The ASP sought to further standardize the shareware model. It provided an ombudsman to mediate disputes, helped shareware authors access credit card payment services, and published a list of values such as "treat users with respect," "promise a minimum level of support," and "[offer a] money-back guarantee."[109] Members promoted the ASP by indicating their membership in the documentation of their software, a mark of legitimacy to reassure potential customers.

In the late 1980s, the shareware economy boomed. Low-cost "IBM-compatible" clones provided shareware authors with a platform for development, and the modem world provided a network for distribution. Several of the biggest BBSs in North America specialized in file sharing, providing convenient hubs for shareware authors wishing to spread their programs and communicate directly with users. In seeming defiance of classical economic theory, the Association of Shareware Professionals boasted that its members were generating tens of millions in annual revenue.

Shareware was especially popular among modem owners. Telecommunications utilities such as Fluegelman's PC-TALK and Smith's Procomm were consistent best-sellers. In spite of the overall scarcity of modems among computer owners, lists of "top," "recommended," or "essential" shareware invariably featured communications-related programs. The commercial success of modem-oriented applications underscored the fitness of the shareware model to the file-sharing practices of the modem world.[110] John Friel, author of Qmodem, argued that the shareware model was uniquely suited to telecommunications because every modem owner needed quality communications software in order to access online services and download files.[111] Consequently, hardware firms directly benefited from the widespread availability of programs like PC-TALK. Modem manufacturers routinely shipped out copies of shareware programs with their new modems, a practice that continued into the 1990s.

The commercial success and circulation of shareware also shaped the decentralized, hierarchical structure of the growing North American BBS network. A handful of large-scale systems, sprinkled across the continent, served as distribution hubs. In the early 1990s, the ASP mailed out diskettes to a list of "approved" BBSs, which were guaranteed to have the latest programs published by ASP members.[112] Independent shareware authors uploaded new programs to these central nodes as well, from which dozens of regional sysops downloaded new files for distribution on their local boards. Commercial online services such as CompuServe served a complementary function as meeting places for BBS sysops and shareware authors.[113] Although the steep costs of long-distance dialing meant that most shareware was downloaded from a local BBS, the decentralized network of "feeder" BBSs and nationwide services enabled files to move quickly from the author's home PC to thousands of regional systems across the continent.

Shareware represented a vast industry of small- and medium-sized software-development firms, many of which were, behind their PO boxes, lone programmers working in their spare time. The shareware business model—try now, pay later, pass it on—depended on bulletin board systems as an infrastructure for the distribution of new software, word-of-mouth marketing, and a decentralized customer-support network. Large-scale BBSs specializing in file sharing deployed racks of CD-ROM and hard disk drives to keep vast libraries of shareware online. For example, the aptly named Infinite Data Source in Alexandria, Virginia, hosted more than fifty gigabytes of files across sixty CD-ROMs near its peak in 1996.[114] Similarly, Exec-PC in Elm Grove, Wisconsin, the self-anointed "World's Largest BBS," advertised a library of "450,000 programs and files" available for free download.[115] As the shareware advocate Rey Barry put it plainly in 1995, without BBSs, the shareware industry would have simply ceased to function.[116]

The initial success of shareware was the subject of some debate in the computer industry. In a 1987 op-ed about the future of media economics, Stewart Brand championed the shareware model as a "major marketing innovation" that positioned microcomputer software as a "service to which you subscribe" rather than a product that you buy. Brand compared shareware favorably to earlier grassroots innovations such as the development of shortwave and packet radio communications by ham radio operators. "Good money was made [by shareware authors]," he remarked, "and the standard software distributors still haven't caught on to the lesson." In Brand's perspective, shareware entrepreneurs were following, rather than fighting, a transition in the economics of information: "It's so easy to copy, send and transform [information] that the price tag gets left far behind."[117]

Not all computer enthusiasts shared Brand's affection for shareware, however. In a letter to the editor, one reader argued that shareware was a failure when measured against more traditional software products. "Would Lotus 1-2-3 or Wordperfect have been successful if they had been distributed for free?" he asked. "Of course not."[118] Shareware authors, meanwhile, tended toward a more nuanced skepticism. John Friel, author of Qmodem, chalked up his own success to "right place, right time." He described the market for PC-compatible shareware as "stalemated" by 1990 because most of the major niches—text editors, spreadsheets, terminal emulators—had been filled. Unless the underlying platform changed substantially, he ventured, a small set of entrenched "winners" would continue to dominate their respective niches.[119]

Shareware might have stalled out if not for a boom in games distributed by modem during the 1990s. Software Creations in Clinton, Massachusetts, became known as a hub for shareware game makers like Apogee Software. With over 134 simultaneous incoming lines, Software Creations might have felt more like one of the nationwide commercial information systems than a local hobbyist "one-liner." Ranked the top BBS in *Boardwatch* magazine's Readers Choice Awards poll from 1993 to 1996, Software Creations was renowned for its comprehensive shareware archives.[120] On the log-in screen, Software Creations dubbed itself the "Home of Authors," and reviewers gushed that it featured "more than 100 new uploads every day."[121] Among the many shareware companies that considered it their primary distribution node, Software Creations was particularly well known for hosting high-quality shareware games from publishers and developers such as Apogee and id Software.

The shareware model depended on the willingness of authors and publishers not only to permit but to encourage the autonomous circulation of their software products. This permissive orientation toward copying facilitated a mutually beneficial relationship with BBS users and sysops, who derived their own benefit from sharing new software. Although a handful of large BBSs like Software Creations were marked as "official" distribution sites for companies like id Software and Epic Megagames, few gamers outside of the 508 area code in Massachusetts could afford to stay on a toll call long enough to download from Software Creations directly. Instead, shareware games like *Doom* were relayed throughout the BBS world by users and sysops who downloaded files from one board and uploaded them to another. There were several motivations for this sort of voluntary labor. Mike Nichols, the sysop of Lamplighter BBS in Hobbs, New Mexico, remembers routinely dialing into BBSs in Dallas, Ft. Worth, and Albuquerque to download the latest shareware files. Nichols considered these occasional toll calls a form of community service for the benefit of fellow BBSers in Hobbs who could not afford to make the long-distance call on their own.[122]

The success of shareware games depended on an innovation in the structure of video-game narratives led by id Software. In 1990, under contract with Apogee, id Software produced *Commander Keen*, a 2-D platformer in which players guided a precocious boy through a humorous adventure battling goofy green aliens. Rather than release the entire game, Apogee packaged the first few levels into an "episode" small enough to fit on a single floppy or download over a 2,400 bps connection. The first episode ended in a cliffhanger, followed by a prompt to call the Apogee sales line and order the rest of the game. Within days of posting the first episode to Software Creations, KEEN1.ZIP had been replicated throughout the North American BBS network, and calls were pouring in from players who wanted to know the rest of the *Keen* story.

The success of *Commander Keen* proved the viability of the shareware model and prompted an explosion in new shareware games. The sudden availability of free games provided a new motivation for joining the modem world. Learning to navigate dial-up BBSs gave gamers access to titles that would not appear in retail stores for months. Likewise, the community functions of the BBS facilitated discussion, debate, and collective intelligence among players grappling with the latest games. In a positive feedback loop, the growing population of PC gamers in the modem world spurred more game publishers to experiment with digital distribution and the shareware business model.

The initial release and reception of *Doom*, a wildly popular first-person shooter from id Software, marked the interdependence of shareware, gaming, and the modem world. In December 1993, the first episode appeared as a single ZIP file on an anonymous FTP server at the University of Wisconsin.[123] Within hours, eager file traders had replicated the shareware across thousands of BBSs. Today, fans remember *Doom* as an instant smash, but it would be months before the game was available in a physical format. In a review for the April 1994 issue of *Compute!*, the critic Denny Atkin enthused, "No computer game you've ever seen has graphics and sound like this."[124] But at the time Atkin's review appeared in print, readers still could not buy *Doom* at the mall. Gamers who wanted to experience the graphics and sound described in Atkin's review needed to either access a BBS themselves or find a friend to download it on their behalf. As anticipation for the game grew, id Software continued to develop, tweak, and polish the game with the input of players, a radically transparent form of participatory play-testing. Yet only those players with a modem and the wherewithal to access a local BBS could fully participate in the growing *Doom* phenomenon. Even when the game was officially released, only the shareware version was available in retail stores.[125] Additional chapters were sold directly to players through mail order using the same model as *Commander Keen*.

Prior to forming id Software, the developers of *Doom* were steeped in the technical culture of hobby computing.[126] *Doom* was the first game designed from the ground up for the norms and values of the modem world. Beyond its episodic structure and online distribution model, *Doom* included a multiplayer game mode in which players connected to one another via modem. In the same way that the availability of shareware games attracted players to BBSs, *Doom*'s multiplayer mode recast the modem as an instrument of fun and entertainment. With so many players discussing the game online, *Doom* became a site of considerable user-driven innovation. Enthusiasts began to circulate modifications, or "mods," for *Doom* that changed the art and sound, altered the game's mechanics, or provided new maps designed for multiple players to explore.[127] The same BBSs that carried the shareware release of *Doom* became repositories for *Doom* mods and maps. Soon, these practices were adopted by other game cultures. By 1995, flight-simulator fans were producing new scenery, mechanical models, and maps of US terrain.[128]

Game-oriented BBSs like Software Creations were not merely distribution nodes but rather community spaces from which a more participatory form of PC gaming culture emerged.

The boom in shareware games at the start of the 1990s occurred in parallel with a second shift in modem speed. The dominance of 2,400 bps was not nearly as long-lived as 300 bps had been. Between 1988 and 1990, as even faster modems came to market, Radio Shack slashed the cost of a 2,400 bps modem in half. By the time *Doom* captured the attention of the PC gaming public in 1994, modem speeds of 9,600 bps and higher were becoming routine. While the adoption of faster modems facilitated the continued growth in shareware, modding, and multiplayer gaming practices, it also accompanied a fundamental shift in the visual culture of BBSing. At 9,600 bps, BBS networks began to traffic in the rapid distribution of digital images.

9,600 BITS PER SECOND

The demand for bandwidth is one of the many continuities from the modem world to the present. Modems dubbed "high speed" in 1983 had become commonplace by 1988, and the market clamored for modems that could hit 9,600 bps and higher. In the summer of 1988, *Byte* ran a cover story on new "ultra-high-speed" devices, profiling more than a dozen modems capable of "accurately sending 3 megabytes across the country in less than an hour."[129] To achieve this four-fold increase in throughput over the same noisy copper telephone lines, modem engineers adapted microchips designed for commercial leased lines with new techniques in modulation, compression, error correction, and signal processing. Housed in molded plastic cases adorned with switches and blinking lights, this gear looked, felt, and sounded high-tech. Plus, at an average price of about $1,350, these were decidedly premium products for a specialist audience.[130] The apparent urgency with which modem makers brought this first wave of 9,600 bps products to market hinted at an emerging battle for the modem world of the 1990s—a battle that would be fought through protocols, standards, brand recognition, and market share.

Between 1988 and 1994, the cost of modems fell across all categories, and the entire metanetwork of dial-up BBSs and online services began to speed up. Initially, the adoption of higher-speed modems was led by BBS sysops who created a brief bandwidth surplus. A reader survey conducted by *Boardwatch* in early 1992 indicated that 38 percent of BBSs supported 9,600 bps connections, while 66 percent of callers remained at 2,400 bps.[131] Leading modem makers like Courier and Hayes actively courted the BBS world with "sysop discounts" and other targeted promotions. For FidoNet sysops and shareware traders, the recurring savings on long-distance telephone calls quickly covered the fixed cost of buying a high-speed modem. By 1990, US Robotics reported that more than five thousand BBSs had adopted one of its high-speed Courier modems.[132]

Expanding the adoption of 9,600 bps modems beyond sysops required a fundamental change in technology and a substantial drop in price. These came in January 1992 when Supra, Inc., known for its cost-sensitive SupraModem, announced a new device combining novel hardware with a "killer" price.[133] Enclosed in an aluminum case approximately the size of "two decks of playing cards," the SupraFAXModem 14400 looked like a miniaturized clone of the Hayes Smartmodem.[134] But inside the shiny housing, the SupraFAXModem employed a microchip made exclusively by Rockwell that supported multiple communication protocols and an astonishing 14,400 bps transfer rate—all for $399. At half the cost of less-capable modems from better-known competitors, the new Supra modem effectively crashed the modem market. The ensuing price war brought the cost of high-speed modems lower and lower. By the start of 1993, a decent 9,600 bps modem could be had for as little as $250. On file-oriented boards across the net, the kilobytes piled up.

With the growing availability of high-speed modems, the standard 2,400 bps modem became a commodity, a cheap add-on for any home computer owner, removing one of the critical barriers to entry for the expanding modem world. In 1991, the commercial online service Prodigy produced a retail "start-up kit" that included a private-label 2,400 bps modem—"$148.95 value for only $49.95."[135] Occasionally offered at a discount for as low as $30, the Prodigy kit was one of the cheapest ways to get your hands on a working modem. Nothing stopped a buyer from using their Prodigy modem to dial into local BBSs, gaming systems, or other commercial networks.[136] Meanwhile, competition drove the price of a new IBM-compatible system below $2,000.[137] PC makers like Compaq and Gateway, to distinguish their beige boxes from their competitors' beige boxes, bundled in modems (along with sound cards, speakers,

CD-ROM drives, printers, and other peripherals). In this frenzied commercial environment, it was not uncommon for a new computer owner to find themselves in the possession of a modem by accident. The expansion in modem ownership and falling cost of higher-end devices contributed to an overall acceleration in transfer speeds. By 1994, all of the major nationwide online services boasted support for 9,600 bps connections, and Radio Shack was selling its own 9,600 bps modem—just in time for *Doom* players to upgrade.

Climbing modem speeds did not immediately transform the moment-to-moment experience of using a BBS. More than a decade after the creation of CBBS, keyboard commands and text menus remained the standard interface to the modem world.[138] Rather, the immediate effect of adopting a high-speed modem was to lower the cost of large file transfers, enabling users to become file explorers, casually downloading files that they would have previously passed over. This new exploratory style of downloading stimulated the production of new types of files that could take advantage of the growing multimedia capabilities of newly upgraded PCs. As the 1990s wore on, BBSs increasingly provided space to trade digitized photos, ray-traced graphics, procedurally generated animations, and short video clips in their downloads areas.

Creating, collecting, and circulating digital images combined the participatory feeling and illicit thrill of textfiles with the visual spectacle of games and demos. Simply put, home computer owners of the 1980s did not expect their machines to display digital photos and videos. The term "graphics" generally referred to the charts produced by spreadsheet software or the pixel art of video games. To see a full-color photographic image on a computer screen was still a remarkable thing in 1990. High-resolution graphics required special software, hardware, and operator expertise, and although creative professionals—from home-video editors to console-game developers—had embraced multimedia computers such as the Apple Macintosh, Atari ST, and Commodore Amiga, the consumer tech industry relegated these colorful machines to a specialized niche.[139] The mainstream home-computing industry converged on beige-boxed PC clones, many of which shipped with monochrome displays by default.[140] As one tech writer put it in 1990, "graphics [were] more of a perk than a foundation" for everyday computer users.[141]

Digitized images of spaceflight watermarked by the popular Aquila and EXEC-PC BBSs. In the late 1980s, digitized photographs served multiple purposes. For some computer owners, the mere possibility of displaying a photographic image was intrinsically exciting. For others, BBSs provided access to categories of images—from satellite photography to amateur pornography—that were otherwise difficult to obtain. Knowing that high-quality images would circulate among collectors, BBS sysops appropriated them as promotional media, stamping them with BBS telephone numbers and access information.

Yet the technical difficulties associated with graphical applications only made them more appealing to computer enthusiasts. Unlike the technical pleasures of programming or telecommunications, the joys of colorful graphics and animation were immediate, visceral, and accessible to nonexperts. What better way to show off your banging new PC to friends and family than with a flashy graphic display? From procedurally generated fractals to three-dimensional ray-traced scenes, the graphics programs and files found on BBSs frequently served as visual marvels rather than practical applications or informative resources. In a retail context, the term "demo" referred to graphical programs serving no purpose other than the delight and surprise of viewers.[142] Artists and programmers traded tips on writing code to defy viewers' expectations and push the limits of a home computer's graphical display.[143]

In addition to impressing others, the graphics files available on BBSs could surprise computer owners themselves, revealing unknown technical features of their machines. Multimedia computers traded on their graphical capabilities, but the typical PC clone required special utility programs to access higher-resolution video modes or decode images stored in new file formats such as CompuServe's Graphics Interchange Format, or GIF.[144] At the start of the 1990s, many shareware authors aimed at unlocking the graphical capabilities of DOS-based PCs. Astute sysops listed popular shareware image-viewing programs like CompuShow in the same download folders as their collections of graphics files.[145] In the same sense that BBSs provided advanced access to games like *Commander Keen* and *Doom*, they offered a glimpse into a radically new visual culture of computing.

Digitized photographs were difficult to create, expensive to transmit, and complicated to view, but users could not get enough of them. The insatiable demand for graphic files across the network drove the creation of one of the most popular—and profitable—BBSs of all time. From 1983 until at least 1996, Jim Maxey, a sysop in Lake Oswego, Oregon, capitalized on the seemingly insatiable demand for digital images among BBS callers. In 1983, Maxey, unemployed and living alone with his six-year-old daughter, founded Event Horizons BBS with the intention of building an online archive of astronomy-related images.[146] Unlike many of his hobbyist contemporaries, finding a way to turn a profit was paramount to his continued participation in BBSing. Although Maxey's space images were exquisite, the business side of Event Horizons picked up only after he began to scan centerfolds from adult magazines.[147] From 1987 to 1993, the hourly rate for access to Event Horizons jumped quickly from $1 to $3 to $10.[148] By 1992, Event Horizons was a profitable small business with office space and ten employees producing a steady stream of new files for the modem world. Journalistic coverage of the "world's most expensive BBS" suggested revenues approaching $8,000 per day, more than $3 million per year.[149]

Maxey and his crew were prolific digitizers. The digital photo library on Event Horizons BBS included many images scanned in-house. Scanning high-resolution images and preparing them for download was painstaking, but this labor justified Event Horizons' premium price.[150] Consistent with the norm of interoperability throughout the modem world, CompuServe's GIF became the de facto standard raster image format on BBSs like Event Horizons.[151] In addition to its use by CompuServe, a wide variety of freeware and shareware programs could create and display GIF files. As one shareware author wrote, GIF was "by design, an INTERCHANGE format [and] the graphics can be 'moved' from one type of computer to another."[152] Rather than a flatbed scanner (which would have been prohibitively expensive in the mid-1980s), the early images on Event Horizons were produced using specialized hardware for capturing still images from composite video streams.[153] To transform the resulting files into GIFs, a second piece of software was required to crop the image, reduce the resolution, transform each hue to one of just sixteen colors, and run the GIF compression algorithm. Finally, a third program was required to overlay captions, titles, or other text on the GIF. Overall, the human labor, computational time, and hard-disk memory required to produce each image was considerable, but for users accustomed to spreadsheets and text-mode terminals, the results were remarkable.

By 1992, hundreds of BBSs offered downloadable images, but the runaway success of Event Horizons seemed to rest on a few specific factors. First, Event Horizons included thousands of unique images not available from other systems, including a particularly voluminous collection of "adult" GIFs. Second, Maxey was committed to educating PC owners about the latent graphics capabilities of their systems. Print advertisements in popular computer magazines assured readers,

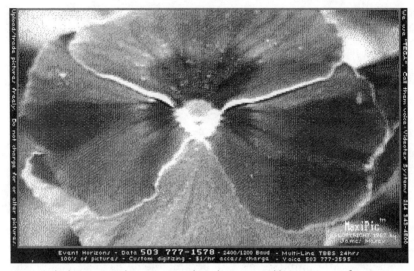

Watermarked "MaxiPic" that appears to have been created by Jim Maxey of Event Horizons BBS around 1987–88. This image depicts a macro photo of a pansy. The source photo is unknown. The white text running around the border of the photograph details the software used to create the image, invites viewers to call Event Horizons, and encourages them to copy and trade images without charge.

"Viewing computer images is much easier than you might think," while also promising a visual thrill: "Experience your computer's maximum graphics ability!"[154] In 1988, Maxey released a freeware program titled Universe that nicely conveyed his commitment to encouraging amateur interest in space. Universe was an educational slideshow program featuring eleven digitized astronomy photos. To ensure maximum compatibility, the images were cropped to 640 by 350 pixels and encoded at a 4-bit color depth—settings that would display correctly on both older and newer graphics hardware.[155] Finally, a short caption appeared at the top of each image, including a title, brief description, and tagline with the Event Horizons BBS telephone number. Even uncompressed, the entire program fit easily on a single floppy, and Maxey explicitly permitted users to share copies with friends and local BBSs.

Event Horizons rightfully earned a reputation as the maker of "mighty fine .GIFs," and its work began to circulate beyond northwestern Oregon.[156] The colorful titles displayed at the top of the Universe images were characteristic of the captions added to each and every "Maxi-Pic" found in the Event Horizons collection.[157] In addition to describing the contents of the image, these captions included the phone number of the Event Horizons BBS. As was the case with shareware, the captions assured that as the images traveled floppy to floppy and BBS to BBS throughout the country, viewers could find their way back to the source. The BBS network may have been decentralized, but Maxey's captions marked a direct route to Event Horizons. One question lurked around this growing community of GIF traders, however: Who owned these digital reproductions?

The small staff at Event Horizons spent hours *digitizing* images, but they were not out in the field with cameras *photographing* images. The value of the resulting GIF depended on the combined labor and ingenuity of both the photographer and the digitizer. When a reporter from the *Oregonian* described Event Horizons' archives as "breath-taking," she was clearly referring to the content of the images—"skiers in midflight, landscapes with mountains or palm trees, [and] real astronomical images from NASA"—not their pixel density, accurate color, and high resolution.[158] Around 1990, with no legal precedent for guidance, Event Horizons issued a confusing policy regarding the redistribution of its images. Though the images were clearly marked "freely distributable," the new policy stated that sysops of other BBSs should limit their collections of "MaxiPics" to just twenty files. The rule was never enforced—indeed, enforcement would have been impractical—but sysops bristled at the notion that they were obligated to follow a policy set by Event Horizons. "I am not a huge BBS," complained Eddie Rowe, the sysop of the HOTLine BBS in Ruston, Louisiana. "It really pisses me off that a company who gets free advertising has such a 'rule.'"[159] Rowe went on to call for a boycott of Event Horizons. He could not abide the inherent contradiction of an enterprise that made its reputation (and fortune) on the free circulation of digital media attempting to constrain the downstream uses of that media.

The question of ownership came to a head on March 28, 1992, when Playboy Enterprises announced that it was suing Event Horizons for copyright and trademark infringement.[160] The copyright claim asserted that Event Horizons was unlawfully selling Playboy's property by charging users to download digital copies of nine photos that originally appeared in *Playboy* magazine. In an article for *Boardwatch* magazine, the legal affairs columnist Lance Rose remarked that unauthorized GIFs had become a "well-known fact of life" for BBS users and that observers had long wondered "who will get nailed by a copyright owner, and when."[161] The trademark claim, however, struck at the crux of the tension between labor and ownership. Playboy argued that because the files were hosted by Event Horizons and Event Horizons had layered its own name and phone number over the images, viewers may have mistakenly believed that the photographs were originally taken by Event Horizons' staff rather than scanned out of an issue of *Playboy* magazine.[162] Rather than answer this charge dead-on, Jim Maxey pointed out that the file libraries on Event Horizons contained numerous images contributed by users, over whom Maxey had little control. Specifically, he argued that the infringing photos were uploaded by an unknown user and that Event Horizons staff had missed them in their routine check for infringing files.[163] With thousands of incoming calls each day and fewer than a dozen employees, the defense was plausible, but the notion that Maxey was not ultimately in control of the files on his own computer was almost incomprehensible to anyone outside of the small population of modem users.[164] Event Horizons ultimately settled the case out of court for a reported sum of $500,000.[165]

At the heart of the short, fiery history of Event Horizons is a tension between Maxey's genuine interest in astronomy and the financial reality that his core business was selling access to porn.[166] By 1992, Event Horizons was known for its collection of X-rated images. The entry in *Boardwatch* magazine's BBS directory read simply, "64 Line Digitized Graphics Image Library—Adult .GIF files."[167] In hindsight, we should see Event Horizons as a vanguard of the commercial web. The opportunity to view pornography at home, without having to venture out to an adult bookstore or video-rental place, was transformative for American computer owners and attracted untold thousands of new users to the modem world. But despite this obvious explosion of interest, sysops like Maxey equivocated.

Just as the promoters of shareware had to contend with the reality of software piracy, the maintainers of large GIF libraries had to make peace with the prevalence of pornographic images online. In 1990, Event Horizons took out a series of ads in print magazines such as *Byte* and *PC Magazine* that seemed to reveal a discomfort with its growing reputation as a source of pornography while acknowledging the allure of this material. A photo at the top of the ad depicted a young white woman with her arms raised and hands behind her head. Cropped just a few inches below her bare shoulders, the photo suggested that the model was topless. Above the photo, logos for Visa and MasterCard flanked the words "Computer Images." At the bottom of the ad, a second photo of the same size appeared. This photo depicted Saturn and several of its moons in sharp detail. Between these contrasting images, the ad copy promised access to images of "astronomy," "nature," and "scenic" subjects, along with a "huge adult section" featuring, simply, "girls." As the board grew more profitable, however, any subtlety vanished from the advertising for Event Horizons. A full-page ad in *Boardwatch* from 1994 featured a young, white woman in a bikini with the tagline, "Heavenly Bodies Online."[168] Astronomy had been reduced to a fuzzy backdrop. After the Playboy settlement, Maxey told reporters that Event Horizons was shifting its resources away from images to focus on "games and programs for children."[169] By that time, of course, BBSing was on decline in the United States. Modemers were increasingly turning to the web in their pursuit of "heavenly" GIFs.

The proliferation of adult GIFs was not without precedent, of course. Digital images were only the latest innovation in the integration of telecomputing and human sexuality. Salacious stories in the spirit and style of *Penthouse* letters had long circulated among textfile collections and messaging networks like USENET.[170] Special-interest boards offered virtual meeting places for a diverse population of modem-equipped swingers, queers, and self-described practitioners of "alternative lifestyles." And the adult-oriented chat rooms, or *messageries roses*, were notoriously popular on Minitel in France.[171] What distinguished Event Horizons from these earlier systems was not its files but its finances. As one anonymous sysop put it, "adult files pay the rent."[172]

Whether or not Jim Maxey was entirely comfortable selling access to pornography, several other sysops were happy to follow his example. With the high cost of image-capture equipment, most of the GIFs in circulation during the late 1980s could be traced back to one of a dozen or so BBSs. Like Event Horizons, the names and numbers of BBSs such as DataShack, Farmer's Daughter, Nitelog, and the Roman Empire appeared alongside the images in their collections. Whereas the production activities at Event Horizons were limited to digitization, a few adult-oriented

BBSs began to create their own images. Perhaps the best-known producer of original BBS erotica was the General BBS in San Diego. The General produced an ongoing series of nude and seminude photos featuring local amateur models known as the "Giffy Girls."[173] The originality of each GIF was emphasized by the Giffy tagline, "On Location in San Diego." Similarly, the Ebony Shack BBS in Toledo, Ohio, boasted "the largest collection of minority images," including a combination of digitized and original photographs.[174] In a library of nearly fifty thousand images and video clips, the Black owned and operated BBS produced an original series of photos featuring amateur women of color identified by filenames beginning with "ES." Outside of these few examples, however, the cost of digitizing equipment was prohibitive for most BBS operators, and everyday computer owners rarely produced their own pornographic images for upload to BBSs. Truly amateur production remained the domain of VHS tapes and Polaroid cameras for several years to come.

BEYOND BITS PER SECOND

The cultural history of the modem world was enmeshed with the technological history of its infrastructure. From 1978 to 1994, the rate at which data flowed between BBSs and their users expanded from 300 to 9,600 bits per second. The same 360 kilobyte floppy disk that would have taken three hours to transmit in 1983 took less than five minutes in 1993. This thirty-two-fold increase happened in bursts, reflecting stepwise innovations in modem design and a competitive market for home computer peripherals. At each step, enthusiasts unleashed new creative practices on the modem world, quickly filling their surplus bandwidth with a panoply of new files: electronic zines, shareware applications, digital images, and game mods. By changing the quantitative capacity of the communication channel, high-speed modems changed the qualitative capabilities of the human communication networks that relied on them.

With the spread of cheap, capable devices like the SupraFAXModem, BBS advocates could dream about even-faster futures for the modem world. But there would be no repeat of the 1980s. Dial-up modems were speeding toward a wall spray-painted with Claude Shannon's mathematical theory of communication. According to Shannon's definition of channel capacity, the maximum throughput of a 3 kilohertz analog phone line is about 33,400 bits per second.[175] With 14.4 kilobit per second (kbps) modems becoming abundant in 1992, *Boardwatch* editor Jack Rickard cautioned, "the party is drawing to a close."[176] Cognizant of the limits of AT&T's copper cabling, modem-world enthusiasts placed bets on the likelihood of digital upgrades to the telephone network and speculated about alternative physical infrastructures like packet radio and fiber optics. In 1988, the likeliest scenario seemed to be systems that extended the capabilities of the existing telephone infrastructure, like the Integrated Services Digital Network, or ISDN. But by 1993, consumer ISDN had yet to arrive at any significant scale.[177] Despite the technical limitations, cyberspace would run on dial-up modems for at least another decade.[178]

At any data-transfer rate, however, the promise of free files motivated millions of computer owners to buy a modem and learn how to use it. For these file hounds, the sheer joy of discovering new files to download preceded—and overshadowed—the potential community functions of the dial-up BBS. As a result, countless BBSs of the 1980s and 1990s functioned mainly as file depots, hidden caches of data tucked away on the side of the information superhighway, with little action in their discussion forums. Yet the ongoing pursuit of files and the affordances of the network produced a range of new technical cultures and software practices—bringing file traders into direct communication with one another. The textfiles, shareware, and images circulating in this period bore traces of the people who created them and the places they were collected: inside jokes, ASCII art, phone numbers, and shout-outs. Files became material markers of memory for otherwise-ephemeral communities. Their README files and watermarked GIFs are the artifacts that remain.

CHAPTER FIVE

Cultivating Community

AT THE START OF 1992, amid rising popular interest in the "information superhighway," *Boardwatch* magazine ran a poll to determine "the best BBS in North America."[1] The winner of the "Reader's Choice" award would be featured in a special issue of the magazine, and the system's owners would be given a free trip to ONE BBSCON, the first major BBS trade show.[2] In addition to naming the "best" BBS, the ballot also included an open response question asking readers to elaborate on their choices. It was the first time that anyone had tried to capture the preferences of the modem world in its totality. The poll promised to address long-standing speculation about what drove users to one BBS over another. For years, enthusiasts had argued over the relative value of well-curated files, convivial discussion forums, and interactive online games. *Boardwatch* editor Jack Rickard encouraged BBS owners to actively campaign by providing a digital ballot for users to download, print, and submit by mail. For Rickard, the poll was more than a popularity contest: it was a survey, an opportunity to gather data on the decentralized BBS movement. In aggregate, the ballots that arrived at his office in Colorado represented a nonrandom sample of highly engaged BBS enthusiasts. From demographic details to qualitative opinions, the reader responses revealed, for the first time, how a vanguard population of modem owners were making sense of the nascent online world.[3]

Top-Ranked BBSs in the *Boardwatch* "Reader's Choice" Poll, 1992

RANK	NAME	AREA CODE	LOCATION	VOTES
1	Canada Remote Systems	416	Mississauga, ON, Canada	462
2	Pleasure Dome	804	Tidewater, VA, USA	416
3	Odyssey	818	Monrovia, CA, USA	360
4	PC-OHIO	216	Cleveland, OH, USA	320
5	Albuquerque ROS	505	Albuquerque, NM, USA	260
6	Micro Message Service	919	Raleigh, NC, USA	217
7	San Diego Connection	619	Spring Valley, CA, USA	207
8	Gay/Lesbian Information Bureau (GLIB)	703	Arlington, VA, USA	164
9	Stanford Palo Alto Computer Exchange (SPACE)	415	Menlo Park, CA, USA	149
10	After Hours	512	Austin, TX, USA	147

Note: For details on the contest rules, results, and supplemental survey, see "Boardwatch Magazine Announces the Boardwatch 100 Reader's Choice BBS Contest," *Boardwatch*, February 1992; David Hakala, "Boardwatch 100 Readers' Choice BBS Contest Update," *Boardwatch*, May 1992; "ONE BBSCON," *Boardwatch*, November 1992.

By the time that the May issue of *Boardwatch* went to press, the editors believed that a clear set of winners was emerging. Of the 4,017 tallied responses, 1,234 of the voters named one of ten BBSs as their favorite. To the editors' surprise, seven of the top ten were categorized as "socially oriented" systems.[4] "Voters Favor Online Communities," proclaimed *Boardwatch* writer David Hakala. The "social" category was admittedly broad, inclusive of any board organized around discussion and chat rather than file downloads, online games, or commercial services. The social boards that topped the poll ranged in content and theme from "G-rated" discussion boards to sexually explicit "swinger's clubs." The precise meaning of "social" notwithstanding, the dominance of person-to-person communication in the poll results was undeniable. "BBSland is not an information utility," enthused Hakala; it is about "people communicating with people."[5]

In retrospect, the use of BBSs for community and communication might seem obvious. Why else would someone build an online database of public messages if not for community use? A "computerized" bulletin board would seem to naturally inherit the community function from its paper-based forebear. Furthermore, the hobbyists who gave life to early BBSs were already members of clearly articulated communities of interest: computer clubs, church groups, Boy Scout troops. If the overwhelming preference for "social boards" in the 1992 poll was surprising, it wasn't because community was a recent development but rather that it had become taken for granted among longtime users.

The overwhelming preference for "social" BBSs among *Boardwatch* readers is a mandate from the past to attend to the everyday culture of the modem world. This mandate comes with a thorny methodological challenge, however. Unlike textfiles or BBS software, the day-to-day messages that gave life to BBSs were rarely saved. On occasion, a particularly humorous, rancorous, or informative post was copied to a floppy, printed out, or, in some cases, stored as a textfile, but for the most part, BBS messages were considered ephemeral by their authors and readers. Every post eventually scrolled up off the top of the screen, never to be read again.

During the 1980s and 1990s, small-scale BBSs were the primary infrastructure for the emergence of computer-mediated "virtual" communities in North America. The visibility of "nationwide" social boards like Canada Remote Systems at the top of the *Boardwatch* list belies the prevalence of thousands of smaller, regional BBSs that were nonetheless vital gathering places for local enthusiasts. In fact, a preference for local BBSs was revealed by the *Boardwatch* poll. An overwhelming majority of readers (78 percent) voted for a BBS in their own area code.[6] In smaller cities and towns, general-purpose BBSs provided local users with a friendly meeting place to chat, flirt, and debate. These were idiosyncratic, individual environments. Their architectures and aesthetics reflected the personalities of the people who ran them. Their atmospheres were comparable to a local donut shop, dive bar, or CB radio channel. At a micro scale, any one of these general-purpose local systems might include fewer than one hundred regular callers. But at a continental scale, tens of thousands of such systems come into view. Considered collectively, the virtual waterholes dotting North America represented a dynamic, decentralized network of computer-mediated communities.

Geography was just one organizing principle for community-oriented BBSs. By the late 1980s, many virtual communities developed around interests or identities other than location, providing discursive space for topics that could not draw enough users from a single area code. On pop culture BBSs like the Batboard in Columbia, Missouri, fans gathered to debate the finer points of favorite texts, while the file areas were filled with fan-made artwork, episode guides, and photos from related conventions.[7] Fantasy sports leagues adopted BBSs, and boards dedicated to sports fandom appeared in West Virginia, Arkansas, Missouri, and Minnesota. Other interest-driven systems appealed to users with religious or ideological affiliations. The sysops of the WinPlus BBS in Kent, Washington, dubbed their system "the largest Christian based BBS" and hosted family-friendly get-togethers such as pizza parties and softball games.[8] Farther down the West Coast, members of Burn This Flag BBS in San Jose, California, prided themselves on having thick skins and exploring the limits of free speech.[9] Still others were exclusively open to members of a profession or guild: the Backdraft BBS in Key Largo, Florida, was populated by firefighters and emergency medical services professionals, and the Dissociation Network in Albany, New York, was devoted to social work and mental health.[10]

In 1992, even a close observer would have been hard-pressed to generalize about the types of communities and activities emerging around BBSs in North America. Modemers were in broad agreement that *something* new and important was happening, but they imagined wildly different futures for these grassroots systems. The editors of *Boardwatch* touted individual economic liberation, a "new cottage industry" that "thousands are leaving corporate America forever to join."[11] Activists like Keith Wade of New York City, a self-proclaimed "lover of freedom," saw the promise of radical social change and described BBSs as "five hundred dollar anarchy machines."[12] Across the country, Colonel Dave Hughes, sysop of the Ross Perot for President BBS, was hard at work campaigning for a candidate who envisioned "national town halls" enacted through interactive TV broadcasts. David Fox, author of *Love Bytes*, meanwhile, encountered BBSs as friendly gathering spaces—"pubs on the information superhighway"—catering to "every interest, every hobby," and packed with "colorful people," some of whom might turn out to be future friends or lovers.[13]

In spite of the divergent social meanings and purposes of these visions of online community, each was produced, fundamentally, by the ritual of dialing into the same system, night after night. In the punctuated temporality of BBSing, relationships developed gradually over weeks, months, and years of asynchronous written communication. Communities did not snap into existence, fully formed, when a BBS came online. They required care and continuity on the part of BBS users and administrators. In the language of community moderators, gardening metaphors were common. Communities "grow" and require "tending." Troublemakers are "weeded out." But what was the object of all this time and attention? What did they hope to make as they set about cultivating virtual communities?

DIAL-UP COMMUNITIES

Community is a difficult concept to define. In the nineteenth century, community principally referred to people living in proximity, such as the residents of a neighborhood or village. By the mid-twentieth century, community had taken on a more abstract meaning, describing relationships based on shared interests or identities such as the Black community, the medical community, the Jewish community, the gay community, or the skateboarding community. Unlike a nation-state, belonging to a community is a matter of social classification rather than citizenship or taxation. You may not even think of yourself as a member of a particular community until someone else hails you as one. In many Western cultures, community is also widely accepted as a good thing. In the 1970s, Raymond Williams observed that "community" had taken on a "warmly persuasive" character in public debate, evoking a sense of authenticity in contrast to the formal politics of government and the state.[14] Since then, the term has continued to convey universally positive sentiments. Politicians of all stripes promise to "strengthen" or "rebuild" the communities of their constituents. Service to the community—in the form of voluntary labor and charitable giving—is to be admired and encouraged. The specific meaning of community may vary widely by context, but everyone agrees that community is good.

One explanation for the expanded meaning of community is that telecommunications media—from postcards to text messages—enable people to experience a sense of communion and affiliation with people living in faraway places.[15] Indeed, the first large-scale computer networks were built at the same time that Raymond Williams was writing his reflections on the meaning of community. While earlier electronic media may have brought about an "annihilation of distance," computer networks seemed to produce new places and proximities.[16] What was a time-sharing computer but a common space for group communication? In the 1970s, educational networks like the Minnesota Education Computing Consortium aimed to provide a medium for students and faculty at different K–12 schools to meet, play, and learn together.[17] Intraorganizational "conferencing" systems like Electronic Information Exchange System used computer systems to structure collaborative decision-making and collective intelligence activities.[18] Hobbyist networks, meanwhile, began as extensions of local computer clubs, only to become meeting places for far-flung computer enthusiasts who did not live close enough to participate in face-to-face club meetings.

During the 1980s, communities flourished across the modem world. Utilitarian applications such as free files attracted new users, but it was the experience of community that kept them coming back. From small-town BBSs to the international FidoNet, modem users spent hours trading messages, building a sense of shared identity without the need to meet in person. The very notion of the "modem world" reflected a growing feeling among modem owners that the online world constituted a unique community, apart from their offline relationships. But while experienced users could see the value of this novel form of community, it was difficult to convey to nonusers. In print and on TV, advertisements for commercial services like America Online and CompuServe highlighted information-retrieval functions such as databases, market reports, and news feeds rather than community-oriented features like chat rooms and multiplayer games. Yet falling barriers to participation and word of mouth spread awareness of the modem world among American computer owners, and by the early 1990s, millions of people were coming online specifically in search of community.

At the same time, community had become a principal focus for a new cohort of cultural critics and academic researchers.[19] In 1993, Howard

Rheingold, longtime modemer and editor of *The Whole Earth Review*, published *The Virtual Community*, an accessible exploration of several thriving online communities.[20] Appearing just months into the Clinton-Gore presidency, *The Virtual Community* offered a glimpse of a possible future for the information superhighway. Faced with a widespread enclosure of public space by commercial interests, Rheingold reasoned that computer networks might provide alternative places for people to gather, debate, learn, and play. In Rheingold's view, virtual community had the potential to transform society, enabling a more egalitarian form of public culture to emerge. "The future of the Net," he argued, "is connected to the future of community, democracy, education, science, and intellectual life."[21] Yet *The Virtual Community* described an online world that was itself on the precipice of change. By the time the book appeared on library shelves, the commercialization of the internet was well under way. The "virtual communities" documented by Rheingold—The WELL, FidoNet, Minitel, USENET—either vanished or were folded into the all-encompassing World Wide Web. Sensing that readers might never experience these systems for themselves, Rheingold cautioned that state surveillance, corporate greed, or regulatory overreach could easily squash the utopian potential of the virtual communities he described.[22] In a review for the *New York Times*, the historian Bruce Mazlish summarized the conflict at the heart of Rheingold's book as a tension between "the despotic and the democratic."[23]

Meanwhile, a cohort of academics—most of them early in their careers—were building the field of internet studies by adapting methods from communication, anthropology, and sociology to understand the social life of computer networks.[24] The democratic possibilities celebrated by Rheingold became a central preoccupation of the nascent field, and researchers set out to examine the growing number of virtual communities on the net. In a retrospective account of this period, the sociologist Lori Kendall identifies group dialogue as one of the fundamental characteristics of computer-mediated communities.[25] Whether in asynchronous conferences or real-time chat, groups of people typing messages back and forth might come to a sense of shared identity and common purpose. For all the excitement over 3-D games and graphics, any messaging system could be adapted to group dialogue, enabling community practices such as collective intelligence, mutual support, discussion and debate, flirting, flaming, and fantasy roleplay. The emergence of virtual community did not depend on complex technology as much as a willingness on the part of users to return, day after day, and participate in ongoing dialogue with the group.[26]

Despite the influence of bulletin board systems on the conceptualization of "virtual community," relatively little systematic research was conducted on BBS communities during their heyday.[27] Researchers studying virtual communities in the early 1990s focused on USENET and IRC, systems that were easily accessible to university students and faculty with internet access but inaccessible to the general public. Yet the virtual communities that developed around dial-up BBSs were shaped by a different set of social, technical, and economic constraints from their counterparts on the internet.

Dial-up BBSs were intrinsically place-based networks. Unlike national systems like Minitel or international networks like USENET, North American BBS communities developed around local area codes, which varied in geographic size by population density. This regional focus provided greater opportunity for offline interactions between users and resulted in less emphasis on escaping from borders into an alternative "cyberspace." BBS users were real people in real places. The cost of long-distance dialing also restricted the choices available to most would-be BBS users. Whereas studies of internet-based communities tended to emphasize limitless choice and the opportunity for users to create highly personalized niches, most BBS users made do with the systems available in their local dialing areas. A side effect of BBS regionalism was that virtual communities formed across multiple bulletin boards, defined more by their shared area codes than the boundaries of any one system.

The architecture of dial-up BBSs allowed them to develop independently from one another and autonomously from large institutions. From the start, BBS host software was designed for tinkering and modification. The aesthetic and interactive features of a given system reflected the individual priorities and personalities of the system's owner. From the structure of the discussion forums to interactive art and multiplayer games, BBSs offered a degree of customization that was simply not available on most other community-oriented networks. The control provided to individual BBS operators by the underlying software extended to their governance as well. For better and worse, there were no central authorities overseeing the practices of BBS operators. While internet advocates debated the merits of the National Science Foundation's Acceptable Use Policy and consumers decried the censorship on commercial platforms, individual BBS operators enjoyed near-total control over the governance of their systems.[28] With the exception of pornography and piracy, which could attract the attention of state authorities, most BBSs existed in a state of benign neglect.

Ultimately, the local culture of each BBS was shaped by the behavior of its system operator, or "sysop." From maintaining the software to resolving disagreements between users, the role of the sysop represented a unique combination of technical and social responsibilities. Sysops enjoyed nearly total control over the design and regulation of their systems, enabling them to freely experiment without prior approval of their users. By modifying the underlying software, sysops could separate users into groups, create exclusive areas of the board, constrain the behaviors of some users, or simply pull the plug, immediately taking the BBS offline. The power of the BBS sysop was limited only by the relatively low cost of exiting the system. If a sysop angered their users enough, the users would simply leave and start their own system. To understand how community developed on BBSs, it is essential to begin with the figure of the sysop.

THE SYSOPS

As the owner of a BBS's host computer, sysops enjoyed almost total authority over their systems. They were responsible for configuring the software, maintaining the hardware, paying the bills. But—as many new sysops discovered by surprise—the job extended far beyond these practical concerns.[29] Sysops were the gatekeepers and moderators. Their personalities, interests, and aesthetic preferences were woven into every facet of the system's operation. They wrote and enforced any social policies, and their behavior set the norms for appropriate behavior. If a user broke the rules, only the sysop could kick them off. In moments of conflict, sysops became mediators and amateur counselors. If operating costs grew too high, it was the sysop who needed to raise money or solicit donations. As one veteran sysop observed, "words do not adequately portray the emotional and physical requirements of this often misunderstood and frequently expensive hobby."[30]

The sysop's authority rested in their proximity to the power switch. In a moment of frustration, they could always pull the plug, shutting down the whole system in an instant. But a sysop's power was limited by the boundaries of their BBS. Outside the system, there remained a parity between sysops and users. The barriers to creating a new BBS were sufficiently low that nearly any user could start a BBS and become a sysop themselves. Longtime modemers joked that every BBS caller would eventually try running a system of their own.[31] The relative accessibility of BBS technology and expertise provided an important check on the power of the sysop. If an individual or group of users found themselves in an unresolvable conflict, they could always quit and start a new board on their own terms. The freedom to leave—so unusual in today's social media—provided a sense of mutual accountability and identification between BBS users and sysops.

So who were the sysops? The number of sysops is difficult to estimate because of the ease with which any BBS user could step into the role, but we can get a rough sense of the population through a few indirect clues. By definition, every active BBS had at least one sysop, so there were at least 100,000 in North America at one time or another. Between 1991 and 1994, the number of people traveling to attend national conventions for BBS operators rose from about 400 at FidoCon in 1991 to 4,000 at ONE BBSCON in 1994.[32] That same year, *Boardwatch*, a BBS specialist magazine, reported a circulation of approximately 80,000, and Phil Becker, maker of the popular TBBS software, claimed that there were 250,000 active sysops.[33] The proportion of modemers starting their own BBSs was relatively high, considering the time and resources required. BBS advocates suggested that approximately one out of every 200 to 250 BBS users became a sysop.[34] Of course, sysops varied in how they viewed their role and their relationship to their BBSs. Some were hobbyists, running their boards purely for fun; others were entrepreneurs, seeking to build a profitable business; and still others operated BBSs for instrumental purposes, serving the needs of a preexisting organization or community group.

The initial pathway from BBS caller to sysop was relatively straightforward. Running a BBS required a computer, modem, home telephone, and host software. By the mid-1980s, a workable system could be set up with secondhand equipment and public domain software for a few hundred dollars. In practice, a more robust 24/7 BBS required a budget in the range of $1,000 to $2,000 to cover a hard drive, high-speed modem, and dedicated phone line.[35] Many sysops took pleasure in tweaking and customizing their BBS software, but the initial configuration could be daunting. One satirical textfile cautioned newbie sysops to expect little from the documentation: "The manual for the BBS software was most likely written by the author's 10 year old and was mimeographed. It got wet in the mail and smeared as well, so at least 30% of the manual will be physically useless. The rest is just procedurally useless."[36] Before opening to the public, a new sysop needed to create a welcome screen, write instructions for new users, define user roles and privileges, organize the structure of the file area, select conference topics, arrange for feeds from the BBS network, and install any third-party games, add-ons, or other external "door" utilities. To figure all of this out, sysops relied on one another for advice. Jerry Shifrin, the sysop of a popular programming BBS out of Northern Virginia, urged newbies to make contact with other sysops: "The vast majority . . . will be happy, even eager, to help you along."[37]

Once the BBS was up and running, the sysop became solely responsible for its day-to-day operations. Routine tasks such as scanning for viruses, backing up the database, and reading system logs mirrored the work of professional system administrators, but the BBS sysop was also responsible for cultivating the community of users. They screened new user applications, started conference topics, tracked down unusual files, and installed new online games. Through this ongoing care work, sysops came to identify with their BBSs. "Sysoping" became a lifestyle.[38] It was the first thing they did in the morning and the last thing at night.[39]

Sysops liked to joke about their thankless job—"Ask any Sysop and he or she will tell you . . . 'It ain't worth it, pal!'"[40]—but there were clear benefits to owning one's own BBS.[41] From the start, many sysops created BBSs as an opportunity to learn more about computing and communications.[42] In the late 1970s, starting a BBS became a popular collaborative project for microcomputer clubs. By the mid-1980s, however, most future sysops were themselves avid BBS callers, calling BBSs around the country and racking up long-distance charges. For these modem junkies, the goal was to reverse the flow of data. Instead of always dialing out, they would wait for the interesting files and people to come to them. Running a BBS also conferred a certain social status within the technical culture of BBSing. "You are the center of attention," wrote one teen sysop in 1983. "You are the owner and controller of the board."[43] Lastly, some sysops saw their work in terms of service to the modem community. Jerry Shifrin cited the notion of "karma," the "Golden Rule," and the Beatles. For Shifrin, running a board was "the love you make."[44]

In their role as hosts, BBS sysops pioneered the difficult practice of community moderation.[45] Sysops may have possessed unlimited power over the technical architecture of their boards, but if they acted like jerks, their users were not likely to return. In 1992, *Boardwatch* readers cited "friendly sysop" as one of the most important criteria in selecting a BBS.[46] Moderation took many forms—from screening new users to implementing strict time limits. By the late 1980s, "voice verification" had become a standard feature of many BBS programs, and sysops grew accustomed to greeting new users over the phone before granting access to their systems. The sysops of boards serving large or diverse groups of users often appointed one or more "co-sysops," distributing authority and responsibility to especially active members of the community. Much of this interpersonal work occurred out of the sight of the casual user, which led some sysops to feel underappreciated. Sysops complaining of "burnout" often cited a lack of feedback from their users.[47] "If only a few people would express a little compassion for the guy that runs their favorite board," wrote John Olson in a piece for *FidoNews*, "it could insure that [the BBS] will be there a while longer."[48] The tenure of a typical sysop seems to have varied quite widely, but there also seems to have been a steady supply of newcomers willing to take a turn at the wheel.

The BBS sysop is a unique figure in the history of the net. Compared to other online communities, from USENET to Facebook, BBS sysops enjoyed an unmatched degree of control over the day-to-day life of their communities.[49] No other class of users experienced the challenges of life online as immediately as BBS sysops did. In 1995, as internet hype was spilling into popular culture and thousands of companies were scrambling to stake a claim, Bob Metcalfe observed that sysops were among the only specialists in the "art" of community building.[50] Indeed, they were among the only living people with practical experience in both the technical design and governance of computer-mediated social spaces. Yet only a few sysops appear to have articulated their unique place at the forefront of this new industry. "You have your finger on the pulse of the next wave of human progress," enthused one anonymous sysop. "You're one of the people making it happen."[51]

A STORY OF TWO AREA CODES

Today, the Whole Earth 'Lectronic Link, or The WELL, is remembered as an ideal instance of "virtual community" by scholars, critics, and former callers. Firsthand accounts by users portray The WELL as an uncommonly collegial space in which participants from many walks of life gathered to share the stories of their lives and debate the topics of the day.[52] Unlike the community-oriented hobby systems that were already spread throughout North America at the time of its founding, however, The WELL was a profit-seeking venture and relied on subscription fees to stay online. According to Fred Turner's historical analysis, The WELL was the latest iteration of an approach to social and industrial organization that was first articulated by Stewart Brand during the publication of the *Whole Earth Catalog* in the 1970s.[53] Under the continued influence of Brand, The WELL served as a working model of a new form of egalitarian community. An important detail often neglected in idealized portrayals of The WELL, however, was the extent to which the intellectual discussions cherished by journalists and futurists were supported financially by the reliable subscription fees of a much larger population of Grateful Dead fans. To fully appreciate the place of The WELL within the larger history of North American BBSing, it is important to keep in mind the political-economic realities that enabled its unmatched community to flourish.

In February 1985, The WELL came online from a small office in Sausalito, California.[54] Thanks to frequent mentions in *Wired* magazine and the firsthand reporting of Howard Rheingold and the tech journalist Katie Hafner, The WELL is now the most well-documented community BBS of the 1980s and 1990s.[55] In *Mondo 2000*'s encyclopedic *User's Guide*, the editors of the magazine defined "The Net" as "an international web of . . . bulletin board systems," but The WELL was one of just two systems mentioned by name.[56] And yet, in spite of this visibility, The WELL was quite an atypical system among its homegrown contemporaries. Whereas most BBSs were hosted on a personal computer with just one dedicated line, The WELL ran on a much more powerful, if aging, VAX server with a bank of modems and phone lines. Further-

more, while most BBSs were operated on a voluntary basis by enthusiasts, The WELL was founded as a profit-seeking business with $90,000
in start-up capital and two paid staffers. The WELL was hardly flush with
cash, but it existed in a different economic sphere from its hobbyist contemporaries. Finally, although its roots were in the Bay Area, The WELL
eventually attracted users from around the globe, many of whom paid
significant long-distance tolls to access the system.[57] And yet, though
this technical infrastructure and political economy were organized like
nationwide commercial systems, The WELL's core community of Bay
Area users more closely matched the kind of regional sociality found on
a dial-up BBS.[58]

Like the organizers of earlier experiments in social computing, the
founders of The WELL shared a commitment to free speech. Instead of
pursuing a radically open architecture to achieve this goal, however, they
implemented a small number of constraints to encourage accountability
among participants. First, users were welcome to adopt pseudonyms,
but they were required to register and reveal their "real" names.[59] Second, each user's past contributions were accessible in a message archive.
This public record of past behavior contributed to a system-wide principle known as "You Own Your Own Words," or "YOYOW."[60] Third, the
messaging area of the system was organized into a large hierarchy of
"conferences," each of which was further divided according to special
topics. For example, the Arts and Letters conference included Art and
Graphics, Beatles, Books, Comics, Design, Jazz, MIDI, Movies, and so
on. Each of these architectural features shaped the types of interactions
that took place on The WELL.

To callers in the late 1980s, The WELL represented a culturally specific ideal community that matched the values of liberal progressives of
a certain age. The founders granted free accounts to well-known "interesting people" in the Bay Area to act as "hosts" and attract users with
similar *habitus*. Rheingold compared The WELL's conferences to an ongoing "Paris salon" with "somewhat more elevated [discourse] than the
usual BBS stuff," an oblique reference to the preponderance of technical
minutiae on hobbyist systems at the time.[61] The intellectual atmosphere
of the salons was not to everyone's taste, of course. *Boardwatch*'s Rickard
described the system as "VERY California" and joked that "at some point
you just damn near choke on all the visionary thinking going on."[62]

Nevertheless, for dedicated WELLites, the system represented an ideal form of computer-mediated public culture.

For its intellectual core, The WELL offered thoughtful discussions of myriad topics from parenting to the social implications of networked technology, but the financial survival of the parent organization depended on revenue generated by an almost wholly distinct second population of users. Grateful Dead fans—the "Deadheads"—were "by far" the biggest collective source of income for The WELL.[63] In 1992, access to The WELL cost $10 per month plus $2.50 per hour, a price comparable to other large-scale subscription BBSs.[64] The WELL's Deadhead conferences provided not only a stream of revenue but also a bridge into a preexisting community with its own norms of sharing and cooperation.[65] And yet Rheingold also distanced the Deadheads of the 1980s from the Deadheads of an earlier generation and, by association, The WELL's countercultural elite. He characterized The WELL's Dead fandom as having "drifted far from its counter-culture origins" and described the majority of Deadheads on The WELL as "blithely unaware" of the high-minded discourse occurring elsewhere on the system.[66] For all that The WELL represented an idealized form of BBSing for its elite users, it was not without its own internal boundaries and social distinctions.

In many ways, The WELL community of the 1980s and 1990s lives up to its mythic reputation. In 1995, *Boardwatch*'s Rickard, a longtime user, characterized The WELL's discussion forums as "somehow a cut above," with a culture of an "immeasurable" quality. "No [sysop] knows quite how to get it," he wrote about the board's culture, "but you can recognize it when you see it."[67] The success of The WELL's community-building effort was not nearly so mysterious as Rickard's poetic description suggests. Unlike hobbyist sysops focused on tweaking the infrastructures of their boards, the founders of The WELL consciously designed a community-oriented system. To this end, they drew together a population of users from a reasonably small geographic area and with shared backgrounds, diverse expertise, and an existing social network. Notable figures in the emerging "cyberculture" were given free accounts and encouraged to take leadership roles on a set of predetermined conference topics. Furthermore, the experimental, niche areas of The WELL were supported by a small but reliable stream of income generated by a large population of tech-savvy Grateful Dead fans. An alternative history of

The WELL might describe it as primarily an interest-driven BBS for fans of the Grateful Dead that occasionally featured salon-style conferences hosted by well-known thinkers on the transformative potential of social computing. But by the 1980s, followers of the Dead were no longer the countercultural vanguard they once might have been, and a Deadhead BBS was hardly headline material.[68] At the same time that The WELL began to gain visibility in the popular press, hundreds of online communities with their own unique cultures were developing elsewhere on not-for-profit boards running on more modest hardware out of the homes of volunteers.

Like The WELL, the TARDIS BBS in Indiana supported a deeply engaged community of local users. Outside of the friendly tone of their forums, however, the two systems differed in nearly every other detail. The WELL was founded as a business, albeit a socially conscious business; the TARDIS began as a hobby project. The WELL charged a fee for access; the TARDIS was free to the public. The WELL could support more than sixteen simultaneous users on its 1980 VAX-11/750 minicomputer; the TARDIS was a "one-liner" running off the floppy drive of an old Apple II+.[69] But the history of the TARDIS offers more than simply a scaled-down complement to the familiar myth of The WELL. As a labor of love run by a hands-on team of sysops whose values, sense of humor, and care for one another were interwoven in the sociotechnical fabric of the system, the TARDIS was a practical realization of the democratic potential of social computing valued by the champions of The WELL. In the words of one former sysop, "All three [of the other sysops] were my best friends and the board showed it."[70]

In the long-running science fiction series *Doctor Who*, the TARDIS is a vehicle for time-travel disguised as an ordinary telephone booth. Fantasy and science fiction inspired the names of many BBSs, but "TARDIS" was an especially popular choice. At various times between 1983 and 1998, more than thirty different BBSs in North America were named after the quirky vessel.[71] One reason for its popularity is that the Doctor's TARDIS and the dial-up BBS play similar roles in the lives of their users. In the same way that the familiar desktop computer belies the complex social world of a BBS, the internal structure of the TARDIS is impossibly large—far greater than the area inside a telephone booth. Further, like the low-powered 8-bit computers that continued to host BBSs well into the 1990s, the Doctor's TARDIS is considered obsolete and unreliable by many of his Time Lord peers. And yet, like the dedicated owners of Commodore and Atari systems, the Doctor and the ship share a deep, affective interdependence.[72] According to *Doctor Who* mythology, the Doctor selected the TARDIS for its "soul" rather than its technical features.[73] The TARDIS and the dial-up BBS are technologies that encourage a long-term commitment to maintain and care for them in the face of forced obsolescence and relentless technological progress.

One of the earliest BBSs named after the TARDIS was founded in 1982 by Thomas O'Nan, an amateur radio operator living in Terre Haute, Indiana, about a ninety-minute drive west from Indianapolis. O'Nan initially ran the BBS over the airwaves, rather than the telephone network, using a "radio BBS" program called Super-Ratt for the Apple II.[74] Like its dial-up counterparts, the radio BBS included messaging and file-transfer features and was occasionally referred to as an "electronic mailbox."[75] Soon, however, O'Nan discovered dial-up BBSs and decided to migrate from the airwaves to the telephone lines.

In the 1980s, Terre Haute shared an area code with several other cities in southern Indiana, including several university campuses, but O'Nan had trouble attracting users to his BBS. In his recollection, the local hams were not interested in microcomputers and "refused to even try" connecting to the bulletin board system.[76] Upon moving to Indianapolis in 1985, however, O'Nan came across new BBS software for the Apple and was inspired to bring his BBS back online. As he designed the first iteration of the system, he incorporated numerous jokes and pranks into its architecture, some of which were fannish references to the board's namesake and others that reflected his own weird sense of humor. On one menu, he included an option to "Chat with the Sysop" by pressing "C" but instead of connecting the caller to a sysop, the "C" command invoked a modified version of ELIZA, Joseph Weizenbaum's infamous natural-language chat bot.[77] More than a few new users found themselves talking in circles before realizing that they had been tricked. Like a funhouse, the architecture of the TARDIS did not aim for efficiency or elegance but was designed to delight and surprise its callers.

One of O'Nan's goals for the new BBS was to ensure that "anybody, using any equipment," could access the system. One of the four system operators, O'Nan's longtime girlfriend, was deaf, and they gradually learned that many of the board's regular users were also deaf or blind.[78] Modemers with a visual impairment generally used "screen readers" to translate standard ASCII characters into sound or touch, but as BBS sysops began to incorporate semigraphical characters in their menus, they inadvertently made their systems inaccessible to visually impaired callers. From 1985 to 1992, the TARDIS ran Prime BBS software on an Apple II+ with few changes, upgrades, or modifications. Beyond the low maintenance costs, sticking with a relatively simple platform ensured that the TARDIS remained accessible to callers with disabilities. In spite of—or perhaps because of—this modest infrastructure, the TARDIS attracted 3,500 registered users, of whom O'Nan considered 750 "regulars" and 40 "daily" callers.[79] At its peak, the TARDIS logged more than five hundred calls per day on its sole incoming telephone line and carried more than eleven million messages between its users.[80]

O'Nan could not have predicted it at the start of the TARDIS, but the Prime BBS host software became known among Apple computer enthusiasts for its long-lasting reliability and accessible source code. In 1989, the last of three programmers responsible for Prime, Daniel Haynes, decided that he no longer had time to maintain the software. Rather than hand it off to someone else, Haynes committed the source code to the public domain, wrote up detailed documentation, and encouraged other Prime BBS sysops to start sharing their upgrades, modifications, and customizations with one another.[81] By the early 1990s, Prime BBS was still being touted as the best host software for running a "smaller" system for ten to two hundred users.[82] In fact, after Prime BBS was released to the public domain, its value rose dramatically, as volunteer programmers developed and shared more than seventy new add-on programs that extended the core features of the system.[83] With the diffusion of IBM-compatible clones at the end of the 1980s, secondhand Apple computers were widely available for as little as $200. In a 1992 article circulated among Apple users on GEnie, the BBS enthusiast Jerry Penner suggested that readers "dig out that unused Apple II [from the] back of the closet" and build a new system on old hardware using Prime BBS.[84] From the initial release of Prime to its revival, the TARDIS lived on, uninterrupted.

The telephone number for the TARDIS was circulated through BBS lists and local newsletters, but new users were not granted access

```
||||||||||||||||||||||||||||||||||||||||||||||||||||||||||||||||||||||||||||||||||||||||

                          PRIME
                Bulletin  Board  System
        (C)opyright 1989            Daniel  Haynes
||||||||||||||||||||||||||||||||||||||||||||||||||||||||||||||||||||||||||||||||||||||||


               1) Install to Floppy Disks
               2) Install to 3.5" Disks
               3) Install to Hard Drive
               4) Install Modem Driver Only
               5) Run PRIME BBS



        |||||||||||||||||||||||||||||||||||||||||||||||||||||||||||||||||
                  SmokeSignal  Software
                   Canton, Michigan
||||||||||||||||||||||||||||||||||||||||||||||||||||||||||||||||||||||||||||||||||||||||
```

Prime BBS installation menu on an Apple II with a monochrome display. In 1989, Daniel Haynes purchased Prime BBS from the original developers, released the source code, and placed the software in the public domain. Written in Applesoft BASIC, Prime was accessible for tinkering, maintenance, and customization. The program's manual promised to "stretch your imagination and creativity to the limit."

immediately. First-time callers were asked to fill out a short questionnaire that included a combination of demographic questions—name, address, phone number, age, gender—and silly questions: planet of origin, species, blood type, favorite M&M, and the rate at which their fingernails grew.[85] All of the questionnaires were reviewed by one of the four sysops before the user was granted access to the system. If the user's answers seemed "bogus," then the sysop would look up their name in the phone book and, in some cases, verify the new user by voice. Prime BBS allowed sysops to define nine different classes of users, and on the TARDIS, users were sorted by age and gender. Certain areas of the board were visible only to users in the "adult" or "female" classes. If a new caller self-identified as a woman, then one of the two female sysops would call them on the phone. New users were usually verified by one of the four sysops within a few hours of their first call.[86]

One of the unique features of the TARDIS was that it provided a safe space for women to gather, apart from the rest of the board. O'Nan recalls that in the 1980s, women experimenting with BBSs frequently experienced harassment from the men they encountered online. One former member described being a woman on other BBSs as a "nightmare" and credited the sysops of the TARDIS for actively intervening to stop harassing behavior on their system.[87] In addition to this hands-on approach to moderating the open forums, all administrative oversight of the TARDIS's exclusive "Ladies only" section was performed by the women in the community. "I stayed out of it," O'Nan later recalled. "[The women] did it all."[88] Users classified as men on the TARDIS could neither see nor access the "Ladies only" area. Even O'Nan himself was restricted. "To this day," he remarked, "I don't know what went on in that room!"[89]

Community and conversation were the central features of the TARDIS BBS, and both the technical and social architectures of the system reflected these priorities. Any user could introduce a new discussion topic on the TARDIS, and there were few constraints on what could be said. O'Nan's quirky sense of humor was evident throughout the board and implicitly encouraged a friendly, casual tone.[90] O'Nan characterized his core user population as "academic, moderate or liberal," and, consequently, the only topics that regularly required sysop intervention were, in O'Nan's judgment, "extreme right wing" themes because they sparked "flame wars."[91] Although O'Nan was the board's founder, moderation duties were distributed throughout the community by the "co-sysop" arrangement he created with his girlfriend and another couple. The TARDIS had no particular theme or core purpose beyond building community. Within that broad mission, however, the system provided invaluable spaces for groups of people who would have been outnumbered, unwelcome, or mistreated on any other BBS.

Like The WELL, the TARDIS attracted a dedicated core group of users who became fiercely loyal and personally invested in the board's culture. O'Nan recalls one instance in which a local technology writer gave the TARDIS an unfavorable review in his monthly BBS column because it offered very few IBM PC files for download. The users felt personally insulted and responded with angry letters arguing that the reviewer misunderstood the purpose of the BBS. The TARDIS was a community constituted through its public and private message forums, not downloading. O'Nan, for his part, did not participate in the controversy, preferring to "let the users do their thing."[92] Consistent with the results of the 1992 *Boardwatch* poll, users valued the everyday culture of a BBS over its technical features or media libraries.

Sadly, by 1992, the infrastructure of the TARDIS began to show its age. Prime BBS could not support connection speeds higher than 2,400 bits per second. For the existing user population, this was hardly a problem, and most were happy to continue using the BBS at the speed they had grown accustomed to. Unfortunately, if a new user attempted to connect with a faster modem, the system could behave erratically and, in some cases, crash altogether. O'Nan recalls that a group of kids "who wanted something destructive to do" discovered this weakness and began to intentionally crash the TARDIS. For two months, they repeatedly brought down the system and hogged the phone lines, preventing any of the regular callers from getting through. Failing to appeal to the boys' better judgment, O'Nan solicited the help of the telephone company. Instead of assisting him, however, the telephone company argued that O'Nan was misusing his residential phone line and threatened to start charging him at a higher business rate. Desperate to stop the assault, O'Nan reported the boys as "nuisance callers," and they were subsequently arrested by the police. The boys' parents became extremely upset and could not understand what their children had done. Worn out from the experience, O'Nan decided to close the TARDIS for good: "I just didn't have the heart to run a system anymore."[93]

The WELL and the TARDIS were dial-up BBSs operating out of two different area codes. Although virtually anyone with a microcomputer, a modem, and a telephone line could have called either board, only nearby callers could access the systems without paying an additional long-distance toll. One consequence of this billing structure was that the core populations of each system were constituted primarily of local callers.[94] The histories of the two boards and the histories of their area codes are, therefore, inextricably intertwined.

The WELL ran on a VAX minicomputer housed in a small office in the waterfront town of Sausalito, California, just across the Golden Gate Bridge from San Francisco.[95] In 1985, Sausalito shared the 415 area code with most of the Bay Area, including the newly transformed "Silicon

Valley," where the microcomputer industry was booming. In contrast, when Tom O'Nan rebooted his TARDIS in Indianapolis in 1985, it took up residence in the 317 area code, covering much of central Indiana. A reasonable guess suggests that the flow of engineers to the Bay Area would support a large number of local BBSs. After all, young engineers have all the money, technical aptitude, and skills required to participate in the modem world. Extant historical BBS lists, however, indicate that the BBSing scene of central Indiana was as active (if not more so) than that of the Bay Area during the same period of time.[96] Indeed, from 1982 until the early 2000s, there was roughly the same ratio of boards to working adults in each area—but among the population of adults working with computers in some fashion, there were nearly twice as many BBSs in central Indiana (2.1 per 100 tech workers) as in the Bay Area (1.12 per 100 tech workers).[97] In other words, during the BBS period, not only did the TARDIS host its own exemplary online community, but it was part of a thriving local BBS scene in metropolitan Indianapolis.

It may seem counterintuitive that BBSing would be more prevalent in Indianapolis than in Silicon Valley. But it comes down to the relationship of BBSs to one another within an area code. The WELL, with its global ambitions, attempted to transcend its local area code. The TARDIS, however, was embedded in a local community, and its callers enjoyed network effects as a result. Each BBS in the 317 area code was, in practice, a node in an internetwork of Indianapolis boards. The TARDIS was known for its intimate, thoughtful community, but it was not necessary for the TARDIS to also offer a large library of downloadable software. Indeed, 317 was already home to several BBSs that specialized in shareware,[98] and gamers might have preferred the Doomsday Dungeon, run by an Indianapolis high school student.[99]

The presence of Silicon Valley may have limited the emergence of a complementary network of BBSs in the Bay Area. Modemers in the Bay Area had access to a far wider variety of networks than those in central Indiana, including local, dial-up access to packet-switching networks, which allowed users to reach BBSs in more than a dozen other area codes for a flat monthly fee. Modemers in Indianapolis, meanwhile, were limited to either costly nationwide commercial services or nearby BBSs run by members of their local community. As a result, BBS callers in each area code developed different spatial imaginaries.

The WELL, from its infrastructure to its political economy to its legion of tech-savvy Deadheads, was in nearly every way atypical. When BBSs are included in the history of networked computing, however, The WELL is often the only system mentioned by name. Unfortunately, this convention has produced a rather skewed picture of BBSing that excludes considerable activity that occurred far from Silicon Valley. The TARDIS, on the other hand, reflected a more widely shared experience of North American BBSing. Although both the TARDIS and The WELL developed unusually warm, welcoming, and thoughtful communities, the roots of the TARDIS reached back much more clearly to the long tradition of amateur telecommunications. Whereas the founders of The WELL endeavored to create a profitable worldwide conferencing system, the TARDIS was operated by four self-described best friends who ran the system at the pleasure of their users. With its modest hardware, focus on local community, and commitment to accessibility, the TARDIS embodied a set of values that enabled the diffusion of computer-mediated communication outside traditional centers of power.

The story of The WELL stands alone. Whether remembered as an Eden or a vision of the future, The WELL is unfailingly singular. The TARDIS, however, is a conjuncture of familiar people, places, and technologies. It is hard to imagine The WELL existing anywhere other than the Bay Area, and it is hard to imagine that the Bay Area would not have hosted a system like The WELL—of course those hippies would have built a weird cybercommune! The TARDIS, on the other hand, challenges the accepted geography of the early internet. If the 317 area code could have played host to such a vibrant online community, why not any other?

COMMUNITIES OF INTEREST

By the late 1980s, BBS sysops increasingly created spaces for communities defined by qualities other than a common location. Groups of people drawn together by niche cultural interests, marginalized sexual or gender identities, new religious movements, and radical political commitments turned to BBSs after being excluded from mainstream media systems such as radio and TV. Like underground newspapers, BBSs operated outside the control of traditional media institutions. For communities that could not safely congregate in person, a BBS offered desirable technical features such as anonymity. For others, it provided a complement to face-to-face meetings and other traditional forms of community organizing. From pornography to political activism, community-oriented BBSing in the late 1980s and early 1990s presaged the diversity of virtual communities on the World Wide Web a decade later. Yet the unusual spatial, technical, and economic characteristics of dial-up BBSs distinguished these early communities from the systems that would come later. For many communities of interest, a social BBS was not a substitute but rather a tactical alternative to other forms of gathering.

Communities defined by sexual interest and gender identity provide exemplary cases for thinking about the tactical use of community BBSs. Sex and sexuality were common themes of adult-oriented BBSs. Many sysops featured forums and games dedicated to dating, hooking up, or personal ads. The use of dial-up BBSs for flirtation, romance, and sex extended the metaphor of the BBS as an after-work hangout. In *Love Bytes*, a "handbook" for BBS dating published in 1995, author David Fox described the adult-only BBS as an idealized "electronic pub" and suggested that online dating was an attractive alternative to the "real-world" dating scene.[100] His initial pitch for the electronic pub invoked familiar tropes of disembodiment—text chat rendering skin color, gender, age, and "physical flaws" invisible—but his narrative centered on the BBS world, a cyberspace that was very much rooted in place, rather than the deterritorialized internet.[101] "When it comes to making contacts with real people, for real-life dates, real relationships, and real commitments," he wrote, "it's tough to beat a good ol' local BBS."[102] "Compu-dating" on a local BBS involved the (potentially thrilling) knowledge that the person on the other end of a sexy chat was dialing in from one's own area code.

At the peak of BBSing in North America, meeting people online was still a generally uncommon practice, and as popular interest in the "information superhighway" began to grow, so did the occasional human-interest story about computer-mediated sex and romance. These accounts tended to approach online interactions as wholly distinct from "traditional" forms of dating and focus on details that emphasized that distinction. For example, in an early "hitch-hiker's guide" to "America's information highway," the *Economist* described "steamy" sex talk on BBSs as the "textual equivalent of grunts and groans."[103] Others focused on the potential for fantastical sexual encounters. In *Erotic Connections*, an early guide to cybersex, the pseudonymous author Billy Wildhack compared an adults-only chat room to "a telepathic costume party" in which the electronic utterances of other users stimulate the imagination and "get the adrenaline going big time."[104] Fox was more pragmatic in *Love Bytes*. If meeting someone at the local singles bar could feel superficial, frustrating, or dangerous, the local singles BBS offered a fun, low-risk opportunity to mingle with a different population of people, all of whom were comfortable expressing themselves in writing. "There is no dressing up, driving across town and getting lost, ordering drinks, or squabbling over bills," enthused Fox. "If the person you end up with turns out to be a geek, jerk, lemon, frump, or nerd, it's easy to mumble some excuse and just hit a few keys, logging yourself off"—that is, assuming that a geeky frump is not exactly what you are looking for.[105]

The asynchronous messaging features of a one-liner BBS could be adapted for online romance, but most adult-oriented BBS were multiline systems with a range of special features specifically designed for matchmaking. By the late 1980s, most BBS host software implemented a modular system for adding external programs from third-party developers, known as "doors." Door programs for matchmaking, such as ProMatch by WoodyWare, were typically customizable, but their default configurations revealed assumptions about the social circumstances within which their authors expected them to be used.[106] Most matchmaker programs presumed a normative heterosexuality, but they also included opportunities for resistance, however superficial. The documentation for Intelligent Match Maker by TcSoft suggested creating three distinct databases: "Generic Match Maker," "Gay Male Match Maker," and "Gay Female Match Maker."[107] Presumably, the "generic" database was for those who were seeking heterosexual relationships, but the program's creator still acknowledged the prevalence of gay BBSers through this recommended setup. ProMatch, meanwhile, stored all of the users in a single database. Whenever users were asked questions related to gender or sexuality, they were presented with a catch-all option such as "Other" or "Plead the fifth." When entering a "Spin the Bottle" game, for example, users were asked whether they wished to kiss "Females," "Males," or "Doesn't Matter." The architecture of programs like Intelligent Match Maker and ProMatch rarely posed a fundamental challenge to the dominance of heterosexuality, but they universally acknowledged the existence and legitimacy of same-sex desire. It was in these small moments that adult BBSs afforded visibility to queer identities, even on boards that were not explicitly coded "queer."

Even as many BBS programs assumed heterosexuality by default, this norm was routinely unsettled in practice. Boards with explicitly sexual themes—say, swinging as opposed to dating—advertised areas dedicated to "alternative lifestyles." For example, Lifestyle Online was an exceptionally popular BBS hosted on Long Island, New York.[108] Although it hosted no explicit GIFs, Lifestyle Online received over sixteen hundred calls per day from users who interacted with one another in subforums dedicated to "Swinging/B&D/S&M/Bi/TV/fetishes."[109] By marking queerness and kink as "interests," the sysops of Lifestyle Online positioned them as accessible options for curious heterosexuals. Indeed, each of these "alternative lifestyles" was presented online to callers in the form of a browsable menu.

As with many preexisting subcultures, swingers constituted a particularly active part of the adult BBS world. The log-in screen for Lifestyle Online boasted, "The Largest Swingers Correspondence Magazine in the World!," an explicit reference to the underground swingers mailing lists that predated the modem world. Swinging, like dating, benefited from both the social and spatial characteristics of BBS culture. "Tom Terrific," the pseudonymous sysop of The Pleasure Dome in Virginia Beach, Virginia, started the board in 1985 as a "meeting place" for the local swingers community; each month, he hosted both "regular parties" and "swing sessions" for his callers.[110] As the system began to attract callers from outside its local area code, Terrific enforced the social focus of the board through the architecture of the underlying software. Between 7 p.m. and midnight every night, the file area was automatically shut down to encourage all users to participate in the late-night chat rooms. The chat features on multiline adult boards like The Pleasure Dome enlarged the space of possibility for many swingers. For some couples, sharing a modem, a screen, and a keyboard offered an accessible, "softer" form of swinging than was previously available.

Consistent with many areas of the modem world, longtime participants in sexually themed adult BBSs unfailingly described their favorite boards in terms of sociality rather than sexuality. In user testimonials, words like "fun," "open-minded," "uncensored," "village," and "home" are common, while details about the particular games, files, or technical features of the BBSs are seldom mentioned. The sexy side of adult systems often provided an illicit edge to an otherwise conventional chat. The Paradise Play Line BBS in Houston, Texas, for example, featured fifty incoming lines and local access numbers throughout the 713 metropolitan area code. With its tropical theme, erotic online games, live trivia, and frequent get-togethers at a local bar, the Paradise Play Line offered an atmosphere more akin to an adults-only cruise ship than a kinky after-hours club.[111] As one reviewer described it, the BBS offered "an island paradise for Internet vacationers everywhere."[112]

While the overwhelming number of men in the modem world enabled gay BBSs to thrive, the exclusion of women from BBSing for over a decade posed an obvious problem for boards with a heterosexual orientation. Wildhack estimated that on most adult boards, men outnumbered women five to one.[113] In the face of this imbalance, some sysops attempted to attract women through segmented pricing. But cost was hardly the reason for women's disinterest in sexually oriented spaces dominated by men. For years, Compu-Erotica offered free access to women, but men continued to make up more than 70 percent of its membership.[114] The Pleasure Dome added a dedicated line for women to call, but the results were similar: men continued to outnumber women two to one.[115] Laura's Lair BBS in Ava, Missouri, was one of a very few adult-oriented BBSs founded by women. Run by a team of four women, including Laura Brito, Laura's Lair featured moderated discussions that went far beyond casual socializing to include collaborative storytelling, safer sex information, and technical advice for producing amateur pornography. Unfortunately, Laura's Lair was a singular exception amid hundreds of clueless men. "We try to create an atmosphere that makes women feel comfortable and unharassed," wrote the sysop of one adults-only BBS, "as we know they are a valuable online commodity."[116]

Of course, for some men seeking heterosexual online encounters, the exclusion of women was not an insurmountable barrier. Text-mode environments provided considerable flexibility for self-presentation, and much of the ostensibly heterosexual sex occurring in "hot" chat rooms was, in fact, the product of two men. Consistent with the dominant media frame of the time, the authors of *Aether Madness* described this as a "tragicomic scenario," but there is little evidence to suggest that all—

or even most—of the men participating in these mediated encounters would have considered them acts of deception.[117] Indeed, the exclusion of women from the modem world was widely known—though seldom described in terms of "exclusion"—as was the possibility, if not the practice, of cross-gender presentation in sex-oriented online spaces. Indeed, in *Love Bytes*, Fox suggested that the possibility of a coded same-sex encounter was "often part of the appeal" for men who participated in sexually explicit chat.[118] On BBSs like Lifestyle Online that encouraged fantasy, the tacit appeal of the "cross-gendered" user was preserved through an absence of voice verification.[119] Beyond paying subscription fees, users were not required to disclose any additional personal information.

The tacit acceptance of gender play on boards like Lifestyle Online reflected a broader acceptance of queer life across BBS culture. For even casual BBS users, queer culture was pervasive. In 1993, *Boardwatch* again invited readers to vote for their favorite BBSs.[120] As the results rolled in, the prevalence of queer life online was undeniable. The Gay and Lesbian Information Bureau, a nonprofit BBS in Arlington, Virginia, serving primarily gay, lesbian, and bisexual users, ranked in the top five.[121] The only systems that ranked higher were "monster BBSs" like Software Creations and Exec-PC, with dozens of incoming lines, exclusive shareware, and commercial support. Further down, the top-one-hundred list also included S-Tek BBS in Montréal—"Montréal's premiere Gay & Lesbian BBS"—and the Zoo BBS, an "adult social network" in Chicago that advertised "gay, bi, straights welcome."[122] In November 1992, The Gay & Lesbian BBS List, just one of the queer-themed BBS lists, included more than 320 systems in North America alone.[123] To participate in the modem world in the late 1980s was to witness the emergence of a newly computerized gay culture: out of the closet and onto the net.

Multicom-4 was one of the largest queer systems in North America. Although it started as a single-line hobbyist BBS in 1979, Multicom-4 grew into a mission-driven, nonprofit online community for gay, lesbian, and bisexual people living in and around Rochester, New York.[124] Sysop Chaz Antonelli described the evolution of the system as a reflection of his own growth: "When I came out of the closet as a gay man in the 80s, my BBS soon followed."[125] To ensure the safety and confidentiality of the BBS community, Antonelli verified nearly every new user, often with a

The Multicom-4 BBS Network &
Internet Service Provider

The World's Largest, Free, Gay/Lesbian/Bisexual
and Adult Bulletin Board System (21 and over)

telnet://multicom.org
http://www.multicom.org
modem:(+716) 756-4300
voice:(+716) 442-1669

EVENTS   PRIDE WEEKEND ROCHESTER   EVENTS

- Pride - Dignity - Diversity -

Gay/Lesbian/Bisexual Parade
Saturday Night, starting at 7pm
downtown at Liberty Pole

BLOCK PARTY to benefit AIDS ROCHESTER
behind Rochester Custom Leathers,
274 N Goodman St after the parade
Food - Music - Games - and More
meet the erotic film star Johnny Rea!

Tickets for the annual Gay/Lesbian/Bisexual Picnic (this Sunday) are
available at Rochester Custom Leathers until 12 noon on Sunday!

Join us for a Multicom-4 Party
on Friday, October 11th
at Muther's 40 Union
starting at 10pm!

$1 donation at door!

M U T H E R ' S

= Free Buffet   = Huge Outdoor Patio
= 50/50 Raffle   = *NEW* MC-4 Access Terminal

= Kitchen and dining room open 'till 1:30am
= New York State instant lottery & Quick Draw!

If you already have a User-ID on Multicom-4, type it in and press RETURN.
Otherwise type "new":

Social and fundraiser event invitations displayed on Multicom-4 BBS during the early
1990s. (Courtesy of Chaz Antonelli; Sysop Chuck, Multicom-4 BBS)

one-on-one voice telephone call. Members without a PC or modem could access the system from public terminals installed in gay-oriented businesses around the city, including Antonelli's own leather shop. In the early 1990s, membership blossomed into the thousands, and with the help of a lawyer from the board, Antonelli created a nonprofit corporation to handle donations and support the growing community. By 1996, Multicom-4 also provided low-cost access to the internet and World Wide Web. At the end of the decade, there were over eighty-five hundred registered accounts in the user database, of which more than two-thirds had been individually verified.

Not all queer BBSs started out as spaces for community. In many cases, virtual communities emerged on services created to share information. Founded in 1986 as a nonprofit service providing health and legal advice to the "gay/lesbian/bi" community of Washington, DC, the Gay and Lesbian Information Bureau quickly became an informal online meeting place for gay men.[126] In addition to health information, GLIB users traded tips on gay nightlife in the nation's capital city. By the time of its *Boardwatch* award in 1992, GLIB was a lively social scene supported by twenty-two incoming telephone lines, live multiuser chat, and personal profiles with GIF images. For gay men—including closeted gay men—with a computer and a modem, GLIB provided a low-risk opportunity to explore the local gay community in DC. "This was a revelation, that you could use your computer to connect with other gay people," remarked GLIB sysop Jon Larimore in an article from 2010 comparing GLIB to gay-oriented mobile social software like Grindr.[127] More adventurous callers might venture out to the GLIB Happy Hour, hosted weekly in Dupont Circle, the city's upscale gay enclave.

For BBS users interested in talking about politics and culture, BBSs like GLIB offered a valuable alternative to the conservative-leaning boards that predominated. Queer bulletin boards, like gay bookstores and other queer-coded spaces offline, served multiple purposes. For local callers, a BBS like GLIB might offer a fruitful cruising opportunity one night and an opportunity to talk about Ross Perot's candidacy on another.[128] In a 1995 guide to modeming, Gary Wolf and Michael Stein avoided characterizing queer BBSs as either hookup sites or information repositories; rather, they focused on the rich communities they encountered on these systems. Queer BBSs, they wrote, were among "the most vibrant electronic subcultures of the online world."[129] Indeed, the authors speculated, the proximity of GLIB to Washington, DC, made it a particularly rich forum for discussing politics, queer and otherwise.

Consistent with the predominance of men in the BBS world, queer BBSs were largely frequented by men who identified as gay and bisexual.[130] As the majority, gay men implicitly dominated the representation of queerness throughout the modem world. The Gay & Lesbian BBS List, for example, included a special designation for "women only" boards, though no similar marker existed for men.[131] Meanwhile, boards such as the Male Box, the Male Room, and the Male Stop were not likely to offer much by way of lesbian interest. In 1996, the anthropologist Kira Hall described the obvious imbalance of the modem world as an "intensification" of gendered discourse.[132] Instead of unsettling or erasing conventional notions of gender, text-mode interactions seemed to exaggerate hegemonic conceptions of femininity and masculinity. In response, a number of women sysops created separate "women-only" bulletin boards. Sappho BBS in New York City, 10% Connection BBS in Chicago, and the Oak Tree BBS in Denver were all open exclusively to women.[133] In a study of a similar space—the SAPPHO mailing list—during the first half of 1993, Hall observed a communal resistance in which participants produced a "female-gendered discourse" that actively opposed the harassment they encountered elsewhere online by crafting an alternative set of social norms.[134] The participants in SAPPHO endeavored to create a cyberfeminist form of discourse distinct from the "poor example" exhibited by the men—gay, straight, and otherwise—who dominated most online spaces. "Exclusion of men," wrote one participant, "is a precondition . . . not the purpose itself" of creating a newly feminist cyberculture.[135] Defining the boundaries of the "women-only" space was an ongoing challenge, as the affordances of the mailing list did not allow for the sort of personal verification that was carried out by the sysops of the "Ladies only" area of the TARDIS. Instead, women on SAPPHO relied on subjective assessment of the content of new participants' posts: usernames, return addresses, signatures, linguistic markers, and the like.

Some of the larger queer BBSs included areas specifically marked as "exclusively for women." GLIB, for example, featured a subboard titled "Lesbians On Line," and anecdotal evidence suggests that lesbian users were an active part of the Backroom BBS.[136] The Backroom

BBS, founded by Arthur Kohn in 1984, similarly appealed to men and women.[137] Indeed, a print advertisement for the Backroom from 1992 depicts both a pair of men and a pair of women gleefully typing to each other through computer terminals with large lambdas on their screens. By and large, however, the presumed user of most queer systems was a gay man, and the systems were structured accordingly. To gain visibility and voice in these spaces, lesbian women were forced either to negotiate space within the existing architectures or to create their own separate spaces.[138] Not all adult boards marked by sexuality were overtly queer, of course. Within boards with a default heterosexual orientation, gender was hailed, performed, and constrained very differently.

At the same time that queer culture was flourishing online, BBSs became vital networks for the circulation of information about HIV and AIDS. In 1986, the year that GLIB opened its electronic doors, thousands were dead and dying from an epidemic exacerbated by fear, homophobia, racism, and misinformation. For radical activist groups like ACT UP, access to media networks was a lifeline. "Silence = Death" not only invoked the unheard voices of those suffering from the disease in isolation but called out the health-care providers, policy makers, and educators who censored themselves. Alongside fax networks and DIY publishing efforts, BBSs offered another medium for the circulation of health information, especially outside major metropolitan areas.[139] For people suffering from HIV and AIDS, access to information could be the difference between living and dying.

Activists turned to dial-up BBSs as a means of distributing information and support to impacted communities. BBSs offered several key advantages from the point of view of activists and health workers. First, the BBS was a file-sharing machine: information could be updated continuously, and files could be circulated without centralized coordination. Second, BBS technology was relatively accessible and could be run by a small number of staff on a volunteer basis. And third, BBSs offered a degree of anonymity and privacy that was critical because of the heavy social stigma attached to both HIV/AIDS and homosexuality. Between 1985 and 1993, more than one hundred bulletin boards were set up specifically to share HIV/AIDS information with fellow users and their local communities. During this period, BBSs became such critical hubs for information and community support that the Centers for Disease Control and Prevention's National AIDS Clearinghouse published "A Selected Guide to AIDS-Related Electronic Bulletin Boards" with step-by-step information about how to access dial-up BBSs.[140]

Misinformation about HIV/AIDS was rampant in the 1980s, and without the careful oversight of trusted figures, BBS file-sharing practices would have been worth very little. In 1990, Sister Mary Elizabeth Clark founded the AIDS Education General Information System (AEGIS), a not-for-profit BBS in her hometown of San Juan Capistrano, California.[141] Drawing together information from a wide array of sources, AEGIS provided basic information about HIV/AIDS and safer sex practices as well as the latest news regarding treatment, clinical research, and related political affairs. AEGIS began as a typical "one-liner," but with the help of private donors, the board grew to accommodate twenty-four incoming lines and, eventually, a gateway to the packet-switched internet and the World Wide Web.[142] By January 1996, AEGIS had 1,265 registered members, received approximately twenty-five to seventy-five calls a day, and stored more than two gigabytes of information, including 104,000 files from the National Library of Medicine's AIDSLINE database.[143]

The information posted to AEGIS was duplicated daily to a network of related BBSs, each of which was dedicated to providing free, often anonymous, access to HIV/AIDS information. AEGIS information also circulated beyond the borders of the United States, through both the grassroots FidoNet network and HIVNET, a European network dedicated to HIV/AIDS information. Because of the fundamental decentralization of BBS messaging networks, it was impossible to know exactly how far this information traveled, but journalistic accounts estimate that AEGIS reached more than twenty-four countries.[144]

During the 1990s, the AEGIS database stretched across the modem world, accessible from BBSs, over the internet, and on the World Wide Web. In practice, the system reflected the social and technical convergence of these components of the emerging internet. Wynn Wagner, creator of Opus BBS, became involved with the organization, contributing graphics for the website and an essay titled "Day One" aimed at people just finding out that they have HIV. In frank, friendly language, the essay offered "five pointers for survival" and directed readers on where to turn for information and support.[145] "Day One" became one of the most widely read pieces on the AEGIS site, where it was linked from the home page, translated into several languages, and frequently reprinted by advocacy organizations.

The information stored in AEGIS served multiple audiences. On the one hand, health-care professionals throughout the world accessed AEGIS in order to provide the best care for their patients. Dial-up medical databases already existed, but none shared AEGIS's focus on HIV/AIDS or its commitment to low-cost access. This was particularly important for doctors working outside major metropolitan areas in North America. Indeed, Sister Mary Elizabeth decided to start AEGIS after meeting people living with HIV/AIDS in rural Missouri who had no access to information about the disease. Her goal was to provide access to information for "your average person with AIDS."[146] The hypothetical "average person" may not have been able to interpret all of the technical information in a newly published clinical trial, but they could use the information to advocate for themselves when meeting with local doctors. One user, after suffering from the side effects of drug therapy in 1995, went to his doctor with a stack of new research that he downloaded from AEGIS.[147] In this ideal case, access to the online database provided a set of resources that facilitated local, face-to-face communication between a doctor and a patient.

BBSs providing access to health information often also encouraged the growth of supportive online communities for visitors. In 1993, the Computerized AIDS Ministries Network (CAM) in New York City was founded under the slogan "There is more to living with AIDS than AIDS."[148] Unlike most dial-up systems, CAM provided access through an 800 number so that callers could reach the system from anywhere in the United States without paying a long-distance toll.[149] CAM was operated by the Health and Welfare Ministries Program of the United Methodist Church's General Board of Global Ministries, and faith played an important role in shaping its community. In addition to providing unrestricted access to basic AIDS information (e.g., "Facts, Fiction, and How to Prevent It"), CAM focused on bringing people suffering from AIDS out of isolation and into a "safe . . . supportive community."[150] Isolation often affected the friends and family of people living with AIDS, and many of the 750 registered members of CAM identified as "caregivers."[151]

CAM was open to all users, and some callers would not have identified as Christian. Although no religious affiliation was required or expected of callers and CAM was not an explicitly evangelical project, the emphasis on support and compassion was understood by many users to be an expression of Christian values. Not all congregations in the United Methodist Church were equally supportive of families and individuals living with AIDS, and CAM provided access to a supportive community that was nonetheless rooted in a familiar faith.[152] One caller from Virginia contrasted the lack of compassion he encountered in his local church, where AIDS was regarded by some members as "a plague sent by God to punish the evil sinners," with his experience dialing into CAM.[153] "While there is no attempt made at CAM to preach or moralize," he remarked, "the love and faith that is found here shines like a beacon."[154] Another caller, who later adopted the pseudonym Rusty, remembered coming to CAM with apprehension after losing a cousin to AIDS. "Although I've known some good people who are Christian," recalled Rusty in a testimonial about her time on the site, "most I met seemed so full of judgment and condemnation."[155] On CAM, however, Rusty was "grateful" to find "a different kind of God," ministered "without condemnation."[156]

For believers, on the other hand, an encounter with AIDS could be a significant challenge to their faith, and CAM provided a supportive space for reflection and information seeking. Debbi Hood Johnson, a devoted Christian and a particularly active user of CAM, joined the BBS after learning that her husband was infected.[157] Although Johnson lost her husband to AIDS in 1993, she continued to participate in the discussion forums on CAM. As a self-described "white heterosexual female in the heart of the conservative South" who was also HIV-positive, Johnson provided considerable support to other women in the community until her own death in 1996.[158] As a regular on CAM, Johnson befriended a community of queer activists who practiced the sort of "unconditional love" and "honest, unflinching AIDS prevention education" that she found lacking in her religious community at home.[159] "What about the rest of us?" she asked. "Where are the mainstream churches?"[160] Rather than undermine her faith, Johnson's experiences on CAM deepened her commitment to a principle of compassion that she associated with Christianity and enabled her to hold her church community to a higher moral standard.[161] Rev. Larry Mason, a regular caller from North Loup,

Nebraska, similarly credited his participation in CAM for helping him achieve a "much deeper understanding and far more acceptance" of gay and lesbian people.[162]

REAL PEOPLE IN REAL PLACES

From the single-line "computerized bulletin board" to worldwide messaging networks like FidoNet, the technical culture of BBSing was driven by a desire for connection between people. The communities that developed on dial-up BBSs were different from those of commercial services or the internet due to the persistence of place and the unique role of the sysop in BBS culture. Whether connecting with nearby computer enthusiasts or far-flung strangers, BBS communities arose out of real people in real places sending messages to one another, day after day, night after night. Some of these users stepped into the role of the sysop, shaping the environment and setting the terms by which communities flourished or floundered. As one former sysop put it, running a BBS was a service, provided to "a very special community of very special people."[163]

The sysops and users who immersed themselves in BBS communities were among the first computer owners to experience the ups and downs of a computer-mediated society. Their experiences chatting, trading files, and playing games online provided a foundation for the popular adoption of the commercial web a decade later. Across the tech and media industries, observers and investors looked to the BBS world as a model for the communication networks of the future. And yet community BBSs like the TARDIS, despite their rich histories, are rarely discussed as antecedents to the internet or social media. The influence of the modem world on the social web was seldom overt. Rather, the sysops and users of community BBSs carried their experiences with them as they filtered into the booming tech industry. From *Slashdot* and gURL pages to Reddit and Facebook, the structures and practices of BBS communities have been continuously reproduced by Silicon Valley, albeit without the autonomy, independence, or control enjoyed by their dial-up ancestors.

CHAPTER SIX

Becoming the Net

TO MOST PEOPLE IN THE United States, the internet arrived in the summer of 1995.[1] From the nightly news to the multiplex to the grocery-store checkout, cyberspace was inescapable. Cover stories in *Time* magazine introduced the general public to "cyber porn," "cyber democracy," and "cyber war." In a feature on the local tech industry, *New York* magazine declared the arrival of "Cyber City."[2] Theater marquees featured one high-tech thriller after another: *Johnny Mnemonic*, *The Net*, *Virtuosity*, *Hackers*, and *Strange Days* all debuted between May and October.[3] Prime-time dramas *Law & Order* and *The X-Files* featured computer-mediated creeps, and *The Simpsons* showed the Comic Book Guy posting on a USENET newsgroup.[4] In speeches and debates, Republicans and Democrats agreed that the "information age" was imminent and the future of US prosperity depended on "electronic cottages" and "information superhighways."[5] Meanwhile, the unexpected success of Netscape's initial public offering (IPO) drew a flood of investment capital to the net.[6] Sales of "multimedia" PCs with built-in modems were booming. Microsoft's new operating system, Windows 95, promised to get every new PC owner online with user-friendly networking features.[7] In cities and towns across the United States, tens of thousands of dial-up bulletin boards were buzzing with callers, files, games, and forums.

And yet, despite all of this excitement for cyberspace, 1995 was the beginning of the end of the modem world as long-time users had come to know it. The dial-up bulletin board system, or BBS, did not survive the cultural, economic, and technological changes brought about by the World Wide Web, the dot-com boom, and the mainstreaming of cyberspace. Buoyed by speculative investment following the Netscape IPO, dozens of new services had begun to compete for modemers' time and money. "Nationwide" platforms like Prodigy sold "start-up" kits through Radio Shack; America Online bombarded middle-class America with free diskettes; and Microsoft bundled the Microsoft Network with every new copy of Windows 95. Gradually, all of these platforms became on-ramps to the internet and the World Wide Web.

By early 1996, BBS activity was in steep decline in North America. BBSs throughout the continent were going permanently offline as their users spent more and more time elsewhere. The number of nodes trading mail on FidoNet began to shrink for the first time in over a decade.[8] While some sysops gave users advanced notice of the shuttering of their systems, others simply pulled the plug after weeks of dormant phone lines and stagnant forums: no forwarding addresses, no thank-you notes for former callers. Longtime modemers grew accustomed to hearing the prerecorded voice of a telephone operator through their PC speakers: "We're sorry. You have reached a number that has been disconnected or is no longer in service. If you feel you have reached this recording in error, please check the number and try your call again."[9] Little evidence remained of the systems that once thrived on the ends of these disconnected numbers. The very term "BBS" began to vanish from the American tech vocabulary. In 1997, the US Census retired a question about BBSs, replacing it with one about the internet. In 1998, even *Boardwatch* magazine—mouthpiece for the BBS industry—dropped "BBS" from its masthead. For some residents of the modem world, the dot-com boom was a bust.

The World Wide Web, in particular, seemed to draw all of the attention away from dial-up BBSs. In the memories of many former users, the web's graphical interface posed an existential threat to the text-oriented BBS. Determined sysops struggled to survive, adopting new graphical software and adding internet features to their boards, but the rhetorical

Taglines from the Cover of *Boardwatch* Magazine, 1991–98

FIRST APPEARANCE	TAGLINE
June 1991	Electronic BBS and Online Information Services
April 1992	Guide to the World of Online Services
May 1992	Guide to Electronic BBS and Online Information Services
December 1993	Guide to Online Information Services and Electronic Bulletin Boards
January 1996	Guide to the Internet, World Wide Web and BBS
March 1998	Guide to Internet Access and the World Wide Web

battle was already lost. As former users tell this morbid tale, the BBS is said to have "fallen" or "died" at the hands of the internet.[10] In the 2006 memoir of the former sysop Rob O'Hara, he described the arrival of the internet as an almost instantaneous event that "crushed" all of the BBSs and dial-up systems into "oblivion."[11] A terminal prognosis for the BBS world propagated almost immediately after the arrival of public access to the web. In August 1996, the software developer Rob Swindell, to occasion the closing of his BBS company, Synchronet, circulated an essay titled, provocatively, "The Internet Killed the BBS Star."[12] As silence spread across North America's BBS networks, few could disagree.

But what did it mean for so many thousands of BBSs to "die"? What other explanations could there be for the sudden disappearance of these dial-up networks? For a forensic analysis of the "killing" of the modem world, we need to take a few steps back, to the years just before the Netscape IPO and the release of Windows 95 and the Telecommunications Act of 1996 and the dot-com boom. At the start of the 1990s, BBS sysops were a vanguard force in the emerging internet economy, some of the only people on Earth with practical experience in the social and technical challenges of maintaining an online community. So how did these longtime users respond when their friends and family started talking about cyberspace? What did they imagine when they heard the president touting the construction of an "information superhighway"? Did they expect "the net" to change their lives? How did they react to the swiftly changing cultural economy of the dot-com boom?

A COMING-OUT PARTY FOR THE BBS INDUSTRY

At the outset of the 1990s, BBS operators optimistically awaited public access to the internet. During the previous decade, the internet had been restricted to research institutions. Commercial uses—including amateur BBSs—were discouraged. By 1990, however, an internal process of privatization promised to open the high-speed data network to the general public and create a competitive internet industry.[13] Unregulated access to the packet-switched internet promised a new medium for linking BBSs together, free of the costs and constraints of the telephone network. The transformation of the internet from public to private paralleled a transformation in the technical culture of BBS operators as well. In August 1991, over four hundred FidoNet sysops and BBS diehards met in Boulder, Colorado, for FidoCon '91. Previous conventions had attracted a smaller number of FidoNet insiders and focused on the immediate problems of network growth and maintenance. An especially contentious battle over forming a nonprofit corporation gave FidoCon a reputation for acrimony and arguing—as well as the unfortunate nickname "Fight-O-Con."[14] But with the growing buzz of internet privatization in the background, the 1991 conference promised something different.

The organizers of FidoCon '91 hoped to change the reputation of the conference. Instead of an administrative meeting aimed at addressing arcane routing issues, they promised that FidoCon '91 would be "the biggest SysOp gathering in history."[15] Drawing on their prior experience running large "cons" for science fiction and fantasy enthusiasts, the organizers explicitly invited BBS users and neophytes to participate.[16] Despite the specific name, FidoCon '91 was broadly aimed at every modem junkie and Echomail addict in the world, a gathering for anyone interested in "international BBSing and electronic communications."[17] It was the first time that anyone had attempted to bring the entire decentralized network of dial-up BBSs together under one roof.

Promotional materials, circulated on BBS networks and computer magazines, promised three days of workshops and events. A preliminary program featured how-to sessions with FidoNet architects Tom

Jennings and Tim Požar, a presentation from John Perry Barlow and Mitch Kapor of the newly founded Electronic Frontier Foundation, a mud-pie-throwing contest to benefit a multiple sclerosis charity, and the "real wedding" of Peter Stewart and Michele Hamilton, two sysops who fell in love over Echomail.[18] The response was overwhelming—the official conference hotel sold out, and vendors occupied all of the available booths. More than twenty sysops attended from overseas, including Australia, Finland, the Netherlands, and Switzerland. One registered sysop from the Soviet Union was reportedly forced to cancel at the last minute due to an attempted coup d'état by members of the Communist Party.[19]

To the hundreds of modemers who showed up, FidoCon '91 was a revelation. After years of BBSing in relative isolation, here they were, shoulder-to-shoulder with hundreds of other people who knew the difference between XMODEM, QMODEM, and ZMODEM, people with whom they had been trading files and messages for years, people who shared a utopian vision for the future of computer-mediated communication. The hallways of the Sheraton buzzed with laughter as attendees met face-to-face, shook hands, and embraced one another. After hours of phone calls and thousands of kilobytes of email, the modem world was meeting itself for the first time. Combining the awkward energy of a first date with the easy humor of old friends, one attendee described the event as more of a "revival" than a convention.[20] Meanwhile, the invited speakers were just as colorful in person as on the boards. Tom Jennings turned up with bleached blond hair and a kill-your-TV T-shirt. Dave Hughes appeared in a cowboy hat and bolo tie. Barlow wore a kerchief around his neck and a Grateful Dead steal-your-face badge on his lapel.[21] Somehow, this hobby didn't seem so marginal after all.

The unexpected turnout at FidoCon '91 raised a new question for BBS sysops: Was BBSing still just a hobby? Or was it becoming something else? A social movement? An industry? While attendees puzzled over this shift in collective identity, two conference sponsors leapt eagerly at the chance to redefine the meaning of "BBS" for the 1990s. Phil Becker, creator of TBBS, and Jack Rickard of *Boardwatch* embraced FidoCon '91 as an opportunity for commercial growth and innovation.[22] Initially, they compared FidoCon to the Dayton Hamfest, an annual gathering of amateur radio operators that combined the commercialism of a trade show with the conviviality of a county fair.[23] But after attending the convention, Rickard came to believe that something bigger was going on. In his next *Boardwatch* column, he described FidoCon '91 as a "turning point" for the "infant" BBS industry.[24] Despite the "grumbling" of some old-timers, the crowd seemed open to commercialization and keen to learn more about the privatization of the internet. Something had happened to BBS culture over the previous year, Rickard marveled: "the kid gained his feet."[25]

Riding the wave of excitement from FidoCon '91, Rickard and Becker announced plans to organize an event of their own in 1992. Dubbed the Online Networking Exposition and BBS Conference, or "ONE BBSCON," the new event sought to cut ties with FidoNet and embrace commercialization of the modem world. Jim Warren, organizer of the legendary West Coast Computer Faire, offered informal mentorship and a degree of legitimacy to the fledging organization.[26] If amateur sysops felt any lingering discomfort with commercialism, they were free to continue running FidoCon independently. To address the concerns of Fido sysops, Rickard submitted an article to *FidoNews* outlining his vision of a "general BBS industry and networking trade show" inclusive of commercial platforms like CompuServe and Prodigy, BBS networks like RelayNet and ILink, and internet services.[27] Tom Jennings added a note of support to the article, emphasizing that he was not opposed to commercialization but rather protective of the autonomy of the Fido network. So long as ONE BBSCON kept "Fido" out of its name, there would be no confusion over the relationship between the amateur FidoNet and the commercial BBS industry.

Tensions over commercialization revealed other fissures in North American BBS culture. Although the population was growing in sheer numbers, white men continued to make up a large majority. At FidoCon '91, nearly everyone dragging a suitcase through the hotel lobby appeared to fit this description. In October, *Boardwatch* ran a FidoCon feature including several pages of snapshots from around the convention halls. Not only were there no women listed as presenters or award recipients, there was not a single woman in any of the photos. One attendee, who identified herself as "the only Black Female" at FidoCon, returned home from the conference feeling very differently from Rickard and Becker. In an "open letter" published by *Boardwatch*, Lisa Downing describing being snubbed and ignored all weekend: "I was relegated to the role of nonperson at this conference."[28] In a brutal irony, she noted the frequency with which the invited speakers hailed the coming of an egalitarian virtual community, free of bias. "Don't fool yourselves," she remarked; "[technology] will not erase the prejudices of the user."[29] Rickard issued a short response, showing little compassion or willingness to engage with Downing's critique. Instead, he dismissed the rudeness of other FidoCon attendees as the harmless behavior of "maladjusted" computer geeks and repeated the utopian belief that BBS users are "more tolerant and accepting than most." Yet Rickard also echoed the racial hostility of the right-wing radio hosts whom he frequently lauded, bitterly suggesting that any conflict that Downing felt at FidoCon stemmed from her own identification as a Black woman: "I doubt you were as unique and out of place as you apparently delight in thinking you were."[30]

Unlike the conflict over commercialization, this startling exchange between Rickard and Downing barely seemed to register in the public discourse of the period. Not one follow-up letter appeared in the pages of *Boardwatch*. Of course, Rickard might have suppressed the topic in the interest of portraying FidoCon in a positive light, but notably, he did not curb a debate over homosexuality that erupted a few weeks later. Rickard did not speak for everyone in the modem world when it came to race and racism—indeed, just six months later, Jennings published an impassioned defense of racial justice activism in *FidoNews*[31]—but the lack of response to Downing's letter reflected an unwillingness on the part of most white men to think seriously about race, class, and gender. Sadly, Downing's experience at FidoCon was not unique. Despite the many contributions of women and Black people to early net culture, the benefits of commercialization—from BBSs to social media—have consistently gone to those who fit the stereotype of the white male computer geek.[32] Downing gave Rickard and the readers of *Boardwatch* an opportunity to follow a different path. They didn't take it.

Over the next three years, the utopian vision of virtual community went mainstream—from niche computer rags to the cover of *Time*—thanks to the privatization of the internet. Commercial online services like Prodigy created "start-up kits" bundling terminal software with cheap modems to help curious computer owners get online, and subscriber numbers spiked. America Online reportedly grew from fewer than 180,000 users in 1992 to over one million in 1994.[33] BBSs saw a parallel spike in activity as thousands of new modem users sought an on-line world beyond the walled gardens of CompuServe, Prodigy, and AOL. The number of people traveling to BBS conventions in North America more than doubled every year, hitting a peak of four thousand at the 1994 meeting of ONE BBSCON in Atlanta.[34]

Dial-up BBSs increasingly acted as local gateways to the newly priva-tized internet, blurring the distinction between the two spheres. As more of the public came online, the biases identified by Downing after Fido-Con '91 only intensified. Despite firsthand accounts of racism and sexual harassment, BBS advocates clung to a vision of cyberspace as a medium free of bias—a "society of the Mind," as John Perry Barlow declared it.[35] But the modem users targeted by harassment had different utopias in mind. By 1994, more than two dozen BBSs were trading messages over AfroNet, a Fido-based network initially organized by the graduate stu-dent Ken Onwere to carry conferences on "African-American themes."[36] Long-running women-only spaces on BBSs like ECHO and The WELL were welcoming new users. And queer spaces like the Gay and Lesbian Information Bureau (GLIB) were taking calls from all over the country. A common purpose to networks like these was helping people to find one another out in cyberspace. The utopia promised by these networks was not a disembodied virtual reality but rather a simultaneous blossoming of translocal communication. Regardless of which utopia you were chas-ing in 1992, the future of cyberspace looked less like the commercial web and more like a worldwide network of BBSs.

STORMING THE INTERNET

Between 1992 and 1995, thousands of BBS sysops set about rebuilding their BBSs as on-ramps and off-ramps to the internet. The energy and ex-perience of the BBS community caught some longtime internet observ-ers by surprise. After more than a decade of parallel development, they could no longer ignore the cooperative, grassroots networks stretching across the globe. Ethernet cocreator Bob Metcalfe joked about his BBS blind spot: "Where have I been while cyberspace was being settled?"[37] From Metcalfe's view, BBS users and sysops were about to transform the social fabric of the internet, bringing in new practices, new exper-tise, and new expectations. Over the next few years, he wrote regularly about BBSs in his column for *InfoWorld* and urged his readers to take the community seriously. Today's BBSs, he predicted, would soon serve as the "local front ends" to the privatized internet. BBS users and sysops would be the ones to grow the web.[38]

In addition to the persistent growth of BBSs in population and geographic reach, they also seemed to be surpassing their UNIX contemporaries in some technical regards. For example, while the user interface of a text-mode BBS might look somewhat out of date next to Prodigy's point-and-click menus, the internet looked downright ancient. In 1991, the internet's user interface was the blinking cursor of a UNIX shell account, indistinguishable from the monochrome BBSs of a decade before. Because BBS sysops and software developers had spent years exploring the limits of ANSI-mode graphics, BBS screens of the early 1990s were interactive, animated, and colorful—worlds away from the UNIX command line. As the internet software developer Brad Clements remarked in 1993, many BBSs "blow-away" existing internet services.[39] In a letter to *Boardwatch*, he offered to collaborate with BBS makers to enable incoming connections from the internet. In Clements's view, internet users would benefit from being able to connect to the BBS world as much as BBS users would be curious to explore the internet.

A convergence of BBS and internet networks seemed mutually beneficial. The internet would provide a robust infrastructure for shuttling data between the many BBS communities already thriving on the dial-up telephone system. In the aftermath of FidoCon '91, Jack Rickard became an increasingly vocal proponent of this convergence. He urged BBS sysops to see themselves as the primary point of contact between the everyday computer owner and the internet's "ivory tower."[40] "The ordinary electronic bulletin board will BE the interface to the Internet," he enthused. "[It will be] the only Internet most people will see for some time to come."[41] Along with Phil Becker, Rickard believed that much of the internet hype was misplaced. After all, so much of what sparked cyberspace mania—virtual community, online learning, e-commerce— was already happening on dial-up BBSs! "Peel away all the mystery," they asserted, and "[the internet] is the world's largest BBS."[42] After meeting with Becker and Rickard at ONE BBSCON in 1993, Bob Metcalfe was convinced that the "fabled" internet was about to undergo a cultural transformation with the arrival of "millions" of users through BBS gateways.[43] "A warning for my friends on the Internet," he wrote in *Info-World*: "[expect] an imminent invasion of BBS sysops."[44]

Sysops eager to interconnect soon discovered that there were substantial hurdles—technical and administrative—to getting on the internet. The complicated process of establishing an internet connection was the subject of numerous textfiles, magazine articles, club meetings, and conference workshops. Since 1985, BBS sysops had been exchanging messages and files with internet networks through intermittent store-and-forward gateways using a file-transfer utility known as Unix-to-Unix Copy, or UUCP.[45] However, these ad hoc points of connection required access to a UNIX machine and an employer who didn't know (or didn't care) what you did with it after hours.[46] Most sysops were out of luck until 1989, when the programmer Tim Požar released UFGATE, a UUCP package for MS-DOS with full support for internet email and USENET newsgroups.[47] Požar made UFGATE available free of charge to noncommercial users and offered to mail a physical copy to anyone who sent him a blank disk and return postage.[48] In 1990, a UFGATE BBS operated in Portland, Oregon, by the FidoNet contributor Randy Bush facilitated the exchange of FidoNet, Echomail, USENET, and internet mail with South Africa.[49]

By 1993, however, many BBS sysops were looking for more than a store-and-forward gateway. They wanted a "real" internet connection with a dedicated IP address and a domain name like "mybbs.com." Such a connection would allow local BBS users to venture out and explore internet services like Gopher and IRC while also accepting incoming connections from people anywhere on the internet. While a standard dial-up modem supported just one user at a time, a packet-switched internet connection could support dozens of users simultaneously. The problem was that the internet's packet-switching protocols, TCP/IP, were not designed for microcomputers. All of the early development of the internet was done using the sorts of computers found at large institutional facilities: mainframes, minicomputers, and workstations with the networking-friendly UNIX operating system.[50] Meanwhile, the modem world ran on IBM-compatible PCs and MS-DOS, which did not support networking by default. Third-party software tools were available for adding the internet protocols to DOS, but they were notoriously difficult to configure. In the preamble to a long how-to guide, the sysop Bernard Aboba urged readers to persevere. "Lots of us are doing this," he wrote. "Don't despair!"[51]

Configuring the software was just one part of the puzzle. Sysops also needed to find an existing internet host willing to provide a connection.[52] In the 1980s, store-and-forward gateways relied on establishing an informal arrangement such as a local university computer lab willing to donate a few hours of telephone time per week. But a packet-switched connection required a more substantial commitment of resources—a 24/7 link to the remote host.[53] Since the ARPANET days, institutional networks relied on dedicated lines leased from the telephone company for thousands of dollars a month—not an option for the typical hobbyist.[54] Yet, despite the official "privatization," in most North American cities and towns, there were simply no internet providers selling access to consumers. A BBS sysop couldn't simply call someone on the phone and order "one internet, please!" In October 1992, *Boardwatch* published a list of internet service providers for readers seeking connections.[55] It included just ten commercial networks. Even the nationwide commercial systems were struggling to move beyond the gateway paradigm.[56]

By 1994, sysops were experimenting with a variety of hacks and alternative infrastructures to bring about the convergence of BBSs and the internet. Consumer satellite services such as Planet Connect offered a "firehose from the sky," complete with USENET, Echomail, and streams of real-time weather and stock market data.[57] Unfortunately, it was noninteractive. The high-bandwidth satellite feed traveled in one direction: from the sky to the ground. Data sent back from the BBS traveled over a standard telephone call. Early cable internet connections, meanwhile, presented a similar problem. Due to the asymmetric design of the typical cable network, BBS users could access the internet at high speed, but internet users could not access the BBS.[58] Despite these constraints, sysops continued to pry open the edges of the internet. Tom Jennings briefly accessed the internet from home by dialing a friend with a connection, attaching their modems, and never hanging up.[59] Thanks to his flat-rate local dialing plan, there was no additional charge, despite being continuously "on the phone" for weeks on end.

Regardless of the technical challenges, nearly five hundred sysops succeeded in adding a two-way, packet-switched internet connection to their BBSs during the early 1990s.[60] Hybrid "internet BBSs" combined the local culture of a dial-up BBS with the global reach of the internet. As the sysop of one internet BBS put it, the BBS offered a friendly, familiar place to "kick back and relax" after "roaming the cold vastness of cyberspace."[61] *Boardwatch* and *BBS Magazine* ran features on internet BBSs and provided technical information to would-be sysops. In the summer of 1992, The WELL announced that it was upgrading its internet email gateway to include incoming and outgoing telnet connections, making it one of the first dial-up systems directly accessible from the internet.[62] Soon after, Women's Wire split off from The WELL and formed its own BBS with connections to USENET and the internet.[63] Toward the end of 1993, the burgeoning internet industry could scarcely keep pace with the demand for interactive services. The BBS-friendly Colorado SuperNet had to briefly suspend its UUCP gateway to provide bandwidth for other customers.[64]

BBS sysops had reason to be optimistic about their future on the internet. Throughout 1994, they had seen considerable growth and innovation among BBSs. From single-line hobbyist boards to large multi-line systems, new BBSs were popping up all over North America. In addition, updated BBS host software took advantage of faster modem

DRAGON KEEP INTERNATIONAL (904)375-3500 Gainesville, Florida since 01/87. Sysop: Dragon & Cerebus. Using WildCat 6.21 with 50 lines on MS-DOS 80486 with 5000 MB storage. US Robotics at 14400 bps. $.25 Hourly fee. Real-time multi-player games, 24 Hr live chat featuring Global Chatlink every night at 10PM. Over 50,000 files, 6 CD-ROM's, MajorNet, NetAccess. Full Internet access (Telnet/IRC/FTP). Telnet to dkeep.com (198.79.54.10) Instant access w/credit card.

Classified ad for Dragon Keep International, a hybrid internet BBS in Gainesville, Florida, from the October 1994 issue of *Boardwatch*. The sysop, Richard Scott Mark, was the maintainer of a widely circulated list of internet-connected BBSs and an advocate for the convergence of BBSs and the web. (Courtesy of *Boardwatch*, now *Light Reading*) speeds, faster processors, and multitasking operating systems to make it easier for sysops to add internet services. In the spring, *BBS Magazine* launched a new trade show, dubbed BBS Expo '94, in Washington, DC, aimed at the Northern Virginia internet industry. In the fall, ONE BBSCON moved to Atlanta, Georgia, and attracted more attendees, vendors, and press than any previous year. The longtime sysop Dave Hughes characterized the crowd as "deadly serious about Internet connectivity" and willing to fight for access at a fair price.[65] Jack Rickard, in his first editorial of 1995, poked fun at "a bevy of latecomers" rushing to publish books and magazines about BBSs and the internet. "It's good to be 'discovered,'" he remarked.[66] Yet the advantages of being first were short-lived. In January, a striking statistic on the cover of *Boardwatch* foreshadowed an abrupt end to the BBS moment: "World Wide Web Traffic . . . 1,814% Growth."

Between January and December 1995, the web became the face of the internet. At first glance, the graphical web would seem at odds with text-mode BBSs, but internet BBSs embraced the new medium, serving as both gateways and destinations. With a few technical modifications, the sysops of internet BBSs could provide users with access to the graphical web using the Serial Line Internet Protocol (SLIP).[67] The procedure for connecting to the graphical web from a BBS was tedious (an article in *Boardwatch* estimated that it took "a few hours" to get everything set up), and the download speeds were agonizing (a site with a few images might take fifteen minutes to load); but it worked about as well as any of the other options available to home computer owners.[68] Even crusty modem-world veterans like Jack Rickard were impressed with the experience of clicking from page to page. "Yes," he admitted, "we got a little excited."[69]

In addition to gateways, however, many internet BBSs also styled themselves as destinations for users of the web. Nearly every sysop created a home page for their BBS. Learning HTML and planning a home page were novel and enjoyable projects, even for experienced programmers. The typical BBS home page was little more than a digital advertisement, inviting readers to leave the site and connect directly to the board via telnet. Several large-scale BBSs went a step further, however, by re-creating their systems within the idiom of the web. In 1995, The WELL debuted an interactive web service that ran in parallel with the existing PicoSpan software.[70] The new point-and-click interface sought to provide

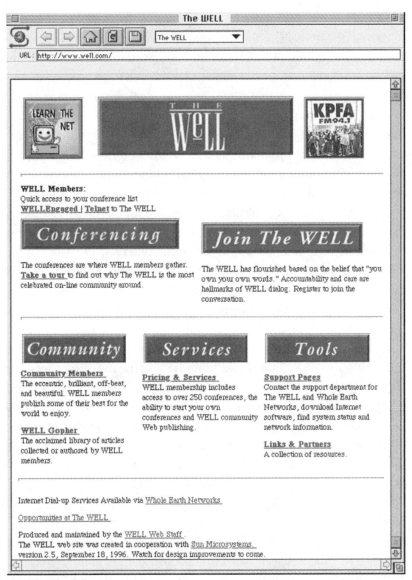

In 1995, The WELL added an interface to the World Wide Web. In this period of transition, the website functioned more as a portal than a replacement for the existing BBS. Links on the site pointed visitors to member home pages, a how-to site for new internet users, a Gopher server run by the community, and instructions for using telnet to access the text-mode BBS. Today, the entire conferencing system is accessible through the web, and the community continues to thrive. (Courtesy of The WELL Group)

a more accessible experience for newcomers while preserving the spirit of the old dial-up system. Similar upgrades were on the way from commercial BBS makers like Galacticomm and Mustang Software, both of which provided out-of-the-box support for the web by 1996.

Sysops chased internet access because it offered a solution to the central constraint on the growth of the modem world: long-distance dialing. While the rest of the world dreamed of virtual reality, BBS enthusiasts saw the internet primarily as a replacement for the telephone network. They imagined a future in which IP addresses and domain names replaced area codes and telephone numbers, a future in which they no longer needed to quickly calculate the cost of a long-distance call before connecting to a new and interesting system. Bernard Aboba compared the experience of internet access to a reconfiguration of space: "It becomes possible for you to communicate with someone half a world away by calling a computer down the street!"[71] For sysops, the appeal of internet access wasn't about particular files or services or communities—there were plenty of all of those in the modem world; rather, it was an infrastructural upgrade with social consequences, a hot-swapping of one medium for another that would bring BBS users and sysops together from around the world. This transition would both reduce the cost of existing networks like FidoNet and enable the growth of interest-oriented community BBSs like the Gay & Lesbian Information Bureau. Longtime modemers were ecstatic to be free of the confines of their local dialing area. One former user described their initial impression of the internet as "a giant virtual convention that would never end."[72]

DEATH OF THE BBS

The transformative events of 1995 interrupted BBS sysops' vision of the internet. As cyberspace splashed into popular culture and the Netscape IPO made headlines, investment capital flooded into the industries associated with data communications. But instead of BBSs, this new money and attention flowed to firms touting the internet and the World Wide Web. Regardless of the expertise and experience of BBS programmers, sysops, and entrepreneurs, thousands were in danger of losing out on the dot-com boom. Despite the convergence of the early 1990s, vocal proponents of the internet had never embraced BBS culture. As a result, anyone wishing to benefit from the boom eventually needed to shed their past associations with the modem world and embrace the internet.

For proponents of the commercial internet, it was important that the web seem cool, new, safe, and profitable.[73] Whereas Jack Rickard argued for an inclusive definition of "online services," internet advocates rejected earlier attempts at building a public data infrastructure. Videotex, time-sharing, commercial services, and dial-up BBSs were all in the past. The web was the future. Too old, too weird, too commercial, and too small, BBSs were rejected, neglected, stigmatized, and forgotten.

The most common explanation for the decline of BBSs is that new users rejected the text-mode technology in favor of the graphical web. This explanation tracks with the representation of the web in popular culture. For years, the "information superhighway" had been presented through the metaphor of "interactive TV"—a vision of the future with roots in *télématique* systems of the late 1970s and early 1980s, such as Minitel.[74] In 1993 and 1994, cover stories in *Time* and *Popular Mechanics* depicted the information superhighway as streams of television images—dramas, sports, news, animation—zipping through space. Dial-up BBSs could not produce the visual spectacle of these images, but neither could the internet. When people accustomed to cable TV and console games heard terms like "cyberspace" and "virtual reality," they were not imagining the blinking cursor of the UNIX shell. The graphical web, as seen through the Mosaic browser, represented the first internet application approaching the realization of interactive TV. As Megan Sapnar Ankerson argues, Mosaic's inline graphics and enjoyable user experience were just good enough for users to imagine what the web might become in the future.[75]

But the snubbing of BBSs cannot be explained solely as a matter of technology or market competition. After more than a decade, the exclusivity of the internet had nurtured a culture of elitism among some users. "Little did we know," observed the sysop Richard Scott Mark in 1996, but some internet users were less than enthusiastic about the arrival of BBS communities.[76] Out of ignorance, they regarded BBS users as unsophisticated and inexperienced in the online world. This snobbishness is evident in the bit of internet folklore known as "Eternal September."[77] Despite the name, "Eternal September" began in the spring of 1994, when America Online first gained access to USENET.[78] As the story goes, USENET was previously restricted to college students, academics, researchers, and other internet insiders.[79] With the arrival of new users from AOL, the quality of discussion on many newsgroups plummeted, as longtime users were overwhelmed by posts from newcomers who hadn't yet learned the norms of behavior. To some internet users, BBSs occupied an even lower social status than commercial services. In September 1994, Bob Metcalfe joked about the perception of BBSs: "If you thought America Online, CompuServe, and Prodigy users were barbarian newbies . . . here come the BBSes."[80] Of course, the sorts of BBS users seeking access to USENET were hardly newcomers. Many had been online for a decade or more. Despite this irony, the negative perception of BBSs seems to have been widespread among internet users.[81]

The low status afforded to BBS networks reflected technical, social, and geographic biases among internet advocates. The norms and values of the early internet were shaped by the unique technical culture of UNIX.[82] Indeed, the internet protocols were initially distributed through a version of UNIX popular with academic computer labs. To many UNIX devotees, microcomputer operating systems like MS-DOS seemed like a technological backwater, safe to ignore.[83] Yet this cultivated disinterest created an inward-facing technical culture that could feel radically open and egalitarian to insiders, while also being structurally closed to outsiders.[84] Likewise, in the early 1990s, champions of the internet's democratic culture tended to elide the inherent elitism of a network accessible only to people with a university affiliation. At best, internet users regarded BBSs as "stepping stones" to the "real" internet, a hierarchical view that overlooked the substantial social and technical innovation that had taken place on BBS networks themselves during the 1980s.

Of course, BBS networks thrived in spite of the neglect of internet users. That neglect was replaced by stigma, however, with the emergence of an internet industry. Dial-up BBSs provided an easy scapegoat for internet spokespeople struggling to present the commercial web as safe and fun. The stigmatization of BBSs was supported by more than a decade of negative coverage. Since 1985, nearly every time that a BBS was mentioned on the nightly news, it was associated with something shady or nefarious: hackers, foreign spies, neo-Nazis, or pornographers.[85] These stories were not without merit, but there was no complementary coverage highlighting the vast majority of community-oriented BBSs and the

sysops who operated them. Indeed, the Electronic Frontier Foundation
was founded in 1990 to support the users and sysop of a BBS that had
been mistakenly targeted by the United States Secret Service.[86]

In 1993, a moral panic began to emerge over the accessibility of pornographic images online.[87] Under the headline "Orgies On-Line," *Time*
magazine published an unsubstantiated claim that a "majority" of BBSs
offered "some form of digital titillation."[88] Whether or not this was true,
it provided cover for heavily moderated platforms like Prodigy, which
sold themselves as a family-friendly alternative. BBS sysops were rightfully frustrated, and the *PC Magazine* columnist John Dvorak decried
their unfair marginalization: "The media equates [BBSs] with child porn
while it equates the Net with 'Information Superhighway'!"[89] By July
1995, however, the "cyberporn" panic threatened to derail the commercialization of the web entirely. A poorly designed study of online pornography prompted a sensational cover story in *Time* magazine claiming
that an overwhelming majority of the images found online were pornographic.[90] In both the original study and the story published by *Time*,
the term "BBS" was used to describe forums on CompuServe, USENET
newsgroups, anonymous FTP sites, and dial-up bulletin boards. The web
was mentioned only once, in passing: a potential "engine of economic
growth."[91]

Unlike the web, internet BBSs were seldom described as a source of
prosperity, despite the enthusiasm of many sysops for entrepreneurship.
Magazines like *Time* framed the runaway commercial success of BBSs
such as Event Horizons and Rusty n Edie's as ill gotten, due to their association with porn and piracy.[92] Yet profit and commercialization were
much less controversial among BBS sysops than in the rarefied culture
of the internet. The problem wasn't that BBSs were anticommercial but
that they were the wrong kind of commercial. Internet businesses were
emerging as national and international players, riding the neoliberal
wave of deregulation and free trade to compete with entrenched tele-
coms. Commercial BBSs, however, tended to be small and medium-
sized enterprises with a regional focus. They were run by families or
groups of friends out of small offices and spare bedrooms. In the lingo
of Silicon Valley, internet BBSs did not "scale."

The final cause of death for the BBS was the ambiguous meaning
of the term "internet" itself.[93] The internet transformed everything that

Caricature of the sysops of Rusty n Edie's BBS being "busted" for alleged copyright infringement. The husband-and-wife team that ran Rusty n Edie's liked to describe their system as "the friendliest BBS in the world." According to the FBI, unlicensed commercial products were available alongside its massive collection of shareware and adult GIFs. As BBSs came under increasing scrutiny from law enforcement, high-profile busts contributed to an association of BBSs with unlawful activity, however undeserved. (Courtesy of *Boardwatch*, now *Light Reading*)

it touched. Once a BBS added an internet connection, it was subsumed into the massive network-of-networks. As BBS networks converged with the internet, "BBS" became a vestigial category. To join the internet was to vanish into the vastness of the internet. After years of being marginalized, ignored, and neglected, many sysops threw in the towel. In 1994, the BBS software maker Scott J. Brinker observed that his company's primary product, The Major BBS, had outgrown the BBS label. It was soon rebranded as Worldgroup—"an open platform for creating your own online service"—and sold as a bridge between corporate intranets and the public web.[94] In 1995, the market research firm Nielsen reclassified all online services under the heading "Internet Access."

Rhetorical closure around the term "internet" made it easier for newcomers to find their way into cyberspace, but it also contributed to a concentration of power on the web. BBS sysops enjoyed a degree of autonomy from one another that was not available on the commercial web. And since BBSs were materially isolated from one another, users' personal data did not follow them from one system to the next. Although dial-up networks were less efficient than the packet-switched internet, they nevertheless distributed control to edges of the network. In addition, the technical architecture of BBSs enforced a kind of local culture that was simply not a priority for the web. By the time former users realized the intimate relationships they had lost, most BBSs were already gone.

BIRTH OF THE ISP

By 1996, a startling number of BBSs had vanished. From America Online to the World Wide Web, millions of modem users found themselves dividing their online time among a much larger number of networks and services. As users spent less time on their local BBSs, they set off a negative feedback loop. Fewer callers today meant fewer messages for tomorrow's callers to read. In short time, BBS activity fell off precipitously. As one former sysop told me, "The lines went dead."

But something else was going on, out of sight of the typical user. Between 1994 and 1996, the telephone number (708) 820-8344 belonged to an office in Aurora, Illinois. Situated just off the historic Ogden Avenue near the junction with Route 59, the office was home to Aquila BBS, "Chicagoland's Largest BBS." An advertisement from *Boardwatch* highlighted some of the attractive features of the BBS: hundreds of discussion areas, a library of over 120,000 files, an internet email gateway, local weather, the digital edition of *USA Today*. By 1996, however, dialing (708) 820-8344 no longer connected you to Aquila BBS. Instead, the number now led to Aquila Internet Services. Operating out of the same office in Aurora, Aquila Internet Services offered dial-up internet access, commercial web design, and free web hosting for subscribers.

The sysops of systems like Aquila abandoned the term "BBS" and reinvented themselves as "internet service providers" (ISPs).[95] The same PCs, modems, hardware, and software used to run an internet BBS could be adapted to running a local ISP. In fact, the makers of high-end BBS software actively encouraged sysops to sell internet access to callers. The fifth version of Wildcat!, released in 1996, promised to give sysops "the power [to] develop into a full-blown Internet Service Provider."[96] As demonstrated by Aquila BBS, the difference between an "internet BBS" and an "internet service provider" was just as often a matter of branding and organizational identity as technology. By adopting the label "ISP," entrepreneurial sysops could avoid the stigma attached to the term "BBS" and take part in the booming internet economy.

It is hard to know precisely how many BBSs transformed into ISPs due to the protean state of the market, the absence of central authorities, and the fuzzy definition of "ISP." However, BBS publications from the period offer some clues. In December 1995, Jack Rickard estimated—somewhat implausibly—that "over 95%" of the ISPs created in the previous eighteen months were run by former BBS sysops.[97] That same year, Richard Scott Mark offered a more conservative estimate: 40 percent of all ISPs in the United States started out as a BBS.[98] These numbers vary, in part, according to the definition of "ISP." Would a BBS offering a USENET feed and internet email gateway count? How about an ISP providing shell accounts and a local BBS but no access to the web? Or what about an internet BBS offering home-page hosting and a web interface but no traditional text-mode services? In 1996, entrepreneurial sysops offered a broad range of network services at highly varied rates. Everyone was still trying to figure out just what it meant to be an "ISP."

Hindsight offers additional evidence of the transformation of BBSs into ISPs. From 1994 to 1996, Richard Scott Mark published an electronic list of BBSs accessible via telnet, to encourage internet users to

In October 1994, Aquila BBS boasted about being "Chicagoland's Largest BBS" with features that rivaled nationwide commercial services. By October 1996, however, it had reinvented itself as "Aquila Internet Services," with the BBS as just one component of its online business. Despite this change of face, the telephone number to reach Aquila remained the same. (Print advertisement courtesy of *Boardwatch*, now *Light Reading*)

explore the growing number of internet BBSs. Mark's list was circulated on USENET, posted to the web, republished in *BBS Magazine*, and eventually compiled into a softcover book. The longest version of the list included 462 BBSs, of which 428 included a link to a page on the World Wide Web.[99] Tracing these BBS home pages through the Internet Archive's Wayback Machine reveals that approximately one-third of the web-enabled boards on Mark's list had explicitly rebranded themselves as ISPs by 1999. Sysops dropped any trace of their former BBSs and adopted the language of the internet economy. The Big Easy BBS had become "the region's premier Internet Service Provider!"; Access Nevada promised to "put your business on the Web!"; and CyberNet sold itself as a provider of "leading-edge Internet/intranet technologies."

At the start of the dot-com boom, thousands of BBSs seemed to disappear within the space of a few months. Of those with an internet connection, however, a substantial proportion reemerged as ISPs. Beyond these direct metamorphoses, we can imagine tens of thousands of former BBS sysops and users carrying their past experiences into new jobs in the nascent internet industry. The years that they spent learning how to build dial-up networks and moderate online communities qualified them for a variety of roles, from infrastructure maintenance and system administration to web design and custom support. As the commercial web became the dominant medium of the twenty-first century, it was shaped—almost invisibly—by a cohort of online professionals who had cut their teeth swapping files and messages on a dial-up BBS.

REMEMBERING A DIFFERENT INTERNET

In 1995, something happened to dial-up BBS networks in North America. A year that seemed poised to bring BBSs into the mainstream instead marked their sudden decline. Today, former users and sysops generally accept that the aesthetic advantages of the graphical web spelled the "death" of the text-mode BBS. But looking back at the events of the early 1990s, a more complicated picture emerges. BBS enthusiasts foresaw a future in which the web was not only a hypertext publishing medium but a platform for computer-mediated communication. To bring about this transformation, they sought a convergence of BBSs and the newly privatized internet. As they endeavored to interconnect, however, BBS sysops encountered resistance on the part of longtime internet users and wound up abandoning the term "BBS." So BBSs did not simply vanish in 1995. They migrated to the internet, giving up their distinct identity in the process.

By accepting a technological explanation for the demise of the dial-up BBS, we have been misremembering the internet and the early web. From the perspective of a home computer owner with a dial-up modem, the web of 1995 was scarcely serviceable. It was tedious to set up and slow to use.[100] To understand why the web generated so much excitement, it is necessary to look at the broader media ecology of the early 1990s. People in North America had been promised high-speed, interactive telematics since the early 1980s, but the political economy of the Bell System breakup left no room for long-range planning or serious investment in digital infrastructure.[101] After nearly two decades pushing the residential telephone network to its limit, BBS enthusiasts were casting about for a new infrastructure. From the perspective of a BBS sysop, public access to the internet's "backbone" looked like an opportunity to expand beyond the local area code, fundamentally reordering the spatial imaginary of the modem world. The point-and-click web interface enabled BBS enthusiasts to envision what it might feel like to navigate a hybridized BBS-internet in the future.

The BBS sysop's optimistic vision of a convergence of BBSs and the internet allows us to remember the early web differently. Instead of seeing the web as a competitor or a replacement for the dial-up BBS, we can see the web as a continuation of the modem world. "Our primary goal was to expand our little BBS community to a world wide audience," recalled sysop Richard Scott Mark when thinking about his motivations for connecting to the internet.[102] In the case of BBSs becoming ISPs, the continuity was even more concrete. The exact same telecommunications apparatus that once carried FidoNet messages and ANSI log-in screens was repurposed to handle HTML pages and animated GIFs. In cities and towns around North America, the internet was literally made of BBSs.

CHAPTER SEVEN

Imagining a Better Future for the Internet

A FEW YEARS AGO, SOMETHING went weird in one of my undergraduate internet history courses. As I was grading final exams, I discovered that a handful of students had come away with an unexpected misunderstanding of early online culture. With deep nostalgia for a past they hadn't experienced, they described AOL as an online service *primarily* for gay, lesbian, bisexual, and trans people to connect with one another. They similarly offered a highly romanticized vision of BBSs as a place of queer, feminist, and antiracist organizing. For them, the history of the social internet was one of decline: once it had been utopia; now it was just Facebook.

I was both puzzled and a little amused by this inaccurate but enthusiastic misunderstanding of the history. As I looked back over my notes from the course, I could see where things had gone awry. I had intended for the course to upend stereotypes about the people who built the internet. While we covered in detail the histories of packet switching, timesharing, and the Cold War, the syllabus was also filled with articles and activities highlighting the contributions of marginalized people to the networks that would become social media. In some ways, these were the most fun aspects to teach. Students' eyes glazed over as I tried to get them to marvel at TCP/IP, but they lit up when we talked about HIV/AIDS support groups, Afrofuturism, and cyberfeminist e-zines.

When I told my friends about the confusion, they laughed. Was AOL, so crucial to our 1990s high school and college experiences, really such ancient history? But I was troubled by the students' misunderstanding. It simply is not true that AOL was overwhelmingly gay or that most BBS networks were experiments in radical organizing. In the early days, as now, the computer-geek stereotype had some basis in fact. White men with modems outnumbered everyone else. In my effort to challenge the standard narrative, I had conveyed the exceptional as the typical. And in doing so, I had stripped these extraordinary events from the conditions of oppression, exclusion, violence, and neglect in which they took place.

In this book, I have offered stories from the modem world as a set of narrative resources, but turning to the past for help with the present is risky. A toxic nostalgia lurks around the history of consumer technology, particularly where men's technical hobbies are concerned. Certainly, some people prefer a past uncomplicated by issues of injustice. It's more fun to kick back and remember the good old days spent tinkering with computers, playing *Legend of the Red Dragon*, and flaming losers online, and that's one way that the history of the modem world could be told.

But as my students' confusion illustrates, it's easy to overcorrect in the other direction. I want to tell a version of the past that celebrates the contributions of those whose stories have not been sufficiently told, but I also want to offer meaningful context. Misogyny, homophobia, and white supremacy were problems on the networks of the 1980s, just as they are today. Even emphasizing the remarkable stories of queer life on BBSs obscures another set of intersectional exclusions. Every BBS in North America operated within a cultural matrix of race and gender marking personal computers as the domain of white men. Replacing one oversimplified story with another is not the way forward.

Nevertheless, the stories from the modem world gathered in this book are real, and they are important. For more than two decades, dial-up bulletin board systems, or BBSs, were a primary form of popular networked computing in North America. The users and sysops of grassroots BBSs stood at the forefront of computer-mediated communication, carving out a space between nationwide commercial services and subsidized university systems. From the moral economy of shareware to the cooperative networks of HIV/AIDS activists, BBS communities adapted the simple idea of a "computerized bulletin board" to an array of socially valuable purposes. Their experiments with file sharing and community building during the 1980s provided a foundation for the blogs, forums, and social network sites that drove the popularization of the World Wide Web more than a decade later. But, today, these systems are almost totally absent from the internet's origin story.

Instead of emphasizing the role of popular innovation and amateur invention, the dominant myths in internet history focus on the trajectory of a single military-funded experiment in computer networking: the ARPANET. Though fascinating, the ARPANET story excludes the everyday culture of personal computing and grassroots internetworking. In truth, the histories of ARPANET and BBS networks were interwoven—socially and materially—as ideas, technologies, and people flowed between them. The history of the internet could be a thrilling tale inclusive of many thousands of networks, big and small, urban and rural, commercial and voluntary. Instead, it is repeatedly reduced to the story of the singular ARPANET.

The tales that we tell about ARPANET and the Cold War, Silicon Valley and the early web have become a founding mythology for the internet—narrative resources that we rely on to make sense of our computer-mediated world.[1] Activists, critics, executives, and policy makers routinely call on this mythology to advance arguments on issues related to technology and society. In debates about censorship, national sovereignty, privacy, net neutrality, cybersecurity, copyright, and more, advocates refer to a few oft-repeated tales in search of fundamental truths about how the internet ought to be governed. The stories that people—especially people in power—believe about the internet of the past affect the lives of everyone who depends on the internet in the present.

Forgetting has high stakes. As wireless broadband approaches ubiquity in many parts of North America, the stories we tell about the origins of the internet are more important than ever. Faced with crises such as censorship and surveillance, policy makers and technologists call on a mythic past for guidance. In times of uncertainty, the most prominent historical figures—the "forefathers" and the "innovators"—are granted a special authority to make normative claims about the future of telecommunications. As long as the modem world is excluded from the internet's origin story, the everyday amateur will have no representation in debates over policy and technology, no opportunity to advocate for a different future.

The paradox running through this book is that the modem world refuses to be a single, stable object of analysis. In life and in memory, it was multiple, different, conflicting networks at the same time. This complexity was written into the architecture of the networks themselves. Before 1996, the modem world was not yet the internet, not yet a single, universal information infrastructure bound together by a shared set of protocols. In the days of USENET and BBSs and Minitel, cyberspace was defined by the interconnection of thousands of small-scale local systems, each with its own idiosyncratic culture and technical design, a dynamic assemblage of overlapping communication systems held together by digital duct tape and a handshake. It looked and felt different depending on where you plugged in your modem.

The standard history of the internet jumps from ARPANET to the web, skipping right past the mess of the modem world. A history that consists of mostly ARPANET and the web isn't incorrect; indeed, it is quite valuable. There is much to learn from these networks about informal collaboration, international cooperation, public-private partnerships, and bottom-up technical innovation.

But we've been telling the same story about ARPANET and the web for twenty-five years, and it isn't satisfying anymore. It doesn't help us understand the social internet we have now: it doesn't explain the emergence of commercial social media, it can't solve the problems of platformization, and it won't help us to imagine what comes after.[2]

Today's social media ecosystem functions more like the modem world of the late 1980s and early 1990s than like the open social web of the early twenty-first century. It is an archipelago of proprietary platforms, imperfectly connected at their borders. Any gateways that do exist are subject to change at a moment's notice. Worse, users have little recourse, the platforms shirk accountability, and states are hesitant to intervene.

Before the widespread adoption of internet email, people complained about having to print up business cards with half a dozen different addresses: inscrutable sequences of letters, numbers, and symbols representing them on CompuServe, GEnie, AOL, Delphi, MCI Mail, and so on.[3] Today, we find ourselves in the same situation. From nail salons to cereal boxes, the visual environment is littered with the logos of incompatible social media brands. Facebook, Google, Twitter, and Instagram are the new walled gardens, throwbacks to the late 1980s.

In recent years, it has become commonplace to blame social media for all our problems. There are good reasons for this. After decades of techno-optimism, a reckoning came due. But I am troubled by how often people—not platforms—are the object of this criticism. We're told that social media is making us vapid, stupid, intolerant, and depressed, that we should be ashamed to take pleasure from social media, that we are "hardwired" to act against our own best interest. Our basic desire to connect is pathologized, as if we should take the blame for our own subjugation. I call shenanigans.

People aren't the problem. The problem is the platforms. By looking to the history of the modem world, we can begin to extricate the technologies of sociality from what we've come to call "social media." Underlying many of the problems we associate with social media are failures of creativity and care. Ironically, for an industry that prides itself on innovation, platform providers have failed to develop business models and operational structures that can sustain healthy human communities.

Silicon Valley did not invent "social media." Everyday people made the internet social. Time and again, users adapted networked computers for communication between people. In the 1970s, the ARPANET enabled remote access to expensive computers, but users made email its killer app. In the 1980s, The Source and CompuServe offered troves of news and financial data, but users spent all their time talking to one another on forums and in chat rooms. And in the 1990s, the web was designed for publishing documents, but users created conversational guest books and message boards. The desire to connect with one another is fundamental. We should not apologize for the pleasures of being online together.

Commercial social media platforms are of a more recent origin. Major services like Facebook formed around 2005, more than a quarter century after the first BBSs came online. Their business was the enclosure of the social web, the extraction of personal data, and the promise of personalized advertising. Through clever interface design and the strategic application of venture capital, platform providers succeeded in expanding access to the online world. Today, more people can get online and find one another than was ever possible in the days of AOL or FidoNet.

Yet commercial social media failed to produce equitable, sustainable business models. Despite massive user populations, remarkable engineering, and pervasive cultural influence, all major social media platforms depend on a revenue stream that has not changed for two decades: the exploitation of personal data for the purposes of advertising. This was true when Google launched Adwords in the year 2000. It was true when Google acquired YouTube in 2006. It was true when Facebook and Twitter went public in 2012. And it was still true in 2021. Despite the "moon shots" and "big bets," these firms draw an overwhelming proportion of their revenue from the mundane business of placing ads on screens.[4]

The modem world shows us that other business models are possible. BBS sysops loved to boast about "paying their own bills." For some, the BBS was an expensive hobby, a money pit not unlike a vintage car. But many sysops sought to make their BBSs self-sustaining. Absent "angel" investors or government contracts, BBSs became sites of commercial experimentation. Many charged a fee for access—experimenting with tiered rates and per-minute or per-byte payment schemes. There were also BBSs organized like a social club. Members paid "dues" to keep the hard drive spinning. Others formed nonprofit corporations, soliciting tax-exempt donations from their users. Even on the hobby boards, sysops sometimes passed the virtual hat, asking everybody for a few bucks to buy a new modem or knock out a big telephone bill.

The other key, and closely related, failure of the social media industry is in its disregard for the needs of the communities that rely on them. In public debate, commercial social media providers like Facebook portray themselves as "tech" firms rather than "media" publishers, merely "neutral platforms."[5] This allows them to disclaim liability for the things that people do on their platform and entitles them to regulate user behavior through capricious "Terms of Service" agreements. Users who rely on these platforms for social support and economic opportunity click through the inscrutable terms without reading them. When harmed, they are left with no recourse, no avenues for redress, and no practical pathways to exit. Of course, the platforms want it both ways.[6] At the same time that they deny responsibility for their users, they promote themselves as places for people to gather and share the intimate details of their lives. These are undemocratic, private spaces masquerading as a public square.

The modem world, again, offers different models. The stewardship of an online community takes work. The literature of the modem world is replete with textfiles, magazine articles, and how-to books about cultivating communities, moderating discussions, handling troublesome users, and avoiding burnout. The role of the bulletin board system operator required a unique mix of technical acumen and care for the community. Former BBS sysops recall late nights spent answering email, verifying new users, tweaking software settings, cleaning up messy files, and trying to quell flame wars.

This work is still being done on platforms like Facebook and reddit. But unlike the sysops who enabled the flourishing of early online communities, the volunteer moderators on today's platforms do not own the infrastructures they oversee. They do not share in the profits generated by their labor.[7] They cannot alter the underlying software or implement new technical interventions or social reforms. Instead of growing in social status, the role of the sysop seems to have been curtailed by the providers of platforms. If there is a future after Facebook, it will be led by a revival of the sysop, a reclamation of the social and economic value of community maintenance and moderation.

Platforms didn't invent the social use of computer networks. Amateurs, activists, educators, students, and small business owners did. Silicon Valley turned their practices into a product, pumped it full of speculative capital, scaled it, and so far refuse to treat the lives we live through it with care. The stories we tell about the early internet must disentangle the grassroots origin of social media from its capture and commodification. I do not expect that new models for online sociality will look exactly like the BBSs did in the 1980s, but the history of the modem world centers on the interests of everyday people, a reorganization of narrative resources from which to envision alternative futures.

While I absolutely need to teach a history of the internet that is accurate, I also want to retain my students' enthusiasm for the extraordinary people who brought the modem world to life. The constellation of historical narratives that will allow us to imagine an internet after Facebook must situate these moments of brilliance and possibility within the complex—often ugly—circumstances in which they originally unfolded. The historian Joy Lisi Rankin urges us to "overwrite" the narrow mythology of Silicon Valley exceptionalism with histories of the many different worlds of computing that have existed since the 1960s.[8] And indeed, there is an abundance of history that remains unwritten.

From the late 1970s to the mid-1990s, millions of people living and working in cities and towns throughout the continent collectively transformed the personal computer into a medium for social communication. They were the first to voluntarily spend hours in front of a computer, typing messages to strangers. Their experiments in community building and information sharing provided a foundation for the practices that now compel us to open our laptops and reach for our smartphones each day: love, learning, commerce, community, and faith.

In the words of one former sysop, the BBS was the original cyberspace.[9] This book offers one set of stories, but there are countless left to be told. These stories remind us that many different internets have already existed. An internet after social media is still possible; the internet of today can still become something better, more just, equitable, and inclusive—a future worth fighting for.

ACKNOWLEDGMENTS

This book is about the millions of amateurs who brought the modem world into being. After years exploring the things they left behind, I am still astounded by the creativity of this sprawling community. There are countless stories yet to be written about the people who transformed computer networks into spaces for human sociality. I look forward to a future in which their legacy is more widely recognized. In this spirit, I wish to honor the memories of Sven and Rik Wallin, Randy Suess, Jack Rickard, Mark "Sparky" Herring, my uncle Fred Ziegler (KB1LLO), and all the modemers who passed away during the writing of this book.

Many BBS users and sysops gave their time to help me understand this history. I was especially fortunate to cross paths with Tom Jennings. His candid and critical perspective stuck with me as I dug deeper into the archives. I am also grateful to Chaz Antonelli, Rey Barry, Frédéric Cambus, Mike Nichols, Tom O'Nan (N9CXI), and Ben Thornton (NI5B) for sharing their experiences and expertise. Brian Grace led me through a hangar of dinosaur bones to see the computer collections at the New Mexico Museum of Natural History and Science.

A special thank-you goes to rogue archivist Jason Scott. This book would have been impossible without Jason's commitment to preserving the material history of BBS culture and passion for making it accessible to the public. I also depended on the archival labor of Benj Edwards, Josh

Renaud, and Kay Savetz. Floppies and tapes and magazines and manuals don't digitize and organize themselves.

I began this work at the Annenberg School for Communication and Journalism at the University of Southern California. Henry Jenkins, my advisor, impressed upon me a spirit of curiosity, a pedagogy of generosity, and a commitment to social justice. My committee members, Alison Trope and François Bar, approached my work with rigor and care. I also benefited from discussions with Sarah Banet-Weiser, G. Thomas Goodnight, Tara McPherson, and Kjerstin Thorson, as well as a "shadow committee" from the Culture Digitally research network: Tim Jordan, Hector Postigo, and Thomas Streeter.

At Microsoft Research New England, I found a home in the Social Media Collective. Special thanks to Nancy Baym, Tarleton Gillespie, Mary L. Gray, Jessa Lingel, Sarah Brayne, Kate Crawford, danah boyd, Sharon Gillett, Andrea Alarcón, Rebecca Hoffman, Stefanie Duguay, Caroline Jack, Nick Seaver, Megan Finn, Dan Greene, Dylan Mulvin, Henry Cohn, Nicolo Fusi, Butler Lampson, Jennifer Listgarten, and Irene Money. Jennifer Chayes and Christian Borgs provided unparalleled leadership and support.

I presented work in progress to several audiences, including ROFLCon II; the Free Art & Technology Lab Public Access program, organized by Bennett Williamson; Comparative Media Studies at MIT; Mistakes Were Made, organized by Laine Nooney; the Boston Hassle Telethon; Computer Networks Histories, organized by Gabriele Balbi, Paulo Bory, and Gianluigi Negro; the German Historical Institute, organized by Elisabeth Engel and Anne Schenderlein; Home Computer Subcultures and Society Before the Internet Age, organized by Gleb Albert, Julia Erdogan, and Markku Reunanen; the Media School colloquium at Indiana University; Web Archiving at the Open University of Israel, organized by Anat Ben-David and Vered Silber-Varod; The Web That Was, organized by Anne Helmond and Michael Stevenson; and the Club for Internet and Society Enthusiasts, organized by Polina Kolozaridi and Leonid Yuldashev.

Thank you to my other fellow travelers in the study of communication, media, and information, including Amelia Acker, Bo An, Megan Sapnar Ankerson, Niels Brügger, Finn Brunton, Dayna Chatman, Paul Dourish, Avery Dame-Griff and the Queer Digital History Project, Joan

Donovan, Barbara Gibbons and everyone in the Department of Media Studies at University of Virginia, Lee Humphreys, Jeremy Hunsinger, Julien Mailland, Annette Markham, Fenwick McKelvey, Camille Paloque-Berges, Joy Lisi Rankin, Valérie Schafer, Nathan Schneider, Stephanie Schulte, Kat Tiidenberg, Fred Turner, and Shawn Walker. Shout out to my dissertation writing group at USC and faculty writing group at UVA.

A small army helped me to wrangle the physical materials for this book, including Parker Bach, Joshua Beckman, Asher Caplan, Dan Goldberg, Hannah Royer, Brittany Shook, and Rahul Zalkikar.

Thank you to Joseph Calamia, Seth Ditchik, Andrew Katz, Karen Olson, and Jeff Schier from Yale University Press for their stewardship of this book. Kate Larson helped me to sharpen my arguments and find my voice. Sarah O'Brien provided valuable advice at a critical stage.

Thank you to my family and friends, especially Mary, Ed, Mark, Katie, Callum, Ronan, Marilyn, Kayte, and, in memoriam, Cooper. Big hugs to Eva Marigold and all of my heart to Lana Swartz.

NOTES

CHAPTER 1. RECALLING THE MODEM WORLD

1. Richard Scott Mark, *Internet BBSs: A Guided Tour* (Greenwich, CT: Manning, 1996), x.
2. See Tim Berners-Lee and Mark Fischetti, *Weaving the Web: The Past, Present and Future of the World Wide Web by Its Inventor* (London: Orion Business, 1999); Megan Sapnar Ankerson, *Dot-Com Design: The Rise of a Usable, Social, Commercial Web* (New York: New York University Press, 2018).
3. Mark, *Internet BBSs*, 155.
4. Mark, ix.
5. Mark, vii.
6. Mark, x.
7. Mark, 6–7.
8. On the politics of coolness and the early web, see Megan Sapnar Ankerson, "How Coolness Defined the World Wide Web of the 1990s," *Atlantic*, July 15, 2014, http://www.theatlantic.com/technology/archive/2014/07/how-coolness -defined-the-world-wide-web-of-the-1990s/374443/.
9. Mark, *Internet BBSs*, 5.
10. Kevin Driscoll, "Demography and Decentralization: Measuring the Bulletin Board Systems of North America," *WiderScreen* 23, nos. 2–3 (June 18, 2020), http://widerscreen.fi/numerot/2020-2-3/demography-and-decentralization -measuring-the-bulletin-board-systems-of-north-america/.
11. Bradley Fidler, "The Evolution of Internet Routing: Technical Roots of the Network Society," *Internet Histories* 3, nos. 3–4 (October 2, 2019): 364–87, https://doi.org/10.1080/24701475.2019.1661583.

12. Kevin Driscoll and Camille Paloque-Berges, "Searching for Missing 'Net Histories,'" *Internet Histories* 1, nos. 1–2 (2017): 47–59, https://doi.org/10.1080/24701475.2017.1307541.

13. Learning about protocols is essential, however, for understanding how user behavior may be regulated and community practices constrained. For a critical look at the "daemons" that possess our networks, see Fenwick McKelvey, *Internet Daemons: Digital Communications Possessed* (Minneapolis: University of Minnesota Press, 2018), https://doi.org/10.5749/9781452961743.

14. Morten Bay, "What Is 'Internet'? The Case for the Proper Noun and Why It Is Important," *Internet Histories* 1, no. 3 (May 4, 2017): 209–11, https://doi.org/10.1080/24701475.2017.1339860.

15. For more detail on networking research at Xerox PARC and the PARC Universal Packet (PUP) protocol, see Paul Dourish, *The Stuff of Bits: An Essay on the Materialities of Information* (Cambridge, MA: MIT Press, 2017), https://mitpress.mit.edu/books/stuff-bits.

16. Janet Abbate, *Inventing the Internet* (Cambridge, MA: MIT Press, 1999), 122; Thomas Streeter, "Internet," in *Digital Keywords*, ed. Benjamin Peters (Princeton, NJ: Princeton University Press, 2016), 184–96.

17. Quarterman's cybergeography began with an informal listing of networks circulated among graduate students at the University of Texas in 1984 and an article for the *Communications of the ACM* in 1996. Following the publication of *The Matrix* in 1990, he founded a consultancy called Matrix Information and Directory Services (MIDS). In addition, he continued to document the growth of the internet in a newsletter titled *Matrix News* and a series of maps and graphs titled *Matrix Maps Quarterly*. See John S. Quarterman, *The Matrix: Computer Networks and Conferencing Systems Worldwide* (Bedford, MA: Digital, 1990); John S. Quarterman and Josiah C. Hoskins, "Notable Computer Networks," *Communications of the ACM* 29, no. 10 (October 1, 1986): 932–71, https://doi.org/10.1145/6617.6618; Quarterman, "About Matrix News (MN)," Matrix Information and Directory Services, January 21, 1998, https://web.archive.org/web/19980121022331/http://www.mids.org/mn/about.html; "Matrix Maps Quarterly," Matrix.net, January 24, 2001, https://web.archive.org/web/20010124082100/http://www.matrix.net/publications/mmq/index.html.

18. Quarterman, *Matrix*, 277–79.

19. Quarterman, xxiii.

20. William J. Clinton, "Address before a Joint Session of the Congress on the State of the Union," January 25, 1994, accessed at American Presidency Project, https://www.presidency.ucsb.edu/documents/address-before-joint-session-the-congress-the-state-the-union-12; Brian McCullough, "She Gave the World a Billion AOL CDs—An Interview with Marketing Legend Jan Brandt," *Internet History* (podcast), August 2014, http://www.internethistorypodcast.com/2014/08/she-gave-the-world-a-billion-aol-cds-an

-interview-with-marketing-legend-jan-brandt/; Matthew Gray, "Web Growth Summary," MIT, 1996, https://www.mit.edu/~mkgray/net/.

21. Philip Elmer-Dewitt and David S. Jackson, "Battle for the Soul of the Internet," *Time* 144, no. 4 (July 25, 1994): 52.

22. America Online's "Internet Center" was an especially critical gateway for the expansion of the 1990s internet. The "Internet Center" was an area within America Online for users to access resources outside of the closed platform. In June 1992, AOL introduced an internet email gateway and provided users with @aol.com addresses. During the winter and spring of 1993–94, it added access to Gopher, USENET, and WAIS. By the end of 1994, it was aggressively opening its platform to the internet through the implementation of a custom web browser and the acquisition of the backbone provider ANS. See "America Online Expands Capacity and Internet Support," *Information Today*, May 1994; Peter H. Lewis, "America Online Buys 2 Internet Companies: A Company Warms Up to the World Wide Web," *New York Times*, November 10, 1994, sec. Business Day; Jared Sandberg, "America Online, Capital Cities/ABC Plan New Service," *Wall Street Journal*, July 7, 1994, sec. Technology and Telecommunications; Kara Swisher, *AOL.com: How Steve Case Beat Bill Gates, Nailed the Netheads, and Made Millions in the War for the Web* (New York: Times Business, 1998).

23. "America's Information Highway: A Hitch-Hiker's Guide," *Economist*, December 25, 1993.

24. In January 1995, Crocker posted a message to the Big-Internet listserv soliciting thoughts on a new typology of internet access. In his initial message, Crocker indicated that it was the discussion around a *New York Times* article that had inspired him to start thinking about definitions. See Dave Crocker, "Who Is ON the Internet?," *Big-Internet@munnari.oz.au*, January 24, 1995; Crocker, "RFC 1775 To Be 'On' the Internet," Network Working Group, March 1995, https://tools.ietf.org/html/rfc1775.

25. With the spread of mobile broadband and affordable smartphones, approximately 90 percent of all American adults now report using the internet. In wealthier cities and towns, internet access is as common as electrical lighting and indoor plumbing. Pew Research Center, "Demographics of Internet and Home Broadband Usage in the United States," Internet & Technology, June 12, 2019, https://www.pewresearch.org/internet/fact-sheet/internet-broadband/.

26. Susannah Fox and Lee Rainie, "The Web at 25 in the U.S.," Internet & Technology, Pew Research Center, February 27, 2014, http://www.pewresearch.org/internet/2014/02/27/the-web-at-25-in-the-u-s/.

27. For further discussion of the strange overlapping temporalities of the early web, see Ankerson, *Dot-Com Design*, 27–29.

28. For a contemporary analysis of this historiographic moment, see Roy Rosenzweig, "Wizards, Bureaucrats, Warriors, and Hackers: Writing the History

of the Internet," *American Historical Review* 103, no. 5 (December 1, 1998): 1530–52, https://doi.org/10.2307/2649970.

29. Ed Krol, *The Whole Internet: User's Guide & Catalog* (Sebastopol, CA: O'Reilly, 1992); Kiersten Conner-Sax and Ed Krol, *The Whole Internet: The Next Generation: A Completely New Edition of the First and Best User's Guide to the Internet* (Sebastopol, CA: O'Reilly, 1999).

30. Krol, *Whole Internet*, 3.

31. Bruce Sterling, "'Internet' [aka 'A Short History of the Internet']," *Magazine of Fantasy and Science Fiction*, February 1993, http://w2.eff.org/Net_culture/internet_sterling.history.txt.

32. "If you don't own a computer and a modem," wrote Sterling, "get one." The essay was stored in the digital archives of the Electronic Frontier Foundation for more than a decade in a folder titled "Net_culture" under the filename "internet_sterling.history." Electronic Frontier Foundation, "EFF 'Net Culture & Cyber-Anthropology' Archive," March 13, 2003, http://w2.eff.org/Net_culture/.

33. The historian Philip Shiman made note of this theme in the title of his review: "Credits for the Information Highway," *Science* 274, no. 5293 (December 6, 1996): 1627–28, https://doi.org/10.1126/science.274.5293.1627.

34. Katie Hafner and Matthew Lyon, *Where Wizards Stay Up Late: The Origins of the Internet* (New York: Simon and Schuster, 1996), 10.

35. The focus on ARPA is even clearer in the cheeky title to the German edition of Hafner and Lyon's book: *ARPA Kadabra oder die Anfänge des Internet* (Heidelberg: Dpunkt-Verl., 2008).

36. The political implications of ARPA funding were thoroughly examined in an academic book published that same year: Paul N. Edwards, *The Closed World Computers and the Politics of Discourse in Cold War America* (Cambridge, MA: MIT Press, 1997). To see how ARPANET fit into the larger goals of the Information Processing Techniques Office (IPTO) at ARPA, see Arthur L. Norberg, Judy E. O'Neill, and Kerry J. Freedman, *Transforming Computer Technology: Information Processing for the Pentagon, 1962–1986* (Baltimore: Johns Hopkins University Press, 1996).

37. For more details on the reception of *Wizards*, see Daniel Akst, "Cyberculture: Sometimes Dry, Detail of Magic of 1st Internet 'Wizards,'" *Los Angeles Times*, August 26, 1996; David Colker, "Looking into the Origins of the Online Universe," *Los Angeles Times*, August 20, 1996; L. Goeller, "Insomniac Wizards Revisited," *IEEE Technology and Society Magazine* 19, no. 2 (2000): 6–9; Laurel Graeber, "New & Noteworthy Paperbacks," *New York Times Book Review*, March 22, 1998; Robert D. Hof, "Where Did the Net Come From, Daddy?," *BusinessWeek*, September 16, 1996; Stephen Manes, "The Info Footpath: How the Internet Got Its Start in the Early Days," *New York Times*, September 8, 1996; Stewart Brand, "The Revolution Will Be Netcast," *Wired*, September 1996; Katie Hafner, "Ghosts in the Machine," *Wired*, July 1999, http://archive.wired.com/wired/archive/4.07/ghosts.html.

38. Abbate, *Inventing the Internet*; Janet Abbate, "From ARPANET to Internet: A History of ARPA-Sponsored Computer Networks, 1966–1988" (PhD diss., University of Pennsylvania, 1994), ProQuest.

39. "In the years since the Internet became a media sensation, a number of more popular books have appeared that deal in some way with its origins, often in heroic manner." Abbate, *Inventing the Internet*, 221n2.

40. For a detailed history of this period from the UK perspective, see Dorian James Rutter, "From Diversity to Convergence: British Computer Networks and the Internet, 1970–1995" (PhD diss., University of Warwick, 2005).

41. Thomas Streeter, *The Net Effect: Romanticism, Capitalism, and the Internet* (New York: New York University Press, 2011).

42. For more information on implementations of TCP/IP for home computers, see J. Saltzer, D. Clark, J. Romkey, and W. Gramlich, "The Desktop Computer as a Network Participant," *IEEE Journal on Selected Areas in Communications* 3, no. 3 (1985): 468–78, https://doi.org/10.1109/JSAC.1985.1146219; Kaare Christian, "Using the Internet: Getting the Clarkson Packet Drivers," *PC Magazine*, May 28, 1991; Ian Wade, *NOSintro: TCP/IP over Packet Radio: An Introduction to the KA9Q Network Operating System* (Dunstable, UK: Dowermain, 1992).

43. Ronald R. Kline, "The Modem That Still Connects Us," in *Historical Studies in Computing, Information, and Society: Insights from the Flatiron Lectures*, ed. William Aspray (Cham, Switzerland: Springer, 2019).

44. Examples of the "modem world": The Nomad, "The Modem Life. Is It Really Worth It?," May 26, 1985, archived at http://www.textfiles.com/100/modemlif.hac; Hanne Borland and Jytte Mansfeld, *Living in a Modem World* (Hørsholm, Denmark: Focus, 1991); Chris, "The Fall of the Modem World," August 1, 1991, archived at http://textfiles.com/bbs/fotmw.txt; Charles P. Hobbs, "The Modem World," 2000, archived at http://textfiles.com/history/modemwld.txt.

45. The brain as a metaphor for a universal information system predates the availability of programmable digital computers. For example, H. G. Wells, *World Brain* (Garden City, NY: Doubleday, Doran, 1938). See also Ronald E. Day, *Indexing It All: The Subject in the Age of Documentation, Information, and Data* (Cambridge, MA: MIT Press, 2014).

46. See, for example, Nathan Ensmenger, *The Computer Boys Take over Computers, Programmers, and the Politics of Technical Expertise* (Cambridge, MA: MIT Press, 2010).

47. For a detailed examination of the role of time-sharing in the production of personal computing, see Joy Lisi Rankin, *A People's History of Computing in the United States* (Cambridge, MA: Harvard University Press, 2018). For a closer look at the technology and commercial exploitation of time-sharing, see Martin Campbell-Kelly and Daniel D. Garcia-Swartz, "Economic Perspectives on the History of the Computer Time-Sharing Industry, 1965–1985," *IEEE Annals of the History of Computing* 30, no. 1 (January 2008): 16–36, https://doi.org/10

.1109/MAHC.2008.3; T. Van Vleck, "Electronic Mail and Text Messaging in CTSS, 1965–1973," *IEEE Annals of the History of Computing* 34, no. 1 (January 2012): 4–6, https://doi.org/10.1109/MAHC.2012.6; D. Hemmendinger, "Messaging in the Early SDC Time-Sharing System," *IEEE Annals of the History of Computing* 36, no. 1 (January 2014): 52–57, https://doi.org/10.1109/MAHC .2013.44; Jens Brammer, "Time-Sharing in Denmark in 1968," in *History of Nordic Computing 4*, ed. Christian Gram, Per Rasmussen, and Søren Duus Østergaard, vol. 447 (Cham, Switzerland: Springer, 2015), 167–70, http:// link.springer.com/10.1007/978-3-319-17145-6_18; Steve Jones and Guillaume Latzko-Toth, "Out from the Plato Cave: Uncovering the Pre-Internet History of Social Computing," *Internet Histories* 1, nos. 1–2 (January 2, 2017): 60–69, https://doi.org/10.1080/24701475.2017.1307544; Alexander Mirowski, "At the Electronic Crossroads Once Again: The Myth of the Modern Computer Utility in the United States," *IEEE Annals of the History of Computing* 39, no. 2 (2017): 13–29, https://doi.org/10.1109/MAHC.2017.12.

48. Joy Rankin, "From the Mainframes to the Masses: A Participatory Computing Movement in Minnesota Education," *Information & Culture* 50, no. 2 (May 1, 2015): 197–216, https://doi.org/10.7560/IC50204.

49. R. M. Fano, "The MAC System: The Computer Utility Approach," *IEEE Spectrum* 2, no. 1 (January 1965): 56–64, https://doi.org/10.1109/MSPEC.1965 .5531878; Mirowski, "At the Electronic Crossroads."

50. Nick Montfort et al., *10 PRINT CHR$(205.5+RND(1));:GOTO 10* (Cambridge, MA: MIT Press, 2013); Jones and Latzko-Toth, "Out from the Plato Cave."

51. Rankin, *People's History of Computing in the United States.*

52. Kristen Haring, *Ham Radio's Technical Culture* (Cambridge, MA: MIT Press, 2008).

53. For a closer look at the emergence of microcomputers, see Martin Campbell-Kelly and William Aspray, *Computer: A History of the Information Machine* (New York: Basic Books, 1996); Paul E. Ceruzzi, *A History of Modern Computing* (Cambridge, MA: MIT Press, 1998).

54. Hobbyist newsletters have proved especially valuable sources for historians of this period. For example, see Kevin Gotkin, "When Computers Were Amateur," *IEEE Annals of the History of Computing* 36, no. 2 (April 2014): 4–14, https://doi.org/10.1109/MAHC.2014.32; Kevin Driscoll, "Professional Work for Nothing: Software Commercialization and 'An Open Letter to Hobbyists,'" *Information & Culture* 50, no. 2 (May 1, 2015): 257–83, https://doi.org/ 10.7560/IC50207; E. Petrick, "Imagining the Personal Computer: Conceptualizations of the Homebrew Computer Club 1975–1977," *IEEE Annals of the History of Computing* 39, no. 4 (October 2017): 27–39, https://doi.org/10.1109/ MAHC.2018.1221045.

55. Martin Campbell-Kelly, William Aspray, Nathan Ensmenger, and Jeffrey R. Yost, *Computer: A History of the Information Machine*, 3rd ed. (New York: Routledge, 2018), 248–49, https://doi.org/10.4324/9780429494017.

56. John J. Welch, "Item 20: To Ward & Randy: History of CBBS???," November 9, 1986, archived at http://textfiles.com/bbs/CBBS/history.cbbs; Ward Christensen, "C(omputerized)BBS—Thanks for Remembering 25th," *Slashdot*, February 17, 2003, https://slashdot.org/comments.pl?sid=54081& cid=5317919.

57. Messages about these other bulletin boards were posted to CBBS itself during the first few months of operation. See Jason Scott, "BBS Textfiles: CBBS: The Dead CBBS Scrolls," textfiles.com, accessed July 2, 2020, http://www .textfiles.com/bbs/CBBS/SCROLLS/.

58. For a reproduction of the CBBS welcome screen, see Ward Christensen and Randy Suess, "Hobbyist Computerized Bulletin Board," *Byte*, November 1978, 154.

59. "What Might Be Called CACHE's On Line Graffitti (COG)," *Byte*, June 1978.

60. Christensen and Suess, "Hobbyist Computerized Bulletin Board."

61. "Small Firm Offers Home Computer Owners Range of Data Features," *Wall Street Journal*, January 30, 1980.

62. "MicroNET," *Byte*, January 1980.

63. On the influence of *WarGames* on US attitudes about computer networks and internet culture, see Stephanie Ricker Schulte, *Cached: Decoding the Internet in Global Popular Culture* (New York: New York University Press, 2013).

64. This regional focus reflected the economics of 1980s telephony in North America. Most people paid a flat monthly fee for unlimited calling within the local area, but calls to another city or state were billed according to duration, distance, and time of day. The ten digits of a North American telephone number included an "area code" and "exchange." A careless long-distance call could cost a hundred dollars or more. Learning to decode these numbers was an essential skill for any BBS explorer who hoped to avoid going into debt. Most BBS users simply stuck to the boards in their local calling area.

65. The Amateur Radio Relay League (ARRL) started in 1914 with the goal of creating a formal messaging network. After more than a century, the ARRL remains a key advocacy group for ham radio in the United States. On the origin of the ARRL, see Susan J. Douglas, *Inventing American Broadcasting, 1899–1922* (Baltimore: Johns Hopkins University Press, 1987), 205–6.

66. C. Partridge, "The Technical Development of Internet Email," *IEEE Annals of the History of Computing* 30, no. 2 (April 2008): 3–29, https://doi.org/10.1109/ MAHC.2008.32; Abbate, *Inventing the Internet*, 106–11.

67. Camille Paloque-Berges, "Mapping a French Internet Experience: A Decade of Unix Networks Cooperation (1983–1993)," in *Routledge Companion to Global Internet Histories*, ed. Gerard Goggin and Mark McLelland (New York: Routledge, 2017), 153–70.

68. In fact, both hobbyists and professional researchers had been bouncing around the idea of networking PCs since before the advent of CBBS. There were letters published in computer magazines and discussion on ARPANET

of building a "PCNET" for microcomputers. See Dave Caulkins, "Personal Computer Network," *People's Computers*, August 1977; Caulkins, "PCNET, 1979," *People's Computers*, October 1977.

69. Jennings's self-description appeared in a newsletter circulated to all FidoNet sysops in 1991: Tom Jennings, "Editorial," *FidoNews*, September 2, 1991.

70. For more information on English-language textfile groups, see Jason Scott, "Textfile Writing Groups," textfiles.com, accessed February 5, 2021, http://www.textfiles.com/groups/.

71. Gleb J. Albert, "From Currency in the Warez Economy to Self-Sufficient Art Form: Text Mode Graphics and the 'Scene,'" *WiderScreen* 20, nos. 1–2 (2017), http://widerscreen.fi/numerot/2017-1-2/from-currency-in-the-warez-economy -to-self-sufficient-art-form-text-mode-graphics-and-the-scene/; Kevin Driscoll, "Hobbyist Inter-Networking and the Popular Internet Imaginary: Forgotten Histories of Networked Personal Computing, 1978–1998" (PhD diss., University of Southern California, 2014), 191, http://digitallibrary.usc.edu/ cdm/compoundobject/collection/p15799coll3/id/444362/rec/2; Michael A. Hargadon, "Like City Lights, Receding: ANSi Artwork and the Digital Underground, 1985–2000" (MA thesis, Concordia University, 2011), http://mhargadon.ca/media/mhargadon-thesis.pdf.

72. Early ANSI artpacks are now accessible on the public web. See 16colo.rs— ANSI/ASCII Archive, accessed July 31, 2019, https://16colo.rs/.

73. For more information on BBS game development, see Josh Renaud, "Break Into Chat," Break Into Chat—BBS Wiki, accessed May 13, 2014, http://breakintochat.com/wiki/Break_Into_Chat.

74. Queer Digital History Project, "The Backroom," accessed February 3, 2021, http://queerdigital.com/items/show/42.

75. J. Scott Christianson and Dan Wendling, "Econet: The Ecology Network," *Boardwatch*, December 1992.

76. Howard Rheingold, *The Virtual Community: Homesteading on the Electronic Frontier* (Reading, MA: Addison-Wesley, 1993); Katie Hafner, "The Epic Saga of The WELL," *Wired*, May 1997, http://www.wired.com/wired/archive/5.05/ ff_well_pr.html; Hafner, *The WELL: A Story of Love, Death, and Real Life in the Seminal Online Community* (New York: Carroll and Graf, 2001); Fred Turner, "Where the Counterculture Met the New Economy: The WELL and the Origins of Virtual Community," *Technology and Culture* 46, no. 3 (2005): 485–512, https://doi.org/10.1353/tech.2005.0154.

77. Chip Berlet and Carol Mason, "Swastikas in Cyberspace: How Hate Went Online," in *Digital Media Strategies of the Far Right in Europe and the United States*, ed. Patricia Anne Simpson and Helga Druxes (Lanham, MD: Lexington Books, 2015), 21–36. See also Jessie Daniels, *Cyber Racism: White Supremacy Online and the New Attack on Civil Rights* (Lanham, MD: Rowman and Littlefield, 2009).

78. For a closer look at the demographics of the modem world, see Driscoll, "Demography and Decentralization."

79. Jason Scott, The TEXTFILES.COM Historical BBS List, accessed June 15, 2021, http://bbslist.textfiles.com/.

80. For a contemporaneous discussion of gender and BBSing, see Stacy Horn, *Cyberville: Clicks, Culture, and the Creation of an Online Town* (New York: Warner Books, 1998).

81. US Census Bureau, "Appendix Table A. Households with a Computer and Internet Use: 1984 to 2009," in *Computer and Internet Use in the United States: 1984 to 2009* (Washington, DC: US Census Bureau, February 2010), https://www.census.gov/data/tables/time-series/demo/computer-internet/computer-use-1984-2009.html.

82. Bob Metcalfe, "Sysops Are Reaping the Benefits in the Wake of a BBS Explosion," *InfoWorld* 16, no. 36 (September 5, 1994): 52; Metcalfe, "Internet Dwellers Beware: BBS Movement Is Planning an Invasion," *InfoWorld* 16, no. 37 (September 12, 1994): 50.

83. Lacking organizational infrastructure and institutional affiliation, BBS networks did not have their needs and interests directly represented at a series of workshops on privatization held by the Harvard Information Infrastructure project in the early 1990s. See Brian Kahin, "RFC 1192 Commercialization of the Internet Summary Report," Network Working Group, November 1990, http://www.rfc-editor.org/info/rfc1192; Brian Kahin, James Keller, and Harvard Information Infrastructure Project, *Public Access to the Internet* (Cambridge, MA: MIT Press, 1995); Brian Kahin, *Building Information Infrastructure: Issues in the Development of the National Research and Education Network* (New York: McGraw-Hill Primis, 1996); Brian Kahin, Ernest J. Wilson, and Global Information Infrastructure Commission, *National Information Infrastructure Initiatives Vision and Policy Design* (Cambridge, MA: MIT Press, 1997). See also Janet Abbate, "Privatizing the Internet: Competing Visions and Chaotic Events, 1987–1995," *IEEE Annals of the History of Computing* 32, no. 1 (2010): 10–22, https://doi.org/10.1109/MAHC.2010.24.

84. For some detail on the use of leased lines, see Fenwick McKelvey and Kevin Driscoll, "ARPANET and Its Boundary Devices: Modems, IMPs, and the Inter-structuralism of Infrastructures," *Internet Histories* 3, no. 1 (January 2, 2019): 31–50, https://doi.org/10.1080/24701475.2018.1548138.

85. On the "cyberporn" panic of 1995 and later moral panics, see Philip Elmer-Dewitt and Hannah Bloch, "On a Screen near You: Cyberporn," *Time* 146, no. 1 (July 3, 1995): 38–45; Alice E. Marwick, "To Catch a Predator? The MySpace Moral Panic," *First Monday* 13, no. 6 (May 19, 2008), https://doi.org/10.5210/fm.v13i6.2152.

86. See Kira Hall's discussion of "cybermasculinity" in "Cyberfeminism," in *Computer-Mediated Communication: Linguistic, Social, and Cross-Cultural Perspectives* (Amsterdam: John Benjamins, 1996), 147–70.

87. Horn, *Cyberville*; Charlton D. McIlwain, *Black Software: The Internet and Racial Justice, from the AfroNet to Black Lives Matter* (New York: Oxford

University Press, 2019); Avery Dame-Griff, "TGNet Map," Mapping TGNet, Queer Digital History Project, 2018, http://queerdigital.com/tgnmap/index .html.

88. McIlwain, *Black Software*.

89. See Tung-Hui Hu, *A Prehistory of the Cloud* (Cambridge, MA: MIT Press, 2015).

90. See Megan Sapnar Ankerson, "Writing Web Histories with an Eye on the Analog Past," *New Media & Society* 14, no. 3 (2011): 384–400, https://doi.org/10.1177/1461444811414834.

91. In 1992 and 1993, FidoNet contributor Randy Bush attempted to extrapolate demographics from the FidoNet nodelist. More recently, Avery Dame-Griff has been mapping queer histories of the modem world through the recon-struction of networks using FidoNet technology such as TGNet. See Randy Bush, "FidoNet: Use, Technology, and Tools," in *Proceedings of INET '92: International Networking Conference, Kobe, Japan, June 15–18, 1992*, ed. Haru-shisa Ishida (Reston, VA: Internet Society, 1992); Bush, "FidoNet: Technol-ogy, Tools, and History," *Communications of the ACM* 36, no. 8 (August 1993): 31–35, https://doi.org/10.1145/163381.163383; Dame-Griff, "TGNet Map." See also Scott, "TEXTFILES.COM Historical BBS List."

92. For a detailed examination of the available sources of demographic data, see Driscoll, "Demography and Decentralization."

93. Kevin Driscoll, "Cooperative Mode for Amateur and Academic Game Histo-ries," *ROMchip* 1, no. 1 (July 1, 2019), http://romchip.org/index.php/romchip -journal/article/view/71.

94. In 1999, Scott cited the lack of BBS material on the web as one of the motiva-tions for creating the site. After searching for the names of BBSs he called as a teenager, he was dismayed that they were not represented on the web. Speaking to the *Denver Post* in 1999, he recalled, "All these important (to me) people and places were nowhere to be found." David Thomas, "Online Pio-neer's Web Site Chronicles Phenomenon's Beginning," *Denver Post*, August 1, 1999, archived at http://www.textfiles.com/thoughts/denver.art.

95. Joe Ashbrook Nickell, "Return of the Living BBS," *Wired*, March 1, 1999, https://www.wired.com/1999/03/return-of-the-living-bbs/.

96. Jason Scott, "TEXTFILES.COM File Statistics," textfiles.com, July 1, 2005, http://www.textfiles.com/filestats.html.

97. Jason Scott, "BBS: A Documentary: The Pitch," BBS: The Documentary, ac-cessed February 2, 2014, http://www.bbsdocumentary.com/longpitch.html.

98. Jason Scott, "BBS Documentaries," Internet Archive, accessed February 2, 2014, https://archive.org/details/bbs_documentary.

99. For a close look at early Apple culture through the lens of *Softalk* magazine, see Laine Nooney, Kevin Driscoll, and Kera Allen, "From Programming to Products: *Softalk* Magazine and the Rise of the Personal Computer User," *Information & Culture* 55, no. 2 (June 18, 2020): 105–29.

100. Driscoll and Paloque-Berges, "Searching for Missing 'Net Histories.'"

CHAPTER 2. COMPUTERIZING HOBBY RADIO

1. "Snowfall a Nuisance Here, Deadly in East," *Chicago Tribune*, January 15, 1978; Roy Halt, "Freight Car Tumbles off Viaduct," *Chicago Tribune*, January 15, 1978.

2. This storm would soon be overshadowed by two even more punishing storms: the "Cleveland Superbomb" from January 25 to 27 in the Midwest and the "Blizzard of '78" from February 5 to 8 in the Northeast.

3. A comment in the source code from January 26, 1978, read, "Originally Written, Sitting Home Snowbound by Ward Christensen." See Ward Christensen, "Comments and Prologues to CBBS up to Version 3.2," BBS Software Directory, 1979, http://software.bbsdocumentary.com/AAA/AAA/CBBS/history.txt.

4. Teleprinters were already in limited use among time-sharing systems and relatively common in surplus and secondhand shops. In fact, teleprinters were previously appropriated by computer hobbyists as interfaces to kit computers such as the Altair 8800. See Martin Campbell-Kelly and William Aspray, *Computer: A History of the Information Machine* (New York: Basic Books, 1996), 238.

5. Much of the CBBS software was burned onto an EEPROM rather than saved on a floppy. As Suess later recalled, the system was under near-constant revision: "Musta re-programmed that sucker 10 times a week for a few months." Ward Christensen and Randy Suess, "The Birth of the BBS," Chinet, 1989, https://www.chinet.com/html/cbbs.html.

6. Ward Christensen and Randy Suess, "Hobbyist Computerized Bulletin Board," *Byte*, November 1978, 157.

7. The January 1975 issue of *Popular Electronics* featured a cover story on the MITS Altair 8800. Sold as a kit, the architecture of the Altair was widely imitated and became a de facto standard for microcomputers of the mid-1970s. Campbell-Kelly and Aspray, *Computer*, 240–44. See also H. Edward Roberts and William Yates, "Altair 8800 Minicomputer, Part 1," *Popular Electronics*, January 1975.

8. Christensen and Suess, "Birth of the BBS."

9. The Hayes modem was designed to fit into the S-100 bus found on kit computers like the Altair 8800. *Byte* magazine ran an early advertisement for the Hayes modem alongside the story about CBBS. Christensen and Suess, "Hobbyist Computerized Bulletin Board," 157.

10. Distributed throughout North America and western Europe, *Byte* was one of the premier venues for learning about new products, techniques, organizations, and ideas in computing. Even in communist states where access to US periodicals could be limited, hobbyists found ways to read *Byte*. The historian Patryk Wasiak found that the members of informal computer clubs in Poland pooled their funds and shared subscriptions to "Western" computer magazines such as *Byte*. See Wasiak, "Playing and Copying: Social Practices of Home Computer Users in Poland during the 1980s," in *Hacking Europe: From Computer Cultures to Demoscenes*, ed. Gerard Alberts and Ruth Oldenziel

(London: Springer, 2014), 129–50. Regarding my circulation estimate, the February 1978 issue included an apology letter from the publisher blaming recent fulfillment problems on the magazine's success: "From its inception in September of 1975, BYTE has experienced colossal growth to a circulation of over 110,000." I rounded this number down to one hundred thousand, reflecting my skepticism at the publisher's statistic while also allowing for an unknown number of readers in circumstances such as those described by Wasiak. See Virginia Peschke Londner, "Letter from the Publisher," *Byte*, February 1978.

11. "People who are successful will of course be known to us, but people who are unsuccessful won't. That's not right, as it gives a falsely biased view of the system's success. I therefore ask people who are unsuccessful in communi- cating to call me, Ward, at (312) 849-6279." Ward Christensen, "Computer Network Poll," *Dr. Dobb's Journal of Computer Calisthenics & Orthodontia*, July 1978.

12. "What Might Be Called CACHE's On Line Graffitti (COG)," *Byte*, June 1978.

13. In personal communication published by Jason Scott, Christensen wrote, "It received almost a quarter million callers on its one phone line over the course of its life." Scott, "Customized: S-100 Kit Computer: CBBS," BBS Soft- ware Directory, accessed February 17, 2021, http://software.bbsdocumentary .com/AAA/AAA/CBBS/.

14. To put the eight pages of Helmers's editorial about modems—and, implicitly, his enthusiasm for CBBS—in context, the modal page length for Helmers's editorials in 1978 was three (mean = 3.67, SD = 3.08).

15. Carl Helmers, "Some Thoughts about Modems," *Byte*, July 1978.

16. Christensen and Suess, "Hobbyist Computerized Bulletin Board."

17. PCNET was a Bay Area organization founded at the first West Coast Com- puter Faire in April 1977. With connections to the ARPANET community, Caulkins and the PCNET group were early to envision networks of micro- computers. In 1989, Christensen and Suess indicated that they were in touch with PCNET and excited about the potential of the idea but "frustrated by the lack of DOERS" in the group. See Dave Caulkins, "Personal Computer Network," *People's Computers*, August 1977; Caulkins, "PCNET, 1979," *People's Computers*, October 1977; Christensen and Suess, "Birth of the BBS."

18. Ward Christensen and Randy Suess, "CBBS—COOKBOOK Rev. 3.5 11/28/81," BBS Software Directory, November 28, 1981, http://software.bbsdocumentary .com/AAA/AAA/CBBS/cookbook.txt.

19. Christensen, "Computer Network Poll."

20. The exact date that Christensen and Suess began to sell CBBS is not clear. It was available for mail order by 1981, as several documents indicate; how- ever, the recollections of the two men from 1989 suggest that it was for sale around the time of the *Byte* article's publication.

21. Christensen and Suess, "Birth of the BBS."

22. Christensen and Suess.

23. Ben Bronson, "Installing a Computer Bulletin Board Program," BBS Software Directory, April 1981, http://software.bbsdocumentary.com/AAA/AAA/CBBS/cpmnet81.apr.txt.

24. Christensen and Suess, "Birth of the BBS."

25. Ward Christensen and Randy Suess, "Part-Time Msg Sys. Phone #s," BBS Software Directory, September 27, 1981, http://software.bbsdocumentary.com/AAA/AAA/CBBS/parttime.txt; Christensen and Suess, "Other Message Sys. Phone #s," BBS Software Directory, December 26, 1981, http://software.bbsdocumentary.com/AAA/AAA/CBBS/parttime.txt; Christensen and Suess, "Midwest Remote CP/M Systems," BBS Software Directory, July 7, 1981, http://software.bbsdocumentary.com/AAA/AAA/CBBS/1981cbbslist.txt; Christensen and Suess, "CBBS Phone #s," BBS Software Directory, December 26, 1981, http://software.bbsdocumentary.com/AAA/AAA/CBBS/parttime.txt.

26. "What Might Be Called CACHE's On Line Graffitti (COG)."

27. John J. Welch, "Item 20: To Ward & Randy: History of CBBS???," November 9, 1986, archived at http://textfiles.com/bbs/CBBS/history.cbbs.

28. Hacking for the sake of hacking mirrors the pursuit of "contacts" of ham radio operators, who pursued two-way wireless communication for the sake of making contact itself rather than exchanging messages. See Susan J. Douglas, *Listening In: Radio and the American Imagination: From Amos 'n' Andy and Edward R. Murrow to Wolfman Jack and Howard Stern* (New York: Times Books, 1999), 333. Also Kristen Haring, "The 'Freer Men' of Ham Radio: How a Technical Hobby Provided Social and Spatial Distance," *Technology and Culture* 44, no. 4 (2003): 734–61, https://doi.org/10.1353/tech.2003.0164.

29. "What Might Be Called CACHE's On Line Graffitti (COG)."

30. Initially titled *The CACHE Flash*.

31. The club formally announced its name, CACHE, in a note to *Byte* magazine published in 1976. "Clubs and Newsletters," *Byte*, February 1976. The number for the hotline was published in the monthly newsletter. *CACHE Register* 6, no. 1 (January 1981). Christensen mentioned the hotline in a post on CBBS in 1986. Welch, "Item 20."

32. In particular, Christensen hoped that club members would use the bulletin board to "modem in" new articles for the newsletter. Welch, "Item 20."

33. Joe Kasser, "The Sky's the Limit," *Byte*, November 1978.

34. CBBS began to take on a mythical status while it was still in operation. In a post to CBBS from 1986, Ward Christensen remarked, "I have told [the origin story] so many times I'm burned out." Indeed, Christensen tried to resist the valorization of his system by downplaying the significance of being first: "It was no big deal. I just happened to be first. It wasn't great, or even very good—but it was first." For a full transcript of Christensen's remarks from 1986, see Welch, "Item 20."

35. For example, see Robert X. Cringely, *Accidental Empires: How the Boys of Silicon Valley Make Their Millions, Battle Foreign Competition, and Still Can't Get a Date* (Reading, MA: Addison-Wesley, 1991).

36. Welch, "Item 20."

37. For more on this case in the context of ARPANET, see Fenwick McKelvey and Kevin Driscoll, "ARPANET and Its Boundary Devices: Modems, IMPs, and the Inter-structuralism of Infrastructures," *Internet Histories* 3, no. 1 (January 2, 2019): 31–50, https://doi.org/10.1080/24701475.2018.1548138.

38. Michel Carpentier, Sylviane Farnoux-Toporkoff, Christian Garric, and C. P Skrimshire, *Telecommunications in Transition* (Chichester, UK: Wiley, 1992), 1.

39. Jared Barton and Tyler Watts, "'I Can't Drive 55': The Economics of the CB Radio Phenomenon," *Independent Review* 15, no. 3 (2011): 383–97.

40. The Amateur Radio Relay League described the adoption of VHF equipment in the 1970s as a "revolution" for ham radio operators. See Jim Maxwell (W6CF), "Amateur Radio: 100 Years of Discovery," *QST*, January 2000, http://www.arrl.org/files/file/About%20ARRL/Ham_Radio_100_Years.pdf.

41. Kevin Gotkin, "When Computers Were Amateur," *IEEE Annals of the History of Computing* 36, no. 2 (April 2014): 4–14, https://doi.org/10.1109/MAHC.2014.32.

42. See Patrick Parsons, *Blue Skies: A History of Cable Television* (Philadelphia: Temple University Press, 2008), 19–21; Paula Petrik, "The Youngest Fourth Estate: The Novelty Toy Printing Press and Adolescence, 1870–1886," in *Small Worlds: Children and Adolescents in America, 1850–1950*, ed. Elliott West and Paula Petrik (Lawrence: University Press of Kansas, 1992), 125–42; Christian Sandvig, "Disorderly Infrastructure and the Role of Government," *Government Information Quarterly* 23, nos. 3–4 (2006): 503–6, doi:10.1016/j.giq.2006.07.008.

43. Kristen Haring, *Ham Radio's Technical Culture* (Cambridge, MA: MIT Press, 2008).

44. In amateur radio, "contact" is a noun that refers to the successful exchange of call signs between two radio operators. For more on the cultural practices, as well as the racial and gendered dimensions, of radio hobbyist communication, see Susan J. Douglas, *Inventing American Broadcasting, 1899–1922* (Baltimore: Johns Hopkins University Press, 1987); Douglas, *Listening In*; Jonathan Sterne, *The Audible Past: Cultural Origins of Sound Reproduction* (Durham, NC: Duke University Press, 2003); Haring, *Ham Radio's Technical Culture*; Art M. Blake, "Audible Citizenship and Audiomobility: Race, Technology, and CB Radio," *American Quarterly* 63, no. 3 (September 1, 2011): 531–53.

45. See Douglas, *Inventing American Broadcasting*; Haring, *Ham Radio's Technical Culture*.

46. Douglas, *Inventing American Broadcasting*, 216–39.

47. Maxim is a central figure in the history of amateur radio in the United States. See Chris Codella, "Hiram Percy Maxim," *QST*, February 2014.

48. Douglas, *Inventing American Broadcasting*, 297.

49. Haring, *Ham Radio's Technical Culture*, 147–48.

50. Gary Pearce, "VHF/UHF-FM, Repeaters, Digital Voice and Data," in *The ARRL Operating Manual for Radio Amateurs*, 9th ed. (Newington, CT: Amateur Radio Relay League, 2010), 2-1–2-29.

51. One notable transceiver produced in this period was the 1969 Motorola HT-220. The HT-220 was a large handheld radio that was used as a prop in numerous police dramas on television and in film. The radio continues to be used today, and a small memorial page is kept online by the HT-220 Preservation Society. "HT-220 Page," Michael Wright Page, accessed February 9, 2014, http://mfwright.com/HT220.html.

52. The size of a transmitting antenna scales proportionally with the wavelength of the signals to be transmitted. While some hams rejected the integrated circuit as an inscrutable black box that resisted tinkering, others welcomed the lower cost of equipment and began to experiment with new applications for the smaller scale components.

53. Pearce, "VHF/UHF-FM, Repeaters, Digital Voice and Data," 2-2.

54. Tom Szerencse (WB9VTZ), "The History of ECRA Repeaters in Elkhart County," Elkhart County Radio Association, accessed February 9, 2014, http://web.archive.org/web/20090926025125/http://www.ecra.us/history.html.

55. Szerencse.

56. More recently, hams have begun to use internet gateways to "link" various repeaters into decentralized networks such as WinLink that cover a much larger area. Although this activity is beyond the scope of the present discussion, it is nevertheless a fitting demonstration of the ongoing culture of innovation in amateur telecommunications.

57. Haring, *Ham Radio's Technical Culture*, 154.

58. Radio Shack, *Radio Shack Catalog* (1965).

59. Ernest Dickinson, "Business Tunes In on Citizens Band: Giants Enter Booming Market for 2-Way Sets," *New York Times*, March 7, 1976, sec. Business & Finance.

60. Radio Shack, *Radio Shack Catalog* (1975); Dickinson, "Business Tunes In on Citizens Band."

61. Dickinson, "Business Tunes In on Citizens Band."

62. "Gay Ballad Is Joined by 'Savage,'" *Billboard*, November 13, 1976.

63. Harvey A. Daniels, "Breaker, Break, Broke: Citizens Band in the Classroom," *English Journal* 65, no. 9 (December 1, 1976): 55, doi:10.2307/815750.

64. Daniels, 55.

65. Art M. Blake, "Audible Citizenship and Audiomobility: Race, Technology, and CB Radio," *American Quarterly* 63, no. 3 (September 1, 2011): 534.

66. Blake.

67. Shawn D. Lewis, "10-4, Bro," *Ebony*, October 1976.

68. Blake, "Audible Citizenship and Audiomobility," 533.

69. Robert Rosenthal, "Busing Foe: South Boston Ready to Defend Itself," *Boston Globe*, April 21, 1976; Blake, "Audible Citizenship and Audiomobility," 544–45.

70. Haring, *Ham Radio's Technical Culture*, 157.

71. The ham and CB radio populations were not as distinct as my narrative might suggest. Dave Hall (N3CVJ) recalls on a webpage about his CB radio

experiences that CBers with "some knowledge and a lot of free time" were capable of setting up a CB repeater in the late 1970s. Hall, "CB Repeater," Spew
Radio Inc., accessed February 11, 2014, http://home.ptd.net/~n3cvj/repeater
.htm.

72. Evidence of the resonance across these activities appears regularly in their archives, e.g., the first nontechnical mailing list on ARPANET was SF-LOVERS
for fans of science fiction. Kristen Haring has also explored some connections among twentieth-century technical cultures in the United States. See
Katie Hafner and Matthew Lyon, *Where Wizards Stay Up Late: The Origins of
the Internet* (New York: Simon and Schuster, 1996), 201; Haring, "'Freer Men'
of Ham Radio."

73. Ham radio mentors are known as "Elmers," and mentoring is known as
"Elmering." For more on the origin of this aspect of ham radio culture, see
Rod Newkirk, "How's DX," *QST*, March 1971.

74. Haring, "'Freer Men' of Ham Radio."

75. Martin Campbell-Kelly and Daniel D. Garcia-Swartz, "Economic Perspectives
on the History of the Computer Time-Sharing Industry, 1965–1985," *IEEE
Annals of the History of Computing* 30, no. 1 (January 2008): 16–36, https://doi
.org/10.1109/MAHC.2008.3.

76. Joy Lisi Rankin, *A People's History of Computing in the United States* (Cambridge, MA: Harvard University Press, 2018); Rankin, "From the Mainframes
to the Masses: A Participatory Computing Movement in Minnesota Education," *Information & Culture* 50, no. 2 (May 1, 2015): 197–216, https://doi.org/
10.7560/IC50204; Rankin, "Toward a History of Social Computing: Children,
Classrooms, Campuses, and Communities," *IEEE Annals of the History of
Computing* 36, no. 2 (2014): 86–88.

77. *Hackers: Wizards of the Electronic Age*, dir. Fabrice Florin, 1984, DVD, http://
hackersvideo.com; Campbell-Kelly and Aspray, *Computer*.

78. On the cultural values of early hobby computing, see E. Petrick, "Imagining
the Personal Computer: Conceptualizations of the Homebrew Computer
Club 1975–1977," *IEEE Annals of the History of Computing* 39, no. 4 (October
2017): 27–39, https://doi.org/10.1109/MAHC.2018.1221045.

79. M. Mitchell Waldrop, *The Dream Machine: J. C. R. Licklider and the Revolution
That Made Computing Personal* (New York: Penguin Books, 2001), 339.

80. Haring, *Ham Radio's Technical Culture*.

81. "73" is an affectionate salutation in the on-air argot of amateur radio.

82. Wayne Green (W2NSD/1), "Computers Are Here—Are You Ready?," *73*, October 1975.

83. In 1969, Ed Roberts and Forest M. Mims III, a pair of Air Force engineers
working out of the Weapons Lab in Albuquerque, cofounded Micro Instru-
mentation and Telemetry Systems (MITS) to provide electronics kits for
model rocket builders. Mims went on to create an influential workbook titled
Getting Started in Electronics that sold through Radio Shack and has remained
in print for more than thirty years. More information about early MITS

products may be found on Mims's personal home page: "About Forrest M. Mims III," Forrest Mims's website, accessed February 18, 2014, http://www .forrestmims.org/biography.html.

84. The parallel rows of lights and switches on the Altair resembled several variants of the front panels in the DEC PDP-11 series of minicomputers. See also Waldrop, *Dream Machine*, 430.

85. The article was authored by Ed Roberts and Microsoft founder Bill Gates, misattributed as "William Yates." See H. Edward Roberts and William Yates, "Altair 8800 Minicomputer, Part 1," *Popular Electronics*, January 1975.

86. Early microcomputer programmers wrote their code by hand using a set of mnemonic "opcodes." For example, the 8080 machine language instruction for halting a program might be the binary value 1111111, but the programmer would use the mnemonic "HLT" when planning out a program. To prepare the program for execution on the Altair, programmers referred to a printed table of opcodes and machine language instructions to translate their program into a list of binary numbers. See Charles Petzold, *Code: The Hidden Language of Computer Hardware and Software* (Redmond, WA: Microsoft Press, 1999), 236.

87. Following the *Popular Electronics* feature, MITS was overwhelmed by orders for the Altair kit and shortly developed a reputation for slow shipping and poor customer service. Further, those who received their kits were likely to become frustrated by the complexity of the kit and the arduous programming experience. To satisfy the needs of this newfound customer base, MITS soon announced bundled systems that included printers, disk drives, tape readers, and keyboards along with the Altair. Unfortunately for MITS, the marketplace had grown more competitive, and it had largely lost its advantage. See also Campbell-Kelly and Aspray, *Computer*; Waldrop, *Dream Machine*, 431.

88. Martin Campbell-Kelly, *From Airline Reservations to Sonic the Hedgehog: A History of the Software Industry* (Cambridge, MA: MIT Press, 2003), 201–28.

89. Rankin, *People's History of Computing in the United States*; Nick Montfort et al., *10 PRINT CHR$(205.5+RND(1));:GOTO 10* (Cambridge, MA: MIT Press, 2013).

90. John Evans Williams (W2BFD), "The Story of Amateur Radio Teletype," *QST*, October 1948.

91. Stanley P. Levy (WB6SQU), "A Morse to RTTY Converter—Using a Microprocessor," in *Hobby Computers Are Here!*, ed. Wayne Green (W2NSD/1) (Peterborough, NH: 73 Publications, 1976), 78–81.

92. Sally O'Dell (KB1O), "Clubs and Computers: A Simple Interface (Club Corner)," *QST*, July 1983.

93. David P. Allen (W1UKZ), "Computer Net Info (Strays)," *QST*, November 1980.

94. The W6TRW swap meet continues to operate monthly in the parking lot of a Northrop Grumman building in Redondo Beach, California. In 1967, this location also served as the setting for an Earth colony on the fictional planet

of Deneva Prime in season 1, episode 29, of *Star Trek*. For more information, see W6TRW Swap Meet, accessed February 18, 2014, http://www.w6trw
.com/swapmeet/index.htm; Memory Alpha, "TRW Space and Defense Park,"
accessed June 4, 2021, https://memory-alpha.fandom.com/wiki/TRW_Space
_and_Defense_Park.

95. Christensen and Suess, "Hobbyist Computerized Bulletin Board."
96. Lary L. Myers, *How to Create Your Own Computer Bulletin Board* (Blue Ridge
Summit, PA: TAB Books, 1983), 202–8.
97. Between 1975 and 1980, 78 of 675 reader letters published in *Byte* mentioned
modems, telecommunications, or radio.

CHAPTER 3. BUILDING AN INTERNET FOR EVERYONE

1. Denise Caruso, "Networking Bulletin Boards," *InfoWorld*, August 27, 1984.
2. John Madill, "FidoNet History," July 30, 1993, archived by Metro Olografix at
http://www.olografix.org/gubi/estate/archivio/fido/fido.htm.
3. Tom Jennings's communication utilities were called Minitel and Telink. The
name "Minitel," occasionally styled "MiniTel," was just a historical coinci-
dence with the French videotex platform.
4. Tom Jennings, "FOSSIL Drivers' Ancient History," *FidoNews*, February 3,
1992, http://www.bbsdocumentary.com/library/PROGRAMS/NETWORK/
FOSSIL/.
5. Madill, "FidoNet History."
6. Tom Jennings, "Some Preliminary Ideas for the FidoNet," April 30,
1984, archived at http://www.textfiles.com/bbs/FIDONET/JENNINGS/
STANDARDS/fidonet.doc.txt.
7. There is some inconsistency in the precise date of this first connection,
but it seems to have happened around May or June 1984. FidoNet on the
Internet, "FOTIs FidoNet Timeline Page," accessed October 12, 2019, http://
www.textfiles.com/fidonet-on-the-internet/tl.htm; "The International FidoNet—15,649 Bulletin Boards Worldwide with a Connection," *Boardwatch*,
October 1992.
8. Tom Jennings, "The History of FidoNet: An Interview with Tom Jennings,"
interview by Marge Robbins, October 1993, archived at http://www.textfiles
.com/bbs/FIDONET/JENNINGS/HISTORY/tomj_mrobbins.txt.
9. Ben Baker, "An Informal History of FidoNet," *FidoNews*, November 23, 1987.
10. Baker.
11. Baker.
12. For a deeper dive on "telephonic" histories of technology, see Gabriele Balbi
and Christiane Berth, "Towards a Telephonic History of Technology," *History and Technology* 35, no. 2 (April 3, 2019): 105–14, https://doi.org/10.1080/
07341512.2019.1652959.
13. Fenwick McKelvey and Kevin Driscoll, "ARPANET and Its Boundary Devices:
Modems, IMPs, and the Inter-structuralism of Infrastructures," *Internet Histories* 3, no. 1 (January 2, 2019): 31–50, https://doi.org/10.1080/24701475.2018
.1548138.

14. The details of the Numbering Plan were first circulated outside of AT&T in a series of memos to the United States Independent Telephone Association (USITA) in 1945. The memos were then published in *Telephony*, the USITA trade magazine, to inform independent telephone companies about the coming changes. In accordance with the universal ambitions of the Numbering Plan, it provided codes for the independent companies, and the new AT&T switching equipment was designed to be interoperable with the older "manual" switchboards in use at many independent exchange offices. Cooperation with independents was essential for the Bell System to convey a sense of universality to North American telephone subscribers. "Nationwide Operator Toll Dialing (Part 1 of 5)," *Telephony* 130 (January 12, 1946): 13–26; "Nationwide Operator Toll Dialing (Part 2 of 5)," *Telephony* 130 (January 19, 1946): 28–30, 46; "Nationwide Operator Toll Dialing (Part 3 of 5)," *Telephony* 130 (January 26, 1946): 16–18, 35; "Nationwide Operator Toll Dialing (Part 4 of 5)," *Telephony* 130 (February 2, 1946): 18–19; "Nationwide Operator Toll Dialing (Part 5 of 5)," *Telephony* 130 (February 2, 1946): 20–26.

15. Billy Wildhack, *Erotic Connections* (Corte Madera, CA: Waite Group, 1994), 21.

16. One rather tedious approach to discovery was to write a program that would systematically dial every telephone number in a given range and log whether a modem answered at the other end. This practice was known colloquially as "war dialing" after it was dramatized in the 1983 film *WarGames*.

17. Tom Jennings, "Fido's Operating Manual," November 1, 1984, archived at http://www.textfiles.com/bbs/FIDONET/JENNINGS/PROGRAMS/FIDO-10/.

18. Tom Jennings, "FidoNet History and Operation," February 8, 1985, archived at http://www.textfiles.com/bbs/FIDONET/JENNINGS/HISTORY/fidohist.1.txt.

19. Jennings.

20. Baker, "Informal History of FidoNet."

21. Jennings, "Fido's Operating Manual."

22. Jennings.

23. Notably, the FidoNet crew were not the first BBS enthusiasts to imagine building a computerized relay network. In 1993, Jennings relayed a story to the historian Marge Robbins about a system that predated FidoNet: "There was a system in Andover Mass run by Wayne something? Andover CNODE it was a CP/M-80 (Zilog Z80) machine he had a whole bunch of harddisks and a lot of programs to download. and about 8 logical drives like from A: to H: or something. He had a MINICBBS BBS (stripped-down version of CBBS . . . utterly minimal) that he would run as a separate program from it. Some user of his system had this idea about what if we had bulletin boards that just hopped a message across the country by going local call to local call to local call. And while it was an intriguing idea, when you stop to think about it mindboggling and ridiculous. But it got some tiny amount of message traffic and of course we put it away like all ideas like that, but it kinda stuck with me." Jennings, "History of FidoNet."

24. Jennings.

25. "The Birth of BYTEnet," *Byte*, October 1984.

26. Cost estimates based on commentary in Tom Jennings, "European Fido," *FidoNews*, December 24, 1984.

27. Tom Jennings, "The First FidoNet Newsletter," *FidoNews*, December 1, 1984.

28. Jennings.

29. Thom Henderson, "Electronic Hate," *FidoNews*, May 13, 1985.

30. Fido sysops jokingly called it "The Snooze." See Michael Schuyler, "Big Dummy's Guide to FidoNet," FidoNet.us, 1992, http://www.fidonet.us/ dummyguide.html.

31. Tom Jennings and others, "FidoNet History," August 20, 1985, archived at http://www.textfiles.com/bbs/FIDONET/JENNINGS/HISTORY/fidohist .2.txt.

32. Plutopia News Network, "Tom Jennings Interview (1993)," *Plutopia Blog*, April 9, 2018, https://plutopia.io/tom-jennings-interview-1993/.

33. Jennings, "Fido's Operating Manual."

34. Tom Jennings, "As you all probably know by now . . . ," *FidoNews*, March 18, 1985.

35. Thom Henderson, "The New Kid on the Block," *FidoNews*, April 1, 1985; Henderson, "Change of Command," *FidoNews*, March 25, 1985; Henderson, "ARC? What's an ARC?," *FidoNews*, October 14, 1985.

36. Henderson, "New Kid on the Block."

37. Tom Jennings, "Hot News," *FidoNews*, January 16, 1985.

38. Ben Baker, "New Look for FidoNet," *FidoNews*, April 22, 1985.

39. Baker.

40. Tom Jennings, "Fido #1 in Net # . . . ," *FidoNews*, April 22, 1985.

41. "FidoNet, Sidekick, Apple, Get Organized!, And Handle," *Byte*, October 1984, 357.

42. "International FidoNet—15,649 Bulletin Boards."

43. Jennings, "Fido #1 in Net #."

44. Baker, "Informal History of FidoNet."

45. Jennings and others, "FidoNet History."

46. Thom Henderson, "Special Issue," *FidoNews*, April 22, 1985.

47. Jennings, "Fido #1 in Net #," 1.

48. Under the new system, net and node numbers could range from 1 to 32,767, the maximum value of a short signed integer in the C programming language. See Jennings, "Fido #1 in Net #"; Ken Kaplan, "Obtaining a Fido Net Number," *FidoNews*, June 3, 1985. For a more detailed explanation of the net/ node system, see also Schuyler, "Big Dummy's Guide to FidoNet."

49. Jennings and others, "FidoNet History."

50. "In the Crowd: Tom Jennings," *Thrasher*, November 1986.

51. Ben Baker, "Coordinators List," *FidoNews*, June 10, 1985.

52. "In the Crowd: Tom Jennings."

53. Ben Baker and Ken Kaplan, "The Duties of a Network or Region Coordinator," *FidoNews*, June 3, 1985.

54. Van Olmstead, "Sauntering Sysops Batman," *FidoNews*, July 22, 1985.

55. Olmstead.

56. Not only had FidoNet reached the 250 node ceiling, but Ken's wife, Sally, had just given birth to a son. A heartfelt notice in *FidoNews* dubbed him "the first FidoBaby" and joked that Ken hadn't yet given him a node number. The young Kaplan's first birthday was also added to the *FidoNews* calendar in 1986, and in 1990, Kaplan noted that his son and multinet Fido were the same age. Baker, "New Look for FidoNet"; "The First FidoBaby," *FidoNews*, June 10, 1985; "The Interrupt Stack," *FidoNews*, April 28, 1986; Ken Kaplan, "Editorial: Happy Birthday FidoNet," *FidoNews*, June 11, 1990.

57. See Thom Henderson, "Any Day Now," *FidoNews*, May 6, 1985; Henderson, "Fido 10i," *FidoNews*, May 20, 1985.

58. Tom Jennings, "Fido's Operating Manual, Fourth Edition," August 1985, archived at http://www.textfiles.com/bbs/FIDONET/JENNINGS/PROGRAMS/FIDO-10/.

59. Ben Baker, "GO! GO! GO!—June 12 Is IT," *FidoNews*, June 10, 1985.

60. Baker, "Informal History of FidoNet."

61. Baker.

62. Thom Henderson, "Editorial: Future Directions," *FidoNews*, November 11, 1985.

63. Baker, "Informal History of FidoNet."

64. Nodelist data in this paragraph are based on an independent analysis of the nodelist published on Friday, October 3, 1986. In March 1986, Ben Baker announced that the nodelist had grown too large to distribute weekly. Instead, they planned to distribute a "NODEDIFF" file representing only those entries that had changed since the last major update. A special utility program was required to update the local nodelist. Ben Baker, "New NODELIST Distribution Method," *FidoNews*, March 3, 1986; Ben Baker, Ken Kaplan, and Henk Wevers, eds., "The International FidoNet Nodelist, Day Number 276," International FidoNet Association, October 3, 1986, http://www.textfiles.com/fidonet-on-the-internet/n1986/nodelist.276.

65. Tom Jennings, "Editorial," *FidoNews*, December 16, 1985.

66. Jennings.

67. Vin McLellan, "Out of the Doghouse," *Digital Review*, August 1985, fido00231.nws.

68. Ken Shackelford, "Fido BBS Christmas Wish List (Early)," *FidoNews*, October 14, 1985.

69. Richard Polunsky, "Fido Catalog Author Seeks Heko," *FidoNews*, April 14, 1986; Polunsky, "Fido Utility Catalog," *FidoNews*, May 5, 1986.

70. Tom Jennings, "HOMOCORE Issues 1 through 7," Sensitive Research, accessed June 15, 2021, https://web.archive.org/web/20210618022530/https://www.sr-ix.com/Etc/HOMOCORE/index.html; Jennings, "Shred of Dignity Skaters Union, ca. 1989," Sensitive Research, accessed June 15, 2021, https://web.archive.org/web/20210618022646/https://www.sr-ix.com/Etc/myQueerSF/Shipley/index.html.

71. Jack Boulware and Silke Tudor, "Shred of Dignity," Gimme Something Better, 2009, http://gimmesomethingbetter.com/excerpts/shred-of-dignity. See also Boulware and Tudor, *Gimme Something Better: The Profound, Progressive, and Occasionally Pointless History of Bay Area Punk from Dead Kennedys to Green Day* (New York: Penguin Books, 2009).

72. Jennings, "[FidoNet Is Growing]."

73. Jennings.

74. Jennings.

75. Jennings.

76. Jennings; Robert Briggs, "Creating Fido Source," *FidoNews*, April 14, 1985; Briggs, "Fido Re-write," *FidoNews*, April 29, 1985; Bob Hartman, "This is simply a request for information . . . ," *FidoNews*, July 15, 1985; Paul Kelly and Jim Lynn, "A Few Ideas about the Rewrite of Fido," *FidoNews*, July 22, 1985; Hartman, "Fido Re-write," *FidoNews*, July 29, 1985; John Plocher, "More Fido Rewrite Ideas," *FidoNews*, December 30, 1985.

77. Bob Hartman, "Rover, Rovermsg, Renum, and the UN*X Gateway," *FidoNews*, December 9, 1985.

78. The meaning of "packet" and "packet switching" in early FidoNet documentation is different from packet-switching networks like CYCLADES or ARPANET. Whereas packet-switching usually refers to real-time "datagram" protocols such as TCP/IP, FidoNet "packets" were compressed bundles of mail transmitted through the store-and-forward network. "For historical reasons, the term 'packet' is used in FidoNet to represent a bundle of messages, as opposed to the more common use as a unit of communication, which is known as a block in FidoNet." Randy Bush, "A Basic FidoNet(tm) Technical Standard, Draft FSC001-9," FidoNet Technical Standards Committee, December 27, 1987, http://ftsc.org/docs/fsc-0001.000.

79. During the production of *BBS: The Documentary*, Jason Scott began collecting BBS programs with an emphasis on software written before 1995. As of 2020, the collection includes 857 BBS programs for thirty-seven platforms. See Scott, BBS Software Directory, accessed August 4, 2020, http://software.bbsdocumentary.com/.

80. See Susan Leigh Star and Martha Lampland, "Reckoning with Standards," in *Standards and Their Stories: How Quantifying, Classifying, and Formalizing Practices Shape Everyday Life*, ed. Martha Lampland and Susan Leigh Star (Ithaca, NY: Cornell University Press, 2009), 3–34.

81. Alexander R. Galloway, *Protocol: How Control Exists after Decentralization* (Cambridge, MA: MIT Press, 2004).

82. See Andrew L. Russell, "'Rough Consensus and Running Code' and the Internet-OSI Standards War," *IEEE Annals of the History of Computing* 28, no. 3 (2006): 48–61; Russell, "OSI: The Internet That Wasn't," *IEEE Spectrum*, July 30, 2013, http://spectrum.ieee.org/computing/networks/osi-the-internet-that-wasnt; Russell, *Open Standards and the Digital Age: History, Ideology, and Networks* (New York: Cambridge University Press, 2014).

83. Caruso, "Networking Bulletin Boards."

84. In 2014, Wynn Wagner III changed his name to Sven Andréas Wallin. He continued to use "Wynn Wagner" as a pen name. For consistency, I will use his former name when referring to events from the past and in citations to his writing. See Sven Andréas Wallin, "Naming Convention," *SAW* (blog), February 1, 2014. http://web.archive.org/web/20160903205902/http://www .svenandreaswallin.com/tag/wynn-wagner/.

85. Wynn Wagner, "History of Opus-CBCS," July 7, 1997, http://web.archive.org/ web/19970707073934/http://www.global.org/opus/history/opushist.html; Wagner, "OPUS Computer-Based Conversation System Version 1.0," ed. John Miller, June 14, 1987, http://cd.textfiles.com/masterdisc/SS/CMM/0004/ OPUSDOC.TXT.

86. Wagner, "History of Opus-CBCS."

87. For a more detailed examination of BBS graphics for the IBM PC platform, see Michael A. Hargadon, "Like City Lights, Receding: ANSi Artwork and the Digital Underground, 1985–2000" (MA thesis, Concordia University, 2011), http://mhargadon.ca/media/mhargadon-thesis.pdf.

88. Wagner, "OPUS Computer-Based Conversation System."

89. Contact information for AIDS-related charities was hard-coded into the Opus executable from its first release in 1986. Initially, Wagner directed funds to the Shanti Project in San Francisco. Later, he asked that donations be sent to AmFAR in Los Angeles. To comply with the donation require- ment, European Opus users found local AIDS-related charities. Although the exact number of donations are not known, one estimate places the number in the range of $1 million. Wagner notes that "Opus Sysops" were listed in the Shanti Project newsletter alongside large corporate donors. See Wagner, "History of Opus-CBCS"; John R. Selig, "Sit Down, Shut-Up and Row: Wynn Wagner Helps Build the HIV/AIDS Information Superhighway," John Selig's website, March 2001, http://www.johnselig.com/commentary/row/.

90. Wagner, "History of Opus-CBCS."

91. Jennings previously documented the message and packet formats along with the "lower layers of the protocol." Tom Jennings, "FidoNet Electronic Mail Protocol," October 20, 1984, archived at http://www.textfiles.com/bbs/ FIDONET/JENNINGS/STANDARDS/fidomail.doc.txt.

92. Randy Bush, "FidoNet Standards Committee," *FidoNews*, July 28, 1986.

93. Thom Henderson, "What a Weekend!," *FidoNews*, August 25, 1986.

94. Allen Miller, "International Fido Conference, August 14–17, 1986," *FidoNews*, September 8, 1986.

95. Thom Henderson, "Editorial: Double Dawns," *FidoNews*, November 10, 1986.

96. Henderson.

97. An archive of documents produced by the FidoNet Technical Standards Committee since 1987 is available on the public web. See FidoNet Technical Standards Committee, "FTSC Documents," accessed August 5, 2020, http:// ftsc.org/docs/.

98. For a closer look at the decision-making practices embedded in the internet community's "Request for Comments" system, see Sandra Braman, "Internet RFCs as Social Policy: Network Design from a Regulatory Perspective," *Proceedings of the American Society for Information Science and Technology* 46, no. 1 (January 1, 2009): 1–29, https://doi.org/10.1002/meet.2009.1450460254; Braman, "The Interpenetration of Technical and Legal Decision-Making for the Internet," *Information, Communication & Society* 13, no. 3 (April 1, 2010): 309–24, https://doi.org/10.1080/13691180903473814; Braman, "The Framing Years: Policy Fundamentals in the Internet Design Process, 1969–1979," *Information Society* 27, no. 5 (October 1, 2011): 295–310, https://doi.org/10.1080/01972243.2011.607027.

99. Bush, "Basic FidoNet(tm) Technical Standard."

100. Bush.

101. Bush.

102. Bush was an ecumenical technician and later brought his expertise to the Internet Engineering Task Force.

103. Notably, the message-storage format used by Fido in 1987 assigned only two characters to the year and was, therefore, not Y2K compliant. For more on the consequences of this and similar design choices, see Dylan Mulvin, "Distributing Liability: The Legal and Political Battles of Y2K," *IEEE Annals of the History of Computing* 42, no. 2 (July 2020): 26–37, doi:10.1109/MAHC.2020.2973630.

104. SEAdog reflected Henderson's opinion that Fido BBS should be broken up into interoperable components. See Thom Henderson, "Public Domain Fido," *FidoNews*, April 14, 1985.

105. In 1987, the nodelist included several codes describing the technical features of each node. The code "#CM" meant "Accepts mail 24 hours per day." The nodelist published on October 16 included 1,880 unique telephone numbers, of which 1,015 included the "#CM" code. See FidoNet on the Internet, "FidoNet Nodelist," October 16, 1987, http://www.textfiles.com/fidonet-on-the-internet/n1987/nodelist.289. The December 1992 nodelist included 18,238 unique telephone numbers, and 15,469 were marked "CM." See FidoNet on the Internet, "FidoNet Nodelist," December 25, 1992, http://www.textfiles.com/fidonet-on-the-internet/n1992/nodediff.360.

106. FrontDoor evolved from a simple add-on utility for Fido into a complete electronic mail system like SEAdog. FrontDoor was originally created by Joaquim Homrighausen, a teenaged programmer living in Sweden. Commercial interest in FrontDoor enabled Homrighausen to travel and work internationally, though his employers and benefactors were not always satisfied. Homrighausen was an occasional contributor to *FidoNews*, and the rocky development of FrontDoor became a subject of gossip for several years. For one perspective, see Peter Adenauer, "fdhist.txt," FidoNet on the Internet, December 1993, http://www.textfiles.com/fidonet-on-the-internet/history/fdhis.txt.

107. The FidoNet addressing scheme referred to single-user nodes as "points." Points were not included on the nodelist. Instead, all mail destined for a

point was routed to a "boss node" that agreed to hold mail for the point. FidoNet point addresses are identifiable by a "dot" notation. For example, in 1987, Thom Henderson's FidoNet address was 1:107/6.1. All of his mail was routed through Node 6 in Net 107.

108. Comparisons between FidoNet and USENET were common in the 1980s, but Echomail provided several functions missing from USENET, such as the option to attach files to messages. For a technical comparison, see Jack Decker, "USENET vs. FidoNet—A Quick Comparison," *FidoNews*, February 24, 1992.

109. Caruso, "Networking Bulletin Boards," 31; Jennings, "Fido's Operating Manual."

110. Wynn Wagner, "History of Echomail," The Documentary Photo Album and Interview Page, accessed June 4, 2021, http://www.bbsdocumentary.com/photos/140wynn/FILES/echomail.txt.

111. Details on the first week of Echomail are based on the account included in the Opus 1.0 manual. See Wagner, "OPUS Computer-Based Conversation System," 96–97.

112. For more details regarding the technical procedures required to participate in Echomail at various points in its history, see John Dashner, "Ham Radio EchoMail Conference," *FidoNews*, October 13, 1986; Steve Bonine, "New-Sysop Orientation Information," International FidoNet Association, February 22, 1988, http://www.textfiles.com/bbs/FIDONET/JENNINGS/STANDARDS/newsysop.txt; Schuyler, "Big Dummy's Guide to FidoNet."

113. See Josh Gordon, "EchoMail and Host Routing: A Plea for Sanity," *FidoNews*, June 9, 1986; Ben Baker, "View from the Top: Echomail," *FidoNews*, June 30, 1986; David James, "EchoMail Can Help You Find Your Roots," *FidoNews*, July 28, 1986; Todd Looney, "Vietnam Veterans Bulletin Board," *FidoNews*, August 11, 1986; Mitch Kessler and Gerrie Blum, "Adult but Not X-Rated," *FidoNews*, August 18, 1986; "Notices," *FidoNews*, August 25, 1986; Todd Looney and Nancy Looney, "A Cry for Support! Dedicated to Vietnam Veterans," *FidoNews*, September 8, 1986; Jim Kay, "I wish to register a loud complaint . . . ," *FidoNews*, September 15, 1986; Randall Kobetich, "I.P.R. Echomail (Interpersonal Relationships)," *FidoNews*, September 22, 1986; Dashner, "Ham Radio EchoMail Conference"; Roger Smith, "Record Collectors EchoMail Conference," *FidoNews*, October 20, 1986.

114. Ben Baker and Tom Jennings seem to have observed this new user behavior independently of each other. Baker, "View from the Top: Echomail"; Jennings, "History of FidoNet."

115. The "origin" line was eventually standardized in the Echomail specification. See Bob Hartman, "FTS-0004 EchoMail Specification Version 3.31," FidoNet Technical Standards Committee, December 12, 1987, http://www.textfiles.com/fidonet-on-the-internet/fs/fts_0004.txt; Mark Kimes, "FSC-0068 A Proposed Replacement For FTS-0004," FidoNet Technical Standards Committee, December 13, 1992, http://www.textfiles.com/fidonet-on-the-internet/fs/fsc_0068.txt.

116. Echomail traffic was a recurring topic in *FidoNews* throughout 1986. See, for example, Gordon, "EchoMail and Host Routing"; J. Brad Hicks, "Echomail, Host-Routing, and Topology," *FidoNews*, June 23, 1986; Baker, "View from the Top: Echomail"; Butch Walker, "Echomail Coordinators," *FidoNews*, October 6, 1986.

117. Thom Henderson, "Editorial: One Year Later," *FidoNews*, March 31, 1986.

118. Wagner, "OPUS Computer-Based Conversation System."

119. Grey Mist, "Conference Report," *FidoNews*, August 25, 1986.

120. For more on the impact of Echomail, see the evolution of FidoNet policy from 1985 to 1986: FidoNet on the Internet, "FidoNet Policy and Procedures Guide Version 2," June 26, 1986, http://www.textfiles.com/fidonet-on-the -internet/history/policy2.txt; FidoNet on the Internet, "FidoNet Policy and Procedures Guide Version 3," October 24, 1986, http://www.textfiles.com/ fidonet-on-the-internet/history/policy3.doc.

121. Thomas Kenny, "I'm very interested in Echomail networking . . . ," *FidoNews*, May 12, 1986.

122. Thomas Kenny, "The First Echomail Conference List," *FidoNews*, March 9, 1987.

123. Kenny.

124. GAYNET and BIBLE were each created within weeks of the introduction of Echomail. Wynn Wagner, "History of Echomail," Opus CBCS, July 7, 1997, http://web.archive.org/web/19970707073957/http://www.global.org/opus/ history/echomail.html.

125. See Wagner's 1997 home page, archived here: http://web.archive.org/web/ 19970707042730/http://www.global.org/wynn/.

126. Baker, "View from the Top: Echomail."

127. Jennings, "History of FidoNet."

128. Bonine, "New-Sysop Orientation Information."

129. The Echomail backbone represented a different topology from FidoNet, with routing independent of the nodelist. See John Souvestre, George Peace, Jim Bodger, and John Johnson, "FidoNet Echomail Backbone," ONE BBSCON 1994, 1994, http://www.textfiles.com/fidonet-on-the-internet/zips/index.htm.

130. Michael G. Fuchs began publishing a list of echoes in 1988. The oldest copy I have been able to track down is from 1991. See Fuchs, "Echomail Conference List Report," FidoNet on the Internet, July 1, 1991, http://www.textfiles.com/ fidonet-on-the-internet/e1991/elist107.txt.

131. Ken Kaplan reported that the head of US Robotics in 1985 told him, "there ain't nobody out there who has anything that can match [FidoNet] right now." McLellan, "Out of the Doghouse"; see also Bob Hartman, "What Is the Story on 9600 Baud Modems," *FidoNews*, March 9, 1987.

132. For more details on PageSat and Planet Connect, providers of FidoNet by satellite, see Jason Scott, "Concepts: Services: Satellites," BBS Documentary Library, accessed February 4, 2021, http://www.bbsdocumentary.com/library/ CONCEPTS/SERVICES/SATELLITES/.

133. Roy Timberman, "FidoNet Basics," ONE BBSCON 1994, 1994, http://www.textfiles.com/fidonet-on-the-internet/zips/index.htm.

134. The earliest gateways between FidoNet and USENET were created in 1985. By the early 1990s, several Echomail conferences were mirrored on USENET as newsgroups. The "k12.*" hierarchy on USENET began as a FidoNet Echo. For more information on gateways, see Hartman, "Rover, Rovermsg, Renum, and the UN*X Gateway"; Tim Požar, "Late Night Software Is Proud to Announce UFGATE," *FidoNews*, January 30, 1989; Tom Jennings and Tim Požar, "Editorial," *FidoNews*, June 3, 1991.

135. See George Peace's comments on internet gateways here: Souvestre et al., "FidoNet Echomail Backbone."

136. Souvestre et al.

137. The creation and dissolution of the International FidoNet Association (IFNA) deserves closer historical attention than is possible here. In short, IFNA aimed to serve as an umbrella organization to represent the interests of BBS sysops, administer the nodelist, and support future efforts at standardization. It was explicitly inspired by the Amateur Radio Relay League (ARRL), a voluntary membership organization supporting ham radio operators.

138. In September 1988, an Alternet-FidoNet gateway went into service, carrying messages between the two networks. See David Dodell and Ben Baker, "FidoNet-Alternet Technical Agreement," *FidoNews*, September 5, 1988.

139. For a more comprehensive account of early othernets, see Ralph Merritt, "A Listing of Known Othernets," *FidoNews*, November 25, 1991; William J. Shefski, *Free Electronic Networks* (Rocklin, CA: Prima, 1994); Adam Michlin, "A Listing of Known Othernets," *NETLAND*, January 1, 1995, http://www.nfbnet.org/files/magazine/NETL0195.ZIP.

140. For access to historical nodelists, see FidoNet Net 282, "The FidoNet Nodelist Historical Analysis," February 2, 2005, http://web.archive.org/web/20170629084903/http://www.rxn.com/~net282/nodelist/; FidoNet on the Internet, "FOTIs FidoNet Nodelist/Nodediff Archive Page," 2004, http://textfiles.com/fidonet-on-the-internet/nodediff.htm.

141. Don Daniels, "IFNA Welcomes Poland to FidoNet," *FidoNews*, September 7, 1987; Jacek Szelozynski, "Something Exotic—Polish Traffic in Net/Echo Mail," *FidoNews*, June 5, 1989, fido00623.nws; Jan Stozek, "FidoNet in Poland," *Pigulki*, June 5, 1991, https://ftp.icm.edu.pl/packages/pigulki/pigulki6.pub.

142. Several issues of *Komputer* are available on the public web via the Internet Archive: https://archive.org/details/computermagazines.

143. Daniels, "IFNA Welcomes Poland to FidoNet"; Szelozynski, "Something Exotic."

144. Szelozynski, "Something Exotic."

145. FidoNet may take a more prominent role in the memories of longtime Russian internet users than in the United States or Europe. Prior to 1991, FidoNet was already functioning in cities throughout the Soviet Union, and

it continued to grow in the years after the fall of the Soviet Union. Anecdotal evidence such as the prevalence of the term "Фидонет" on Twitter and a comparative analysis of the relevant Russian Wikipedia entries underscores the important technological and cultural connections between the historical FidoNet and the Russian internet, or "Runet." For a closer look at the local histories of the internet in Russia, see the latest work of Polina Kolozaridi and the Club for Internet and Society Enthusiasts, e.g., Gregory Asmolov and Polina Kolozaridi, "The Imaginaries of RuNet," *Russian Politics* 2, no. 1 (March 9, 2017): 54–79, https://doi.org/10.1163/2451-8921-00201004; Polina Kolozaridi and Dmitry Muravyov, "The Narratives We Inherit: The Local and Global in Tomsk's Internet History," *Internet Histories* 4, no. 1 (January 2, 2020): 49–65, https://doi.org/10.1080/24701475.2020.1723980.

146. The debate took place over an Echomail conference for members of the International FidoNet Association. To date, I have not found records of this conference, so my characterization of the debate is based on a report published in *FidoNews*.

147. See Don Daniels, "IFNA Status Report for October 1987," *FidoNews*, October 5, 1987.

148. Randy Bush, "FidoNet: Technology, Tools, and History," *Communications of the ACM* 36, no. 8 (August 1993): 31–35, https://doi.org/10.1145/163381.163383.

149. For more details on Bush's gateways, see Randy Bush, "How FidoNet™ Tunnels the Internet," September 21, 1992, archived at http://www.textfiles.com/bbs/FIDONET/JENNINGS/STANDARDS/tunnel.msg.txt.

150. Travis Good, "Building the LATINO Net," *FidoNews*, November 9, 1987; Pablo Kleinman, "FidoNet en Sudamerica," *FidoNews*, November 23, 1987.

151. Juan Davila, Pablo Kleinman, and Travis Good worked together on the creation of Latin American network links for FidoNet, including economical routing paths, Spanish-language Echomail conferences, and region and zone coordination. See Good, "Building the LATINO Net"; Juan Davila, "Como Obtener un Número de Nodo en FidoNet 367 (RED de Puerto Rico)," *FidoNews*, February 1, 1988; Kleinman, "FidoNet en Sudamerica."

152. For the history of FidoNet in China, also known as "CFido," see Bo An, "Infrastructure, Amateurism, and Radical Networking: FidoNet in China (1995–1998)" (paper presented at Computer Networks Histories: Local, National and Transnational Perspectives, Università della Svizzera italiana, Lugano, Switzerland, 2017), https://www.infoclio.ch/en/computer-networks-histories-local-national-and-transnational-perspectives.

CHAPTER 4. SHARING FILES WITH STRANGERS

1. John Markoff, "In Focus: Personal Computers Communicate," *InfoWorld*, November 1, 1982.

2. For more variations of the name of Rich Schinnell's BBS, see the TEXTFILES.COM Historical BBS List: http://bbslist.textfiles.com/301/oldschool.html.

3. The members of the Communications SIG of the Capital PC User's Group (CPCUG) made several key contributions to the BBS infrastructure of the early 1980s. HostComm, the first program used by Schinnell's BBS, was written by Don Withrow on a dare. Schinnell bet him a "steak dinner" that he couldn't do it. While Withrow went on to sell copies of HostComm, several members of the SIG began to play with a program called RBBS-PC, written by Russ Lane. CPCUG shortly took over the development of RBBS, adding countless features and bug fixes. RBBS gained a reputation as an accessible, extensible host program and powered thousands of systems running on IBM-compatible PC hardware. Documentation of the early development of HostComm and RBBS is plentiful but scattered. See D. Thomas Mack and Jon Martin, "Remote Bulletin Board System for the IBM Personal Computer Version CPC12.1," BBS Software Directory, January 29, 1984, http://software .bbsdocumentary.com/IBM/DOS/RBBS/rbbs121.txt; D. Thomas Mack, Ken Goosens, and Doug Azzarito, "Remote Bulletin Board System for the Personal Computer Version 17.4: Technical Reference Guide," BBS Software Directory, June 21, 1992, http://software.bbsdocumentary.com/IBM/DOS/ RBBS/; Markoff, "In Focus"; Jason Scott, "A Story of RBBS (and PC-Talk, and Andrew Fluegelman)," ASCII by Jason Scott (blog), September 2, 2008, http://ascii.textfiles.com/archives/1440.

4. Rich Schinnell, "Rich's Ramblings January 2004," Rich Schinnell's website, January 2004, https://web.archive.org/web/20040211225245/http:// schinnell.org:80/ramb/ramb0401.html.

5. Markoff, "In Focus."

6. To PC owners in 1982, "free software" referred strictly to price, e.g., "free as in beer." The free and open-source software movement associated with the GNU Project and Free Software Foundation had not yet begun and did not cross over from UNIX systems to personal computing until the early 1990s.

7. "In Focus," InfoWorld, June 27, 1983.

8. Tom Shea, "Free Software," InfoWorld, June 27, 1983.

9. John Markoff, "Freeware Hunt with IBM PC Shoots Numerous Prey," Info-World, June 27, 1983.

10. Paul E. Ceruzzi, A History of Modern Computing (Cambridge, MA: MIT Press, 1998), 236.

11. Bill Gates, "An Open Letter to Hobbyists," Computer Notes, February 1976.

12. Kevin Driscoll, "Professional Work for Nothing: Software Commercialization and 'An Open Letter to Hobbyists,'" Information & Culture 50, no. 2 (May 1, 2015): 257–83, https://doi.org/10.7560/IC50207.

13. Alf Rehn, "The Politics of Contraband: The Honor Economies of the Warez Scene," Journal of Socio-Economics 33, no. 3 (July 1, 2004): 359–74, https://doi .org/10.1016/j.socec.2003.12.027; Markku Reunanen, "How Those Crackers Became Us Demosceners," WiderScreen 17, nos. 1–2 (April 15, 2014), http:// widerscreen.fi/numerot/2014-1-2/crackers-became-us-demosceners/; Gavin Mueller, "Piracy as Labour Struggle," TripleC: Communication, Capitalism &

Critique: Open Access Journal for a Global Sustainable Information Society 14, no. 1 (May 15, 2016): 333–45; Patryk Wasiak, "Telephone Networks, BBSes, and the Emergence of the Transnational 'Warez Scene,'" *History and Technology* 35, no. 2 (April 3, 2019): 177–94, https://doi.org/10.1080/07341512.2019 .1652432; safe crackers, "The Art of Warez," video, 2019, https://safecrackers .com/.

14. Kevin Driscoll and Joshua Diaz, "Endless Loop: A Brief History of Chiptunes," *Transformative Works and Cultures* 2 (March 15, 2009), https://doi .org/10.3983/twc.2009.096; Markku Reunanen, "Times of Change in the Demoscene: A Creative Community and Its Relationship with Technology" (University of Turku, Finland, 2017), http://doria32-kk.lib.helsinki.fi/handle/ 10024/130915.

15. For a closer look at the social implications of the ASCII character set, see Daniel Pargman and Jacob Palme, "ASCII Imperialism," in *Standards and Their Stories: How Quantifying, Classifying, and Formalizing Practices Shape Everyday Life*, ed. Martha Lampland and Susan Leigh Star (Ithaca, NY: Cornell University Press, 2008), 177–206.

16. American Telegraph and Telephone Company, "Data Set 103 A," March 1963; "Data Set 103F Interface Specification," *Bell System Data Communications Technical Reference*, American Telephone and Telegraph Company, May 1964; American Telegraph and Telephone Company, "Data Set 103A Type Identification and Operation," *Bell System Practices: Plant Series*, no. 5 (January 1967); American Telegraph and Telephone Company, "Data Set 103A Interface Specification," *Bell System Data Communications Technical Reference*, February 1967.

17. Charles P. Bourne and Trudi Bellardo Hahn, *A History of Online Information Services, 1963–1976* (Cambridge, MA: MIT Press, 2004).

18. Lee Felsenstein, "Build 'Pennywhistle': The Hobbyist's Modem," *Popular Electronics*, March 1976.

19. "Hayes Stack," *Byte*, June 1981.

20. "The Phone Link Acoustic Modem," *Byte*, December 1980.

21. "Cat Calls," *Byte*, December 1979.

22. "The Hayes Micromodem II," *Byte*, December 1981.

23. "Cat Calls."

24. The fantasy of a worldwide supercomputer has roots in a collection of speculative essays by the science fiction author H. G. Wells published in 1938. Although Wells had imagined the world brain as a precursor to global harmony, by the 1960s, the all-knowing supercomputer had become a symbol of antihuman technocracy. See H. G. Wells, *World Brain* (Garden City, NY: Doubleday, Doran, 1938); Kevin Driscoll, "From Punched Cards to 'Big Data': A Social History of Database Populism," *Communication +1* 1, no. 1 (August 29, 2012), http://scholarworks.umass.edu/cpo/vol1/iss1/4.

25. Stan Miastkowski, "Information Unlimited: The Dialog Information Retrieval Service," *Byte*, June 1981, 108.

26. Steven K. Roberts, "Online Information Retrieval: Promise and Problems," *Byte*, December 1981.

27. Miastkowski, "Information Unlimited," 108.

28. Outside the United States, public videotex projects such as Minitel in France and Telidon in Canada aimed to bring database access to the general public. By 1983, computer enthusiasts in the United States would have been hearing about videotex from a variety of sources, including a special issue of *Byte*. See "Videotex," *Byte*, July 1983; Julien Mailland and Kevin Driscoll, *Minitel: Welcome to the Internet* (Cambridge, MA: MIT Press, 2017); Valérie Schafer and Benjamin G. Thierry, *Le Minitel: L'enfance numérique de la France* (Paris: Nuvis, 2012).

29. Janet Abbate, *Inventing the Internet* (Cambridge, MA: MIT Press, 1999), 106–10; Joy Rankin, "From the Mainframes to the Masses: A Participatory Computing Movement in Minnesota Education," *Information & Culture* 50, no. 2 (May 1, 2015): 197–216, https://doi.org/10.7560/IC50204; Rankin, *A People's History of Computing in the United States* (Cambridge, MA: Harvard University Press, 2018).

30. Craig W. Vaughan, "Bulletin-Board Evolution Enhances Communication," *InfoWorld*, May 25, 1981, 33.

31. See Lary L. Myers, *How to Create Your Own Computer Bulletin Board* (Blue Ridge Summit, PA: TAB Books, 1983), 202–8.

32. Vaughan, "Bulletin-Board Evolution," 33.

33. Myers, *How to Create Your Own Computer Bulletin Board*.

34. Myers, 7.

35. Myers, 7.

36. Myers, 8–9.

37. Myers, 36.

38. Myers, 36.

39. Myers, 36–37.

40. On the political consequences of software defaults, see Wendy Hui Kyong Chun, *Control and Freedom: Power and Paranoia in the Age of Fiber Optics* (Cambridge, MA: MIT Press, 2006).

41. Wayne Bell, *WWIV*, version v3.21d (1986).

42. The documentation for later versions suggested that the "G-files" section might be divided into separate sections for "Communications files," "Humorous files," and "ANSI pictures." Wig De Moville, "The User's Guide to WWIV," *WWIV*, version 4.21a (1991).

43. Eric Katz and Rony Daher, *Oblivion/2 Bulletin Board System*, version 2.40 (Darkflame Enterprises, 1995).

44. Mindcrime, ANSI Gallery, version 1.00 (ACiDic, a division of ACiD Productions, 1994), ARTSCENE: The Textfiles.com Computer Art Collection, http://artscene.textfiles.com/acid/BBSMODS/.

45. Jason Scott, "Why I Prefer Textfiles," February 27, 1987, archived at http://www.textfiles.com/groups/OCTOTHORPE/whytext.oct.

46. The unauthorized transcription of text documents seems not to have at-tracted the legal scrutiny of publishers. One reason for this may have been the fact that many important texts were already in the public domain, so creating a digital copy was not only legal but socially valuable. Also, PCs were not yet seen as devices for reading long texts, and printing a long text would be costly; so publishers may have regarded digital bootlegging as mostly harmless.

47. "Plain text" is a colloquialism and not a technical term. In practice, "text" comes in a variety of formats, most of which are at least partially inter-operable. See Pargman and Palme, "ASCII Imperialism."

48. See Stephen Duncombe, *Notes from Underground: Zines and the Politics of Alternative Culture* (London: Verso, 1997); Megan Sapnar Ankerson, *Dot-Com Design: The Rise of a Usable, Social, Commercial Web* (New York: New York University Press, 2018); Kate Anastas, "Underground Newspapers: The Social Media Networks of the 1960s and 1970s," Mapping American Social Movements through the 20th Century, University of Washington, accessed February 6, 2020, http://depts.washington.edu/moves/altnews_geography .shtml.

49. Although computing was scarcely mentioned in *HOMOCORE*, Jennings ac-cepted submissions on floppy disk or cassette tape. In 2010, he told me that all of the text was formatted in raw T_EX. Tom Jennings, "HOMOCORE Issues 1 through 7," Sensitive Research, accessed June 15, 2021, https://web.archive .org/web/20210618022530/https://www.sr-ix.com/Etc/HOMOCORE/index .html.

50. Jason Scott, "518 Area Code BBSes through History," The TEXTFILES.COM Historical BBS List, accessed April 28, 2014, http://bbslist.textfiles.com/518/. For history of Factsheet Five and the milieu it served, see Duncombe, *Notes from Underground*.

51. Mark Frauenfelder, "bOING bOING Advertisement in Factsheet Five #33 (1989)," *Boing Boing*, August 7, 2009, http://boingboing.net/2009/08/19/ boing-boing-advertis.html. In 2013, *Boing Boing* reorganized its site from a blog-and-comments format to a blog-and-BBS format. Editor Rob Beschizza joked that the new format would be "a bulletin board system, accessible exclusively via dial-up modem," which prompted several readers to reminisce about their favorite BBSs. "I would have been so stoked if you had really gone dial up BBS for comments," wrote one reader. "Can you still play the dial-up modem tones when we log-in to our accounts?" asked another. See Beschizza, "Can We Talk?," *Boing Boing*, June 27, 2013, http://web.archive .org/web/0/https://boingboing.net/2013/06/27/can-we-talk.html.

52. Jason Scott, "Overview of The Works," July 16, 1986, archived at http://www .textfiles.com/groups/OCTOTHORPE/allworks.bbs.

53. Between 1978 and 2003, 914 was home to over five hundred bulletin board systems. Jason Scott, "914 Area Code BBSes through History," The TEXTFILES.COM Historical BBS List. accessed April 29, 2014, http://bbslist .textfiles.com/914/.

54. Jason Scott, The Works BBS, cache cow, accessed April 29, 2014, http://web
    .archive.org/web/20011115192625/http://cache.cow.net/works/.

55. Scott, "Overview of The Works."

56. doctor_x, "Curt Vendel on the BBS Documentary," AtariAge, May 18,
    2010, http://atariage.com/forums/topic/163089-curt-vendel-on-the-bbs
    -documentary/?p=2016015.

57. The textfiles produced by Octothorpe are available in Scott's archive. See
    Jason Scott, "Groups: Octothorpe Productions," accessed April 29, 2014,
    archived at http://www.textfiles.com/groups/OCTOTHORPE/.

58. Jason Scott and The Cruiser, "The Guide to Real Works Users," February 26,
    1987, archived at http://www.textfiles.com/groups/OCTOTHORPE/works2
    .oct.

59. The Works BBS was uncommonly well preserved among contemporary
    systems. When Scott moved to Boston to attend Emerson College in 1988,
    one of his users took over as the primary sysop of the BBS, and The Works
    continued for another five years from the new sysop's home in Lexington,
    Massachusetts. In the late 1990s, Scott began to collect and curate the digital
    history of networked personal computing at textfiles.com, a project that
    led ultimately to the production of BBS, a documentary series on BBSing,
    released on DVD in 2005. Scott's preservation efforts in this area are un-
    matched. See Jason Scott, "Does the BBS Guy Run a BBS?," ASCII by Jason
    Scott (blog), October 21, 2003, http://ascii.textfiles.com/archives/753.

60. For a closer reading of Phrack in the context of hacker culture, see Douglas
    Thomas, "Representing Hacker Culture: Reading Phrack," in Hacker Culture
    (Minneapolis: University of Minnesota Press, 2002), 115–40.

61. Joseph Menn, Cult of the Dead Cow: How the Original Hacking Supergroup
    Might Just Save the World (New York: PublicAffairs, 2019).

62. Jason Scott's collection of e-zines includes more than four hundred unique ti-
    tles founded during the 1980s and 1990s. See Scott, "Electronic Magazines,"
    textfiles.com, accessed April 30, 2014, http://textfiles.com/magazines/.

63. Swamp Rat, "The Infamous . . . Gerbil Feed Bomb," Cult of the Dead Cow,
    1985, http://textfiles.com/groups/CDC/cDc-0001.txt.

64. To access Cult of the Dead Cow textfiles from the 1980s, see Jason Scott,
    "Groups: The Cult of the Dead Cow," textfiles.com, accessed February 4,
    2021, http://textfiles.com/groups/CDC/.

65. For contemporaneous analysis of the Legion of Doom case, see volume 10
    of the TELECOM Digest mailing list: Patrick Townson, TELECOM Digest
    Archives, accessed February 4, 2021, http://massis.lcs.mit.edu/.

66. Jim Thomas and Gordon Meyer, "Statement of Intent," Computer Under-
    ground Digest, March 28, 1990, http://www.textfiles.com/digest/CUD/
    cud0100.txt.

67. During the production of BBS: The Documentary, Jason Scott collected a
    small number of files related to Chip Berlet's study of racist BBSs during the
    mid-1980s. Despite a minor media panic in the mid-1980s, Scott concluded
    that racist BBSs were so few in number—he dubbed them an "anomaly"—

that they did not merit inclusion in the documentary. See Scott, "Controversy: BBSes of Evil and Fear: Racist BBSes," BBS Documentary Library, 1985, http://bbsdocumentary.com/library/CONTROVERSY/EVIL/RACISTBBSES/.

68. Chip Berlet and Carol Mason, "Swastikas in Cyberspace: How Hate Went Online," in *Digital Media Strategies of the Far Right in Europe and the United States*, ed. Patricia Anne Simpson and Helga Druxes (Lanham, MD: Lexington Books, 2015), 21–36.

69. Berlet and Mason, 27–28.

70. CBS, "Computer Network / Neo-Nazi Network," *CBS Evening News*, May 10, 1985, https://tvnews.vanderbilt.edu/broadcasts/303493; ABC, "Special Assignment (The Radical Right) (Part II)," *ABC Evening News*, May 30, 1985, https://tvnews.vanderbilt.edu/broadcasts/96423.

71. Three days after a segment on Neo-Nazi BBSs ran on *CBS Evening News*, Thom Henderson wrote an article for *FidoNews* reporting on his experience logging onto the BBS of a hate group in Texas. Alarmed by the violent, racist materials he encountered there, Henderson solicited help from his fellow Fido sysops. "I am at somewhat of a loss as to exactly what we should do," he admitted. "Does anyone have any suggestions?" Despite Henderson's concern, there was no further discussion in *FidoNews*. See Thom Henderson, "Electronic Hate," *FidoNews*, May 13, 1985.

72. The sociologist Jessie Daniels notes that hate groups struggled to find a foothold on commercial services like Prodigy or America Online due to the active moderation policies on those systems. The flourishing of racist sites on the commercial internet was due, in part, to the decentralized, peer-to-peer structure of the participatory web. See Daniels, *Cyber Racism: White Supremacy Online and the New Attack on Civil Rights* (Lanham, MD: Rowman and Littlefield, 2009), 91–116.

73. Catherine Driscoll, "Girl Culture, Revenge and Global Capitalism: Cybergirls, Riot Grrls, Spice Girls," *Australian Feminist Studies* 14, no. 29 (1999): 173–93, doi:10.1080/08164649993425; Melanie A. Ferris, "Resisting Mainstream Media: Girls and the Act of Making Zines," *Canadian Woman Studies* 21, no. 1 (April 1, 2001), http://pi.library.yorku.ca/ojs/index.php/cws/article/view/6906; Alison Piepmeier, *Girl Zines: Making Media, Doing Feminism* (New York: New York University Press, 2009); Janice Radway, "Zines, Half-Lives, and Afterlives: On the Temporalities of Social and Political Change," *PMLA* 126, no. 1 (January 1, 2011): 140–50, doi:10.1632/pmla.2011.126.1.140.

74. See Ellen Balka, "Womantalk Goes On-Line: The Use of Computer Networks in the Context of Feminist Social Change" (PhD diss., Simon Fraser University, 1991), https://core.ac.uk/download/pdf/56369048.pdf.

75. Rob O'Hara, *Commodork: Sordid Tales from a BBS Junkie* (self-published, 2006), 28.

76. O'Hara, 28.

77. Blue was an experienced developer of BBS software for the Apple II. He is also the cocreator, along with Craig Vaughn, of the Apple Bulletin Board Sys-

tem (ABBS) and the People's Message System (PMS). Mack, Goosens, and
Azzarito, "Remote Bulletin Board System," 27-1.

78. Bill Blue and Mark Robbins, *ASCII Express "The Professional,"* version 3.4x
(Santee, CA: Southwestern Data Systems, 1982).

79. Omega, Lord Vision, and Rock 'n Roll Doctor, "Getting AE/CATFUR to Work
with Apple-Net," July 9, 1986, archived at http://www.textfiles.com/apple/
applenet.txt.

80. James A. Pope, "Apple-CAT II: A Communications System from Novation,"
Byte, January 1983.

81. International Telecommunication Union, "ITU-T Recommendation V.22 Bis:
2400 Bits per Second Duplex Modem Using the Frequency Division Technique Standardized for Use on the General Switched Telephone Network
and on Point-to-Point 2-Wire Leased Telephone-Type Circuits" (International
Telecommunication Union, 1988).

82. Kim Maxwell, "High-Speed Dial-Up Modems," *Byte*, December 1984.

83. Maxwell, 182.

84. John J. Hunter, "Three V.22bis Modems, One Clear Winner," *InfoWorld*,
September 1986.

85. "$109 2400 Baud Modem," *Byte*, June 1988.

86. Curiously, the print-based distribution mechanism produced its own cottage
industry. Typing services such as Amtype Corporation charged a small fee to
transcribe programs and mail them on diskette. Kudos to the Atari historian
Kevin Savetz for spotting the Amtype Corp. advertisement and posting it
to Twitter: @KaySavetz, "1/Saw this ad . . . ," Twitter, November 16, 2017,
https://twitter.com/KevinSavetz/status/931045389247037440.

87. See Alison Gazzard, *Now the Chips Are Down: The BBC Micro* (Cambridge,
MA: MIT Press, 2016).

88. The historian Martin Campbell-Kelly describes VisiCalc's place in computing lore as "the 'killer app' hypothesis." While his analysis suggests that any
number of "productivity" programs might have similarly launched the early
PC software industry, VisiCalc remained a top-selling PC product for another
half decade. In 1983, VisiCalc continued to top the market for productivity
software, selling more than twice as many licensed copies as its nearest competitor. See Campbell-Kelly, *From Airline Reservations to Sonic the Hedgehog: A
History of the Software Industry* (Cambridge, MA: MIT Press, 2003), 215.

89. B. Grad, "The Creation and the Demise of VisiCalc," *IEEE Annals of the History of Computing* 29, no. 3 (July 2007): 20–31, https://doi.org/10.1109/MAHC
.2007.4338439.

90. Martin Campbell-Kelly, "Number Crunching without Programming: The
Evolution of Spreadsheet Usability," *IEEE Annals of the History of Computing*
29, no. 3 (July 2007): 8, https://doi.org/10.1109/MAHC.2007.4338438.

91. Benjamin M. Rosen, "VisiCalc: Breaking the Personal Computer Bottleneck,"
Morgan Stanley Electronics Letter, July 11, 1979, http://www.bricklin.com/
history/rosenletter.htm.

92. At the peak of VisiCalc's success, a quarter of PC software sales were through mail order, and half came via retail chains such as ComputerLand. See Richard P. Rumelt and Julia Watt, "VisiCorp 1978–1984 (Revised)" (Los Angeles, CA: Anderson School at UCLA, 1985, rev. 2003), archived at http://web .archive.org/web/20031101141127/http://www.anderson.ucla.edu/faculty/dick .rumelt/Docs/Cases/Visicorp.pdf.

93. David Kushner, *Masters of Doom: How Two Guys Created an Empire and Transformed Pop Culture* (New York: Random House, 2003), 61.

94. Russ Walter, *Secret Guide to Computers* (Somerville, MA: Self-published, 1995), 65.

95. Rey Barry, *Guide to Free Software* (Charlottesville, VA: Freeware Hall of Fame, 1995), xi–xiii.

96. E.g., Doug Clapp, "Clapp-Trapp," *InfoWorld*, November 21, 1983; Markoff, "Freeware Hunt"; Katie Seger, "From One Program to Another," *PC Magazine*, January 1983.

97. The capitalization of software titles is inconsistent in the literature of this period. In this text, I have followed the author's own capitalization whenever possible.

98. Jim Knopf, "The Origin of Shareware," Association of Software Professionals, 1995, http://web.archive.org/web/0/http://www.asp-software.org/users/ history-of-shareware.asp.

99. Knopf.

100. "Shareware lets the software explain itself." Wallace, quoted in Michael E. Callahan, aka Dr. File Finder, "The History of Shareware," Paul's Picks Shareware Library, 1999, https://web.archive.org/web/20090403094743/http:// paulspicks.com:80/history.asp.

101. John Markoff, "Word-Processing Package Costs $10 under New Marketing Scheme," *InfoWorld*, September 19, 1983.

102. Callahan, "History of Shareware."

103. The Association of Shareware Professionals promotes the simultaneous inventions of shareware by Fluegelman, Knopf, and Wallace as "the history of shareware." See Nelson Ford, "The History of Shareware & PsL," Association of Software Professionals, 2000, http://web.archive.org/web/ 20100522020415/http://www.asp-software.org/users/history-of-shareware .asp.

104. Fluegelman's background as a writer shaped his transition into software. He later claimed that his motivation for writing the first version of PC-TALK was to facilitate trading drafts of a manuscript with his coauthor. Dennis Erokan and Mary Eisenhart, "Andrew Fluegelman: PC-Talk and Beyond," *MicroTimes*, May 1985, 22.

105. Bob Wallace left Microsoft with $15,000 in the bank and the goal of creating software to "empower people and advance society." Mike Callahan and Nick Anis, *Dr. File Finder's Guide to Shareware* (Berkeley, CA: Osborne McGraw-Hill, 1990), 33.

106. There are many variations on this sentiment. For example, Michael Callahan profiled Sammy Mitchell, author of QEdit, in 1990. In 1985, Mitchell quit a "cushy, safe, well-paid job" to write shareware full-time. Shareware allowed the authors of QEdit "to write software for a living": "which is what we love to do." Callahan and Anis, 55.

107. Wallace remembers reading the term "shareware" in a computer magazine. It seems likely that he encountered it in an article by Jay Lucas for *InfoWorld*. I have not found the original article, but there are plenty of references in subsequent issues of *InfoWorld*, including a letter to the editor from June 27, 1983. In a recollection from 1993, Bob Metcalfe pins the Lucas article to May 30, 1983. Metcalfe, "Shareware Should Not Be Shunned at All," *InfoWorld*, March 15, 1993. See also John C. Dvorak, Chris Pirillo, and Wendy Taylor, "The History of Shareware," in *Online! The Book* (Upper Saddle River, NJ: Prentice Hall Professional, 2004), 226–28.

108. Markoff, "Freeware Hunt with IBM PC."

109. Ford, "History of Shareware & PsL."

110. The use of shareware to distribute shareware suggests a comparison with the "recursive public" of free and open-source software. See Christopher M. Kelty, *Two Bits: The Cultural Significance of Free Software* (Durham, NC: Duke University Press, 2008).

111. John Friel: "[The] Shareware [model] works better for communication programs than any other type of Shareware," as quoted in Callahan and Anis, *Dr. File Finder's Guide to Shareware*, 47.

112. Jay Caplan, "Effective Shareware Distribution via the BBS Channel, Version 1.2," August 10, 1992, archived at http://textfiles.com/bbs/bbstip12.txt.

113. For a discussion of the economic barriers to CompuServe as a shareware-trading space, see Ford, "History of Shareware & PsL."

114. Richard Scott Mark, *Internet BBSs: A Guided Tour* (Greenwich, CT: Manning, 1996), 203.

115. Exec-PC, "Sorry Prodigy," *Boardwatch*, May 1992.

116. Barry, *Guide to Free Software*, xii.

117. Stewart Brand, "Finding a Balance in the Slippery Economics of an Information Age," *Los Angeles Times*, November 8, 1987, sec. Part IV.

118. David W. Batterson, "Information Age Is Coming, but 'Freeware,' 'Shareware' Won't Be There Making Money," *Los Angeles Times*, November 22, 1987, http://articles.latimes.com/1987-11-22/business/fi-23979_1_shareware-freeware-bullet-train.

119. Callahan and Anis, *Dr. File Finder's Guide to Shareware*, 46–47.

120. Dvorak Telecommunications Awards, "1995 Dvorak Awards Winners," accessed April 25, 2014, http://web.archive.org/web/19961031202539/http://www.citivu.com/dvorak/95awds.html#bbswebsite; Thomas J. Glover and Millie M. Young, *Pocket PCRef*, 3rd ed. (Littleton, CO: Sequoia, 1993), 484.

121. Mark, *Internet BBSs*, 283.

122. Mike Nichols, telephone interview with the author, April 15, 2014.

123. Kushner, *Masters of Doom*, 151–52.

124. Denny Atkin, "We're DOOMed," *Compute!*, April 1994.

125. In 1994, I saw *Doom* shareware diskettes sold near the cash register along-side other "impulse buys" at a video-game store in a mall in Massachusetts.

126. John Romero, the designer of *Doom*, began his career in the early 1980s selling games to magazines such as *inCider* that published them in print as source-code listings. See Retro Gamer, "John Romero," January 17, 2014, http://www.retrogamer.net/profiles/developer/john-romero/; MobyGames, "Scout Search for Apple II (1984)," accessed April 25, 2014, http://www.mobygames.com/game/scout-search.

127. David Kushner, "It's a Mod, Mod World," *IEEE Spectrum* 40, no. 2 (February 2003): 56–57, https://doi.org/10.1109/MSPEC.2003.1176517; Kushner, *Masters of Doom*; Sue Morris, "WADs, Bots and Mods: Multiplayer FPS Games as Co-creative Media," in *Level Up Conference Proceedings* (University of Utrecht, 2003), http://www.digra.org/wp-content/uploads/digital-library/05150.21522 .pdf; Hector Postigo, "Of Mods and Modders Chasing Down the Value of Fan-Based Digital Game Modifications," *Games and Culture* 2, no. 4 (October 1, 2007): 300–313, doi:10.1177/1555412007307955.

128. Robin Nelson, "The Spirit of Cyberflight," *Popular Science*, April 1995.

129. John H. Humphrey and Gary S. Smock, "High-Speed Modems," *Byte*, June 1988.

130. The *Byte* article listed prices for sixteen models and configurations (mean = $1,355.38, *SD* = $370.75). Humphrey and Smock.

131. David Hakala, "Best BBS Contest Update," *Boardwatch*, April 1992.

132. Lamont Wood and Dana Blankenhorn, "State of the BBS Nation," *Byte*, January 1990.

133. Jonathan Roy, "SupraFAXModem," *freenet.sci.comp.atari.news*, February 1, 1992, http://web.archive.org/web/20030109030157/http://www.atariarchives .org/cfn/12/03/0028.php.

134. Roy.

135. "Prodigy Numbers," *Boardwatch*, June 1992; Prodigy, "Prodigy Interactive Personal Service Start-Up Kit," 1991, The Henry Ford Museum, Dearborn, MI, accessed June 15, 2021, https://www.thehenryford.org/collections-and -research/digital-collections/artifact/361296.

136. Gayle Ehrenman, "Prodigy Interactive Personal Service," *PC Magazine*, February 23, 1993.

137. Peter H. Lewis, "Low-Cost, High-Feature PCs," *PC Magazine*, February 23, 1993.

138. While the makers of "multimedia" PCs touted their ability to display high-resolution imagery, only a few games or CD-ROM applications took advantage of these capabilities. Even in point-and-click environments such as the Apple Macintosh, BBS terminal software tended to favor interoperability over innovation when it came to user interface design. Several BBS software packages supported graphical interfaces including the NAPLPS standard used by

Prodigy and the proprietary RIPscrip by TeleGrafix Communications, Inc., but they were not widely adopted. See "Online Graphics—The Next Frontier," *Boardwatch*, October 1992; "NAPLPS Graphics Gains Legs," *Boardwatch*, December 1992; John Kwasnik, "RIP Graphics," John Kwasnik's website, July 2015, http://www.kwasstuff.altervista.org/RIP/index.html.

139. Reviewers of both the Atari ST and Amiga families of PCs tended to focus on their large color palettes and high-resolution displays, but, generally, they portrayed these systems being used to create new computer art and special effects, rather than manipulating digitized photographs. Indeed, Andy Warhol was famously commissioned by Commodore International to create a series of original drawings using the new Amiga 1000 in 1985. Instead of incorporating the Amiga into his well-known photographic silkscreen process, Warhol doodled on-screen using the Amiga mouse. Rich McCormick, "Andy Warhol's Amiga Computer Art Found 30 Years Later," *The Verge*, April 24, 2014, http://www.theverge.com/2014/4/24/5646554/andy-warhols-lost-amiga-computer-art-photo-essay; Jimmy Maher, *The Future Was Here: The Commodore Amiga* (Cambridge, MA: MIT Press, 2012), 43–44; Emily Meyer, "Press Release: The Andy Warhol Museum Announces Newly Discovered Amiga Experiments," Andy Warhol Museum, April 24, 2014, http://www.warhol.org/uploadedFiles/Warhol_Site/Warhol/Content/The_Museum/Press_room/documents/The_Warhol_Amiga_Project_Release_4-24-14.pdf.

140. Nearly every PC dealer advertising in the May 1990 issue of *PC Magazine* charged $200–$600 extra for color and high-resolution displays. All base PC packages remained monochrome.

141. Bradley Dyck Kliewer, "VGA to the Max," *Byte*, December 1990, 360.

142. Reunanen, "Times of Change in the Demoscene." See also the discussion of the Amiga "Boing Ball" demo in Maher, *Future Was Here*.

143. Some systems focused on the generation of novel computer art rather than digitized copies of existing photos. Leo's Graphics in Torrance, California, offered four CD-ROMs of files related to computer graphics *programming* including source code in C, C++, Pascal, and BASIC. Markus W. Pope, *Que's BBS Directory* (Indianapolis, IN: Que, 1994), 123. For more on personal computers and ray tracing, see Kliewer, "VGA to the Max"; Steve Upstill, "Graphics Go 3-D," *Byte*, December 1990.

144. For a snapshot of the state of image compression in 1992, see Lori Grunin, "Something Lossed, Something Gained: Image Compression for PC Graphics," *PC Magazine*, April 28, 1992, http://books.google.com/books?id=HERlooBgpGYC&lpg=PP1&dq=supervga&pg=PT321#v=onepage&q=targa&f=false.

145. Within a year of VESA's Super VGA standards, *Byte* magazine reported that "several shareware programs" already supported the new standard. Kliewer, "VGA to the Max." Rey Barry's *Guide to Free Software* lists more than twenty different freeware image viewers (22).

146. Fran Gardner, "Entrepreneur Hits Bulletin Board Bull's Eye," *Oregonian*, February 10, 1994; Nick Jones, "Jim Maxey Interview," *Boston Sun*, July 19, 2003, http://www.bostonsun.com/archives/story_a1933_part1.htm.

147. "America's Information Highway: A Hitch-Hiker's Guide," *Economist*, December 25, 1993.

148. Jim Maxey, "README.TXT," *Universe* (Event Horizons, 1988), http://cd .textfiles.com/multimediamania/GAMES/UNIVERS/README.TXT; Jack Rickard, "Home-Grown BB$," *Wired*, October 1993. http://www.wired.com/ wired/archive/1.04/bbs.html.

149. "Playboy Magazine Sues Event Horizons BBS for Copyright Infringement," *Boardwatch*, May 1992; Rickard, "Home-Grown BB$."

150. Gardner, "Entrepreneur Hits Bulletin Board Bull's Eye."

151. Jason Eppink, "A Brief History of the GIF (So Far)," *Journal of Visual Culture* 13, no. 3 (December 1, 2014): 298–306, https://doi.org/10.1177/ 1470412914553365.

152. Bob Berry, "Q&A.DOC," *CompuShow*, version Standard Version 8.50a (Sedona, AZ: Canyon State Systems and Software, 1992).

153. The description of Event Horizons' production process is based on investigative work by Benj Edwards of the *Vintage Computing and Gaming* blog. See Edwards, "Digitized Autumn Leaves," *Vintage Computing and Gaming* (blog), January 11, 2013, http://www.vintagecomputing.com/index.php/archives/918.

154. Event Horizons, "Computer Images," *PC Magazine*, December 1990.

155. For further detail concerning the screen resolutions and color depth of PCs in this period, see Adam Bellin and Pier Del Frate, "True Color for Windows," *Byte*, December 1990.

156. Eddie Rowe, "A New Call to Arms—Event Horizons vs. Joe Sysop?," *FidoNews*, October 28, 1991, http://www.textfiles.com/bbs/FIDONET/ FIDONEWS/fido0843.nws.

157. "MaxiPic" was one of several graphics-related terms coined by Maxey, including (purportedly) the term "Super VGA," which later became an industry standard. Kliewer, "VGA to the Max."

158. Gardner, "Entrepreneur Hits Bulletin Board Bull's Eye."

159. Rowe, "New Call to Arms."

160. Lance Rose, "Playboy's New Playmate—Event Horizons BBS," *Boardwatch*, June 1992.

161. Rose.

162. In the mid-2000s, image-oriented blogs began to watermark the images on their sites. Once again, watermarking was at the center of public conflicts regarding authorship and labor in the production of digitized images. For an example of one such conflict, see the back-and-forth published in Jason Scott, "The Passion of the Scanner," *ASCII by Jason Scott* (blog), March 11, 2006, http://ascii.textfiles.com/archives/950. For an analysis of the broader context within which this new form of watermarking emerged, see Ryan M. Milner, *The World Made Meme: Public Conversations and Participatory Media* (Cambridge, MA: MIT Press, 2016).

163. Maxey also told *Boardwatch* that Playboy had sent "an enormous man" to the Event Horizons office to intimidate his staff. Further, he claimed that this "250–300 pound" man had "smashed the receptionist against the door," causing her to miss a month of work while she recovered from a hip injury. Rose, "Playboy's New Playmate."

164. Notably, Playboy had yet to build a BBS of its own, although it was still reportedly working "furiously" to build one in 1993. Rickard, "Home-Grown BB$."

165. Rickard.

166. Maxey was not alone, of course. Few champions of the internet wanted to acknowledge the role of pornography in driving adoption!

167. "National List of Electronic Bulletin Board Systems and On-Line Information Services," *Boardwatch*, May 1992.

168. Event Horizons, "World's Most Expensive BBS," *Boardwatch*, September 1994.

169. Gardner, "Entrepreneur Hits Bulletin Board Bull's Eye."

170. Apuleius, "The Alt.Sex.Stories.* Hierarchy and Related Groups FAQ, Version 2.03," Alt Sex Stories Text Repository, June 19, 2000, https://www.asstr.org/files/FAQs_and_Information/ass_faq.txt.

171. Mailland and Driscoll, *Minitel*.

172. Billy Wildhack, *Erotic Connections* (Corte Madera, CA: Waite Group, 1994), 73.

173. Wildhack, 89.

174. "The Ebony Shack BBS," *BBS Magazine*, August 1995.

175. The reality of dial-up networking is that 56 kilobits per second (kbps) is rarely achieved over standard analog telephone lines. In the 1990s, optimists mused about "anti-Shannon" devices capable of dynamically detecting and canceling nonrandom sources of noise—but these devices could only deliver marginal improvements. Meaningful growth in capacity depended on moving beyond the infrastructure of the twentieth-century Bell System.

176. "What Happened to ISDN?," *Boardwatch*, December 1992, 29.

177. Humphrey and Smock, "High-Speed Modems"; John H. Humphrey and Gary S. Smock, "Whither the Modem?," *Byte*, January 1989.

178. Pew Research Center, "Broadband vs. Dial-Up Adoption over Time," Internet & Technology, accessed October 21, 2015, http://www.pewinternet.org/data-trend/internet-use/connection-type/.

CHAPTER 5. CULTIVATING COMMUNITY

1. "Boardwatch Magazine Announces the Boardwatch 100 Reader's Choice Bulletin Board Contest," *Boardwatch*, May 1992.

2. Jack Rickard, "Editor's Notes," *Boardwatch*, February 1992.

3. A few biases of the *Boardwatch* poll should be noted. First, the raw count of votes necessarily favored large-scale, centralized boards over intimate, local systems. Only two "one-liners" appeared in the Top 100. Second, with an emphasis on commercialization and professionalism, *Boardwatch* appealed to an older subset of the modem-using population. While teenage boards

were flourishing in the early 1990s, more than 50 percent of the voters in the *Boardwatch* poll identified their ages falling between thirty and fifty years old (reported range: eight to seventy-seven years old).The outcomes of the poll reflected the preferences of an older, more tech-savvy sample of North American BBSers. David Hakala, "Best BBS Contest Update," *Boardwatch*, April 1992; Hakala, "Boardwatch 100 Readers' Choice BBS Contest Update," *Boardwatch*, May 1992.

4. "Voters Favor Online Communities," *Boardwatch*, May 1992.

5. Hakala, "Boardwatch 100 Readers' Choice BBS Contest Update," 23.

6. Hakala, 23.

7. Markus W. Pope, *Que's BBS Directory* (Indianapolis, IN: Que, 1994), 109.

8. Gary Wolf and Michael Stein, *Aether Madness: An Offbeat Guide to the Online World* (Berkeley, CA: Peachpit, 1995), 128–29.

9. Pope, *Que's BBS Directory*, 111.

10. "Backdraft Bulletin Board System," *ModemNews Magazine*, 1993; Pope, *Que's BBS Directory*, 115.

11. "Subscribe to Boardwatch Magazine," *Boardwatch*, May 1992.

12. Keith Wade, *The Anarchist's Guide to the BBS* (Port Townsend, WA: Loompanics Unlimited, 1990), 2.

13. David Fox, *Love Bytes: The Online Dating Handbook* (Corte Madera, CA: Waite Group, 1995), 3.

14. Raymond Williams, *Keywords: A Vocabulary of Culture and Society* (New York: Oxford University Press, 1976), 76.

15. The routine practice of checking a bulletin board for new messages was essential to sustaining a sense of community and shared temporality among participants. James W. Carey identified "the maintenance of society in time" as one of the characteristics of the "ritual" view of communication. Carey, "A Cultural Approach to Communication," in *Communication as Culture: Essays on Media and Society* (Boston: Unwin Hyman, 1989), 11–28.

16. The phrase "annihilation of distance" was first used to describe the transatlantic telegraph in the mid-nineteenth century. See "The Atlantic Telegraph: General Manifesto of the Directors to the People of Both Continents; Organization of the Company Official History of the Great Enterprise, Interesting and Important Report of Preliminary Electrical Experiments," *New York Times*, August 27, 1857, sec. Archives, https://www.nytimes.com/1857/08/27/archives/the-atlantic-telegraph-general-manifesto-of-the-directors-to-the.html.

17. Joy Rankin, "Toward a History of Social Computing: Children, Classrooms, Campuses, and Communities," *IEEE Annals of the History of Computing* 36, no. 2 (2014): 86–88; Rankin, "From the Mainframes to the Masses: A Participatory Computing Movement in Minnesota Education," *Information & Culture* 50, no. 2 (May 1, 2015): 197–216, https://doi.org/10.7560/IC50204; Rankin, *A People's History of Computing in the United States* (Cambridge, MA: Harvard University Press, 2018).

18. Starr Roxanne Hiltz and Murray Turoff, *The Network Nation: Human Communication via Computer* (Reading, MA: Addison-Wesley, 1978); Murray Turoff

and Starr Roxanne Hiltz, "An Overview of Research Activities in Computer Mediated Communications from 1976 to 1991 Conducted by the Computerized Conferencing and Communications Center," New Jersey Institute of Technology, 1992, https://web.njit.edu/~turoff/Administrative/ccc.htm.

19. See, for example, Ellen Balka, "Womantalk Goes On-Line: The Use of Computer Networks in the Context of Feminist Social Change" (PhD diss., Simon Fraser University, 1991), https://core.ac.uk/download/pdf/56369048.pdf; Nancy K. Baym, "Interpreting Soap Operas and Creating Community: Inside a Computer-Mediated Fan Culture," *Journal of Folklore Research* 30, nos. 2–3 (1993): 143–76; Baym, "From Practice to Culture on Usenet," *Sociological Review* 42, no. S1 (May 1, 1994): 29–52, https://doi.org/10.1111/j.1467-954X .1994.tb03408.x; Baym, "Communication, Interpretation, and Relationship: A Study of a Computer-Mediated Fan Community" (PhD diss., University of Illinois, 1994), http://hdl.handle.net/2142/19011; Eric E. Butow, "A Content Analysis of Rule Enforcement in the Virtual Communities of FidoNet Echomail Conferences" (master's thesis, California State University, Fresno, 1996); Shelley Correll, "The Ethnography of an Electronic Bar: The Lesbian Cafe," *Journal of Contemporary Ethnography* 24, no. 3 (October 1, 1995): 270–98, https://doi.org/10.1177/089124195024003002; humdog, "Pandora's Vox: On Community in Cyberspace," 1994, *Alphaville Herald*, May 2004, http://alphavilleherald.com/2004/05/introducing_hum.html; Michael L. James, "An Exploratory Study of the Perceived Benefits of Electronic Bulletin Board Use and Their Impact on Other Communication Activities" (PhD diss., Florida State University, 1992); Steven G. Jones, *CyberSociety: Computer-Mediated Communication and Community* (Thousand Oaks, CA: Sage, 1996); Jones, *Virtual Culture: Identity and Communication in Cybersociety* (London: Sage, 1997); Kenneth Lansing, "FidoNet: A Study of Computer Networking" (master's thesis, Texas Tech University, 1991); Annette N. Markham, *Life Online: Researching Real Experience in Virtual Space* (Walnut Creek, CA: AltaMira, 1998); David Martin Myers Jr., "Putting It on the Line: The Evolution of Home Computer Networks" (PhD diss., University of Texas at Austin, 1984); Christine Ogan, "Listserver Communication during the Gulf War: What Kind of Medium Is the Electronic Bulletin Board?," *Journal of Broadcasting & Electronic Media* 37, no. 2 (March 1, 1993): 177–96. https://doi.org/10.1080/08838159309364214; Elizabeth M. Reid, "Electropolis: Communication and Community on Internet Relay Chat" (University of Melbourne, 1991), http://www.aluluei.com/electropolis.htm; Rob Shields, *Cultures of Internet: Virtual Spaces, Real Histories, Living Bodies* (London: Sage, 1996); Carla G. Surratt, *Netlife: Internet Citizens and Their Communities* (Commack, NY: Nova Science, 1998); Richard Clark MacKinnon, "Searching for the Leviathan in Usenet" (master's thesis, San Jose State University, 1992), https://doi.org/10.31979/etd.vzvh-hkn4.

20. Howard Rheingold, *The Virtual Community: Homesteading on the Electronic Frontier* (Reading, MA: Addison-Wesley, 1993). For a closer look at the reception and influence of *The Virtual Community*, see Fred Turner, "Where the

Counterculture Met the New Economy: The WELL and the Origins of Virtual Community," *Technology and Culture* 46, no. 3 (2005): 486–87n4, https://doi .org/10.1353/tech.2005.0154.

21. Howard Rheingold, introduction to the electronic version of *The Virtual Community*, accessed February 4, 2021, https://www.rheingold.com/vc/book/ intro.html.

22. For a closer look at some of the thorny problems that accompanied early on-line communities, see Finn Brunton, *Spam: A Shadow History of the Internet* (Cambridge, MA: MIT Press, 2013).

23. Bruce Mazlish, "A Highway or a Trap?," *New York Times*, October 31, 1993, sec. Books, https://www.nytimes.com/1993/10/31/books/a-highway-or-a-trap .html.

24. For a thorough review of the virtual community research of this period, see David Silver, "Looking Backwards, Looking Forward: Cyberculture Studies 1990–2000," in *Web.Studies: Rewiring Media Studies for the Digital Age*, ed. David Gauntlett (Oxford: Oxford University Press, 2000), 19–30, http://rccs .usfca.edu/intro.asp.html; Nicholas W. Jankowski, "Creating Community with Media: History, Theories and Scientific Investigations," in *Handbook of New Media*, ed. Leah A. Lievrouw and Sonia M. Livingstone, Social Shaping and Consequences of ICTs (London: Sage, 2002), 39–49, https://hdl .handle.net/2027/uc1.32106011430425; Lori Kendall, "Virtual Community," in *Encyclopedia of New Media*, ed. Steve Jones (Thousand Oaks, CA: Sage, 2003), 467–70, https://hdl.handle.net/2027/mdp.39015055882594; David Ellis, Rachel Oldridge, and Ana Vasconcelos, "Community and Virtual Community," *Annual Review of Information Science and Technology* 38, no. 1 (September 22, 2005): 145–86, https://doi.org/10.1002/aris.1440380104; Jan Fernback, "Beyond the Diluted Community Concept: A Symbolic Inter-actionist Perspective on Online Social Relations," *New Media & Society* 9, no. 1 (February 1, 2007): 49–69, https://doi.org/10.1177/1461444807072417; Lori Kendall, "Community and the Internet," in *The Handbook of Internet Studies* (New York: Wiley, 2011), 309–25, https://doi.org/10.1002/9781444314861.ch14.

25. Kendall, "Community and the Internet."

26. For a contemporary reflection on the rise and fall of a virtual community, see Amy Bruckman and Carlos Jensen, "The Mystery of the Death of Medi-aMOO: Seven Years of Evolution of an Online Community," in *Building Virtual Communities: Learning and Change in Cyberspace*, ed. K. Ann Renninger and Wesley Shumar (Cambridge: Cambridge University Press, 2002), 21–33.

27. Notable early studies of BBSs include Myers, "Putting It on the Line"; Sheizaf Rafaeli, "The Electronic Bulletin Board: A Computer-Driven Mass Medium," *Computers and the Social Sciences* 2 (1986): 123–36, https://doi.org/10.1177/ 089443938600200302; Lansing, "FidoNet"; Benjamin J. Bates and Kenneth P. Lansing, "The New World of Democratic Telecommunications: FidoNet as an Example of the New Horizontal Information Networks" (paper presented at 42nd annual conference of the International Communication Association, Miami, FL, 1992); M. James, "Exploratory Study"; Joseph Charles Maille,

"Virtually Gutenberg: Computer Bulletin Boards and the First Amendment through United States v. Riggs and Neidorf" (master's thesis, San Jose State University, 1993).

28. For more on the role of the Acceptable Use Policy in the debate over privatization of NSFNET, see Janet Abbate, "Privatizing the Internet: Competing Visions and Chaotic Events, 1987–1995," *IEEE Annals of the History of Computing* 32, no. 1 (2010): 10–22, https://doi.org/10.1109/MAHC.2010.24.

29. Jerry Shifrin, "So You Want to Start a BBS?," May 23, 1987, archived at http://www.textfiles.com/bbs/start-bb.txt.

30. James C. Goldbloom, "SysOp Suicide! (A Day in the Life of a System Operator)," March 1988, archived at http://www.textfiles.com/bbs/sysopsui.txt.

31. "How to Become an Unsuccessful, Burned-Out SysOp," n.d., archived at http://www.textfiles.com/100/howtobbs.txt.

32. "ONE BBSCON," *Boardwatch*, November 1992.

33. Dave Hughes, "The Year of Internet at BBSCON '94," *Cook Report on Internet–> NREN*, October 1994; Bob Metcalfe, "Sysops Are Reaping the Benefits in the Wake of a BBS Explosion," *InfoWorld* 16, no. 36 (September 5, 1994): 52.

34. "ONE BBSCON—Getting It All Together," *Boardwatch*, July 1992, 47; Randy Bush, "FidoNet: Technology, Tools, and History," *Communications of the ACM* 36, no. 8 (August 1993): 32, https://doi.org/10.1145/163381.163383.

35. For example budgets, see Goldbloom, "SysOp Suicide!"; Pazuzu, "Tips on Starting Your Own BBS," November 11, 1993, archived at http://www.textfiles.com/bbs/startbbs.txt.

36. Wally Byczek, "So You Want to Be a Sysop?," 1989, archived at http://textfiles.com/bbs/be-sysop.txt.

37. Shifrin, "So You Want to Start a BBS?"

38. The use of "sysoping" as a verb seems to have been relatively rare. For context, see Tim Knight, "Establishing Your Own Bulletin Board Service," *SoftSide*, November 1983.

39. Mike Butler, "A Day in the Life of an Overworked UK Sysop—or—How to Survive a Business, BBS and Family without Cracking Up," *FidoNews*, February 3, 1992; Mitchell Harding, "A Day in the Life of a Teenage Sysop," *FidoNews*, February 24, 1992.

40. Goldbloom, "SysOp Suicide!"

41. For a firsthand discussion of the benefits of running a BBS, see Shifrin, "So You Want to Start a BBS?"; Byczek, "So You Want to Be a Sysop?"

42. Tony Frey, "The UltraViolet Cafe's Guide to Better Modeming Cuisine," 1989, archived at http://www.textfiles.com/bbs/guide.txt.

43. Knight, "Establishing Your Own Bulletin Board Service."

44. Shifrin, "So You Want to Start a BBS?"

45. For a closer look at BBS moderation practices, see Kevin Driscoll, "Thou Shalt Love Thy BBS: Distributed Experimentation in Community Moderation," in *Computer Network Histories: Hidden Streams from the Internet Past*, ed. Paolo Bory, Gianluigi Negro, and Gabriele Balbi, Histoire et

Informatique / Geschichte und Informatik 21 (Zürich: Chronos Verlag, 2019), 15–34, 10.33057/chronos.1539.

46. Hakala, "Best BBS Contest Update"; Hakala, "Boardwatch 100 Readers' Choice BBS Contest Update."

47. "How to Become an Unsuccessful, Burned-Out SysOp"; John Olson, "How to Avoid Sysop Burnout," *FidoNews*, April 14, 1986; Kris Lewis, "Abuse.BBS," 1987, archived at http://www.textfiles.com/bbs/abuse.txt.

48. Olson, "How to Avoid Sysop Burnout."

49. One caveat to the total control of the BBS sysop is in the case of Echomail conferences. FidoNet conferences, or "echoes," were moderated separately from the local BBS conferences. Each echo had its own moderator who created rules specific to their conference. If a user broke the rules or caused trouble in the echo, the moderator of the echo and the local BBS sysop were supposed to collaborate in resolving the problem. For more detail on this arrangement, see Butow, "Content Analysis of Rule Enforcement."

50. Bob Metcalfe, "How Many Sysops Will Show up for BBSCon—and Just What Is a Sysop?," *InfoWorld* 17, no. 5 (January 30, 1995): 49.

51. "One Sysops Opinion," n.d., archived at http://www.textfiles.com/bbs/opinion.txt.

52. Katie Hafner, *The WELL: A Story of Love, Death, and Real Life in the Seminal Online Community* (New York: Carroll and Graf, 2001); Rheingold, *Virtual Community*.

53. Fred Turner, *From Counterculture to Cyberculture: Stewart Brand, the Whole Earth Network, and the Rise of Digital Utopianism* (Chicago: University of Chicago Press, 2006), 141.

54. Ron Pernick, "WELL Historical Timeline—the Good, Great Place," Well.com, 1995, http://www.well.com/conf/welltales/timeline.html.

55. Hafner, *WELL*; Rheingold, *Virtual Community*.

56. The other BBS mentioned in *Mondo 2000*'s awesomely weird book was Private Idaho, a system run out of Boise, Idaho. The sysop Robert Carr was described as "the man who brought you the famous Mac programs Momonoids from the Deep, Porno Writer, and MacJesus." Rudy von Bitter Rucker, R. U. Sirius, and Queen Mu, *Mondo 2000: A User's Guide to the New Edge* (New York: HarperPerennial, 1992), 188.

57. Rheingold, *Virtual Community*, 54–55.

58. The comparison with nationwide commercial systems is not coincidental. NETI, the company responsible for The WELL's software infrastructure, also designed the software for General Electric's nationwide GEnie service. See Jack Rickard, "The New BBS on the Web—Whole Earth 'Lectronic Link," *Boardwatch*, October 1995.

59. Rheingold, *Virtual Community*, 49.

60. In this context, "owning" your words took on two meanings. Colloquially, it meant that each user was responsible for and accountable to their posts. Legally, however, it meant that The WELL considered each post the prop-

erty of its owners. This was intended both to protect the property rights of contributors and to limit the organization's liability for unlawful speech acts such as copyright infringement, libel, and obscenity.

61. Rheingold, *Virtual Community*, 42.

62. Rickard, "New BBS on the Web," 44.

63. Rheingold, *Virtual Community*, 49.

64. "National List of Electronic Bulletin Board Systems and On-Line Information Services," *Boardwatch*, May 1992, 73.

65. When Grateful Dead guitarist Jerry Garcia passed away in 1995, Gail Ann Williams, director of The WELL, posted a short reflection on her experience with the band's fans. "The Dead have a lot to do with why I fell in love with cyberspace," she wrote. In Williams's estimation, Dead fandom represented a "true virtual community" that was "simply looking for a medium" when The WELL came along. See Williams, "Grateful for Jerry, the Dead, the Deadheads," Gail Williams's pages, August 10, 1995, http://web .archive.org/web/19961220053904/http://www.well.com/user/gail/grateful -dead.html.

66. Rheingold, *Virtual Community*, 49.

67. Rickard, "New BBS on the Web," 42.

68. The WELL wasn't the only dial-up system for Deadheads. Indeed, several other boards were organized specifically for Dead fandom. The Mars Hotel BBS in Roachdale, Indiana, and Terrapin Station in Darien, Connecticut, were each named after Grateful Dead albums.

69. Both The WELL and the TARDIS were upgraded occasionally during their lifetimes, but neither changed substantially from its original architecture until 1995, when The WELL opened a portal on the World Wide Web.

70. Tragically, three of the sysops of the TARDIS were killed by a drunk driver at the peak of their board's popularity. Tom O'Nan, email to the author, March 26, 2014.

71. These data are drawn from the historical BBS database at BBSmates.com.

72. A 2011 episode of the *Doctor Who* TV series explores the emotional relationship between the TARDIS and the Doctor when the "matrix" of the ship is transferred into the body of a human woman and the two can finally speak "with mouths." See "The Doctor's Wife (TV Story)," Tardis Data Core: Doctor Who Wiki, accessed March 21, 2014, http://tardis.wikia.com/wiki/The _Doctor%27s_Wife_(TV_story).

73. "When the Doctor first decided to leave Gallifrey, he had the chance to take a Type 53, but dismissed it as 'soulless' in favour of the Type 40." See "Doctor's Wife."

74. Timothy Daniel (N8RK), "Super-Ratt RTTY/CW Program with RBBS," *73*, September 1983.

75. Robert J. Foster (WB7QWG/9), "Unlock the New Electronic Mailboxes," *73*, April 1983.

76. O'Nan, email to the author.

77. ELIZA has been reproduced many times, and readers will have no trouble locating a version of the program to try on their own computers. For Weizenbaum's original description of the program, see Joseph Weizenbaum, "ELIZA: A Computer Program for the Study of Natural Language Communication between Man and Machine," *Communications of the ACM* 9, no. 1 (January 1966): 36–45, doi:10.1145/365153.365168.

78. The precise number of callers with disabilities was not known. The decision not to keep records regarding the board's users was a political decision. As O'Nan put it, "I didn't believe in classifying people that way" (email to the author).

79. Thomas O'Nan, email to jason@textfiles.com, "Love Your Site," November 17, 2006, archived at http://textfiles.com/history/onan.txt.

80. Jason Scott, "317 BBS List," The TEXTFILES.COM Historical BBS List, accessed March 21, 2014, http://bbslist.textfiles.com/317/.

81. "Prime Bulletin Board System: Zippety-Doo-Dah! Zippety-Day!," BBS Software Directory, [1992?], http://software.bbsdocumentary.com/APPLE/II/PRIME/primebbs.txt.

82. Jerry Penner, "Running Your Own BBS!," *GEnieLamp*, August 1, 1992, http://software.bbsdocumentary.com/APPLE/II/PRIME/primebbs.genie.txt.

83. "Prime Bulletin Board System."

84. Penner, "Running Your Own BBS!"

85. O'Nan, email to the author.

86. O'Nan.

87. Scott, "317 BBS List."

88. O'Nan, "About the T.A.R.D.I.S. BBS."

89. O'Nan.

90. All over the TARDIS, O'Nan made offhand references to a "red button." If users opted to "push the red button" from the main menu, they were humorously logged off and disconnected from the system. See Scott, "317 BBS List."

91. O'Nan, "About the T.A.R.D.I.S. BBS."

92. O'Nan.

93. O'Nan.

94. Some savvy modemers reduced the cost of long-distance calling by subscribing to a packet-switched intermediary service such as PC Pursuit. Less scrupulous users avoided the tolls by using stolen calling cards. Neither case was typical of all modemers, however.

95. Rheingold's account of visiting The WELL's office in 1985 is a wonderful example of a user paying loving tribute to their favorite system (*Virtual Community*, 38–39).

96. The best-known record of historical BBSs was compiled by Jason Scott with the help of other retrocomputing enthusiasts. Area-code splits are a vexing problem because some BBSs are listed twice under various area codes. This bias would seem to favor the Bay Area since it experienced two splits. To the extent that this error is present in the current analysis, it does not undermine

the conclusions. For human-readable access to the data, see Jason Scott, The TEXTFILES.COM Historical BBS List, accessed June 15, 2021, http://bbslist .textfiles.com/.

97. "Tech workers" include individuals in one of three categories defined in the 1980 US Census: "Engineers," "Technologists and technicians, except health," and "Computer equipment operators." See, for example, US Census Bureau, *General Social and Economic Characteristics: California* (Washington, DC: US Census Bureau, 1983); US Census Bureau, *General Social and Economic Characteristics: Indiana* (Washington, DC: US Census Bureau, 1983).

98. Wolf and Stein, *Aether Madness*, 153.

99. Scott, "317 BBS List."

100. Fox, *Love Bytes*, 4.

101. Adult BBSs such as Compu-Erotica in Chicago provided digitizing services so that users would have a photograph to upload. For some, this may have been the first time they had seen themselves depicted in a digital image.

102. Fox, *Love Bytes*, 4.

103. "America's Information Superhighway: Hitch-Hiker's Guide," *Economist*, December 25, 1993.

104. Billy Wildhack, *Erotic Connections* (Corte Madera, CA: Waite Group, 1994), 51.

105. Fox, *Love Bytes*, 14.

106. Jerry Woody, *ProMatch*, version 3.0 (Cullman, AL: WoodyWare, 1995).

107. Tom Cunha, *TcSoft's Intelligent Match Maker*, version 4.9 (San Antonio, TX: TcSoft, Inc., 1995).

108. Wildhack, *Erotic Connections*, 193.

109. Richard Scott Mark, *Internet BBSs: A Guided Tour* (Greenwich, CT: Manning, 1996), 218.

110. Phil Robinson and Nancy Tamosaitis, *The Joy of Cybersex: The Underground Guide to Electronic Erotica* (New York: Brady, 1993).

111. Wildhack, *Erotic Connections*, 206

112. Mark, *Internet BBSs*, 261.

113. Wildhack, *Erotic Connections*, 54.

114. Wildhack, 54.

115. Jason Scott, "Commented BBS List," The TEXTFILES.COM Historical BBS List, accessed May 10, 2014, http://bbslist.textfiles.com/comments.html.

116. Mark, *Internet BBSs*, 159.

117. Wolf and Stein, *Aether Madness*, 101.

118. Fox, *Love Bytes*, 30.

119. Mark, *Internet BBSs*, 218.

120. "Announcing Winners in the Boardwatch 100 Readers' Choice BBS Contest 1993," *Boardwatch*, 1993, http://www.bbsdocumentary.com/mp3/ 93BBSCON/bw100.txt.

121. Queer Digital History Project, "Gay and Lesbian Information Bureau (GLIB)," accessed February 16, 2021, https://queerdigital.com/items/show/55.

122. "Announcing Winners."

123. Leedell J. Miller, "The Gay & Lesbian BBS List," soc.motss, November 2, 1992, https://groups.google.com/forum/#!original/soc.motss/mdXaPe3cw2k/NWGHea0z0KkJ.

124. Chaz Antonelli, "The BBS Documentary and Multicom-4," *When Pigs Fly*, November 7, 2015, https://mc4bbs.livejournal.com/246094.html; *The Empty Closet*, July 1992, Digital Collections, University of Rochester, https://digitalcollections.lib.rochester.edu/ur/empty-closet-1971-current; Rochester Public Library, "Guide to the Gay Alliance of the Genesee Valley Ephemera Collection 2017.023," 2017, https://roccitylibrary.org/special-collections/; Queer Digital History Project, "Multicom-4," accessed February 16, 2021, https://queerdigital.com/items/show/72.

125. Antonelli, "BBS Documentary."

126. Community Educational Services Foundation, "Welcome to GLIB," Gay and Lesbian Information Bureau, accessed May 9, 2014, http://web.archive.org/web/19970228045752/http://www.glib.org/.

127. Hugh Ryan, Brian Joseph Ferree, and Jennifer Livingston, "You Can Buy Gaydar at the Apple Store," *Details*, February 16, 2010, http://www.details.com/sex-relationships/dating-and-cheating/201003/gay-fool-proof-hookups-tech-savy.

128. Perot's candidacy was felt throughout the modem world in many and surprising ways. In June 1992, a group of Perot supporters created an internet mailing list specifically to "facilitate the education of potential presidential candidate Ross Perot about bisexuals, gays, lesbians, &c, and our issues and concerns." The list was titled, appropriately, "Bisexual Gay Lesbian & Other Educating Perot mailing list," or "bglo-teach-perot" for short. See bglo-teach-perot, "New Mailing List for an Impromptu Task Force," June 8, 1992, 18:20:52 PDT, http://www.qrd.org/qrd/electronic/1992/perot.glb.email-06.08.92.

129. Wolf and Stein, *Aether Madness*, 58.

130. See also David F. Shaw, "Gay Men and Computer Communication: A Discourse of Sex and Identity in Cyberspace," in *Virtual Culture: Identity and Communication in Cybersociety*, ed. Steven Jones (London: Sage, 1997), 123–32.

131. Miller, "Gay & Lesbian BBS List."

132. Kira Hall, "Cyberfeminism," in *Computer-Mediated Communication: Linguistic, Social, and Cross-Cultural Perspectives* (Amsterdam: John Benjamins, 1996).

133. Miller, "Gay & Lesbian BBS List."

134. Hall, "Cyberfeminism," 148.

135. Hall, 163.

136. Nina Wakeford, "New Technologies and 'Cyber-Queer' Research," in *Handbook of Lesbian and Gay Studies*, ed. Diane Richardson and Steven Seidman (London: Sage, 2002), 119.

137. For a closer look at the culture of mutual support that developed on the Backroom, see Kathryn Brewster and Bonnie Ruberg, "SURVIVORS: Archiving

the History of Bulletin Board Systems and the AIDS Crisis," *First Monday* 25, no. 10 (October 2020), https://doi.org/10.5210/fm.v25i10.10290.

138. See Cait McKinney, *Information Activism: A Queer History of Lesbian Media Technologies* (Durham, NC: Duke University Press, 2020).

139. Cait McKinney, "Printing the Network: AIDS Activism and Online Access in the 1980s," *Continuum* 32, no. 1 (January 2, 2018): 7–17, https://doi.org/10.1080/10304312.2018.1404670.

140. CDC National AIDS Clearinghouse, "A Selected Guide to AIDS-Related Electronic Bulletin Boards," US Department of Health and Human Services, April 2, 1993, http://cd.textfiles.com/internetinfo/answers/sci/aids-faq/part4.

141. Wolf and Stein, *Aether Madness*, 171–72.

142. Jean O. Pasco, "A Life of Service: Sister Mary, Whose Past Has Seen Many Painful Twists and Turns, Now Brings Comfort to Others with the World's Most Comprehensive Web Site on AIDS and HIV," *Los Angeles Times*, December 1, 1997, http://ww1.aegis.org/news/lt/1997/lt971201.html.

143. Sister Mary Elizabeth, "AEGIS Affidavit in ACLU, et al. v. Reno," ACLU, February 25, 1996, https://www.aclu.org/technology-and-liberty/aegis-affidavit-aclu-et-al-v-reno.

144. American Health Consultants, Inc., "AIDS Computer Bulletin Boards Gaining Popularity," *AIDS ALERT*, November 1993, http://web.archive.org/web/19961018135646/http://hwmin.gbgm-umc.org/CAM/unique.html.

145. Wynn Wagner, "HIV+: Day One," AEGIS, 1996, http://web.archive.org/web/20000818090555/http://www.aegis.com/topics/dayone/.

146. Abe Opincar, "Holy Megabytes: In Her Crusade against AIDS, a Social Justice Nun Goes Online to the World," *Reader*, October 8, 1992.

147. Pasco, "Life of Service."

148. Computerized AIDS Ministries, home page, March 7, 1996, http://web.archive.org/web/19961018015652/http://hwbbs.gbgm-umc.org/.

149. United Methodist News Service, "Computer AIDS Network Offers Support without Judgment," Computerized AIDS Ministries, August 1995, http://web.archive.org/web/19980425034431/http://gbgm-umc.org/CAM/camnews.html.

150. Mark, *Internet BBSs*, 126.

151. United Methodist News Service, "Computer AIDS Network Offers Support."

152. The AIDS ministry out of which CAM was built was part of a larger UMC community in New York City with a long history of supporting gay and lesbian people. The Washington Square United Methodist Church was renowned for its support of the gay and lesbian communities of New York City. In 1970, for example, the church hosted meetings of the Gay Liberation Front. Later, the openly gay pastor Rev. Paul Abels served as the church's pastor from 1973 until 1984, when the national UMC voted to bar "practicing homosexuals" from the clergy. See "Gay Liberation Front Meeting at Washington Square Methodist Church," Digital Collections, Manuscripts and Archives Division, New York Public Library, accessed June 17, 2021, https://

digitalcollections.nypl.org/items/510d47e3-57c4-a3d9-e040-e00a18064a99;
Anne Hughes-Hinnen, "My Memories of Washington Square United
Methodist Church, 1981–2005," *People of the Village* (blog), accessed May 8,
2014, http://peopleblog.churchofthevillage.org/my-memories-of-washington
-square-united-methodist-church-1981-2005/.

153. Richard B. Cory, "The UMC, CAM, and Me," Computerized AIDS Ministries,
July 26, 1995, http://web.archive.org/web/19970129083713/http://gbgm-umc
.org/CAM/cam-me.html.

154. Cory.

155. Rusty, "Testimony and Thank You," Computerized AIDS Ministries, June 14,
1995, http://web.archive.org/web/19980425034516/http://gbgm-umc.org/
CAM/rusty.html.

156. Rusty.

157. Debbi Hood Johnson, "I Wear a Red Ribbon," Computerized AIDS Ministries, 1994, http://web.archive.org/web/19980425032633/http://gbgm-umc
.org/cam/i-wear.html.

158. Tragically, Johnson was killed in a car accident on February 24, 1996
(Johnson).

159. Johnson.

160. Johnson.

161. The comments quoted in this paragraph draw on a short essay that Johnson
first posted to CAM that was then republished through both the UMC's
Health and Welfare Ministries and Sister Mary Elizabeth's AEGIS network.

162. United Methodist News Service, "Computer AIDS Network Offers Support."

163. "One Sysops Opinion."

CHAPTER 6. BECOMING THE NET

1. Numerous accounts of internet history, from the scholarly to the biographical, mark 1995 as a year of transition.

2. Michael Krantz, "The Great Manhattan Geek Rush of 1995," *New York*, November 13, 1995.

3. Eric S. Faden, "The Cyberfilm: Hollywood and Computer Technology," *Strategies: Journal of Theory, Culture & Politics* 14, no. 1 (May 2001): 77–90, https://
doi.org/10.1080/10402130120042370.

4. Ed Sherin, dir., "Rebels," *Law & Order*, NBC, September 27, 1995; David Nutter, dir., "2Shy," *The X-Files*, Fox, November 3, 1995, https://web.archive.org/
web/20010331101254/http://www.thexfiles.com/episodes/season3/3x06.html;
Susie Dietter, dir., "Radioactive Man," *The Simpsons*, Fox, September 24, 1995,
https://simpsons.fandom.com/wiki/Radioactive_Man; Alan Siegel, "How alt
.tv.simpsons Embiggened a Generation of Obsessive Fans," *Slate*, September 26, 2013, https://slate.com/culture/2013/09/the-history-of-simpsons
-message-board-alt-tv-simpsons.html.

5. The "electronic cottage" refers to a vision of telework outlined by the futurist
Alvin Toffler. Newt Gingrich, Republican Speaker of the House and *Time*

"Man of the Year" for 1995, routinely referenced Toffler's futurist literature. For background, see Toffler, "The Electronic Cottage," *Creative Computing*, December 1980; Tom Forester, "The Myth of the Electronic Cottage," *Futures* 20, no. 3 (June 1, 1988): 227–40, https://doi.org/10.1016/0016-3287 (88)90079-1; Karen Tumulty and Paul Gray, "Inside the Minds of Gingrich's Gurus," *Time* 145, no. 3 (January 23, 1995): 20. Faith in the information economy was similarly axiomatic for elected Democrats. The American Presidency Project lists sixty-seven occasions when President Clinton used the phrases "information age" or "information superhighway" in remarks in 1995. See https://www.presidency.ucsb.edu.

6. For a rich history of the boom, see Megan Sapnar Ankerson, *Dot-Com Design: The Rise of a Usable, Social, Commercial Web* (New York: New York University Press, 2018).

7. Joshua Quittner and Tom Curry, "Ho, Ho, Ho, Crash!," *Time* 145, no. 1 (January 9, 1995): 61; Judy Brown, "Microsoft Gives Business View from Windows 95 Preview Copies of the Long-Awaited New Operating System Are Available," *Milwaukee Journal*, March 27, 1995, sec. Business, 95.

8. From RXN's site about the 1:282 Net: "FidoNet (TM) is an amateur electronic mail network, established in 1984, that had grown by 1995 to include almost 40,000 electronic bulletin board systems world-wide. It has since decreased in size . . . :(" See FidoNet Net 282, March 28, 2004, http://web.archive.org/web/20160310164528/http://www.rxn.com/~net282/.

9. The exact wording of this message varied throughout North America. Examples of these "intercept recordings" may be heard today thanks to several enthusiast collections on the web, e.g., Telephone World, "Telephone Sounds & Recordings," accessed June 15, 2021, https://web.archive.org/web/20190701182135/http://www.phworld.org/sounds/.

10. One notable variant of the BBS death narrative involves the mass mailing of AOL diskettes. See The Vann Cave, "Telegraph Road; Social Media before the Internet," YouTube, March 20, 2019, https://www.youtube.com/watch?v=FYY82inv4rc.

11. Rob O'Hara, *Commodork: Sordid Tales from a BBS Junkie* (self-published, 2006), 14.

12. Rob Swindell, "The Digital Manifesto: 'The Internet Killed the BBS Star,'" Synchronet Wiki, August 1996, http://wiki.synchro.net/history:manifesto; Sash, "Adventures in BBSing: BBSing Nostalgia in the Twin Cities or 'Internet Killed the BBS Star,'" 2000, archived at http://www.textfiles.com/history/minn.txt.

13. On the conditions and consequences of privatization, see Janet Abbate, "Privatizing the Internet: Competing Visions and Chaotic Events, 1987–1995," *IEEE Annals of the History of Computing* 32, no. 1 (2010): 10–22, https://doi.org/10.1109/MAHC.2010.24.

14. Jack Rickard later described it as a "tough crowd" that turned off potential sponsors. See Rickard, "Editor's Notes," *Boardwatch*, June 1991.

15. "The 1991 International BBSing and Electronic Communications Conference," *FidoNews*, August 12, 1991.

16. Zone 1 Region Coordinators and Zone 1 Zone Coordinator, "FidoCon 1991—The New Beginning," *FidoNews*, July 30, 1990.

17. See ad in *Boardwatch*, June 1991, 37.

18. See ad in *Boardwatch*, June 1991, 37.

19. "FidoCon 91—408 Attend Biggest BBS Bash Ever," *Boardwatch*, October 1991.

20. Stephen Laliberte, "A Tale of Two Cities: Impressions of FidoCon91 and the VIA Convention," *Boardwatch*, October 1991, 31.

21. See the photos published in the October 1991 issue of *Boardwatch*.

22. Earlier in the summer, Rickard had announced a "coming out party" for the BBS industry at COMDEX in Las Vegas, but a disagreement with the trade-show organizers led to the BBS pavilion falling through. The experience of attending FidoCon appeared to restore Rickard's resolve to promote the modem world as an industry. See Rickard, "Editor's Notes," June 1991.

23. Rickard.

24. Jack Rickard, "Editor's Notes," *Boardwatch*, October 1991.

25. Rickard.

26. Rickard.

27. Jack Rickard, "FidoCon91, Commercialization, and The ONE BBSCON," *FidoNews*, September 9, 1991.

28. "Letters," *Boardwatch*, October 1991.

29. "Letters."

30. "Letters."

31. Tom Jennings, "Editorial," *FidoNews*, May 11, 1992.

32. For a rich account of the contributions of Black people to the technology and culture of BBSs and the early internet, see Charlton D. McIlwain, *Black Software: The Internet and Racial Justice, from the AfroNet to Black Lives Matter* (New York: Oxford University Press, 2019).

33. Accurate data from the big commercial services are scarce. My estimates here are based on data reported in the business press. See, for example, William Grimes, "Computer as a Cultural Tool: Chatter Mounts on Every Topic," *New York Times*, December 1, 1992, sec. The Arts; Daniel Southerland, "America Online's Rapid Rise: It's the Hottest Player in Dial-Up Computer Services, but Stiff Competition Looms," *Washington Post*, November 8, 1993; Sandra Sugawara, "Coaxing GEnie Out of Its Bottle: GE Has at Least 3 Wishes for On-Line Service: Profits, Growth and a Beefed-Up Product," *Washington Post*, June 15, 1994; Sugawara, "Washington Business: On-Line and on the Move Vienna's Computer Service Attracts the Attention of Consumers, Competitors," *Washington Post*, August 8, 1994; Jared Sandberg, "America Online, Capital Cities/ABC Plan New Service," *Wall Street Journal*, July 7, 1994, sec. Technology and Telecommunications; Steve Lohr, "Steve Case at a Crossroad: America Online Is a Leader, but He's Watching the Rear-View Mirror," *New York Times*, August 14, 1995, sec. Business Day.

34. FidoNet sysops continued to organize meetings in North America and Europe (as EuroCon) for several years. These meetings tended to be smaller in size, self-organized, and less commercial than either FidoCon '91 or the subsequent ONE BBSCON trade shows. The organizers of FidoCon '91 created the nonprofit International BBSing and Electronic Communication Conference (IBECC) in 1992 to run head-to-head with ONE BBSCON. The first (and only) meeting of the IBECC was held in Denver across town from ONE BBSCON. The IBECC '92 theme was "Socially Responsible Computing" and featured a compelling program on topics ranging from education to science fiction. Few people made it to both events, however. Even Tom Jennings failed to make an appearance despite being in Denver for the BBSCON. After 1992, the IBECC organizers focused their energies on the Anaconism science fiction convention. See "IBECC," *BBS Magazine*, May 1992; Tom Jennings, "Editorial: (I'm about to) Snooze," *FidoNews*, August 17, 1992.

35. In addition to the firsthand experiences of early modem users, as academic researchers began to study virtual community, they quickly poked holes in the characterization of computer-mediated communication as free of prejudice. See, for example, Amy Bruckman, "Gender Swapping on the Internet," in *High Noon on the Electronic Frontier: Conceptual Issues in Cyberspace*, ed. Peter Ludlow (Cambridge, MA: MIT Press, 1996), 317–26; Byron Burkhalter, "Reading Race Online," in *Communities in Cyberspace*, ed. Marc A. Smith and Peter Kollock (London: Routledge, 1999), 60–75; Lisa Nakamura, *Cybertypes: Race, Ethnicity, and Identity on the Internet* (New York: Routledge, 2002); Megan Boler, "Hypes, Hopes and Actualities: New Digital Cartesianism and Bodies in Cyberspace," *New Media & Society* 9, no. 1 (February 1, 2007): 139–68, https://doi.org/10.1177/1461444807067586.

36. By 1994, more than two dozen BBSs had joined AfroNet. See McIlwain, *Black Software*, 91–106.

37. Bob Metcalfe, "On the Wild Side of Computer Networking," *InfoWorld*, March 29, 1993.

38. Bob Metcalfe, "How Many Sysops Will Show Up for BBSCon—and Just What Is a Sysop?," *InfoWorld* 17, no. 5 (January 30, 1995): 49.

39. See letter from Brad Clements in "Letters to the Editor," *Boardwatch*, April 1993.

40. Jack Rickard, "The BBS to Internet Connection," *Boardwatch*, February 1992.

41. "Letters to the Editor," *Boardwatch*, June 1993.

42. Rickard, "Editor's Notes," June 1991. Jack Rickard was not the only one describing the internet as a "large" or "overgrown" BBS. See also Erik Delfino, "'Transfer, Please'—The Low-Down on Downloading," *Online* 18, no. 3 (May 1994): 112.

43. Bob Metcalfe, "Internet Dwellers Beware: BBS Movement Is Planning an Invasion," *InfoWorld* 16, no. 37 (September 12, 1994): 50.

44. Bob Metcalfe, "Sysops Are Reaping the Benefits in the Wake of a BBS Explosion," *InfoWorld* 16, no. 36 (September 5, 1994): 52.

45. The overlapping interests and duplicate efforts of UUCP and BBS networks was a point of frustration for people with access to both systems. As Richard P. Wilkes complained to Tom Jennings in 1984, "People in the micro BBS environ often are totally unaware that there is a working, FREE, network of mini and microcomputers exchanging gigabytes of mail around the country (by phone)." Wilkes, "FidoNet: Response," May 24, 1984, archived at http://www.textfiles.com/bbs/FIDONET/JENNINGS/STANDARDS/fidonet.rpw.txt.

46. Hartman's gateway started as a one-way link from UUCP to FidoNet and relied on connections paid for by Hartman's employer. See Bob Hartman, "Fido <==> UNIX Mail," FidoNews, August 19, 1985.

47. UFGATE grew out of a prior collaboration between Tim Požar and John Gilmore and included contributions from several others. In 1987, Gilmore wrote an implementation of the Unix-to-Unix Copy Protocol (UUCP) in the C programming language. Požar added modifications for compatibility with MS-DOS and created UFGATE, enabling PCs to trade files and messages with UNIX networks. UFGATE also included code contributed by John Galvin and Garry Paxinos. Požar thanked Randy Bush, David Dodell, and "a host of others" for testing the software. In 1988, Lee Damon, Lisa Gronke, and Dale Weber published the first how-to guide for sending internet email from a BBS running UFGATE. And in January 1989, Požar officially announced UFGATE in FidoNews. John Gilmore, Uuslave, version hoptoad-1.11 (1987); Lee Damon, Dale Weber, and Lisa Gronke, "How to Use the UUCP <===> Fido-Net<tm>," December 9, 1988, archived at https://www.lns.com/papers/ufgate/UFGATE.HOW; Tim Požar, "Late Night Software Is Proud to Announce UFGATE," FidoNews, January 30, 1989; Tom Jennings and Tim Požar, "Editorial," FidoNews, June 3, 1991. See also Požar's personal recollections and an archived copy of the UFGATE software: Požar, "UFGATE—FidoNet/UUCP Gateway," Late Night Software, accessed October 1, 2020, https://www.lns.com/papers/ufgate/.

48. The mere availability of UFGATE did not guarantee interconnection, of course. The sysops of a FidoNet node in South Africa obtained a copy of UFGATE but were not able to bring up a working gateway. See Mike Lawrie, "History of the Internet in South Africa," Uninet Home Page, 1997, accessed June 15, 2021, http://web.archive.org/web/20041205093635/http://www2.frd.ac.za/uninet/history/.

49. In September 1990, Bush traveled to Makhanda, South Africa (known at the time as "Grahamstown"), to participate in a special FidoCon celebrating the start of Zone 5. For a firsthand account of the conference, see Niel Uys, "FidoCon 1990—Zone 5," FidoNews, October 8, 1990.

50. Of course, there were thriving networks running on Commodore Amiga, Atari ST, and Apple Macintosh systems, but these were exceptions. In North America, IBM-compatible PCs were the dominant BBS platform of the early 1990s.

51. Bernard Aboba, "TCP/IP on the IBM PC—an Introduction," Boardwatch, June 1993.

52. For details regarding the availability of internet access to BBS sysops in the early 1990s, see the recurring "Internet News" column in *Boardwatch* magazine from 1991 to 1995.

53. See, for example, Jeff Torello, "Accessing the Internet," *Major News*, Spring 1994.

54. Fenwick McKelvey and Kevin Driscoll, "ARPANET and Its Boundary Devices: Modems, IMPs, and the Inter-structuralism of Infrastructures," *Internet Histories* 3, no. 1 (January 2, 2019): 31–50, https://doi.org/10.1080/24701475.2018.1548138.

55. "How and Why to Access the Internet," *Boardwatch*, October 1992.

56. The World in Brookline, Massachusetts, was one of the few services selling consumer internet access. See "Internet Access at $3 per Month—Delphi Makes the Global Connection," *Boardwatch*, April 1993; Spike Ilacqua, "The First ISP," *USENIX*, March 15, 1999, https://web.archive.org/web/20100603211424/http://www.usenix.org/publications/login/1999-2/isp.html.

57. Tracy Mickley, "Planet Connect Satellite System—FidoNet/USENET Mail Firehose from the Sky," *Boardwatch*, January 1994.

58. Bernard Aboba, "Cable Data: The Shape of Things to Come," *Boardwatch*, January 1994.

59. Tom Jennings, Q&A with Tom Jennings, ROFLcon II, May 1, 2010.

60. Richard Scott Mark, "Guide to Select BBS's on the Internet (SBI List)," August 1995, archived at http://cd.textfiles.com/group42/FAQS/AINTBBS.TXT; Mark, *Internet BBSs: A Guided Tour* (Greenwich, CT: Manning, 1996).

61. Mark, *Internet BBSs*, 6.

62. "The WELL Now Available via Internet," *Boardwatch*, May 1992.

63. Claire L. Evans, *Broad Band: The Untold Story of the Women Who Made the Internet* (New York: Portfolio/Penguin, 2018).

64. Jack Rickard, "Rumors & Factoids," *Boardwatch*, January 1994.

65. Dave Hughes, "The Year of Internet at BBSCON '94," *Cook Report on Internet -> NREN*, October 1994.

66. Jack Rickard, "Editor's Notes," *Boardwatch*, January 1995.

67. Internet BBSs needed to support either SLIP or PPP to provide access to the graphical web. The Serial Line Internet Protocol (SLIP) and Point-to-Point Protocol (PPP) were essential to the provision of dial-up internet services. In 1984, Rick Adams, the future founder of UUNET, implemented SLIP for UNIX systems. In 1988, the Internet Engineering Task Force published a specification of SLIP and example implementation as RFC 1055. By 1996, it was common to see "SLIP/PPP" in the fine print of advertisements for commercial ISPs. See John L. Romkey, "RFC 1055: Nonstandard for Transmission of IP Datagrams over Serial Lines: SLIP," Network Working Group, June 1988, http://tools.ietf.org/html/rfc1055; Drew D. Perkins, "RFC 1134: The Point-to-Point Protocol: A Proposal for Multi-protocol Transmission of Datagrams over Point-to-Point Links," Network Working Group, November 1989, http://tools.ietf.org/html/rfc1134; Aboba, "TCP/IP on the IBM PC."

68. To actually visit a webpage, the user would first dial into their local BBS, enter their log-in information, invoke the SLIP command on the remote system, start up Trumpet Winsock on their local machine, wait for the connection to be verified, start Mosaic, enter a URL, and wait fifteen minutes or more for the page to load.

69. Jack Rickard, "Mosaic and the World Wide Web," *Boardwatch*, January 1994.

70. The reinvention of The WELL began in 1994, when Bruce Katz, founder of the Rockport Shoe Company and longtime modem user, took ownership of the system. Under Katz's direction, The WELL not only became a web BBS but also provided dial-up internet access to the Bay Area. See Jack Rickard, "The New BBS on the Web—Whole Earth 'Lectronic Link," *Boardwatch*, October 1995.

71. Bernard Aboba, *The BMUG Guide to Bulletin Boards and Beyond* (Berkeley, CA: BMUG, 1992).

72. The Extremist, "Dead Alive," March 12, 2000, archived at http://www.textfiles .com/history/dalive.

73. See Ankerson, *Dot-Com Design*.

74. See John Carey and Martin C. J. Elton, "The Other Path to the Web: The Forgotten Role of Videotex and Other Early Online Services," *New Media & Society* 11, nos. 1–2 (2009): 241–60; Hallvard Moe and Hilde Van den Bulck, eds., *Teletext in Europe: From the Analog to the Digital Era* (Göteborg: Nordicom, 2016); Julien Mailland and Kevin Driscoll, *Minitel: Welcome to the Internet* (Cambridge, MA: MIT Press, 2017).

75. Ankerson, *Dot-Com Design*, 41.

76. Mark, *Internet BBSs*, xv.

77. See Michael Hauben and Ronda Hauben, *Netizens: On the History and Impact of Usenet and the Internet* (Los Alamitos, CA: IEEE Computer Society, 1997), http://www.columbia.edu/~hauben/netbook/; Bradley Fidler, "Eternal October and the End of Cyberspace," *IEEE Annals of the History of Computing* 39, no. 1 (January 2017): 6–7, https://doi.org/10.1109/MAHC.2017.9.

78. Historically, USENET users associated the month of September with the disruptive arrival of college freshmen. With the popularization of internet access, "Eternal September" or "the September that never ended" implied an end to this seasonal cycle. Instead of arriving all at once, new users would now arrive continuously. Over time, "Eternal September" has been mistakenly described as the arrival of America Online users in the fall of 1993. But, in fact, America Online did not open a USENET portal until the spring of 1994. Furthermore, one possible origin of the phrase "Eternal September" is a January 1994 post on alt.folklore.computers by the artist Dave Fischer. America Online is not mentioned in Fischer's post. Instead, Fischer was commenting on "the Imminent Death of the Net" as a recurring topic on USENET, harking back to the arrival of FidoNet users in 1985. Unfortunately, this error is enshrined in the Jargon File and has been reproduced in multiple places on Wikipedia. See Wendy Grossman, "The Making of an Underclass: AOL," chapter 3 in *Net.Wars* (New York: New York University Press, 1999), https://

web.archive.org/web/20110505003755/http://www.nyupress.org/netwars/
pages/chapter03/ch03_.html; Dave Fischer, "Longest USENET Thread Ever,"
alt.folklore.computers, January 25, 1994, https://groups.google.com/g/alt
.folklore.computers/c/wF4CpYbWuuA/m/jS6ZOyJd1osJ; Eric S. Raymond,
"September That Never Ended," Jargon File, version 4.4.7, December 29,
2003, http://www.catb.org/jargon/html/S/September-that-never-ended.html.

79. Although gateways existed between FidoNet and USENET, anecdotal evidence suggests that FidoNet users were a relatively small proportion of the
overall USENET population.

80. Metcalfe, "Internet Dwellers Beware."

81. Another possible explanation for the negative perception of BBSs is that
many college students of the early 1990s had cut their teeth on "kiddie
boards" of the late 1980s. For these former users, the move from BBSs to the
internet coincided with the transition from high school to university, from
adolescence to adulthood. It is difficult to assess the prevalence of this life
path, but it seems like a plausible explanation for at least some of the anti-
BBS sentiment among college-aged internet users.

82. See Janet Abbate, *Inventing the Internet* (Cambridge, MA: MIT Press, 1999);
Tara McPherson, "U.S. Operating Systems at Mid-century: The Intertwining
of Race and UNIX," in *Race after the Internet*, ed. Lisa Nakamura, and Peter
Chow-White (New York: Routledge, 2012), 21–37; Camille Paloque-Berges,
"Mapping a French Internet Experience: A Decade of Unix Networks Coop-
eration (1983–1993)," in *Routledge Companion to Global Internet Histories*, ed.
Gerard Goggin and Mark McLelland (New York: Routledge, 2017), 153–70.

83. A thorough examination is beyond the scope of this book, but debates over
UNIX and microcomputing routinely appeared in the pages of *Byte* magazine
during the 1980s.

84. For example, the founding of the GNU Project in 1983 marked the beginning of the free and open-source software movement, but GNU software was
not available to microcomputer users until the creation of the Linux kernel
almost a decade later.

85. Examples of negative BBS coverage from the Vanderbilt TV News Archive
include CBS, "Computer Network / Neo-Nazi Network," *CBS Evening News*,
May 10, 1985, https://tvnews.vanderbilt.edu/broadcasts/303493; ABC, "New
Jersey / Teenage Computer Hackers," *ABC Evening News*, July 17, 1985,
https://tvnews.vanderbilt.edu/broadcasts/97232; CBS, "Computer Virus /
Morris," *CBS Evening News*, November 8, 1988, https://tvnews.vanderbilt
.edu/broadcasts/319238; NBC, "Espionage / New Orleans, Louisiana /
Computer Spy Ring," *NBC Evening News*, March 4, 1989, https://tvnews
.vanderbilt.edu/broadcasts/567753; NBC, "Focus (Cyberspace Pornography),"
NBC Evening News, July 30, 1994, https://tvnews.vanderbilt.edu/broadcasts/
600970.

86. Tom Jennings, "Are All Sysops Criminals?," *FidoNews*, November 26, 1990;
Electronic Frontier Foundation, "A History of Protecting Freedom Where Law
and Technology Collide," October 7, 2011, https://www.eff.org/about/history.

87. Alice E. Marwick, "To Catch a Predator? The MySpace Moral Panic," *First Monday* 13, no. 6 (May 19, 2008), https://doi.org/10.5210/fm.v13i6.2152.

88. Philip Elmer-Dewitt, "Orgies On-Line," *Time* 141, no. 22 (May 31, 1993): 61.

89. John C. Dvorak, "Stagnant Ponds and Bill Clinton," *Boardwatch*, January 1994.

90. Marty Rimm, "Marketing Pornography on the Information Superhighway: A Survey of 917,410 Images, Descriptions, Short Stories, and Animations Downloaded 8.5 Million Times by Consumers in over 2000 Cities in Forty Countries, Provinces, and Territories," *Georgetown Law Journal* 83 (1994–95): 1849–1934; Philip Elmer-Dewitt and Hannah Bloch, "On a Screen near You: Cyberporn," *Time* 146, no. 1 (July 3, 1995): 38–45.

91. Elmer-Dewitt and Bloch, "On a Screen near You," 40.

92. The *Time* story on cyberporn described pornography as "a big moneymaker" and implied that the profitability of all large BBSs depended on the allure of "X-rated material." Elmer-Dewitt and Bloch, "On a Screen near You," 40.

93. Thomas Streeter, "Internet," in *Digital Keywords*, ed. Benjamin Peters (Princeton, NJ: Princeton University Press, 2016), 184–96.

94. Scott J. Brinker, "President's Corner," *Major News*, Spring 1994.

95. Jack Rickard of *Boardwatch* claims to have coined the term "internet service provider."

96. *Wildcat!*, Version 5.0 (Mustang Software, Inc., 1996).

97. Jack Rickard, "Editor's Notes," *Boardwatch*, December 1995, 66.

98. Mark, *Internet BBSs*, 6.

99. Mark.

100. Netscape was the first web browser designed to work well over a dial-up connection. Previous browsers, including Mosaic, were made for people with high-speed institutional connections to the internet. For a contemporary account of Mosaic by modem, see Jack Rickard, "Editor's Notes: Webulism and the Cable Fable," *Boardwatch*, December 1994. See also Ankerson, *Dot-Com Design*, 39–41.

101. In the early 1990s, articles in *Boardwatch* and *InfoWorld* often lamented the stymied diffusion of digital ISDN. See, for example, "What Happened to ISDN?," *Boardwatch*, December 1992.

102. Mark, *Internet BBSs*, xiii.

CHAPTER 7. IMAGINING A BETTER FUTURE FOR THE INTERNET

1. Thomas Streeter, *The Net Effect: Romanticism, Capitalism, and the Internet* (New York: New York University Press, 2011).

2. Anne Helmond, "The Platformization of the Web: Making Web Data Platform Ready," *Social Media + Society* 1 (2015), https://doi.org/10.1177/2056305115603080.

3. See Jack Rickard, "Internet News," *Boardwatch*, May 1991.

4. See Google, Inc., "Annual Report, Form 10-K" (Washington, DC: US Securities and Exchange Commission, December 31, 2006), https://www.sec.gov/

Archives/edgar/data/0001652044/000165204421000010/goog-20201231
.htm; Facebook, Inc., "Annual Report, Form 10-K" (Washington, DC: US
Securities and Exchange Commission, December 31, 2012), https://www.sec
.gov/Archives/edgar/data/1326801/000132680113000003/fb-12312012x10k
.htm; Alphabet, Inc., "Annual Report, Form 10-K" (Washington, DC: US
Securities and Exchange Commission, December 31, 2020), https://www
.sec.gov/Archives/edgar/data/0001652044/000165204421000010/goog
-20201231.htm.

5. Tarleton Gillespie, *Custodians of the Internet: Platforms, Content Moderation,
and the Hidden Decisions That Shape Social Media* (Cambridge, MA: MIT
Press, 2018).

6. Tarleton Gillespie, "The Politics of 'Platforms,'" *New Media & Society* 12, no. 3
(May 1, 2010): 347–64, https://doi.org/10.1177/1461444809342738.

7. For a closer examination of the history of volunteer moderation on commercial services, see Hector Postigo, "Emerging Sources of Labor on the
Internet: The Case of America Online Volunteers," *International Review
of Social History* 48, no. S11 (December 2003): 205–23, https://doi.org/10
.1017/S0020859003001329; Postigo, "America Online Volunteers: Lessons
from an Early Co-production Community," *International Journal of Cultural Studies* 12, no. 5 (September 1, 2009): 451–69, https://doi.org/10.1177/
1367877909337858.

8. Joy Lisi Rankin, *A People's History of Computing in the United States* (Cambridge, MA: Harvard University Press, 2018), 242.

9. Joe Draganosky (Kaboom), "BBSing.com, Remembering the Original Cyberspace," bbsing.com, accessed June 18, 2021, http://web.archive.org/web/
20041205085956/http://www.bbsing.com/.

Abbate, Janet. "From ARPANET to Internet: A History of ARPA-Sponsored Computer Networks, 1966–1988." PhD diss., University of Pennsylvania, 1994.

———. *Inventing the Internet*. Cambridge, MA: MIT Press, 1999.

———. "Privatizing the Internet: Competing Visions and Chaotic Events, 1987–1995." *IEEE Annals of the History of Computing* 32, no. 1 (2010): 10–22. https://doi.org/10.1109/MAHC.2010.24.

ABC. "New Jersey / Teenage Computer Hackers." *ABC Evening News*, July 17, 1985. https://tvnews.vanderbilt.edu/broadcasts/97232.

———. "Special Assignment (The Radical Right) (Part II)." *ABC Evening News*, May 30, 1985. https://tvnews.vanderbilt.edu/broadcasts/96423.

Aboba, Bernard. *The BMUG Guide to Bulletin Boards and Beyond*. Berkeley, CA: BMUG, 1992.

———. "Cable Data: The Shape of Things to Come." *Boardwatch*, January 1994.

———. "TCP/IP on the IBM PC—an Introduction." *Boardwatch*, June 1993.

Adenauer, Peter. "fdhist.txt." FidoNet on the Internet, December 1993. http://www.textfiles.com/fidonet-on-the-internet/history/fdhis.txt.

Akst, Daniel. "Cyberculture: Sometimes Dry, Detail of Magic of 1st Internet 'Wizards.'" *Los Angeles Times*, August 26, 1996.

Albert, Gleb J. "From Currency in the Warez Economy to Self-Sufficient Art Form: Text Mode Graphics and the 'Scene.'" *WiderScreen* 20, nos. 1–2 (2017). http://widerscreen.fi/numerot/2017-1-2/from-currency-in-the-warez -economy-to-self-sufficient-art-form-text-mode-graphics-and-the-scene/.

Allen, David P. (W1UKZ). "Computer Net Info (Strays)." *QST*, November 1980.

Alphabet, Inc. "Annual Report, Form 10-K." Washington, DC: US Securities and Exchange Commission, December 31, 2020. https://www.sec.gov/Archives/edgar/data/0001652044/000165204421000010/goog-20201231.htm.

American Health Consultants, Inc. "AIDS Computer Bulletin Boards Gaining Popularity." *AIDS ALERT*, November 1993. http://web.archive.org/web/19961018135646/http://hwmin.gbgm-umc.org/CAM/unique.html.

American Telephone and Telegraph Company. "Data Set 103A." March 1963.

———. "Data Set 103A Interface Specification." *Bell System Data Communications Technical Reference*, February 1967.

———. "Data Set 103A Type Identification and Operation." *Bell System Practices: Plant Series*, no. 5 (January 1967).

———. "Data Set 103F Interface Specification." *Bell System Data Communications Technical Reference*, May 1964.

"America Online Expands Capacity and Internet Support." *Information Today*, May 1994.

"America's Information Highway: A Hitch-Hiker's Guide." *Economist*, December 25, 1993.

An, Bo. "Infrastructure, Amateurism, and Radical Networking: FidoNet in China (1995–1998)." Paper presented at Computer Networks Histories: Local, National and Transnational Perspectives, Università della Svizzera italiana, Lugano, Switzerland, 2017. https://www.infoclio.ch/en/computer-networks-histories-local-national-and-transnational-perspectives.

Anastas, Kate. "Underground Newspapers: The Social Media Networks of the 1960s and 1970s." Mapping American Social Movements through the 20th Century, University of Washington. Accessed February 6, 2020. http://depts.washington.edu/moves/altnews_geography.shtml.

Ankerson, Megan Sapnar. *Dot-Com Design: The Rise of a Usable, Social, Commercial Web*. New York: New York University Press, 2018.

———. "How Coolness Defined the World Wide Web of the 1990s." *Atlantic*, July 15, 2014. http://www.theatlantic.com/technology/archive/2014/07/how-coolness-defined-the-world-wide-web-of-the-1990s/374443/.

———. "Writing Web Histories with an Eye on the Analog Past." *New Media & Society* 14, no. 3 (2011): 384–400. https://doi.org/10.1177/1461444811414834.

"Announcing Winners in the Boardwatch 100 Readers' Choice BBS Contest 1993." *Boardwatch*, 1993. http://www.bbsdocumentary.com/mp3/93BBSCON/bw100.txt.

Antonelli, Chaz. "The BBS Documentary and Multicom-4." *When Pigs Fly*, November 7, 2015. https://mc4bbs.livejournal.com/246094.html.

Apuleius. "The Alt.Sex.Stories.* Hierarchy and Related Groups FAQ, Version 2.03." Alt Sex Stories Text Repository, June 19, 2000. https://www.asstr.org/files/FAQs_and_Information/ass_faq.txt.

Aquila Internet Services. October 23, 1996. http://web.archive.org/web/19961023022329/http://www.aquila.com/.

Asmolov, Gregory, and Polina Kolozaridi. "The Imaginaries of RuNet." *Russian Politics* 2, no. 1 (March 9, 2017): 54–79. https://doi.org/10.1163/2451-8921-00201004.

Atkin, Denny. "We're DOOMed." *Compute!*, April 1994.

"Atlantic Telegraph, The: General Manifesto of the Directors to the People of Both Continents. Organization of the Company Official History of the Great Enterprise, Interesting and Important Report of Preliminary Electrical Experiments." *New York Times*, August 27, 1857, sec. Archives. https://www .nytimes.com/1857/08/27/archives/the-atlantic-telegraph-general-manifesto -of-the-directors-to-the.html.

"Backdraft Bulletin Board System." *ModemNews Magazine*, 1993.

Baker, Ben. "Coordinators List." *FidoNews*, June 10, 1985.

———. "GO! GO! GO!—June 12 Is IT." *FidoNews*, June 10, 1985.

———. "An Informal History of FidoNet." *FidoNews*, November 23, 1987.

———. "New Look for FidoNet." *FidoNews*, April 22, 1985.

———. "New NODELIST Distribution Method." *FidoNews*, March 3, 1986.

———. "View from the Top: Echomail." *FidoNews*, June 30, 1986.

Baker, Ben, and Ken Kaplan. "The Duties of a Network or Region Coordinator." *FidoNews*, June 3, 1985.

Baker, Ben, Ken Kaplan, and Henk Wevers, eds. "The International FidoNet Nodelist, Day Number 276." International FidoNet Association, October 3, 1986. http://www.textfiles.com/fidonet-on-the-internet/n1986/nodelist.276.

Balbi, Gabriele, and Christiane Berth. "Towards a Telephonic History of Technology." *History and Technology* 35, no. 2 (April 3, 2019): 105–14. https://doi.org/ 10.1080/07341512.2019.1652959.

Balka, Ellen. "Womantalk Goes On-Line: The Use of Computer Networks in the Context of Feminist Social Change." PhD diss., Simon Fraser University, 1991. https://core.ac.uk/download/pdf/56369048.pdf.

Barry, Rey. *Guide to Free Software*. Charlottesville, VA: Freeware Hall of Fame, 1995.

Barton, Jared, and Tyler Watts. "'I Can't Drive 55': The Economics of the CB Radio Phenomenon." *Independent Review* 15, no. 3 (2011): 383–97.

Bates, Benjamin J., and Kenneth P. Lansing. "The New World of Democratic Telecommunications: FidoNet as an Example of the New Horizontal Information Networks." Paper presented at 42nd annual conference of the International Communication Association, Miami, FL, 1992.

Batterson, David W. "Information Age Is Coming, but 'Freeware,' 'Shareware' Won't Be There Making Money." *Los Angeles Times*, November 22, 1987. http://articles.latimes.com/1987-11-22/business/fi-23979_1_shareware -freeware-bullet-train.

Bay, Morten. "What Is 'Internet'? The Case for the Proper Noun and Why It Is Important." *Internet Histories* 1, no. 3 (May 4, 2017): 203–18. https://doi.org/ 10.1080/24701475.2017.1339860.

Baym, Nancy K. "Communication, Interpretation, and Relationship: A Study of a Computer-Mediated Fan Community." PhD diss., University of Illinois, 1994. http://hdl.handle.net/2142/19011.

———. "From Practice to Culture on Usenet." *Sociological Review* 42, no. S1 (May 1, 1994): 29–52. https://doi.org/10.1111/j.1467-954X.1994.tb03408.x.

————. "Interpreting Soap Operas and Creating Community: Inside a Computer-Mediated Fan Culture." *Journal of Folklore Research* 30, nos. 2–3 (1993): 143–76.

Bell, Wayne. *WWIV.* Version v3.21d. 1986.

Bellin, Adam, and Pier Del Frate. "True Color for Windows." *Byte,* December 1990.

Berlet, Chip, and Carol Mason. "Swastikas in Cyberspace: How Hate Went Online." In *Digital Media Strategies of the Far Right in Europe and the United States,* edited by Patricia Anne Simpson and Helga Druxes, 21–36. Lanham, MD: Lexington Books, 2015.

Berners-Lee, Tim, and Mark Fischetti. *Weaving the Web: The Past, Present and Future of the World Wide Web by Its Inventor.* London: Orion Business, 1999.

Berry, Bob. "Q&A.DOC." *CompuShow.* Version Standard Version 8.50a. Sedona, AZ: Canyon State Systems and Software, 1992.

Beschizza, Rob. "Can We Talk?" *Boing Boing,* June 27, 2013. http://web.archive .org/web/0/https://boingboing.net/2013/06/27/can-we-talk.html.

bglo-teach-perot. "New Mailing List for an Impromptu Task Force." June 8, 1992, 18:20:52 PDT. http://www.qrd.org/qrd/electronic/1992/perot.glb.email-06 .08.92.

"Birth of BYTEnet, The." *Byte,* October 1984.

Blake, Art M. "Audible Citizenship and Audiomobility: Race, Technology, and CB Radio." *American Quarterly* 63, no. 3 (September 1, 2011): 531–53.

Blue, Bill, and Mark Robbins. *ASCII Express "The Professional."* Version 3.4x. Santee, CA: Southwestern Data Systems, 1982.

"Boardwatch Magazine Announces the Boardwatch 100 Reader's Choice Bulletin Board Contest." *Boardwatch,* May 1992.

Boler, Megan. "Hypes, Hopes and Actualities: New Digital Cartesianism and Bodies in Cyberspace." *New Media & Society* 9, no. 1 (February 1, 2007): 139–68. https://doi.org/10.1177/1461444807067586.

Bonine, Steve. "New-Sysop Orientation Information." International FidoNet Association, February 22, 1988. http://www.textfiles.com/bbs/FIDONET/ JENNINGS/STANDARDS/newsysop.txt.

Borland, Hanne, and Jytte Mansfeld. *Living in a Modem World.* Hørsholm, Denmark: Focus, 1991.

Boulware, Jack, and Silke Tudor. *Gimme Something Better: The Profound, Progressive, and Occasionally Pointless History of Bay Area Punk from Dead Kennedys to Green Day.* New York: Penguin Books, 2009.

————. "Shred of Dignity." Gimme Something Better, 2009. http:// gimmesomethingbetter.com/excerpts/shred-of-dignity.

Bourne, Charles P., and Trudi Bellardo Hahn. *A History of Online Information Services, 1963–1976.* Cambridge, MA: MIT Press, 2004.

Braman, Sandra. "The Framing Years: Policy Fundamentals in the Internet Design Process, 1969–1979." *Information Society* 27, no. 5 (October 1, 2011): 295–310. https://doi.org/10.1080/01972243.2011.607027.

———. "Internet RFCs as Social Policy: Network Design from a Regulatory Perspective." *Proceedings of the American Society for Information Science and Technology* 46, no. 1 (January 1, 2009): 1–29. https://doi.org/10.1002/meet .2009.1450460254.

———. "The Interpenetration of Technical and Legal Decision-Making for the Internet." *Information, Communication & Society* 13, no. 3 (April 1, 2010): 309–24. https://doi.org/10.1080/13691180903473814.

Brammer, Jens. "Time-Sharing in Denmark in 1968." In *History of Nordic Computing 4*, edited by Christian Gram, Per Rasmussen, and Søren Duus Østergaard, vol. 447, 167–70. Cham, Switzerland: Springer, 2015. http://link .springer.com/10.1007/978-3-319-17145-6_18.

Brand, Stewart. "Finding a Balance in the Slippery Economics of an Information Age." *Los Angeles Times*, November 8, 1987, sec. Part IV.

———. "The Revolution Will Be Netcast." *Wired*, September 1996.

Brewster, Kathryn, and Bonnie Ruberg. "SURVIVORS: Archiving the History of Bulletin Board Systems and the AIDS Crisis." *First Monday* 25, no. 10 (October 2020). https://doi.org/10.5210/fm.v25i10.10290.

Briggs, Robert. "Creating FIDO Source." *FidoNews*, April 14, 1985.

———. "Fido Re-write." *FidoNews*, April 29, 1985.

Brinker, Scott J. "President's Corner." *Major News*, Spring 1994.

Bronson, Ben. "Installing a Computer Bulletin Board Program." BBS Software Directory, April 1981. http://software.bbsdocumentary.com/AAA/AAA/ CBBS/cpmnet81.apr.txt.

Brown, Judy. "Microsoft Gives Business View from Windows 95 Preview Copies of the Long-Awaited New Operating System Are Available." *Milwaukee Journal*, March 27, 1995, sec. Business.

Bruckman, Amy. "Gender Swapping on the Internet." In *High Noon on the Electronic Frontier: Conceptual Issues in Cyberspace*, edited by Peter Ludlow, 317–26. Cambridge, MA: MIT Press, 1996.

Bruckman, Amy, and Carlos Jensen. "The Mystery of the Death of MediaMOO: Seven Years of Evolution of an Online Community." In *Building Virtual Communities: Learning and Change in Cyberspace*, edited by K. Ann Renninger and Wesley Shumar, 21–33. Cambridge: Cambridge University Press, 2002.

Brunton, Finn. *Spam: A Shadow History of the Internet*. Cambridge, MA: MIT Press, 2013.

Burkhalter, Byron. "Reading Race Online." In *Communities in Cyberspace*, edited by Marc A. Smith and Peter Kollock, 60–75. London: Routledge, 1999.

Bush, Randy. "A Basic FidoNet(tm) Technical Standard, Draft FSC001-9." FidoNet Technical Standards Committee, December 27, 1987. http://ftsc.org/docs/fsc -0001.000.

———. "FidoNet Standards Committee." *FidoNews*, July 28, 1986.

———. "FidoNet: Technology, Tools, and History." *Communications of the ACM* 36, no. 8 (August 1993): 31–35. https://doi.org/10.1145/163381.163383.

————. "FidoNet: Use, Technology, and Tools." In *Proceedings of INET '92: International Networking Conference, Kobe, Japan, June 15–18, 1992*, ed. Harushisa Ishida. Reston, VA: Internet Society, 1992.

————. "How FidoNet™ Tunnels the Internet." September 21, 1992. Archived at http://www.textfiles.com/bbs/FIDONET/JENNINGS/STANDARDS/tunnel .msg.txt.

Butler, Mike. "A Day in the Life of an Overworked UK Sysop—or—How to Survive a Business, BBS and Family without Cracking Up." *FidoNews*, February 3, 1992.

Butow, Eric E. "A Content Analysis of Rule Enforcement in the Virtual Communities of FidoNet Echomail Conferences." Master's thesis, California State University, Fresno, 1996.

Byczek, Wally. "So You Want to Be a Sysop?" 1989. Archived at http://textfiles .com/bbs/be-sysop.txt.

CACHE Register 6, no. 1 (January 1981).

Callahan, Michael E., aka Dr. File Finder. "The History of Shareware." Paul's Picks Shareware Library, 1999. https://web.archive.org/web/20090403094743/ http://paulspicks.com:80/history.asp.

Callahan, Mike, and Nick Anis. *Dr. File Finder's Guide to Shareware*. Berkeley, CA: Osborne McGraw-Hill, 1990.

Campbell-Kelly, Martin. *From Airline Reservations to Sonic the Hedgehog: A History of the Software Industry*. Cambridge, MA: MIT Press, 2003.

————. "Number Crunching without Programming: The Evolution of Spreadsheet Usability." *IEEE Annals of the History of Computing* 29, no. 3 (July 2007): 6–19. https://doi.org/10.1109/MAHC.2007.4338438.

Campbell-Kelly, Martin, and William Aspray. *Computer: A History of the Information Machine*. New York: Basic Books, 1996.

Campbell-Kelly, Martin, William Aspray, Nathan Ensmenger, and Jeffrey R. Yost. *Computer: A History of the Information Machine*. 3rd ed. New York: Routledge, 2018. https://doi.org/10.4324/9780429494017.

Campbell-Kelly, Martin, and Daniel D. Garcia-Swartz. "Economic Perspectives on the History of the Computer Time-Sharing Industry, 1965–1985." *IEEE Annals of the History of Computing* 30, no. 1 (January 2008): 16–36. https://doi .org/10.1109/MAHC.2008.3.

Caplan, Jay. "Effective Shareware Distribution via the BBS Channel, Version 1.2." August 10, 1992. Archived at http://textfiles.com/bbs/bbstip12.txt.

Carey, James W. "A Cultural Approach to Communication." In *Communication as Culture: Essays on Media and Society*, 11–28. Boston: Unwin Hyman, 1989.

Carey, John, and Martin C. J. Elton. "The Other Path to the Web: The Forgotten Role of Videotex and Other Early Online Services." *New Media & Society* 11, nos. 1–2 (2009): 241–60.

Carpentier, Michel, Sylviane Farnoux-Toporkoff, Christian Garric, and C. P Skrimshire. *Telecommunications in Transition*. Chichester, UK: Wiley, 1992.

Caruso, Denise. "Networking Bulletin Boards." *InfoWorld*, August 27, 1984.

"Cat Calls." *Byte*, December 1979.

Caulkins, Dave. "PCNET, 1979." *People's Computers*, October 1977.

———. "Personal Computer Network." *People's Computers*, August 1977.

CBS. "Computer Network / Neo-Nazi Network." *CBS Evening News*, May 10, 1985. https://tvnews.vanderbilt.edu/broadcasts/303493.

———. "Computer Virus / Morris." *CBS Evening News*, November 8, 1988. https://tvnews.vanderbilt.edu/broadcasts/319238.

CDC National AIDS Clearinghouse. "A Selected Guide to AIDS-Related Electronic Bulletin Boards." US Department of Health and Human Services, April 2, 1993. http://cd.textfiles.com/internetinfo/answers/sci/aids-faq/part4.

Ceruzzi, Paul E. *A History of Modern Computing*. Cambridge, MA: MIT Press, 1998.

Chris. "The Fall of the Modem World." August 1, 1991. Archived at http://textfiles.com/bbs/fotmw.txt.

Christensen, Ward. "Comments and Prologues to CBBS up to Version 3.2." BBS Software Directory, 1979. http://software.bbsdocumentary.com/AAA/AAA/CBBS/history.txt.

———. "C(omputerized)BBS—Thanks for Remembering 25th." *Slashdot*, February 17, 2003. https://slashdot.org/comments.pl?sid=54081&cid=5317919.

———. "Computer Network Poll." *Dr. Dobb's Journal of Computer Calisthenics & Orthodontia*, July 1978.

Christensen, Ward, and Randy Suess. "The Birth of the BBS." Chinet, 1989. https://www.chinet.com/html/cbbs.html.

———. "CBBS—COOKBOOK Rev. 3.5 11/28/81." BBS Software Directory, November 28, 1981. http://software.bbsdocumentary.com/AAA/AAA/CBBS/cookbook.txt.

———. "CBBS Phone #s." BBS Software Directory, December 26, 1981. http://software.bbsdocumentary.com/AAA/AAA/CBBS/parttime.txt.

———. "Hobbyist Computerized Bulletin Board." *Byte*, November 1978.

———. "Midwest Remote CP/M Systems." BBS Software Directory, July 7, 1981. http://software.bbsdocumentary.com/AAA/AAA/CBBS/1981cbbslist.txt.

———. "Other Message Sys. Phone #s." BBS Software Directory, December 26, 1981. http://software.bbsdocumentary.com/AAA/AAA/CBBS/parttime.txt.

———. "Part-Time Msg Sys. Phone #s." BBS Software Directory, September 27, 1981. http://software.bbsdocumentary.com/AAA/AAA/CBBS/parttime.txt.

Christian, Kaare. "Using the Internet: Getting the Clarkson Packet Drivers." *PC Magazine*, May 28, 1991.

Christianson, J. Scott, and Dan Wendling. "Econet: The Ecology Network." *Boardwatch*, December 1992.

Chun, Wendy Hui Kyong. *Control and Freedom: Power and Paranoia in the Age of Fiber Optics*. Cambridge, MA: MIT Press, 2006.

Clapp, Doug. "Clapp-Trapp." *InfoWorld*, November 21, 1983.

Clinton, William J. "Address before a Joint Session of the Congress on the State of the Union." January 25, 1994. Accessed at American Presidency Project,

https://www.presidency.ucsb.edu/documents/address-before-joint-session
-the-congress-the-state-the-union-12.

"Clubs and Newsletters." *Byte*, February 1976.

Codella, Chris. "Hiram Percy Maxim." *QST*, February 2014.

Colker, David. "Looking into the Origins of the Online Universe." *Los Angeles Times*, August 20, 1996.

Community Educational Services Foundation. "Welcome to GLIB." Gay and Lesbian Information Bureau. Accessed May 9, 2014, http://web.archive.org/web/19970228045752/http://www.glib.org/.

Computerized AIDS Ministries. Home page. March 7, 1996. http://web.archive.org/web/19961018015652/http://hwbbs.gbgm-umc.org/.

Conner-Sax, Kiersten, and Ed Krol. *The Whole Internet: The Next Generation: A Completely New Edition of the First and Best User's Guide to the Internet*. Sebastopol, CA: O'Reilly, 1999.

Correll, Shelley. "The Ethnography of an Electronic Bar: The Lesbian Cafe." *Journal of Contemporary Ethnography* 24, no. 3 (October 1, 1995): 270–98. https://doi.org/10.1177/089124195024003002.

Cory, Richard B. "The UMC, CAM, and Me." Computerized AIDS Ministries, July 26, 1995. http://web.archive.org/web/19970129083713/http://gbgm-umc.org/CAM/cam-me.html.

Cringely, Robert X. *Accidental Empires: How the Boys of Silicon Valley Make Their Millions, Battle Foreign Competition, and Still Can't Get a Date*. Reading, MA: Addison-Wesley, 1991.

Crocker, David. "RFC 1775 To Be 'On' the Internet." Network Working Group, March 1995. https://tools.ietf.org/html/rfc1775.

———. "Who Is ON the Internet?" *Big-Internet@munnari.oz.au*, January 24, 1995.

Cunha, Tom. *TcSoft's Intelligent Match Maker*. Version 4.9. San Antonio, TX: TcSoft, Inc., 1995.

Dame-Griff, Avery. "TGNet Map." Mapping TGNet, Queer Digital History Project, 2018. http://queerdigital.com/tgnmap/index.html.

Damon, Lee, Dale Weber, and Lisa Gronke. "How to Use the UUCP <===> Fido-Net<tm>." December 9, 1988. Archived at https://www.lns.com/papers/ufgate/UFGATE.HOW.

Daniel, Timothy (N8RK). "Super-Ratt RTTY/CW Program with RBBS." *73*, September 1983.

Daniels, Don. "IFNA Status Report for October 1987." *FidoNews*, October 5, 1987.

———. "IFNA Welcomes Poland to FidoNet." *FidoNews*, September 7, 1987.

Daniels, Harvey A. "Breaker, Break, Broke: Citizens Band in the Classroom." *English Journal* 65, no. 9 (December 1, 1976): 52–57. https://doi.org/10.2307/815750.

Daniels, Jessie. *Cyber Racism: White Supremacy Online and the New Attack on Civil Rights*. Lanham, MD: Rowman and Littlefield, 2009.

Dashner, John. "Ham Radio EchoMail Conference." *FidoNews*, October 13, 1986.

Davila, Juan. "Como Obtener un Número de Nodo en FidoNet 367 (RED de Puerto Rico)." *FidoNews*, February 1, 1988.

Day, Ronald E. *Indexing It All: The Subject in the Age of Documentation, Information, and Data*. Cambridge, MA: MIT Press, 2014.

Decker, Jack. "USENET vs. FidoNet—A Quick Comparison." *FidoNews*, February 24, 1992.

Delfino, Erik. "'Transfer, Please'—The Low-Down on Downloading." *Online* 18, no. 3 (May 1994): 112.

De Moville, Wig. "The User's Guide to WWIV." *WWIV*. Version 4.21a. 1991.

Dickinson, Ernest. "Business Tunes In on Citizens Band: Giants Enter Booming Market for 2-Way Sets." *New York Times*, March 7, 1976, sec. Business & Finance.

Dietter, Susie, dir. "Radioactive Man." *The Simpsons*. Fox. September 24, 1995. https://simpsons.fandom.com/wiki/Radioactive_Man.

"Doctor's Wife, The (TV Story)." Tardis Data Core: The Doctor Who Wiki. Accessed March 21, 2014. http://tardis.wikia.com/wiki/The_Doctor%27s_Wife_(TV_story).

doctor_x. "Curt Vendel on the BBS Documentary." *AtariAge*, May 18, 2010, http://atariage.com/forums/topic/163089-curt-vendel-on-the-bbs-documentary/?p=2016015.

Dodell, David, and Ben Baker. "FidoNet-Alternet Technical Agreement." *FidoNews*, September 5, 1988.

Douglas, Susan J. *Inventing American Broadcasting, 1899–1922*. Baltimore: Johns Hopkins University Press, 1987.

———. *Listening In: Radio and the American Imagination: From Amos 'n' Andy and Edward R. Murrow to Wolfman Jack and Howard Stern*. New York: Times Books, 1999.

Dourish, Paul. *The Stuff of Bits: An Essay on the Materialities of Information*. Cambridge, MA: MIT Press, 2017.

Draganosky, Joe (Kaboom). "BBSing.com, Remembering the Original Cyberspace." bbsing.com. Accessed June 18, 2021. http://web.archive.org/web/20041205085956/http://www.bbsing.com/.

Driscoll, Catherine. "Girl Culture, Revenge and Global Capitalism: Cybergirls, Riot Grrls, Spice Girls." *Australian Feminist Studies* 14, no. 29 (1999): 173–93. doi:10.1080/08164649993425.

Driscoll, Kevin. "Cooperative Mode for Amateur and Academic Game Histories." *ROMchip* 1, no. 1 (July 1, 2019). http://romchip.org/index.php/romchip-journal/article/view/71.

———. "Demography and Decentralization: Measuring the Bulletin Board Systems of North America." *WiderScreen* 23, nos. 2–3 (June 18, 2020). http://widerscreen.fi/numerot/2020-2-3/demography-and-decentralization-measuring-the-bulletin-board-systems-of-north-america/.

————. "From Punched Cards to 'Big Data': A Social History of Database Populism." *Communication +1* 1, no. 1 (August 29, 2012). http://scholarworks.umass.edu/cpo/vol1/iss1/4.

————. "Hobbyist Inter-Networking and the Popular Internet Imaginary: Forgotten Histories of Networked Personal Computing, 1978–1998." PhD diss., University of Southern California, 2014.

————. "Professional Work for Nothing: Software Commercialization and 'An Open Letter to Hobbyists.'" *Information & Culture* 50, no. 2 (May 1, 2015): 257–83. https://doi.org/10.7560/IC50207.

————. "Thou Shalt Love Thy BBS: Distributed Experimentation in Community Moderation." In *Computer Network Histories: Hidden Streams from the Internet Past*, edited by Paolo Bory, Gianluigi Negro, and Gabriele Balbi, 15–34. Histoire et Informatique / Geschichte und Informatik 21. Zürich, Switzerland: Chronos Verlag, 2019. 10.33057/chronos.1539.

Driscoll, Kevin, and Joshua Diaz. "Endless Loop: A Brief History of Chiptunes." *Transformative Works and Cultures* 2 (March 15, 2009). https://doi.org/10.3983/twc.2009.096.

Driscoll, Kevin, and Camille Paloque-Berges. "Searching for Missing 'Net Histories.'" *Internet Histories* 1, nos. 1–2 (2017): 47–59. https://doi.org/10.1080/24701475.2017.1307541.

Duncombe, Stephen. *Notes from Underground: Zines and the Politics of Alternative Culture*. London: Verso, 1997.

————. "Stagnant Ponds and Bill Clinton." *Boardwatch*, January 1994.

Dvorak, John C., Chris Pirillo, and Wendy Taylor. "The History of Shareware." In *Online! The Book*, 226–28. Upper Saddle River, NJ: Prentice Hall Professional, 2004.

Dvorak Telecommunications Awards. "1995 Dvorak Awards Winners." Accessed April 25, 2014. http://web.archive.org/web/19990218160124/http://www.citivu.com/dvorak/.

"Ebony Shack BBS, The." *BBS Magazine*, August 1995.

Edwards, Benj. "Digitized Autumn Leaves." *Vintage Computing and Gamin* (blog), January 11, 2013, http://www.vintagecomputing.com/index.php/archives/918.

Edwards, Paul N. *The Closed World Computers and the Politics of Discourse in Cold War America*. Cambridge, MA: MIT Press, 1997.

Ehrenman, Gayle. "Prodigy Interactive Personal Service." *PC Magazine*, February 23, 1993.

Electronic Frontier Foundation. "EFF 'Net Culture & Cyber-Anthropology' Archive." March 13, 2003. http://w2.eff.org/Net_culture/.

————. "A History of Protecting Freedom Where Law and Technology Collide." October 7, 2011. https://www.eff.org/about/history.

Elizabeth, Sister Mary. "AEGIS Affidavit in ACLU, et al. v. Reno." ACLU, February 25, 1996. https://www.aclu.org/technology-and-liberty/aegis-affidavit-aclu-et-al-v-reno.

Ellis, David, Rachel Oldridge, and Ana Vasconcelos. "Community and Virtual Community." *Annual Review of Information Science and Technology* 38, no. 1 (September 22, 2005): 145–86. https://doi.org/10.1002/aris.1440380104.

Elmer-Dewitt, Philip. "Orgies On-Line." *Time* 141, no. 22 (May 31, 1993): 61.

Elmer-Dewitt, Philip, and Hannah Bloch. "On a Screen near You: Cyberporn." *Time* 146, no. 1 (July 3, 1995): 38–45.

Elmer-Dewitt, Philip, and David S. Jackson. "Battle for the Soul of the Internet." *Time* 144, no. 4 (July 25, 1994): 50–56.

Empty Closet, The. July 1992. Digital Collections, University of Rochester. https://digitalcollections.lib.rochester.edu/ur/empty-closet-1971-current.

Ensmenger, Nathan. *The Computer Boys Take over Computers, Programmers, and the Politics of Technical Expertise.* Cambridge, MA: MIT Press, 2010.

Eppink, Jason. "A Brief History of the GIF (So Far)." *Journal of Visual Culture* 13, no. 3 (December 1, 2014): 298–306. https://doi.org/10.1177/1470412914553365.

Erokan, Dennis, and Mary Eisenhart. "Andrew Fluegelman: PC-Talk and Beyond." *MicroTimes*, May 1985.

Evans, Claire L. *Broad Band: The Untold Story of the Women Who Made the Internet.* New York: Portfolio/Penguin, 2018.

Event Horizons. "Computer Images." *PC Magazine*, December 1990.

———. "World's Most Expensive BBS." *Boardwatch*, September 1994.

Exec-PC. "Sorry Prodigy." *Boardwatch*, May 1992.

Extremist, The. "Dead Alive." March 12, 2000. Archived at http://www.textfiles.com/history/dalive.

Facebook, Inc. "Annual Report, Form 10-K." Washington, DC: US Securities and Exchange Commission, December 31, 2012. https://www.sec.gov/Archives/edgar/data/1326801/000132680113000003/fb-12312012x10k.htm.

Faden, Eric S. "The Cyberfilm: Hollywood and Computer Technology." *Strategies: Journal of Theory, Culture & Politics* 14, no. 1 (May 2001): 77–90. https://doi.org/10.1080/10402130120042370.

Fano, R. M. "The MAC System: The Computer Utility Approach." *IEEE Spectrum* 2, no. 1 (January 1965): 56–64. https://doi.org/10.1109/MSPEC.1965.5531878.

Felsenstein, Lee. "Build 'Pennywhistle': The Hobbyist's Modem." *Popular Electronics*, March 1976.

Fernback, Jan. "Beyond the Diluted Community Concept: A Symbolic Interactionist Perspective on Online Social Relations." *New Media & Society* 9, no. 1 (February 1, 2007): 49–69. https://doi.org/10.1177/1461444807072417.

Ferris, Melanie A. "Resisting Mainstream Media: Girls and the Act of Making Zines." *Canadian Woman Studies* 21, no. 1 (April 1, 2001). http://pi.library.yorku.ca/ojs/index.php/cws/article/view/6906.

Fidler, Bradley. "Eternal October and the End of Cyberspace." *IEEE Annals of the History of Computing* 39, no. 1 (January 2017): 6–7. https://doi.org/10.1109/MAHC.2017.9.

———. "The Evolution of Internet Routing: Technical Roots of the Network Society." *Internet Histories* 3, nos. 3–4 (October 2, 2019): 364–87. https://doi.org/10.1080/24701475.2019.1661583.

"FidoCon 91—408 Attend Biggest BBS Bash Ever." *Boardwatch*, October 1991.

FidoNet Net 282. March 28, 2004. http://web.archive.org/web/20160310164528/http://www.rxn.com/~net282/.

———. "The FidoNet Nodelist Historical Analysis." February 2, 2005. http://web.archive.org/web/20170629084903/http://www.rxn.com/~net282/nodelist/.

FidoNet on the Internet. "FidoNet Nodelist." October 16, 1987. http://www.textfiles.com/fidonet-on-the-internet/n1987/nodelist.289.

———. "FidoNet Nodelist." December 25, 1992. http://www.textfiles.com/fidonet-on-the-internet/n1992/nodediff.360.

———. "FidoNet Policy and Procedures Guide Version 2." June 26, 1986. http://www.textfiles.com/fidonet-on-the-internet/history/policy2.txt.

———. "FidoNet Policy and Procedures Guide Version 3." October 24, 1986. http://www.textfiles.com/fidonet-on-the-internet/history/policy3.doc.

———. "FOTIs FidoNet Nodelist/Nodediff Archive Page." 2004. http://textfiles.com/fidonet-on-the-internet/nodediff.htm.

———. "FOTIs FidoNet Timeline Page." Accessed October 12, 2019. http://www.textfiles.com/fidonet-on-the-internet/tl.htm.

"FidoNet, Sidekick, Apple, Get Organized!, And Handle." *Byte*, October 1984.

FidoNet Technical Standards Committee. "FTSC Documents." Accessed August 5, 2020. http://ftsc.org/docs/.

"First FidoBaby, The." *FidoNews*, June 10, 1985.

Fischer, Dave. "Longest USENET Thread Ever." alt.folklore.computers, January 25, 1994. https://groups.google.com/g/alt.folklore.computers/c/wF4CpYbWuuA/m/jS6ZOyJd1osJ.

Ford, Nelson. "The History of Shareware & PsL." Association of Software Professionals, 2000. http://web.archive.org/web/20100522020415/http://www.asp-software.org/users/history-of-shareware.asp.

Forester, Tom. "The Myth of the Electronic Cottage." *Futures* 20, no. 3 (June 1, 1988): 227–40. https://doi.org/10.1016/0016-3287(88)90079-1.

Foster, Robert J. (WB7QWG/9). "Unlock the New Electronic Mailboxes." *73*, April 1983.

Fox, David. *Love Bytes: The Online Dating Handbook*. Corte Madera, CA: Waite Group, 1995.

Fox, Susannah, and Lee Rainie. "The Web at 25 in the U.S." Internet & Technology, Pew Research Center, February 27, 2014. http://www.pewresearch.org/internet/2014/02/27/the-web-at-25-in-the-u-s/.

Frauenfelder, Mark. "bOING bOING Advertisement in Factsheet Five #33 (1989)." *Boing Boing*, August 7, 2009. http://boingboing.net/2009/08/19/boing-boing-advertis.html.

Frey, Tony. "The UltraViolet Cafe's Guide to Better Modeming Cuisine." 1989. Archived at http://www.textfiles.com/bbs/guide.txt.

Fuchs, Michael G. "Echomail Conference List Report." FidoNet on the Internet, July 1, 1991. http://www.textfiles.com/fidonet-on-the-internet/e1991/elist107.txt.

Galloway, Alexander R. *Protocol: How Control Exists after Decentralization*. Cambridge, MA: MIT Press, 2004.

Gardner, Fran. "Entrepreneur Hits Bulletin Board Bull's Eye." *Oregonian*, February 10, 1994.

Gates, Bill. "An Open Letter to Hobbyists." *Computer Notes*, February 1976.

"Gay Ballad Is Joined by 'Savage.'" *Billboard*, November 13, 1976.

"Gay Liberation Front Meeting at Washington Square Methodist Church." Digital Collections, Manuscripts and Archives Division, New York Public Library. Accessed June 17, 2021. https://digitalcollections.nypl.org/items/510d47e3-57c4-a3d9-e040-e00a18064a99.

Gazzard, Alison. *Now the Chips Are Down: The BBC Micro*. Cambridge, MA: MIT Press, 2016.

Gillespie, Tarleton. *Custodians of the Internet: Platforms, Content Moderation, and the Hidden Decisions That Shape Social Media*. Cambridge, MA: MIT Press, 2018.

———. "The Politics of 'Platforms.'" *New Media & Society* 12, no. 3 (May 1, 2010): 347–64. https://doi.org/10.1177/1461444809342738.

Gilmore, John. *Uuslave*. Version hoptoad-1.11. 1987.

Glover, Thomas J., and Millie M. Young. *Pocket PCRef*. 3rd ed. Littleton, CO: Sequoia, 1993.

Goeller, Lee. "Insomniac Wizards Revisited." *IEEE Technology and Society Magazine*, 19, no. 2 (Summer 2000): 6–9.

Goldbloom, James C. "SysOp Suicide! (A Day in the Life of a System Operator)." March 1988. Archived at http://www.textfiles.com/bbs/sysopsui.txt.

Good, Travis. "Building the LATINO Net." *FidoNews*, November 9, 1987.

Google, Inc. "Annual Report, Form 10-K." Washington, DC: US Securities and Exchange Commission, December 31, 2006. https://www.sec.gov/Archives/edgar/data/0001652044/000165204421000010/goog-20201231.htm.

Gordon, Josh. "EchoMail and Host Routing: A Plea for Sanity." *FidoNews*, June 9, 1986.

Gotkin, Kevin. "When Computers Were Amateur." *IEEE Annals of the History of Computing* 36, no. 2 (April 2014): 4–14. https://doi.org/10.1109/MAHC.2014.32.

Grad, B. "The Creation and the Demise of VisiCalc." *IEEE Annals of the History of Computing* 29, no. 3 (July 2007): 20–31. https://doi.org/10.1109/MAHC.2007.4338439.

Graeber, Laurel. "New & Noteworthy Paperbacks." *New York Times Book Review*, March 22, 1998.

Gray, Matthew. "Web Growth Summary." MIT, 1996. https://www.mit.edu/~mkgray/net/.

Green, Wayne (W2NSD/1). "Computers Are Here—Are You Ready?" *73*, October 1975.

Grey Mist. "Conference Report." *FidoNews*, August 25, 1986.

Grimes, William. "Computer as a Cultural Tool: Chatter Mounts on Every Topic." *New York Times*, December 1, 1992, sec. The Arts.

Grossman, Wendy. "The Making of an Underclass: AOL." Chapter 3 in *Net.Wars*. New York: New York University Press, 1999. https://web.archive.org/web/20110505003755/http://www.nyupress.org/netwars/pages/chapter03/ch03_.html.

Grunin, Lori. "Something Lossed, Something Gained: Image Compression for PC Graphics." *PC Magazine*, April 28, 1992.

Hackers: Wizards of the Electronic Age. Directed by Fabrice Florin. 1984. DVD. http://hackersvideo.com.

Hafner, Katie. "The Epic Saga of The WELL." *Wired*, May 1997. http://www.wired.com/wired/archive/5.05/ff_well_pr.html.

———. "Ghosts in the Machine." *Wired*, July 1999. http://archive.wired.com/wired/archive/4.07/ghosts.html.

———. *The WELL: A Story of Love, Death, and Real Life in the Seminal Online Community*. New York: Carroll and Graf, 2001.

Hafner, Katie, and Matthew Lyon. *ARPA Kadabra oder die Anfänge des Internet*. Heidelberg: Dpunkt-Verlag, 2008.

———. *Where Wizards Stay Up Late: The Origins of the Internet*. New York: Simon and Schuster, 1996.

Hakala, David. "Best BBS Contest Update." *Boardwatch*, April 1992.

———. "Boardwatch 100 Readers' Choice BBS Contest Update." *Boardwatch*, May 1992.

Hall, Dave (N3CVJ). "CB Repeater." Spew Radio Inc., Accessed February 11, 2014. http://home.ptd.net/~n3cvj/repeater.htm.

Hall, Kira. "Cyberfeminism." In *Computer-Mediated Communication: Linguistic, Social, and Cross-Cultural Perspectives*, 147–70. Amsterdam: John Benjamins, 1996.

Halt, Roy. "Freight Car Tumbles off Viaduct." *Chicago Tribune*, January 15, 1978.

Harding, Mitchell. "A Day in the Life of a Teenage Sysop." *FidoNews*, February 24, 1992.

Hargadon, Michael A. "Like City Lights, Receding: ANSi Artwork and the Digital Underground, 1985–2000." MA thesis, Concordia University, 2011. http://mhargadon.ca/media/mhargadon-thesis.pdf.

Haring, Kristen. "The 'Freer Men' of Ham Radio: How a Technical Hobby Provided Social and Spatial Distance." *Technology and Culture* 44, no. 4 (2003): 734–61. https://doi.org/10.1353/tech.2003.0164.

———. *Ham Radio's Technical Culture*. Cambridge, MA: MIT Press, 2008.

Hartman, Bob. "Fido Re-write." *FidoNews*, July 29, 1985.

———. "Fido <==> UNIX Mail." *FidoNews*, August 19, 1985.

———. "FTS-0004 EchoMail Specification Version 3.31." FidoNet Technical Standards Committee, December 12, 1987. http://www.textfiles.com/fidonet-on-the-internet/fs/fts_0004.txt.

———. "Rover, Rovermsg, Renum, and the UN*X Gateway." *FidoNews*, December 9, 1985.

———. "This is simply a request for information . . ." *FidoNews*, July 15, 1985.

———. "What Is the Story on 9600 Baud Modems." *FidoNews*, March 9, 1987.

Hauben, Michael, and Ronda Hauben. *Netizens: On the History and Impact of Usenet and the Internet*. Los Alamitos, CA: IEEE Computer Society, 1997. http://www.columbia.edu/~hauben/netbook/.

"Hayes Micromodem II, The." *Byte*, December 1981.

"Hayes Stack." *Byte*, June 1981.

Helmers, Carl. "Some Thoughts about Modems." *Byte*, July 1978.

Helmond, Anne. "The Platformization of the Web: Making Web Data Platform Ready." *Social Media + Society* 1 (2015). https://doi.org/10.1177/2056305115603080.

Hemmendinger, D. "Messaging in the Early SDC Time-Sharing System." *IEEE Annals of the History of Computing* 36, no. 1 (January 2014): 52–57. https://doi.org/10.1109/MAHC.2013.44.

Henderson, Thom. "Any Day Now." *FidoNews*, May 6, 1985.

———. "ARC? What's an ARC?" *FidoNews*, October 14, 1985.

———. "Change of Command." *FidoNews*, March 25, 1985.

———. "Editorial: Double Dawns." *FidoNews*, November 10, 1986.

———. "Editorial: Future Directions." *FidoNews*, November 11, 1985.

———. "Editorial: One Year Later." *FidoNews*, March 31, 1986.

———. "Electronic Hate." *FidoNews*, May 13, 1985.

———. "Fido 10i." *FidoNews*, May 20, 1985.

———. "The New Kid on the Block." *FidoNews*, April 1, 1985.

———. "Public Domain Fido." *FidoNews*, April 14, 1985.

———. "Special Issue." *FidoNews*, April 22, 1985.

———. "What a Weekend!" *FidoNews*, August 25, 1986.

Hicks, J. Brad. "Echomail, Host-Routing, and Topology." *FidoNews*, June 23, 1986.

Hiltz, Starr Roxanne, and Murray Turoff. *The Network Nation: Human Communication via Computer*. Reading, MA: Addison-Wesley, 1978.

Hobbs, Charles P. "The Modem World." 2000. Archived at http://textfiles.com/history/modemwld.txt.

Hof, Robert D. "Where Did the Net Come From, Daddy?" *BusinessWeek*, September 16, 1996.

Horn, Stacy. *Cyberville: Clicks, Culture, and the Creation of an Online Town*. New York: Warner Books, 1998.

"How and Why to Access the Internet." *Boardwatch*, October 1992.

"How to Become an Unsuccessful, Burned-Out SysOp." N.d. Archived at http://www.textfiles.com/100/howtobbs.txt.

"HT-220 Page." Michael Wright Page. Accessed February 9, 2014. http://mfwright.com/HT220.html.

Hu, Tung-Hui. *A Prehistory of the Cloud*. Cambridge, MA: MIT Press, 2015.

Hughes, Dave. "The Year of Internet at BBSCON '94." *Cook Report on Internet ->
NREN*, October 1994.

Hughes-Hinnen, Anne. "My Memories of Washington Square United Methodist Church, 1981–2005." *People of the Village* (blog), April 8, 2014. http://
peopleblog.churchofthevillage.org/my-memories-of-washington-square
-united-methodist-church-1981-2005/.

humdog. "Pandora's Vox: On Community in Cyberspace." 1994. *Alphaville
Herald*, May 2004. http://alphavilleherald.com/2004/05/introducing_hum
.html.

Humphrey, John H., and Gary S. Smock. "High-Speed Modems." *Byte*, June 1988.
———. "Whither the Modem?" *Byte*, January 1989.

Hunter, John J. "Three V.22bis Modems, One Clear Winner." *InfoWorld*, September 1986.

"IBECC." *BBS Magazine*, May 1992.

Ilacqua, Spike. "The First ISP." *USENIX*, March 15, 1999. https://web.archive
.org/web/20100603211424/http://www.usenix.org/publications/login/1999
-2/isp.html.

"In Focus." *InfoWorld*, June 27, 1983.

"International FidoNet—15,649 Bulletin Boards Worldwide with a Connection,
The." *Boardwatch*, October 1992.

International Telecommunication Union. "ITU-T Recommendation V.22 Bis:
2400 Bits per Second Duplex Modem Using the Frequency Division Technique Standardized for Use on the General Switched Telephone Network
and on Point-to-Point 2-Wire Leased Telephone-Type Circuits." 1988.

"Internet Access at $3 per Month—Delphi Makes the Global Connection." *Board-
watch*, April 1993.

"Interrupt Stack, The." *FidoNews*, April 28, 1986.

"In the Crowd: Tom Jennings." *Thrasher*, November 1986.

James, David. "EchoMail Can Help You Find Your Roots." *FidoNews*, July 28,
1986.

James, Michael L. "An Exploratory Study of the Perceived Benefits of Electronic
Bulletin Board Use and Their Impact on Other Communication Activities."
PhD diss., Florida State University, 1992.

Jankowski, Nicholas W. "Creating Community with Media: History, Theories
and Scientific Investigations." In *Handbook of New Media*, edited by Leah A.
Lievrouw and Sonia M. Livingstone, 39–49. Social Shaping and Consequences of ICTs. Thousand Oaks, CA: Sage, 2002. https://hdl.handle.net/
2027/uc1.32106011430425.

Jennings, Tom. "Are All Sysops Criminals?" *FidoNews*, November 26, 1990.
———. "As you all probably know by now . . ." *FidoNews*, March 18, 1985.
———. "Editorial." *FidoNews*, December 16, 1985.
———. "Editorial." *FidoNews*, September 2, 1991.
———. "Editorial." *FidoNews*, May 11, 1992.

———. "Editorial: (I'm about to) Snooze . . ." *FidoNews*, August 17, 1992.

———. "European Fido." *FidoNews*, December 24, 1984.

———. "FidoNet Electronic Mail Protocol." October 20, 1984. Archived at http:// www.textfiles.com/bbs/FIDONET/JENNINGS/STANDARDS/fidomail.doc .txt.

———. "FidoNet History and Operation." February 8, 1985. Archived at http:// www.textfiles.com/bbs/FIDONET/JENNINGS/HISTORY/fidohist.1.txt.

———. "Fido #1 in Net # . . ." *FidoNews*, April 22, 1985.

———. "Fido's Operating Manual." November 1, 1984. Archived at http://www .textfiles.com/bbs/FIDONET/JENNINGS/PROGRAMS/FIDO-10/.

———. "Fido's Operating Manual, Fourth Edition." August 1985. Archived at http://www.textfiles.com/bbs/FIDONET/JENNINGS/PROGRAMS/FIDO-10/.

———. "The First FidoNet Newsletter." *FidoNews*, December 1, 1984.

———. "FOSSIL Drivers' Ancient History." *FidoNews*, February 3, 1992.

———. "The History of FidoNet: An Interview with Tom Jennings." Interview by Marge Robbins. October 1993. Archived at http://www.textfiles.com/bbs/ FIDONET/JENNINGS/HISTORY/tomj_mrobbins.txt.

———. "HOMOCORE Issues 1 through 7." Sensitive Research. Accessed June 15, 2021. https://web.archive.org/web/20210618022530/https://www.sr-ix.com/ Etc/HOMOCORE/index.html.

———. "Hot News." *FidoNews*, January 16, 1985.

———. Q&A with Tom Jennings. ROFLcon II. May 1, 2010.

———. "Shred of Dignity Skaters Union, ca. 1989." Sensitive Research. Accessed June 15, 2021. https://web.archive.org/web/20210618022646/https://www.sr -ix.com/Etc/myQueerSF/Shipley/index.html

———. "Some Preliminary Ideas for the FidoNet." April 30, 1984. Archived at http://www.textfiles.com/bbs/FIDONET/JENNINGS/STANDARDS/fidonet .doc.txt.

Jennings, Tom, and Tim Požar. "Editorial." *FidoNews*, June 3, 1991.

Jennings, Tom, and others. "FidoNet History." August 20, 1985. Archived at http://www.textfiles.com/bbs/FIDONET/JENNINGS/HISTORY/fidohist .2.txt.

Johnson, Debbi Hood. "I Wear a Red Ribbon." Computerized AIDS Ministries, 1994. http://web.archive.org/web/19980425032633/http://gbgm-umc.org/ cam/i-wear.html.

Jones, Nick. "Jim Maxey Interview." *Boston Sun*, July 19, 2003. http://www .bostonsun.com/archives/story_a1933_part1.htm.

Jones, Steve, and Guillaume Latzko-Toth. "Out from the PLATO Cave: Uncovering the Pre-Internet History of Social Computing." *Internet Histories* 1, nos. 1–2 (January 2, 2017): 60–69. https://doi.org/10.1080/24701475.2017 .1307544.

Jones, Steven. *CyberSociety: Computer-Mediated Communication and Community.* Thousand Oaks, CA: Sage, 1996.

————. *Virtual Culture: Identity and Communication in Cybersociety*. London: Sage, 1997.

Kahin, Brian. *Building Information Infrastructure: Issues in the Development of the National Research and Education Network*. New York: McGraw-Hill Primis, 1996.

————. "RFC 1192 Commercialization of the Internet Summary Report." Network Working Working Group, November 1990. http://www.rfc-editor.org/info/rfc1192.

Kahin, Brian, James Keller, and Harvard Information Infrastructure Project. *Public Access to the Internet*. Cambridge, MA: MIT Press, 1995.

Kahin, Brian, Ernest J. Wilson, and Global Information Infrastructure Commission. *National Information Infrastructure Initiatives Vision and Policy Design*. Cambridge, MA: MIT Press, 1997.

Kaplan, Ken. "Editorial: Happy Birthday FidoNet." *FidoNews*, June 11, 1990.

————. "Obtaining a Fido Net Number." *FidoNews*, June 3, 1985.

Kasser, Joe. "The Sky's the Limit." *Byte*, November 1978.

Katz, Eric, and Rony Daher. *Oblivion/2 Bulletin Board System*. Version 2.40. Darkflame Enterprises, 1995.

Kay, Jim. "I wish to register a loud complaint . . ." *FidoNews*, September 15, 1986.

Kelly, Paul, and Jim Lynn. "A Few Ideas about the Rewrite of Fido." *FidoNews*, July 22, 1985.

Kelty, Christopher M. *Two Bits: The Cultural Significance of Free Software*. Durham, NC: Duke University Press, 2008.

Kendall, Lori. "Community and the Internet." In *The Handbook of Internet Studies*, 309–25. New York: Wiley, 2011. https://doi.org/10.1002/9781444314861.ch14.

————. "Virtual Community." In *Encyclopedia of New Media*, edited by Steve Jones, 467–70. Thousand Oaks, CA: Sage, 2003.

Kenny, Thomas. "The First Echomail Conference List." FidoNet on the Internet, January 13, 1987. http://www.textfiles.com/fidonet-on-the-internet/e1987/elist701.txt

————. "The First Echomail Conference List." *FidoNews*, March 9, 1987.

————. "I'm very interested in Echomail networking . . ." *FidoNews*, May 12, 1986.

Kessler, Mitch, and Gerrie Blum. "Adult but Not X-Rated." *FidoNews*, August 18, 1986.

Kimes, Mark. "FSC-0068 A Proposed Replacement For FTS-0004." FidoNet Technical Standards Committee, December 13, 1992. http://www.textfiles.com/fidonet-on-the-internet/fs/fsc_0068.txt.

Kleinman, Pablo. "FidoNet en Sudamerica." *FidoNews*, November 23, 1987.

Kliewer, Bradley Dyck. "VGA to the Max," *Byte*, December 1990.

Kline, Ronald R. "The Modem That Still Connects Us." In *Historical Studies in Computing, Information, and Society: Insights from the Flatiron Lectures*, edited by William Aspray. Cham, Switzerland: Springer, 2019.

Knight, Tim. "Establishing Your Own Bulletin Board Service." *SoftSide*, November 1983.

Knopf, Jim. "The Origin of Shareware." Association of Software Professionals, 1995. http://web.archive.org/web/0/http://www.asp-software.org/users/history-of-shareware.asp.

Kobetich, Randall. "I.P.R Echomail (Interpersonal Relationships)." *FidoNews*, September 22, 1986.

Kolozaridi, Polina, and Dmitry Muravyov. "The Narratives We Inherit: The Local and Global in Tomsk's Internet History." *Internet Histories* 4, no. 1 (January 2, 2020): 49–65. https://doi.org/10.1080/24701475.2020.1723980.

Krantz, Michael. "The Great Manhattan Geek Rush of 1995." *New York*, November 13, 1995.

Krol, Ed. *The Whole Internet: User's Guide & Catalog*. Sebastopol CA: O'Reilly, 1992.

Kushner, David. "It's a Mod, Mod World." *IEEE Spectrum* 40, no. 2 (February 2003): 56–57. https://doi.org/10.1109/MSPEC.2003.1176517.

———. *Masters of Doom: How Two Guys Created an Empire and Transformed Pop Culture*. New York: Random House, 2003.

Kwasnik, John. "RIP Graphics." John Kwasnik's website, July 2015. http://www.kwasstuff.altervista.org/RIP/index.html.

Laliberte, Stephen. "A Tale of Two Cities: Impressions of FidoCon91 and the VIA Convention." *Boardwatch*, October 1991.

Lansing, Kenneth. "FidoNet: A Study of Computer Networking." Master's thesis, Texas Tech University, 1991.

Lawrie, Mike. "History of the Internet in South Africa." Uninet Home Page, 1997. Accessed June 15, 2021. http://web.archive.org/web/20041205093635/http://www2.frd.ac.za/uninet/history/.

"Letters." *Boardwatch*, October 1991.

"Letters to the Editor." *Boardwatch*, April 1993.

"Letters to the Editor." *Boardwatch*, June 1993.

Levy, Stanley P. (WB6SQU). "A Morse to RTTY Converter—Using a Microprocessor." In *Hobby Computers Are Here!*, edited by Wayne Green (W2NSD/1), 78–81. Peterborough, NH: 73 Publications, 1976.

Lewis, Kris. "Abuse.BBS." 1987. Archived at http://www.textfiles.com/bbs/abuse.txt.

Lewis, Peter. "Low-Cost, High-Feature PCs." *PC Magazine*, February 23, 1993.

Lewis, Peter H. "America Online Buys 2 Internet Companies: A Company Warms Up to the World Wide Web." *New York Times*, November 10, 1994, sec. Business Day.

Lewis, Shawn D. "10-4, Bro." *Ebony*, October 1976.

Lohr, Steve. "Steve Case at a Crossroad: America Online Is a Leader, but He's Watching the Rear-View Mirror." *New York Times*, August 14, 1995, sec. Business Day.

Londner, Virginia Peschke. "Letter from the Publisher." *Byte*, February 1978.

Looney, Todd. "Vietnam Veterans Bulletin Board." *FidoNews*, August 11, 1986.

Looney, Todd, and Nancy Looney. "A Cry for Support! Dedicated to Vietnam Veterans." *FidoNews*, September 8, 1986.

Mack, D. Thomas, Ken Goosens, and Doug Azzarito. "Remote Bulletin Board System for the Personal Computer Version 17.4: Technical Reference Guide." BBS Software Directory, June 21, 1992. http://software.bbsdocumentary.com/IBM/DOS/RBBS/.

Mack, D. Thomas, and Jon Martin. "Remote Bulletin Board System for the IBM Personal Computer Version CPC12.1." BBS Software Directory, January 29, 1984. http://software.bbsdocumentary.com/IBM/DOS/RBBS/rbbs121.txt.

MacKinnon, Richard Clark. "Searching for the Leviathan in Usenet." Master's thesis, San Jose State University, 1992. https://doi.org/10.31979/etd.vzvh-hkn4.

Madill, John. "FidoNet History." July 30, 1993. Archived by Metro Olografix at http://www.olografix.org/gubi/estate/archivio/fido/fido.htm.

Maher, Jimmy. *The Future Was Here: The Commodore Amiga.* Cambridge, MA: MIT Press, 2012.

Mailland, Julien, and Kevin Driscoll. *Minitel: Welcome to the Internet.* Cambridge, MA: MIT Press, 2017.

Maille, Joseph Charles. "Virtually Gutenberg: Computer Bulletin Boards and the First Amendment through United States v. Riggs and Neidorf." Master's thesis, San Jose State University, 1993.

Manes, Stephen. "The Info Footpath: How the Internet Got Its Start in the Early Days." *New York Times,* September 8, 1996.

Mark, Richard Scott. "Guide to Select BBS's on the Internet (SBI List)." August 1995. Archived at http://cd.textfiles.com/group42/FAQS/AINTBBS.TXT.

———. *Internet BBSs: A Guided Tour.* Greenwich, CT: Manning, 1996.

Markham, Annette N. *Life Online: Researching Real Experience in Virtual Space.* Walnut Creek, CA: AltaMira, 1998.

Markoff, John. "In Focus: Personal Computers Communicate." *InfoWorld,* November 1, 1982.

———. "Freeware Hunt with IBM PC Shoots Numerous Prey." *InfoWorld,* June 27, 1983.

———. "Word-Processing Package Costs $10 under New Marketing Scheme." *InfoWorld,* September 19, 1983.

Marwick, Alice E. "To Catch a Predator? The MySpace Moral Panic." *First Monday* 13, no. 6 (May 19, 2008). https://doi.org/10.5210/fm.v13i6.2152.

"Matrix Maps Quarterly." Matrix.net, January 24, 2001. https://web.archive.org/web/20010124082100/http://www.matrix.net/publications/mmq/index.html.

Maxey, Jim. "README.TXT." *Universe.* Event Horizons, 1988. http://cd.textfiles.com/multimediamania/GAMES/UNIVERS/README.TXT.

Maxwell, Jim (W6CF). "Amateur Radio: 100 Years of Discovery." *QST,* January 2000. http://www.arrl.org/files/file/About%20ARRL/Ham_Radio_100_Years.pdf.

Maxwell, Kim. "High-Speed Dial-Up Modems." *Byte,* December 1984.

Mazlish, Bruce. "A Highway or a Trap?" *New York Times*, October 31, 1993, sec. Books. https://www.nytimes.com/1993/10/31/books/a-highway-or-a-trap.html.

McCormick, Rich. "Andy Warhol's Amiga Computer Art Found 30 Years Later." *The Verge*, April 24, 2014. http://www.theverge.com/2014/4/24/5646554/andy-warhols-lost-amiga-computer-art-photo-essay.

McCullough, Brian. "She Gave the World a Billion AOL CDs—An Interview with Marketing Legend Jan Brandt." *Internet History* (podcast), August 2014. http://www.internethistorypodcast.com/2014/08/she-gave-the-world-a-billion-aol-cds-an-interview-with-marketing-legend-jan-brandt/.

McIlwain, Charlton D. *Black Software: The Internet and Racial Justice, from the AfroNet to Black Lives Matter*. New York: Oxford University Press, 2019.

McKelvey, Fenwick. *Internet Daemons: Digital Communications Possessed*. Minneapolis: University of Minnesota Press, 2018. https://doi.org/10.5749/9781452961743.

McKelvey, Fenwick, and Kevin Driscoll. "ARPANET and Its Boundary Devices: Modems, IMPs, and the Inter-structuralism of Infrastructures." *Internet Histories* 3, no. 1 (January 2, 2019): 31–50. https://doi.org/10.1080/24701475.2018.1548138.

McKinney, Cait. *Information Activism: A Queer History of Lesbian Media Technologies*. Durham, NC: Duke University Press, 2020.

———. "Printing the Network: AIDS Activism and Online Access in the 1980s." *Continuum* 32, no. 1 (January 2, 2018): 7–17. https://doi.org/10.1080/10304312.2018.1404670.

McLellan, Vin. "Out of the Doghouse." *Digital Review*, August 1985. fido0231.nws.

McPherson, Tara. "U.S. Operating Systems at Mid-century: The Intertwining of Race and UNIX." In *Race after the Internet*, edited by Lisa Nakamura and Peter Chow-White, 21–37. New York: Routledge, 2012.

Memory Alpha. "TRW Space and Defense Park." Accessed June 15, 2021. https://memory-alpha.fandom.com/wiki/TRW_Space_and_Defense_Park.

Menn, Joseph. *Cult of the Dead Cow: How the Original Hacking Supergroup Might Just Save the World*. New York: PublicAffairs, 2019.

Merritt, Ralph. "A Listing of Known Othernets." *FidoNews*, November 25, 1991.

Metcalfe, Bob. "How Many Sysops Will Show Up for BBSCon—and Just What Is a Sysop?" *InfoWorld* 17, no. 5 (January 30, 1995): 49.

———. "Internet Dwellers Beware: BBS Movement Is Planning an Invasion." *InfoWorld* 16, no. 37 (September 12, 1994): 50.

———. "On the Wild Side of Computer Networking." *InfoWorld*, March 29, 1993.

———. "Shareware Should Not Be Shunned at All." *InfoWorld*, March 15, 1993.

———. "Sysops Are Reaping the Benefits in the Wake of a BBS Explosion." *InfoWorld* 16, no. 36 (September 5, 1994): 52.

Meyer, Emily. "Press Release: The Andy Warhol Museum Announces Newly Discovered Amiga Experiments." Andy Warhol Museum, April 24, 2014.

http://www.warhol.org/uploadedFiles/Warhol_Site/Warhol/Content/The
_Museum/Press_room/documents/The_Warhol_Amiga_Project_Release_4
-24-14.pdf.

Miastkowski, Stan. "Information Unlimited: The Dialog Information Retrieval Service." *Byte*, June 1981.

Michlin, Adam. "A Listing of Known Othernets." *NETLAND*, January 1, 1995. http://www.nfbnet.org/files/magazine/NETL0195.ZIP.

Mickley, Tracy. "Planet Connect Satellite System—FidoNet/USENET Mail Fire-hose from the Sky." *Boardwatch*, January 1994.

"MicroNET." *Byte*, January 1980.

Miller, Allen. "International Fido Conference, August 14–17, 1986." *FidoNews*, September 8, 1986.

Miller, Leedell J. "The Gay & Lesbian BBS List." soc.motss, November 2, 1992. https://groups.google.com/forum/#!original/soc.motss/mdXaPe3cw2k/NWGHeaoz0KkJ.

Milner, Ryan M. *The World Made Meme: Public Conversations and Participatory Media.* Cambridge, MA: MIT Press, 2016.

Mims, Forrest M., III. "About Forrest M. Mims III." Forrest Mims's webpage. Accessed February 18, 2014. http://www.forrestmims.org/biography.html.

Mindcrime. ANSI Gallery. Version 1.00. ACiDic, a division of ACiD Productions, 1994. ARTSCENE: The Textfiles.com Computer Art Collection. http://artscene.textfiles.com/acid/BBSMODS/.

Mirowski, Alexander. "At the Electronic Crossroads Once Again: The Myth of the Modern Computer Utility in the United States." *IEEE Annals of the History of Computing* 39, no. 2 (2017): 13–29. https://doi.org/10.1109/MAHC.2017.12.

MobyGames. "Scout Search for Apple II (1984)." Accessed April 25, 2014. http://www.mobygames.com/game/scout-search.

Moe, Hallvard, and Hilde Van den Bulck, eds. *Teletext in Europe: From the Analog to the Digital Era.* Göteborg: Nordicom, 2016.

Montfort, Nick, Patsy Baudoin, John Bell, Ian Bogost, Jeremy Douglass, Mark C. Marino, Michael Mateas, Casey Reas, Mark Sample, and Noah Vawter. *10 PRINT CHR$(205.5+RND(1));:GOTO 10.* Cambridge, MA: MIT Press, 2013.

Morris, Sue. "WADs, Bots and Mods: Multiplayer FPS Games as Co-creative Media." In *Level Up Conference Proceedings*, University of Utrecht, 2003.

Mueller, Gavin. "Piracy as Labour Struggle." *TripleC: Communication, Capitalism & Critique: Open Access Journal for a Global Sustainable Information Society* 14, no. 1 (May 15, 2016): 333–45.

Mulvin, Dylan. "Distributing Liability: The Legal and Political Battles of Y2K." *IEEE Annals of the History of Computing* 42, no. 3 (July 2020): 26-37. doi:10.1109/MAHC.2020.2973630.

Myers, David Martin, Jr. "Putting It on the Line: The Evolution of Home Computer Networks." PhD diss., University of Texas at Austin, 1984.

Myers, Lary L. *How to Create Your Own Computer Bulletin Board.* Blue Ridge Summit, PA: TAB Books, 1983.

Nakamura, Lisa. *Cybertypes: Race, Ethnicity, and Identity on the Internet.* New York: Routledge, 2002.

"NAPLPS Graphics Gains Legs." *Boardwatch*, December 1992.

"National List of Electronic Bulletin Board Systems and On-Line Information Services," *Boardwatch*, May 1992.

"Nationwide Operator Toll Dialing (Part 1 of 5)." *Telephony* 130 (January 12, 1946): 13–26.

"Nationwide Operator Toll Dialing (Part 2 of 5)." *Telephony* 130 (January 19, 1946): 28–30, 46.

"Nationwide Operator Toll Dialing (Part 3 of 5)." *Telephony* 130 (January 26, 1946): 16–18, 35.

"Nationwide Operator Toll Dialing (Part 4 of 5)." *Telephony* 130 (February 2, 1946): 18–19.

"Nationwide Operator Toll Dialing (Part 5 of 5)." *Telephony* 130 (February 2, 1946): 20–26.

NBC. "Espionage / New Orleans, Louisiana / Computer Spy Ring." *NBC Evening News*, March 4, 1989. https://tvnews.vanderbilt.edu/broadcasts/567753.

———. "Focus (Cyberspace Pornography)." *NBC Evening News*, July 30, 1994. https://tvnews.vanderbilt.edu/broadcasts/600970.

Nelson, Robin. "The Spirit of Cyberflight." *Popular Science*, April 1995.

Newkirk, Rod. "How's DX." *QST*, March 1971.

Nickell, Joe Ashbrook. "Return of the Living BBS." *Wired*, March 1, 1999. https://www.wired.com/1999/03/return-of-the-living-bbs/.

"1991 International BBSing and Electronic Communications Conference, The." *FidoNews*, August 12, 1991.

Nomad, The. "The Modem Life. Is It Really Worth It?" May 26, 1985. Archived at http://www.textfiles.com/100/modemlif.hac.

Nooney, Laine, Kevin Driscoll, and Kera Allen. "From Programming to Products: *Softalk* Magazine and the Rise of the Personal Computer User." *Information & Culture* 55, no. 2 (June 18, 2020): 105–29.

Norberg, Arthur L., Judy E. O'Neill, and Kerry J. Freedman. *Transforming Computer Technology: Information Processing for the Pentagon, 1962–1986.* Baltimore: Johns Hopkins University Press, 1996.

"Notices." *FidoNews*, August 25, 1986.

Nutter, David, dir. "2Shy." *The X-Files.* Fox. November 3, 1995. https://web.archive.org/web/20010331101254/http://www.thexfiles.com/episodes/season3/3x06.html.

O'Dell, Sally (KB1O). "Clubs and Computers: A Simple Interface (Club Corner)." *QST*, July 1983.

Ogan, Christine. "Listserver Communication during the Gulf War: What Kind of Medium Is the Electronic Bulletin Board?" *Journal of Broadcasting & Electronic Media* 37, no. 2 (March 1, 1993): 177–96. https://doi.org/10.1080/08838159309364214.

O'Hara, Rob. *Commodork: Sordid Tales from a BBS Junkie.* Self-published, 2006.

Olmstead, Van. "Sauntering Sysops Batman." *FidoNews*, July 22, 1985.

Olson, John. "How to Avoid Sysop Burnout." *FidoNews*, April 14, 1986.

Omega, Lord Vision, and Rock 'n Roll Doctor. "Getting AE/CATFUR to Work with Apple-Net." July 9, 1986. Archived at http://www.textfiles.com/apple/applenet.txt.

O'Nan, Thomas. Email to jason@textfiles.com. "Love Your Site." November 17, 2006. Archived at http://textfiles.com/history/onan.txt.

"ONE BBSCON." *Boardwatch*, November 1992.

"ONE BBSCON—Getting It All Together." *Boardwatch*, July 1992.

"$109 2400 Baud Modem." *Byte*, June 1988.

"One Sysops Opinion." N.d. Archived at http://www.textfiles.com/bbs/opinion.txt.

"Online Graphics—The Next Frontier." *Boardwatch*, October 1992.

Opincar, Abe. "Holy Megabytes: In Her Crusade against AIDS, a Social Justice Nun Goes Online to the World." *Reader*, October 8, 1992.

Paloque-Berges, Camille. "Mapping a French Internet Experience: A Decade of Unix Networks Cooperation (1983–1993)." In *Routledge Companion to Global Internet Histories*, edited by Gerard Goggin and Mark McLelland, 153–70. New York: Routledge, 2017.

Pargman, Daniel, and Jacob Palme. "ASCII Imperialism." In *Standards and Their Stories: How Quantifying, Classifying, and Formalizing Practices Shape Everyday Life*, edited by Martha Lampland and Susan Leigh Star, 177–206. Ithaca, NY: Cornell University Press, 2008.

Parsons, Patrick. *Blue Skies: A History of Cable Television*. Philadelphia: Temple University Press, 2008.

Partridge, C. "The Technical Development of Internet Email." *IEEE Annals of the History of Computing* 30, no. 2 (April 2008): 3–29. https://doi.org/10.1109/MAHC.2008.32.

Pasco, Jean O. "A Life of Service: Sister Mary, Whose Past Has Seen Many Painful Twists and Turns, Now Brings Comfort to Others with the World's Most Comprehensive Web Site on AIDS and HIV." *Los Angeles Times*, December 1, 1997.

Pazuzu. "Tips on Starting Your Own BBS." November 11, 1993. Archived at http://www.textfiles.com/bbs/startbbs.txt.

Pearce, Gary. "VHF/UHF-FM, Repeaters, Digital Voice and Data." In *The ARRL Operating Manual For Radio Amateurs*, 9th ed., 2-1–2-29. Newington, CT: Amateur Radio Relay League, 2010.

Penner, Jerry. "Running Your Own BBS!" *GEnieLamp*, August 1, 1992. http://software.bbsdocumentary.com/APPLE/II/PRIME/primebbs.genie.txt.

Perkins, Drew D. "RFC 1134: The Point-to-Point Protocol: A Proposal for Multi-protocol Transmission of Datagrams over Point-to-Point Links." Network Working Group, November 1989. http://tools.ietf.org/html/rfc1134.

Pernick, Ron. "WELL Historical Timeline—the Good, Great Place." Well.com, 1995. http://www.well.com/conf/welltales/timeline.html.

Petrik, Paula. "The Youngest Fourth Estate: The Novelty Toy Printing Press and Adolescence, 1870–1886." In *Small Worlds: Children and Adolescents in America, 1850–1950*, edited by Elliott West and Paula Petrik, 125–42. Lawrence: University Press of Kansas, 1992.

Petrick, E. "Imagining the Personal Computer: Conceptualizations of the Homebrew Computer Club 1975–1977." *IEEE Annals of the History of Computing* 39, no. 4 (October 2017): 27–39. https://doi.org/10.1109/MAHC.2018.1221045.

Petzold, Charles. *Code: The Hidden Language of Computer Hardware and Software.* Redmond, WA: Microsoft Press, 1999.

Pew Research Center. "Broadband vs. Dial-Up Adoption over Time." Internet & Technology. Accessed October 21, 2015. http://www.pewinternet.org/data-trend/internet-use/connection-type/.

———. "Demographics of Internet and Home Broadband Usage in the United States." Internet & Technology, June 12, 2019. https://www.pewresearch.org/internet/fact-sheet/internet-broadband/.

"Phone Link Acoustic Modem, The." *Byte*, December 1980.

Piepmeier, Alison. *Girl Zines: Making Media, Doing Feminism.* New York: New York University Press, 2009.

"Playboy Magazine Sues Event Horizons BBS for Copyright Infringement." *Boardwatch*, May 1992.

Plocher, John. "More Fido Rewrite Ideas." *FidoNews*, December 30, 1985.

Plutopia News Network. "Tom Jennings Interview (1993)." *Plutopia Blog*, April 9, 2018. https://plutopia.io/tom-jennings-interview-1993/.

Polunsky, Richard. "Fido Catalog Author Seeks Heko." *FidoNews*, April 14, 1986.

———. "Fido Utility Catalog." *FidoNews*, May 5, 1986.

Pope, James A. "Apple-CAT II: A Communications System from Novation." *Byte*, January 1983.

Pope, Markus W. *Que's BBS Directory.* Indianapolis, IN: Que, 1994.

Postigo, Hector. "America Online Volunteers: Lessons from an Early Co-production Community." *International Journal of Cultural Studies* 12, no. 5 (September 1, 2009): 451–69. https://doi.org/10.1177/1367877909337858.

———. "Emerging Sources of Labor on the Internet: The Case of America Online Volunteers." *International Review of Social History* 48, no. S11 (December 2003): 205–23. https://doi.org/10.1017/S0020859003001329.

———. "Of Mods and Modders Chasing Down the Value of Fan-Based Digital Game Modifications." *Games and Culture* 2, no. 4 (October 1, 2007): 300–313, doi:10.1177/1555412007307955.

Požar, Tim. "Late Night Software Is Proud to Announce UFGATE." *FidoNews*, January 30, 1989.

———. "UFGATE—FidoNet/UUCP Gateway." Late Night Software. Accessed October 1, 2020. https://www.lns.com/papers/ufgate/.

"Prime Bulletin Board System: Zippety-Doo-Dah! Zippety-Day!" BBS Software Directory, [1992?]. http://software.bbsdocumentary.com/APPLE/II/PRIME/primebbs.txt.

Prodigy. "Prodigy Interactive Personal Service Start-Up Kit." 1991. The Henry Ford Museum, Dearborn, MI. Accessed June 15, 2021. https://www .thehenryford.org/collections-and-research/digital-collections/artifact/ 361296.

"Prodigy Numbers." *Boardwatch*, June 1992.

Quarterman, John S. "About *Matrix News* (MN)." Matrix Information and Directory Services, January 21, 1998. https://web.archive.org/web/19980121022331/ http://www.mids.org/mn/about.html.

———. *The Matrix: Computer Networks and Conferencing Systems Worldwide*. Bedford, MA: Digital, 1990.

Quarterman, John S., and Josiah C. Hoskins. "Notable Computer Networks." *Communications of the ACM* 29, no. 10 (October 1, 1986): 932–71. https://doi .org/10.1145/6617.6618.

Queer Digital History Project. "The Backroom." Accessed February 3, 2021. http://queerdigital.com/items/show/42.

———. "Gay and Lesbian Information Bureau (GLIB)." Accessed February 16, 2021. https://queerdigital.com/items/show/55.

———. "Multicom-4." Accessed February 16, 2021. https://queerdigital.com/ items/show/72.

Quittner, Joshua, and Tom Curry. "Ho, Ho, Ho, Crash!" *Time* 145, no. 1 (January 9, 1995): 61.

Radio Shack. *Radio Shack Catalog*. 1965.

———. *Radio Shack Catalog*. 1975.

Radway, Janice. "Zines, Half-Lives, and Afterlives: On the Temporalities of Social and Political Change." *PMLA* 126, no. 1 (January 1, 2011): 140–50. doi:10.1632/ pmla.2011.126.1.140.

Rafaeli, Sheizaf. "The Electronic Bulletin Board: A Computer-Driven Mass Medium." *Computers and the Social Sciences* 2 (1986): 123–36. https://doi.org/10 .1177/089443939860020302.

Rankin, Joy Lisi. "From the Mainframes to the Masses: A Participatory Computing Movement in Minnesota Education." *Information & Culture* 50, no. 2 (May 1, 2015): 197–216. https://doi.org/10.7560/IC50204.

———. *A People's History of Computing in the United States*. Cambridge, MA: Harvard University Press, 2018.

———. "Toward a History of Social Computing: Children, Classrooms, Campuses, and Communities." *IEEE Annals of the History of Computing* 36, no. 2 (2014): 86–88.

Raymond, Eric S. "September That Never Ended." Jargon File. Version 4.4.7. December 29, 2003. http://www.catb.org/jargon/html/S/September-that-never -ended.html.

Rehn, Alf. "The Politics of Contraband: The Honor Economies of the Warez Scene." *Journal of Socio-Economics* 33, no. 3 (July 1, 2004): 359–74. https://doi .org/10.1016/j.socec.2003.12.027.

Reid, Elizabeth M. "Electropolis: Communication and Community on Internet Relay Chat." University of Melbourne, 1991. http://www.aluluei.com/electropolis.htm.

Renaud, Josh. "Break Into Chat." Break Into Chat—BBS Wiki. Accessed May 13, 2014. http://breakintochat.com/wiki/Break_Into_Chat.

Retro Gamer. "John Romero." January 17, 2014. http://www.retrogamer.net/profiles/developer/john-romero/.

Reunanen, Markku. "How Those Crackers Became Us Demosceners." Wider-Screen 17, nos. 1–2 (April 15, 2014). http://widerscreen.fi/numerot/2014-1-2/crackers-became-us-demosceners/.

———. "Times of Change in the Demoscene: A Creative Community and Its Relationship with Technology." University of Turku, 2017. http://doria32-kk.lib.helsinki.fi/handle/10024/130915.

Rheingold, Howard. Introduction to the electronic version of The Virtual Community. Accessed February 4, 2021. https://www.rheingold.com/vc/book/intro.html.

———. The Virtual Community: Homesteading on the Electronic Frontier. Reading, MA: Addison-Wesley, 1993.

Rickard, Jack. "The BBS to Internet Connection." Boardwatch, February 1992.

———. "Editor's Notes." Boardwatch, June 1991.

———. "Editor's Notes." Boardwatch, October 1991.

———. "Editor's Notes." Boardwatch, February 1992.

———. "Editor's Notes." Boardwatch, January 1995.

———. "Editor's Notes." Boardwatch, December 1995.

———. "Editor's Notes: Webulism and the Cable Fable." Boardwatch, December 1994.

———. "FidoCon91, Commercialization, and The ONE BBSCON." FidoNews, September 9, 1991.

———. "Home-Grown BB$." Wired, October 1993. http://www.wired.com/wired/archive/1.04/bbs.html.

———. "Internet News." Boardwatch, May 1991.

———. "Mosaic and the World Wide Web." Boardwatch, January 1994.

———. "The New BBS on the Web—Whole Earth 'Lectronic Link." Boardwatch, October 1995.

———. "Rumors & Factoids." Boardwatch, January 1994.

Rimm, Marty. "Marketing Pornography on the Information Superhighway: A Survey of 917,410 Images, Descriptions, Short Stories, and Animations Downloaded 8.5 Million Times by Consumers in over 2000 Cities in Forty Countries, Provinces, and Territories." Georgetown Law Journal 83 (1994–95): 1849–1934.

Roberts, H. Edward, and William Yates. "Altair 8800 Minicomputer, Part 1." Popular Electronics, January 1975.

Roberts, Steven K. "Online Information Retrieval: Promise and Problems." Byte, December 1981.

Robinson, Phil, and Nancy Tamosaitis. *The Joy of Cybersex: The Underground Guide to Electronic Erotica*. New York: Brady, 1993.

Rochester Public Library. "Guide to the Gay Alliance of the Genesee Valley Ephemera Collection 2017.023." 2017. https://roccitylibrary.org/special-collections/.

Romkey, John L. "RFC 1055: Nonstandard for Transmission of IP Datagrams over Serial Lines: SLIP." Network Working Group, June 1988. http://tools.ietf.org/html/rfc1055.

Rose, Lance. "Playboy's New Playmate—Event Horizons BBS." *Boardwatch*, June 1992.

Rosen, Benjamin M. "VisiCalc: Breaking the Personal Computer Bottleneck." *Morgan Stanley Electronics Letter*, July 11, 1979. http://www.bricklin.com/history/rosenletter.htm.

Rosenthal, Robert. "Busing Foe: South Boston Ready to Defend Itself." *Boston Globe*, April 21, 1976.

Rosenzweig, Roy. "Wizards, Bureaucrats, Warriors, and Hackers: Writing the History of the Internet." *American Historical Review* 103, no. 5 (December 1, 1998): 1530–52. https://doi.org/10.2307/2649970.

Rowe, Eddie. "A New Call to Arms—Event Horizons vs. Joe Sysop?" *FidoNews*, October 28, 1991. http://www.textfiles.com/bbs/FIDONET/FIDONEWS/fido0843.nws.

Roy, Jonathan. "SupraFAXModem." *freenet.sci.comp.atari.news*, February 1, 1992. http://web.archive.org/web/20030109030157/http://www.atariarchives.org/cfn/12/03/0028.php.

Rucker, Rudy von Bitter, R. U. Sirius, and Queen Mu. *Mondo 2000: A User's Guide to the New Edge*. New York: HarperPerennial, 1992.

Rumelt, Richard P., and Julia Watt. "VisiCorp 1978–1984 (Revised)." Los Angeles, CA: Anderson School at UCLA, 1985, rev. 2003. Archived at http://web.archive.org/web/20031101141127/http://www.anderson.ucla.edu/faculty/dick.rumelt/Docs/Cases/Visicorp.pdf.

Russell, Andrew L. *Open Standards and the Digital Age: History, Ideology, and Networks*. New York: Cambridge University Press, 2014.

———. "OSI: The Internet That Wasn't." *IEEE Spectrum*, July 30, 2013. http://spectrum.ieee.org/computing/networks/osi-the-internet-that-wasnt.

———. "'Rough Consensus and Running Code' and the Internet-OSI Standards War." *IEEE Annals of the History of Computing* 28, no. 3 (2006): 48–61.

Rusty. "Testimony and Thank You." Computerized AIDS Ministries, June 14, 1995. http://web.archive.org/web/19980425034516/http://gbgm-umc.org/CAM/rusty.html.

Rutter, Dorian James. "From Diversity to Convergence: British Computer Networks and the Internet, 1970–1995." PhD diss., University of Warwick, 2005.

Ryan, Hugh, Brian Joseph Ferree, and Jennifer Livingston. "You Can Buy Gaydar at the Apple Store." *Details*, February 16, 2010. http://www.details.com/sex-relationships/dating-and-cheating/201003/gay-fool-proof-hookups-tech-savy.

safe crackers. "The Art of Warez." 2019. Video. https://safecrackers.com/.

Saltzer, J., D. Clark, J. Romkey, and W. Gramlich. "The Desktop Computer as a Network Participant." *IEEE Journal on Selected Areas in Communications* 3, no. 3 (1985): 468–78. https://doi.org/10.1109/JSAC.1985.1146219.

Sandberg, Jared. "America Online, Capital Cities/ABC Plan New Service." *Wall Street Journal*, July 7, 1994, sec. Technology and Telecommunications.

Sandvig, Christian. "Disorderly Infrastructure and the Role of Government." *Government Information Quarterly* 23, nos. 3–4 (2006): 503–6. doi:10.1016/j.giq.2006.07.008.

Sash. "Adventures in BBSing: BBSing Nostalgia in the Twin Cities or 'Internet Killed the BBS Star.'" 2000. Archived at http://www.textfiles.com/history/minn.txt.

Schafer, Valérie, and Benjamin G. Thierry. *Le Minitel: L'enfance numérique de la France*. Paris: Nuvis, 2012.

Schinnell, Rich. "Rich's Ramblings January 2004." Rich Schinnell's website, January 2004. https://web.archive.org/web/20040211225245/http://schinnell.org:80/ramb/ramb0401.html.

Schulte, Stephanie Ricker. *Cached: Decoding the Internet in Global Popular Culture*. New York: New York University Press, 2013.

Schuyler, Michael. "Big Dummy's Guide to FidoNet." FidoNet.us, 1992. http://www.fidonet.us/dummyguide.html.

Scott, Jason. "BBS: A Documentary: The Pitch." BBS: The Documentary. Accessed February 2, 2014. http://www.bbsdocumentary.com/longpitch.html.

———. "BBS Documentaries." Internet Archive. Accessed February 2, 2014. https://archive.org/details/bbs_documentary.

———. BBS Software Directory. Accessed August 4, 2020. http://software.bbsdocumentary.com/.

———. "BBS Textfiles: CBBS: The Dead CBBS Scrolls." textfiles.com. Accessed July 2, 2020. http://www.textfiles.com/bbs/CBBS/SCROLLS/.

———. "Commented BBS List." The TEXTFILES.COM Historical BBS List. Accessed May 10, 2014. http://bbslist.textfiles.com/comments.html.

———. "Concepts: Services: Satellites." BBS Documentary Library. Accessed February 4, 2021. http://www.bbsdocumentary.com/library/CONCEPTS/SERVICES/SATELLITES/.

———. "Controversy: BBSes of Evil and Fear: Racist BBSes." BBS Documentary Library, 1985. http://bbsdocumentary.com/library/CONTROVERSY/EVIL/RACISTBBSES/.

———. "Customized: S-100 Kit Computer: CBBS." BBS Software Directory. Accessed February 17, 2021. http://software.bbsdocumentary.com/AAA/AAA/CBBS/.

———. "Does the BBS Guy Run a BBS?" *ASCII by Jason Scott* (blog), October 21, 2003. http://ascii.textfiles.com/archives/753.

———. "Electronic Magazines." textfiles.com. Accessed April 30, 2014. http://textfiles.com/magazines/.

———. "518 Area Code BBSes through History." The TEXTFILES.COM Historical BBS List. Accessed April 28, 2014. http://bbslist.textfiles.com/518/.

———. "Groups: Octothorpe Productions." Accessed April 29, 2014. Archived at http://www.textfiles.com/groups/OCTOTHORPE/.

———. "Groups: The Cult of the Dead Cow." textfiles.com. Accessed February 4, 2021. http://textfiles.com/groups/CDC/.

———. "914 Area Code BBSes through History." The TEXTFILES.COM Historical BBS List. Accessed April 29, 2014. http://bbslist.textfiles.com/914/.

———. "Overview of The Works." July 16, 1986. Archived at http://textfiles.com/groups/OCTOTHORPE/allworks.bbs.

———. "The Passion of the Scanner." *ASCII by Jason Scott* (blog), March 11, 2006. http://ascii.textfiles.com/archives/950.

———. "A Story of RBBS (and PC-Talk, and Andrew Fluegelman)." *ASCII by Jason Scott* (blog), September 2, 2008. http://ascii.textfiles.com/archives/1440.

———. "TEXTFILES.COM File Statistics." textfiles.com, July 1, 2005. http://www.textfiles.com/filestats.html.

———. The TEXTFILES.COM Historical BBS List. Accessed June 15, 2021. http://bbslist.textfiles.com/.

———. "Textfile Writing Groups." textfiles.com. Accessed February 5, 2021. http://www.textfiles.com/groups/.

———. "317 BBS List." The TEXTFILES.COM Historical BBS List. Accessed March 21, 2014. http://bbslist.textfiles.com/317/.

———. "Why I Prefer Textfiles." February 27, 1987. Archived at http://www.textfiles.com/groups/OCTOTHORPE/whytext.oct.

———. The Works BBS. cache cow. Accessed April 29, 2014. http://web.archive.org/web/20011115192625/http://cache.cow.net/works/.

Scott, Jason, and The Cruiser. "The Guide to Real Works Users." February 26, 1987. Archived at http://www.textfiles.com/groups/OCTOTHORPE/works2.oct.

Seger, Katie. "From One Program to Another." *PC Magazine*, January 1983.

Selig, John R. "Sit Down, Shut-Up and Row: Wynn Wagner Helps Build the HIV/AIDS Information Superhighway." John Selig's website, March 2001. http://www.johnselig.com/commentary/row/.

Shackelford, Ken. "Fido BBS Christmas Wish List (Early)." *FidoNews*, October 14, 1985.

Shaw, David F. "Gay Men and Computer Communication: A Discourse of Sex and Identity in Cyberspace." In *Virtual Culture: Identity and Communication in Cybersociety*, edited by Steven Jones, 123–32. London: Sage, 1997.

Shea, Tom. "Free Software." *InfoWorld*, June 27, 1983.

Shefski, William J. *Free Electronic Networks*. Rocklin, CA: Prima, 1994.

Sherin, Ed, dir. "Rebels." *Law & Order*. NBC. September 27, 1995.

Shields, Rob. *Cultures of Internet: Virtual Spaces, Real Histories, Living Bodies.* London: Sage, 1996.

Shifrin, Jerry. "So You Want to Start a BBS?" May 23, 1987. Archived at http://www.textfiles.com/bbs/start-bb.txt.

Shiman, Philip. "Credits for the Information Highway." *Science* 274, no. 5293 (December 6, 1996): 1627–28. https://doi.org/10.1126/science.274.5293.1627.

Siegel, Alan. "How alt.tv.simpsons Embiggened a Generation of Obsessive Fans." *Slate*, September 26, 2013. https://slate.com/culture/2013/09/the-history-of-simpsons-message-board-alt-tv-simpsons.html.

Silver, David. "Looking Backwards, Looking Forward: Cyberculture Studies 1990–2000." In *Web.Studies: Rewiring Media Studies for the Digital Age*, edited by David Gauntlett, 19–30. Oxford: Oxford University Press, 2000. http://rccs.usfca.edu/intro.asp.html.

16colo.Rs—ANSI/ASCII Archive. Accessed July 31, 2019. https://16colo.rs/.

"Small Firm Offers Home Computer Owners Range of Data Features." *Wall Street Journal*, January 30, 1980.

Smith, Roger. "Record Collectors EchoMail Conference." *FidoNews*, October 20, 1986.

"Snowfall a Nuisance Here, Deadly in East." *Chicago Tribune*, January 15, 1978.

Southerland, Daniel. "America Online's Rapid Rise: It's the Hottest Player in Dial-Up Computer Services, but Stiff Competition Looms." *Washington Post*, November 8, 1993.

Souvestre, John, George Peace, Jim Bodger, and John Johnson. "FidoNet Echomail Backbone." ONE BBSCON 1994, 1994. http://www.textfiles.com/fidonet-on-the-internet/zips/index.htm.

Star, Susan Leigh, and Martha Lampland. "Reckoning with Standards." In *Standards and Their Stories: How Quantifying, Classifying, and Formalizing Practices Shape Everyday Life*, edited by Martha Lampland and Susan Leigh Star, 3–34. Ithaca, NY: Cornell University Press, 2009.

Sterling, Bruce. "'Internet' [aka 'A Short History of the Internet']." *Magazine of Fantasy and Science Fiction*, February 1993. http://w2.eff.org/Net_culture/internet_sterling.history.txt.

Sterne, Jonathan. *The Audible Past: Cultural Origins of Sound Reproduction*. Durham, NC: Duke University Press, 2003.

Stozek, Jan. "FidoNet in Poland." *Pigulki*, June 5, 1991. https://ftp.icm.edu.pl/packages/pigulki/pigulki6.pub.

Streeter, Thomas. "Internet." In *Digital Keywords*, edited by Benjamin Peters, 184–96. Princeton, NJ: Princeton University Press, 2016.

———. *The Net Effect: Romanticism, Capitalism, and the Internet*. New York: New York University Press, 2011.

"Subscribe to Boardwatch Magazine." *Boardwatch*, May 1992.

Sugawara, Sandra. "Coaxing GEnie Out of Its Bottle: GE Has at Least 3 Wishes for On-Line Service: Profits, Growth and a Beefed-Up Product." *Washington Post*, June 15, 1994.

———. "Washington Business: On-Line and on the Move Vienna's Computer Service Attracts the Attention of Consumers, Competitors." *Washington Post*, August 8, 1994.

Surratt, Carla G. *Netlife: Internet Citizens and Their Communities*. Commack, NY: Nova Science, 1998.

Swamp Rat. "The Infamous . . . Gerbil Feed Bomb." Cult of the Dead Cow, 1985. http://textfiles.com/groups/CDC/cDc-0001.txt.

Swindell, Rob. "The Digital Manifesto: 'The Internet Killed the BBS Star.'" Synchronet Wiki, August 1996. http://wiki.synchro.net/history:manifesto.

Swisher, Kara. *AOL.com: How Steve Case Beat Bill Gates, Nailed the Netheads, and Made Millions in the War for the Web*. New York: Times Business, 1998.

Szelozynski, Jacek. "Something Exotic—Polish Traffic in Net/Echo Mail." *FidoNews*, June 5, 1989. fido0623.nws.

Szerencse, Tom (WB9VTZ). "The History of ECRA Repeaters in Elkhart County." Elkhart County Radio Association. Accessed February 9, 2014. http://web .archive.org/web/20090926025125/http://www.ecra.us/history.html.

Telephone World. "Telephone Sounds & Recordings." Accessed June 15, 2021. https://web.archive.org/web/20190701182135/http://www.phworld.org/sounds/.

Thomas, David. "Online Pioneer's Web Site Chronicles Phenomenon's Beginning." *Denver Post*, August 1, 1999. Archived at http://www.textfiles.com/ thoughts/denver.art.

Thomas, Douglas. "Representing Hacker Culture: Reading Phrack." In *Hacker Culture*, 115–40. Minneapolis: University of Minnesota Press, 2002.

Thomas, Jim, and Gordon Meyer. "Statement of Intent." *Computer Underground Digest*, March 28, 1990. http://www.textfiles.com/digest/CUD/cud0100.txt.

Timberman, Roy. "FidoNet Basics." ONE BBSCON 1994, 1994. http://www .textfiles.com/fidonet-on-the-internet/zips/index.htm.

Toffler, Alvin. "The Electronic Cottage." *Creative Computing*, December 1980.

Torello, Jeff. "Accessing the Internet." *Major News*, Spring 1994.

Townson, Patrick. TELECOM Digest Archives. Accessed February 4, 2021. http:// massis.lcs.mit.edu/.

Tumulty, Karen, and Paul Gray. "Inside the Minds of Gingrich's Gurus." *Time* 145, no. 3 (January 23, 1995): 20.

Turner, Fred. *From Counterculture to Cyberculture: Stewart Brand, the Whole Earth Network, and the Rise of Digital Utopianism*. Chicago: University of Chicago Press, 2006.

———. "Where the Counterculture Met the New Economy: The WELL and the Origins of Virtual Community." *Technology and Culture* 46, no. 3 (2005): 485–512. https://doi.org/10.1353/tech.2005.0154.

Turoff, Murray, and Starr Roxanne Hiltz. "An Overview of Research Activities in Computer Mediated Communications from 1976 to 1991 Conducted by the Computerized Conferencing and Communications Center." New Jersey Institute of Technology, 1992. https://web.njit.edu/~turoff/Administrative/ ccc.htm.

United Methodist News Service. "Computer AIDS Network Offers Support without Judgment." Computerized AIDS Ministries, August 1995. http://web.archive .org/web/19980425034431/http://gbgm-umc.org/CAM/camnews.html.

Upstill, Steve. "Graphics Go 3-D." *Byte*, December 1990.

US Census Bureau. "Appendix Table A. Households with a Computer and Internet Use: 1984 to 2009." In *Computer and Internet Use in the United States: 1984 to 2009*. Washington, DC: US Census Bureau, February 2010. https:// www.census.gov/data/tables/time-series/demo/computer-internet/computer -use-1984-2009.html.

———. *General Social and Economic Characteristics: California*. Washington, DC: US Census Bureau, 1983.

———. *General Social and Economic Characteristics: Indiana*. Washington, DC: US Census Bureau, 1983.

Uys, Niel. "FidoCon 1990—Zone 5." *FidoNews*, October 8, 1990.

Vann Cave, The. "Telegraph Road; Social Media before the Internet." YouTube, March 20, 2019. https://www.youtube.com/watch?v=FYY82ınv4rc.

Van Vleck, T. "Electronic Mail and Text Messaging in CTSS, 1965–1973." *IEEE Annals of the History of Computing* 34, no. 1 (January 2012): 4–6. https://doi.org/ 10.1109/MAHC.2012.6.

Vaughan, Craig W. "Bulletin-Board Evolution Enhances Communication." *Info-World*, May 25, 1981.

"Videotex." *Byte*, July 1983.

"Voters Favor Online Communities." *Boardwatch*, May 1992.

Wade, Ian. *NOSintro: TCP/IP over Packet Radio: An Introduction to the KA9Q Network Operating System*. Dunstable, UK: Dowermain, 1992.

Wade, Keith. *The Anarchist's Guide to the BBS*. Port Townsend, WA: Loompanics Unlimited, 1990.

Wagner, Wynn. "History of Echomail." Opus CBCS. July 7, 1997. http://web .archive.org/web/19970707073957/http://www.global.org/opus/history/ echomail.html.

———. "History of Echomail." The Documentary Photo Album and Interview Page. Accessed June 4, 2021. http://www.bbsdocumentary.com/photos/ 140wynn/FILES/echomail.txt.

———. "History of Opus-CBCS." Opus CBCS. July 7, 1997. http://web.archive .org/web/19970707073934/http://www.global.org/opus/history/opushist .html.

———. "HIV+: Day One." AEGIS, 1996. http://web.archive.org/web/ 20000818090555/http://www.aegis.com/topics/dayone/.

———. "OPUS Computer-Based Conversation System Version 1.0." Edited by John Miller. June 14, 1987. Archived at http://cd.textfiles.com/masterdisc/SS/ CMM/0004/OPUSDOC.TXT.

Wakeford, Nina. "New Technologies and 'Cyber-Queer' Research." In *Handbook of Lesbian and Gay Studies*, edited by Diane Richardson and Steven Seidman, 115–45. London: Sage, 2002.

Waldrop, M. Mitchell. *The Dream Machine: J. C. R. Licklider and the Revolution That Made Computing Personal.* New York: Penguin Books, 2001.

Walker, Butch. "Echomail Coordinators." *FidoNews,* October 6, 1986.

Wallin, Sven Andréas. "Naming Convention." *SAW* (blog), February 1, 2014. http://web.archive.org/web/20160903205902/http://www.svenandreaswallin.com/tag/wynn-wagner/.

Walter, Russ. *The Secret Guide to Computers.* Somerville, MA: Self-published, 1995.

Wasiak, Patryk. "Playing and Copying: Social Practices of Home Computer Users in Poland during the 1980s." In *Hacking Europe: From Computer Cultures to Demoscenes,* edited by Gerard Alberts and Ruth Oldenziel, 129–50. London: Springer, 2014.

———. "Telephone Networks, BBSes, and the Emergence of the Transnational 'Warez Scene.'" *History and Technology* 35, no. 2 (April 3, 2019): 177–94. https://doi.org/10.1080/07341512.2019.1652432.

Weizenbaum, Joseph. "ELIZA: A Computer Program for the Study of Natural Language Communication between Man and Machine." *Communications of the ACM* 9, no. 1 (January 1966): 36–45. doi:10.1145/365153.365168.

Welch, John J. "Item 20: To Ward & Randy: History of CBBS???" November 9, 1986. Archived at http://textfiles.com/bbs/CBBS/history.cbbs.

"WELL Now Available via Internet, The." *Boardwatch,* May 1992.

Wells, H. G. *World Brain.* Garden City, NY: Doubleday, Doran, 1938.

"What Happened to ISDN?" *Boardwatch,* December 1992.

"What Might Be Called CACHE's On Line Graffitti (COG)." *Byte,* June 1978.

Wildcat! Version 5.0. Mustang Software, Inc., 1996.

Wildhack, Billy. *Erotic Connections.* Corte Madera, CA: Waite Group, 1994.

Wilkes, Richard P. "FidoNet: Response." May 24, 1984. Archived at http://www.textfiles.com/bbs/FIDONET/JENNINGS/STANDARDS/fidonet.rpw.txt.

Williams, Gail Ann. "Grateful for Jerry, the Dead, the Deadheads." Gail Williams's pages, August 10, 1995. http://web.archive.org/web/19961220053904/http://www.well.com/user/gail/grateful-dead.html.

Williams, John Evans (W2BFD). "The Story of Amateur Radio Teletype." *QST,* October 1948.

Williams, Raymond. *Keywords: A Vocabulary of Culture and Society.* New York: Oxford University Press, 1976.

Wolf, Gary, and Michael Stein. *Aether Madness: An Offbeat Guide to the Online World.* Berkeley, CA: Peachpit, 1995.

Wood, Lamont, and Dana Blankenhorn. "State of the BBS Nation." *Byte,* January 1990.

Woody, Jerry. *ProMatch.* Version 3.0. Cullman, AL: WoodyWare, 1995.

W6TRW Swap Meet. Accessed February 18, 2014. http://www.w6trw.com/swapmeet/index.htm.

Zone 1 Region Coordinators and Zone 1 Zone Coordinator. "FidoCon 1991—The New Beginning." *FidoNews,* July 30, 1990.

INDEX